Commodity Trading, Globalization and the Colonial World

T0362059

Commodity Trading, Globalization and the Colonial World: Spinning the Web of the Global Market provides a new perspective on economic globalization in the nineteenth and twentieth centuries. Instead of understanding the emergence of global markets as a mere result of supply and demand or as the effect of imperial politics, this book focuses on a global trading firm as an exemplary case of the actors responsible for conducting economic transactions in a multicultural business world. The study focuses on the Swiss merchant house Volkart Bros., which was one of the most important trading houses in British India after the late nineteenth century and became one of the biggest cotton and coffee traders in the world after decolonization.

The book examines the following questions: How could European merchants establish business contacts with members of the mercantile elite from India, China or Latin America? What role did a shared mercantile culture play for establishing relations of trust? How did global business change with the construction of telegraph lines and railways and the development of economic institutions such as merchant banks and commodity exchanges? And what was the connection between the business interests of transnationally operating capitalists and the territorial aspirations of national and imperial governments?

Based on a five-year-long research endeavor and the examination of 24 public and private archives in seven countries and on three continents, *Commodity Trading, Globalization and the Colonial World: Spinning the Web of the Global Market* goes well beyond a mere company history as it highlights the relationship between multinationally operating firms and colonial governments, and the role of business culture in establishing notions of trust, both within the firm and between economic actors in different parts of the world. It thus provides a cutting-edge history of globalization from a micro-perspective. Following an actor-theoretical perspective, the book maintains that the global market that came into being in the nineteenth century can be perceived as the consequence of the interaction of various actors. Merchants, peasants, colonial bureaucrats and industrialists were all involved in spinning the individual threads of this commercial web.

By connecting established approaches from business history with recent scholarship in the fields of global and colonial history, *Commodity Trading, Globalization and the Colonial World: Spinning the Web of the Global Market* offers a new perspective on the emergence of global enterprise and provides an important addition to the history of imperialism and economic globalization.

Christof Dejung is a professor in modern history at the University of Bern, Switzerland.

Routledge International Studies in Business History

Series editors:
Jeffrey Fear and Christina Lubinski

For a full list of titles in this series, please visit www.routledge.com

Commodity Trading, Globalization and the Colonial World
Spinning the Web of the Global Market

Christof Dejung
Translated by Paul Cohen

Routledge
Taylor & Francis Group

NEW YORK AND LONDON

First published 2018
by Routledge
605 Third Avenue, New York, NY 10017

and by Routledge
2 Park Square, Milton Park, Abingdon, Oxon OX14 4RN

First issued in paperback 2020

Routledge is an imprint of the Taylor & Francis Group, an informa business

Library of Congress Cataloging-in-Publication Data
Names: Dejung, Christof, author.
Title: Commodity trading, globalization and the colonial world :
    spinning the web of the global market / by Christof Dejung ;
    translated by Paul Cohen.
Other titles: Fèaden des globalen Marktes. English
Description: New York, NY : Routledge, 2018. | Includes
    bibliographical references and index.
Identifiers: LCCN 2017049541 | ISBN 9781138181687 (hardback) |
    ISBN 9781315646831 (ebook)
Subjects: LCSH: Volkart AG—History. | Trading companies—
    Switzerland—History.
Classification: LCC HD9015.S93 V639513 2018 | DDC
    332.64/409494—dc23
LC record available at https://lccn.loc.gov/2017049541

ISBN 13: 978-0-367-73528-9 (pbk)
ISBN 13: 978-1-138-18168-7 (hbk)

Typeset in Sabon
by Apex CoVantage, LLC

The translation of this work was funded by Geisteswissenschaften
International—Translation Funding for Work in the Humanities and
Social Sciences from Germany, a joint initiative of the Fritz Thyssen
Foundation, the German Federal Foreign Office, the collecting
society VG WORT and the Börsenverein des Deutschen Buchhandels
(German Publishers & Booksellers Association).

Contents

Tables and Figures

Tables

Figures

Acknowledgements

This book would have never been possible without the support of many people around the world. I would like to express my special thanks to Andreas Reinhart, who gave me access to the Volkart archive and thus made this study possible in the first place, as well as to Veronika Lüscher and Inge Corti from the Volkart Foundation, who took it in stride that I occupied their conference room for months on end so I could rummage through dusty old files. It should be explicitly noted, though, that this study was not conducted on behalf of the Volkart company, nor was it financed by it. I would also like to thank my interview partners in Switzerland and Central America who agreed to provide me with information on Volkart's involvement in the coffee business.

Furthermore, my thanks to Jürgen Osterhammel, who immediately showed an interest in the topic and whose suggestion to submit an application to the German Research Foundation laid the cornerstone for this study. His extensive knowledge of global historical processes and ongoing encouragement have done far more to benefit this work than he probably realizes.

Hartmut Berghoff made it possible for me to spend a research semester at the Georg August University in Göttingen, which gave me an opportunity to delve deeper into the historical aspects of international trade. I would also like to thank Sven Beckert for his treasured input on the global history of cotton and for an invitation to Harvard University in the spring of 2008. The opportunity to present the project at a workshop that he organized on the political economy of modern capitalism gave my work new momentum at just the right moment. My heartfelt thanks to Tom Tomlinson and William Gervase Clarence-Smith for making it possible for me to spend four months in their guest residency program at the School of Oriental and African Studies in London.

Many other researchers have made valuable contributions to this work. I would particularly like to mention Christiane Berth, Margrit Müller, Niels P. Petersson, Roman Rossfeld, Jakob Tanner and Andreas Zangger for countless discussions and tips, and for reading individual sections of this work. Moreover, this work benefited from exchanges with Ravi Ahuja, Mark Casson, Alexander Engel, Harald Fischer-Tiné, Bernd-Stefan Grewe,

Harold James, Geoffrey Jones, Gesine Krüger, Takafumi Kurosawa, Alf Lüdtke, Aditya Mukherjee, Gertrud Peters, Shalini Randeria, Tirthankar Roy, Mario Samper, Hansjörg Siegenthaler, Steven Topik, Thomas Welskopp and Dorothee Wierling.

What's more, I owe a debt of gratitude to all of the archivists and librarians who so generously gave me advice and support. With their knowledge of the particular conventions of the archives and libraries in their respective countries, Pedro Monzón (in Guatemala), Andrea Montero (in Costa Rica) and Shripad Wagale (in Mumbai, India) were of invaluable assistance during my stays abroad.

I am deeply grateful to the German Research Foundation for their generous financial support of this project. Additional support that contributed to the success of this work was received from the Schnitter Fund for the History of Technology of the ETH Zurich, the Swiss National Science Foundation and the "Cultural Foundations of Integration" Center of Excellence at the University of Konstanz.

Generous funding from Geisteswissenschaften International has made it possible to translate the manuscript into English after it was originally published in German in 2013. I would like to thank Routledge and the publishers of the series for their willingness to add this study to the Routledge International Studies in Business History. I would also like to thank the two anonymous readers for their recommendations on revising the manuscript for translation. David Varley, Brianna Ascher, Megan Smith and Mary Del Plato from Routledge have handled the production of the book with great care. I am also grateful to our project manager, Deborah Kopka. My heartfelt thanks go to Paul Cohen for his meticulous translation work and keen sense of style. His unflagging dedication to the book has been invaluable.

I thank my parents for their constant support and interest in this work. And, finally, I would like to thank Karin S. Moser, who not only read and re-read parts of this work and helped to improve it with her astute comments and constant encouragement, but also ensured that our household continued to function during my stays abroad. I thank my daughter Liora for luring me away from my computer from time to time and for helping me take my mind off academic matters at playgrounds, riding stables and swimming pools.

Introduction

This book is a micro-historical study of the modern trade in commodities based on the example of the Swiss trading company Volkart Brothers. The Volkart company was founded in 1851 by the brothers Salomon and Johann Georg Volkart, with offices in Winterthur, a small city north of Zurich, and in Bombay. By the end of the nineteenth century, the firm had risen to become one of the largest cotton exporters in India and during the twentieth century it joined the ranks of the world's leading cotton and coffee trading companies, making it one of the leading companies in Switzerland.[1] The fact that a Swiss merchant house during the colonial era could so successfully engage in business activities on the Indian subcontinent shows the degree to which countries that did not possess any overseas territories of their own were nevertheless integrated into the colonial world order. This study thus ties into recent research efforts to shed light on Swiss involvement in colonialism.[2] Furthermore, it illustrates that even during the Imperial Age markets were often not congruent with imperial borders. Even during the colonial era, the key sales markets for Indian raw cotton—for many years the main product traded by Volkart—were not within the confines of the British Empire, but rather in continental Europe and East Asia. Furthermore, the present work follows up on recent endeavors to look beyond the formal empire when examining India's economic history during the late nineteenth and early twentieth centuries.[3]

By examining such phenomena, this book offers a new perspective on economic globalization in the nineteenth and twentieth centuries. Instead of comprehending the emergence of global markets as merely the result of supply and demand, or as a consequence of imperial policies, this work focuses on a single global trading firm in a bid to reveal more about the players who were responsible for conducting economic transactions in a multicultural business environment. The question is how European merchants could establish business contacts with members of the mercantile elite of Asia, and in other parts of the world, and what role a shared mercantile culture played in establishing relationships based on mutual trust. Moreover, the present volume examines how global business practices changed with the construction of telegraph lines and railways and the development of economic institutions such as merchant banks and commodity exchanges after the mid-nineteenth century. And, finally, the text explores the relationship between the business interests of transnationally operating capitalists and the territorial aspirations of national and imperial governments.

Private trading firms were responsible for a large proportion of cross-border commercial transactions during the nineteenth and early twentieth centuries.[4] Although one can hardly deny the vital importance of internationally active trading companies for the development of the modern global economy, experts in the fields of corporate and world history have shown relatively little interest in the history of these globally active companies.[5] The present study thus closes a gap in the research that has been frequently bemoaned[6] and is the first study of the history of Volkart that meets academic standards.[7] By connecting established approaches in the area of business history with recent achievements in the fields of global and colonial history, this book goes well beyond a mere company history. It aims to highlight the relationship between multinational firms and both national and imperial governments, while underscoring the role of business culture in establishing notions of trust between economic players in different parts of the world. Based on an actor-theoretical perspective, the book maintains that the global market that came into being in the nineteenth century can be viewed as the consequence of the interaction of various players. Merchants, peasants, colonial bureaucrats and industrialists were all involved in spinning the web of the global market.[8]

The Individual Threads of the Web of Global Trade

How best to imagine the functioning of a modern trading company? An initial response to this question is offered by a diagram that shows the firm's procurement and sales organization and was originally printed in the 1926 jubilee publication that marked the company's 75th anniversary.

Five years earlier, the trading company had given a very similar flowchart to its customers and employees and commented on it with the following words:

> The entire organization manifests itself as a vast spiderweb, with Winterthur at its center. This central location reveals at a glance the pivotal role that the Winterthur headquarters has been called upon to play in overseeing our movements of goods. This is where the threads of the points of purchasing and selling intersect, and it is from here that buying and selling is regulated and financed.[9]

In contrast to earlier representations, in 1926 Winterthur was no longer alone at the heart of the corporate "spiderweb," but had been joined by the London branch, which five years earlier had been merely portrayed as an office. This image was a more accurate reflection of the reality of the

EINKAUFS- UND VERKAUFS-ORGANISATION DER FIRMA GEBR. VOLKART

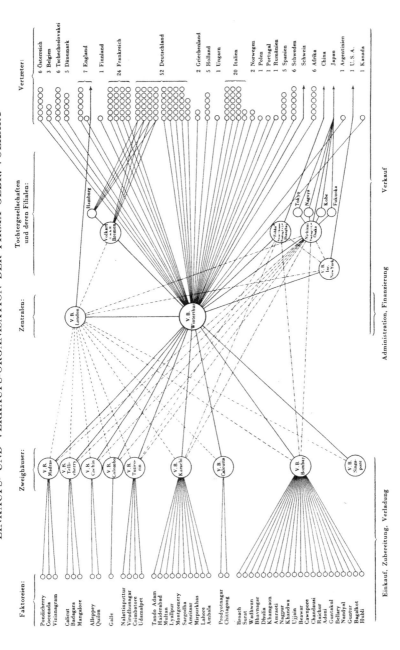

Figure 0.1 Buying and sales organization of the Volkart Brothers company in 1926 (from: Reinhart, Gedenkschrift, 1926, 38–39.)

company's business, since both main offices—the headquarters in Winterthur and the branch in London—were jointly responsible for coordinating and financing the firm's commercial activities. Yet in both cases the chart showed on the left-hand side the agencies and branches in India and Singapore that were responsible for the procurement of commodities, and on the right-hand side the subsidiaries and offices in Europe, East Asia and the US that sold the goods to the industrial enterprises in those parts of the world. The traded commodities were of course never shipped to the company headquarters, but instead transferred directly from the ports of arrival to the relevant industrial districts.

This chart follows in a long tradition of creating diagrams designed to impress upon viewers and potential customers the efficiency and productivity of the companies in question. As German historian Karl Schlögel remarked, it is a common practice of "big companies and banks" to publish maps of their worldwide organizations to demonstrate that "the global presence is an objective fact that no one, anywhere, can escape." Such a representation is not self-explanatory, though, and highly open to interpretation: "Maps speak the language of their makers and remain silent on what the cartographer does not, or cannot, speak of," Schlögel notes.[10] In essence, this representation of the procurement and sales networks of the Volkart company provides no information on how the company was able to establish and maintain business ties with merchants in a multitude of regions of the world. It also reveals nothing about how the company owners acquired loans for their commercial transactions or how they ensured that their employees throughout the world followed the instructions of the headquarters in Winterthur. Furthermore, the diagram raises the question of the relationship between the company's cross-border transactions and the territorial ambitions of national governments. What was the relationship between Volkart as a Swiss company and the British colonial government in India? And to what extent did the trading company benefit from the efforts of the colonial powers to open Asian countries to Western merchants?

One means of pursuing such questions is to interpret the diagram as a representation of interconnected actions. Every large and small circle, every agency and branch office, can be viewed as a social hub that was connected with the rest of the company and the firm's surroundings in a myriad of ways. At each of these hubs the company's employees and partners maintained their own individual business ties to a wide range of players, including peasants, moneylenders and colonial officials in India, compradors in China, bankers in London and Zurich, insurance agents, customs officials, commodity exchange brokers and factory owners. And each of the connecting lines was synonymous with the physical movement of commodities like cotton, coffee, coconut fibers, spices and rubber, which were all transported by rail and steamship from the South Asian backcountry to the industrial regions of East Asia, Europe and America.

The corporate "spiderweb" of the Volkart company thus represented an important link in the global commodity chains of diverse raw materials.[11] This network was connected with economic structures in various parts of the world that, as a whole, formed a system that could be referred to as the global market, which in turn could also be conceived of as a web-like structure of interconnected actions. A number of years before the publication of the abovementioned diagram, German historian Paul Arndt described the global economy in a manner that was very similar to the approach chosen by the managers at Volkart in 1921. Arndt saw the global economy in 1913 as a worldwide web with regional centers "in the civilized world" whose "threads . . . connect each individual enterprise . . . with millions of other enterprises."[12] In accordance with this image, the corporate structure of Volkart was but one component of this global web of economic exchanges of goods and every business relationship between the diverse branches of the company, and between the company and its customers, constituted its threads.

Based on these observations, the history of the Volkart company will serve as the starting point for reconstructing the social and cultural-historical foundations of global trade in the second half of the nineteenth century and during the twentieth century. Special focus here will be on the question of how trading companies embedded their transactions on various continents in the relevant social and economic company settings.[13] How were global trading networks established and how did companies like Volkart ensure that the individual threads of these networks remained stable and did not simply snap when strained?

Volkart thus serves as a paradigm to describe the socio-cultural processes that accompany economic exchanges on a worldwide scale, and often make them possible in the first place, bearing in mind that the actions of individual players transpired within a very specific and highly dynamic political and economic environment. In order to describe the dynamic interaction between these determining factors and the authority of individual players to act, this study is characterized by a constant shift between a micro- and a macro-perspective.[14] On the following pages of this introduction, diverse aspects will be presented that are relevant to this study along with an explanation of how it fits in with the current state of research. First, it will be explained why markets can be interpreted as structures that emerge through the actions of individual players, and are thus also characterized by the culturally interpreted patterns that form the basis for these actions. Second, it will be demonstrated that trading companies doing business overseas serve an important function, not least of all because they provide market information and can thus reduce information and transaction costs. The third section deals with the political context within which Volkart moved. It will be shown that the activities of trading companies during the late nineteenth century and the twentieth century were influenced by the rise of the West and the global inequality that followed in its wake. It will also be shown that the populations in the respective host countries had a certain local power to act, and that globally active companies had to take this into account, for example, when they cooperated with indigenous merchants. The fourth section aims to shed light on the relationship between territoriality and global capitalism, with particular focus on the scope of action available to multinational firms. The fifth and last section examines the internal structure that a trading company like Volkart required to exercise its intermediary function in a volatile business sector such as the commodities trade.

Global Markets as a Result of Social Interaction

The unprecedented growth of global trade, which increased by a factor of more than 10 from 1850 to 1913, has been the subject of intense research for many years. Experts in modern economic history generally explain this expansion by pointing to technological and infrastructural innovations—the telegraph, railways, steamships and the construction of the Suez Canal—and the establishment of the gold standard as key developments that steadily paved the way for smoother operational procedures in the international exchange of goods. The focus of such an account is on the economic policies of diverse national governments and fluctuations in the volume of trade between various nation-states.[15] Accordingly, the general view in the literature is that an initial wave of economic globalization was followed by a phase of deglobalization in which global trade stagnated. This phase began with World War I and culminated in the global economic turmoil of the Great Depression in the early 1930s.[16]

This relatively simplistic periodization can be challenged by examining the economic players who were responsible for conducting these international commercial transactions. During the nineteenth and early twentieth centuries, these were primarily private trading companies that served as intermediaries between buyers and sellers across national and continental borders, particularly when it came to the global trade of commodities. Trading firms had an entrepreneurial organization that was capable of providing manufacturers in industrialized countries with specific quantities of raw materials at an agreed point in time. They guaranteed the quality of the goods, handled the financing of the transport and bore the risk of fluctuating prices between the moment of purchase in the growing countries and the sale of the merchandise in the industrialized countries.

In a very general sense, the history of trading companies reveals that markets do not automatically emerge as a result of supply and demand. Instead, as this study intends to show, it takes economic players to create these markets based on their specific sets of skills and expertise. They do this by offering certain services—such as selecting and preparing goods, organizing transport, warehousing, granting credit and establishing customer contacts—that allow physically separated buyers and sellers to enter into a relationship.[17]

Economists like John Hicks and Carsten Herrmann-Pillath see merchants as vital intermediaries of economic transactions and ascribe them a central role in the formation of markets.[18] Hence, market structures are the result of evolving regular economic exchanges that establish routines and obligations and channel the actions of market players. Such an understanding of markets, based on the theories of structuration put forward by Max Weber and Anthony Giddens, ties in with recent approaches to global history.[19] Jürgen Osterhammel and Niels P. Petersson, for example, argue—in reference to the work of Manuel Castells—[20] that it is necessary "to approach globalization by studying interactions between individuals and groups" that can "transform themselves into networks [and] . . . gain stability."[21]

Such an action-theoretical approach has consequences for the importance of culturally interpreted patterns in economic exchanges.[22] According to Clifford Geertz, culture can be interpreted as a web of meaning that guides human activity.[23] Weber, to whom Geertz explicitly refers, pointed out that every action can only be seen as a social action if it has an intended purpose. It is only when actions by a number of actors mutually relate to each other that a social relationship is formed. This only achieves a certain degree of stability through the establishment of specific norms, which lead to sanctions if they are violated.[24] It thus stands to reason that economic transactions always take place within certain cultural parameters. Economic exchanges are only possible if there exists a minimum of shared ideologies and a degree of trust; and engendering mutual trust can be seen as a fundamental precondition for economic players to be willing to enter into a business relationship in the first place.[25] Nonetheless, trust is not an institution in the sense of a guiding norm, but instead is based on certain preconditions, such as information on potential or actual business partners or the existence of institutions that provide assurances that contracts can be fulfilled.[26]

Yet another consequence of such an actor-centered approach to global trade is that it raises critical questions about the abovementioned postulate, namely that a Victorian globalization was followed by a phase of deglobalization after 1918. A number of business historians have pointed out that the interwar era was by no means a historic period in which companies restricted their activities to their home markets. In fact, it was during this period that many companies began to do business on a global scale, in part in reaction to the growing protectionism of the day.[27] This also holds true for Volkart, which after 1918 evolved from a company that primarily focused on British India to a truly global player. The historical data suggest that the development of global trade should not be viewed as a teleological process in which differentiations can only be made between phases of globalization and deglobalization. Instead, as Frederick Cooper has noted, researchers should focus on possible asynchronicities and contradictions within such globalization processes and pay particular attention to possible discrepancies between the actions of diverse global players.[28]

Trading Companies and the History of Global Trade

An examination of the literature on the economic history of the nineteenth and twentieth centuries could easily lead any reader to conclude that trading companies were of little importance to the modern global economy. Most studies deal with the history of manufacturing companies or explore the emergence of today's consumer society, but rarely focus on trading companies. Even the current extensive literature on multi- and transnational corporations deals first and foremost with foreign direct investments along with the conditions for globally distributed production, and gives short shrift to trading companies.[29] It appears that among economic and business historians these firms are basically viewed as relics of the preindustrial age. This supposition is supported by the observation that there is an overwhelming wealth of literature on trading history and trading companies for the period prior to 1800, ranging from Germany's Fugger family of bankers and traders to the Venetians, the Arab and Indian trading networks, the Hanseatic League and the British and Dutch East India companies.[30]

Why have trading companies received such little attention in the historiography of the industrial age? It cannot be a reflection of their actual importance. Internationally operating trading companies played a key role in shaping global trade during the nineteenth and twentieth centuries. Although global trade was characterized by the general political conditions of the day, concrete business ties were forged exclusively by private economic initiatives, especially with regard to the flourishing trade in natural commodities like cotton, wool, grain, coffee, tea and sugar, which formed the basis for the modern industrial and consumer society. The formation of a global market was primarily made possible by the business activities of globally operating merchants.[31] In contrast to the views of contemporary observers, along with modern economists like John Dunning, the activities of mercantile houses were not limited to trading in commodities.[32] To be sure, many of the large-scale enterprises that were founded in the sectors of mechanical engineering, chemical production and the food industry during the course of the second wave of industrialization in the late nineteenth century set up their own branch offices abroad to promote the sales of their products, and in some cases also shifted their production to the relevant countries. But there were many instances in which—depending on the order volume and the structure of the relevant markets—it was more efficient to market their products by engaging the services of well-established local mercantile houses.[33]

A first—and relatively banal—reason that modern trading companies have been so widely disregarded by historians is probably that these companies have a low profile in the public consciousness. While large-scale industrial production with sprawling factories, smoke-belching chimneys and new housing settlements for workers have left clearly recognizable traces in the landscape, and the products of the modern consumer society remain ubiquitous on the billboards of today's cities and in contemporary house-holds, the activities of import and export companies are only known to a small circle of economic players. What's more, trading firms often display a strong propensity for discretion. Since they are usually privately owned, they are not required to divulge their balance sheets. Given this level of secrecy, publicly available figures pertaining to their sales and profits are often entirely based on rough estimates.

In addition to this obvious and not to be underestimated source-related problem, there is a second—and far more fundamental—reason. The sparse research literature on modern trading companies is not least a consequence of the way in which economists and economic historians conceive the emer-gence of modern markets. Many researchers appear to agree that the market develops more or less automatically when plants and factories are suffi-ciently productive, when the necessary means of information and transport are available, and when political authorities place no constraints on the invisible hand of the market. This notion finds its equivalent in the neoclas-sical view of markets as an abstract model, which allows experts to identify feasible market prices by plotting the intersection of supply and demand curves.[34] This model has proven enormously effective, yet it fails to address a number of problems faced by real-life market players, most notably the costs associated with using the market, i.e., the information and transac-tion costs. Transaction costs is the term used by institutional economics to denote the usage costs of the market, in other words, the costs incurred by economic players when they have to make provisions for the actual, or at least potential, dishonesty of business partners and employees.[35] Mar-ket players can reduce transaction costs in two different ways. First, they can attempt to minimize them by introducing certain rules and regulations, in other words, institutions—with a distinction made here between formal institutions (contracts, trade regulations, etc.) and informal institutions (customs, concepts of honor, etc.).[36] Second, entrepreneurs can reduce trans-action costs by integrating certain operations into their own companies. As Ronald Coase postulated in his pioneering article for the field of institu-tional economics, "The Nature of the Firm," the emergence of companies is largely a reflection of the fact that by internalizing operations within a firm there are fewer transaction costs than if the same transactions had been concluded on the open market.[37]

A number of researchers feel that trading companies have been largely ignored in the study of the modern global economy mainly because many experts in the field have underestimated the importance of transaction costs to the smooth functioning of global trade.[38] Overseas trading was—and remains in many respects even today—an extremely risky business: buyers and sellers had to do business with people whom they did not know on a personal basis and who often lived on other continents. They had to take out loans and pay advances, sell goods that did not yet belong to them and whose exact qualities were often unknown to them, not to mention ship goods for which they had not yet found buyers. These activities often entailed considerable risk because formal institutions were often lacking in the sector or they simply provided insufficient security. In the second half of the nineteenth century, influential industry organizations like the cotton traders' associations in Bremen and Liverpool, the silk merchants in Lyon and the Chicago Board of Trade introduced standard contracts and an elaborate arbitration system that was binding for all players in the respective trading venues.[39] But this private type of regulation did not work in Asia for many years (with the exception of Japan) because there were no strong associations or efficiently run commodity exchanges like the ones in Europe and North and South America. To make matters worse, even in the Atlantic trade commercial transactions were fraught with risk, as arbitration procedures and legal disputes were often extremely protracted and the risk of payment defaults could never be entirely ruled out. By being prepared to take these risks, trading companies could internalize some of the usage costs of the market and offer this as a service to other market players. Moreover, by being able to bridge common gaps in information and confidence in long-distance transactions, they served a key function in the emergence of a global market.[40]

Trade History as a Key Component of Global History

For more than 100 years after its establishment, the Volkart company shipped commodities from colonial India to the industrial regions of Europe and East Asia and exported European consumer and industry goods to Asia. Its history spans the globe and must be understood within the context of the European expansion during the nineteenth century and the rise of the West to political and economic supremacy.[41] Nevertheless, the history of Volkart goes well beyond the colonial historical context. First of all, Volkart was a Swiss company. Although it had a main office in London, it would be historically inaccurate to confine the company's story to a tale of the relationship between the metropole and colonial periphery in the days of the British Empire. Second, the company had a geographical operating range that extended well beyond the confines of the British Empire and it outlived British colonial rule. Even during the colonial era, Volkart maintained business contacts with companies in countries like China (which was only indirectly subject to British imperial dominion), Japan and the US (which were both independent of Britain). Likewise, the firm engaged in intensive business activities in Latin America after the end of the colonial era.

A broader approach to the tale of a European global trading company is provided by the world-systems theory, which was developed by Immanuel Wallerstein to describe the history of the capitalist global economy and the international state system from the sixteenth century onwards.[42] According to Wallerstein, this world-system has its roots in Europe and gradually incorporated other regions of the world to establish a global division of labor between the European core and the countries of the periphery. While the economy of the core is characterized by a highly developed industrial means of production, he argues that the role of the periphery is to provide the core with cheap raw materials and labor. Starting in the 1970s, the world-systems theory was one of the leading macro-historical approaches to the development of the modern world, but it has fallen somewhat out of favor in recent years.[43] One of the weaknesses of this approach is that it posits an existing supremacy of the European economy from the early modern period onward and sees non-European players as only having a very limited ability to act. This Eurocentric perspective has been rejected by many researchers in recent years. Kenneth Pomeranz, for instance, emphasizes from a macro-historical perspective the fundamental similarity between England and the China of the Yangtze Delta until the inception of the Industrial Revolution.[44] Numerous researchers have also shown that during pre-colonial times South Asia ranked among the most highly developed economic regions in the world, and the regions surrounding the Indian Ocean pursued intensive economic exchanges as well.[45] In effect, even before the arrival of the Europeans, the peoples of Asia engaged in a bustling foreign trade that was complemented and further developed by European expansion. India in particular became the key link between two trading circles—an Indian-European and an Indian-East Asian circle—that were gradually integrated into a single global economy.[46] This did not necessarily mean that Europe or the US were the destinations of commodities produced in the periphery. Trade often flowed differently than it should have according to the world-systems theory, such as when most of the cotton from colonial India was used in Japan from the 1890s onwards (and not in Britain or even in Europe), and when the industrial upswing in India, China and Japan prompted these Asian countries to begin importing an increasing amount of cotton from the US starting in the 1920s.[47]

Instead of conceiving the global economy that emerged in the nineteenth century as a trend toward globalization that emanated solely from Europe, researchers would be well advised to view this as a number of different coexisting economic zones that were each dominated by a highly developed, highly capitalized core region, in line with what Fernand Braudel has suggested for the early modern era.[48] Even though the London of the nineteenth century and New York from the 1920s onwards were the worldwide leading centers of trade and finance, there also existed other centers of commerce that had a profound influence on specific economic regions. In Asia, for instance, Japan undoubtedly played such a role from the 1890s onwards. In recent years, a number of Japanese historians have therefore suggested that the economic history of Asian during the nineteenth and twentieth centuries should not be merely viewed as a process of European expansion followed by an Asian reaction, but rather that research should focus more on studying the economic relationships between individual Asian countries.[49]

The subject of the present work also represents a departure from a Eurocentric perspective in favor of a polycentric history of the global economy, as the connections between diverse commercial centers and their relevant peripheries were maintained in large part by merchants conducting business in the overseas trade sector.[50] In recent years, researchers have increasingly recognized that global history is not so much a "history of everything" and that it cannot be a matter of inevitably choosing the entire planet as one's realm of inquiry. Instead, historians should endeavor to develop a sensitivity for possible global interdependencies. However, such an orientation toward historical interactions does not necessarily mean that individual actors had similar opportunities to assert their interests. Both in the colonial and post-colonial context, interactions were invariably characterized by the imbalances of power in the modern world.[51] When it comes to the history of global trade, this means that flows of goods and business ties were intertwined with economic, political and military power relationships. A number of factors allowed European companies to dominate global trade from the mid-nineteenth century, including the Industrial Revolution, colonial rule, the emergence of modern stock exchanges and the fact that an efficient banking system was established in mid-century, which allowed the Old Continent to become the world's leading exporter of capital from the 1870s onwards.[52] Particularly in the commodities trading sector, merchants in the growing countries—who until then had often played an astonishingly big role in the exporting of goods to industrialized countries—were increasingly forced out of the export business from the mid-nineteenth century onwards.[53]

The history of global trade thus draws our attention to a complex web of shared histories.[54] Although long-distance trade by definition deals with transporting goods from far-flung corners of the world, it was often local social and power structures that determined the success or failure of business ventures. With the advent of commercial banks, commodity exchanges and telegraph communications, transport between ports of shipment in South Asia and Latin America and the industrial regions of Europe, Japan and the US became fairly manageable for mercantile houses in the commodities trading sector. It was significantly more difficult, however, to finance purchases in the hinterland of foreign countries, establish contact with local peasants and middlemen, and enforce contractual terms in an unfamiliar business environment. Researchers like David Washbrook, C. A. Bayly and Rajat Kanta Ray have shown that European merchants in Asia, even during the colonial era, were reliant upon native intermediaries who made credit available and ensured that their European clients could establish business contacts in remote, virtually inaccessible regions.[55] It goes without saying that the Volkart company also relied upon the cooperation of local merchants when doing business in foreign countries. In this sense, global trade was highly characterized by processes of "glocalization," as Roland Robertson referred to these dialectical amalgamations of local and global structures. This confirms Arjun Appadurai's theory that globalization generally does not eliminate local elements, but that instead local and global forces often mutually "cannibalize" each other.[56] By tracing such processes, this study intends to take a closer look at the spatial aspects of global economic interactions.[57]

It is important to note, however, that collaborations among European trading companies and non-European merchants were only possible if both parties had a similar understanding of how commercial transactions were to be conducted. But did such commonalities actually exist? Or did European merchants in foreign lands meet with cultural barriers and business partners whose actions were geared to a different economic rationality? When examining the history of a European trading company that was active in Asia during the better part of its existence, it would appear logical to focus on the differences between the European and Asian cultural environments, based on the assumption that both cultures are inherently homogenous and there exist significant differences between them. Such a hypothesis is advocated in a range of sweeping historical studies that deal with the rise of the West during the course of the Industrial Revolution, including recent works by David S. Landes and Gregory Clark.[58] Rudyard Kipling summed it up in his famous poem "Ballad of East and West" with the words "East is East, and West is West, and never the twain shall meet." European culture was widely portrayed as rational and modern in such juxtapositions, while Asia was characterized as an archaic and mystical "wonderland" in which Western-style economic rationality had no place. This would mean that there existed widely divergent concepts of honesty, trustworthiness and economic rationality in Europe and Asia, and that it was precisely these differences that made commercial transactions with Asia so difficult for Europeans.

A number of researchers, most notably Jack Goody, have called into question such a difference between both regions.[59] Aside from the fact that comparing such diverse major world regions like Europe and Asia is per se rather questionable, a number of empirical studies suggest that the differences between European and Asian business cultures, at least in terms of merchant traditions, are much less pronounced than what is often assumed. C. A. Bayly, for example, has shown that Indian merchants adapted very similar business practices, such as double-entry bookkeeping and issuing bills of exchange, and had a similar concept of the merchant's code of honor as their European counterparts. In fact, it was precisely these similarities that allowed the British East India Company to establish commercial ties with Indian mercantile houses and tie into the economy of the subcontinent.[60] The merchants' customary law, the *lex mercatoria*, whose sole principle is that contracts are to be fulfilled, and which has been characterized by German legal theorist Gunther Teubner as a "global law without a state," thus constituted a highly effective institutional foundation for the Asian trade.[61]

It was a similar story in other parts of the world, such as in North America and Latin America. Hence, the economic exchange between European and non-European merchants can be interpreted as a social interaction that was able to take place because both parties had internalized specific mercantile cultures that were sufficiently similar to serve as the basis for a business relationship.[62] During their economic expansion, Europeans encountered a mercantile elite that adhered to similar guiding principles and practices. It was only based on such a shared cultural foundation that an understanding could be reached about the way in which business was to be conducted and about the nature of partnerships, and it was only based on such a cornerstone that business relationships could be maintained over considerable periods of time. A shared mercantile culture engendered a sense of trust and helped the Europeans to embed their transactions in an unfamiliar Asian business environment. This mercantile culture can be construed as an informal institution as formulated by Douglass North, in other words, as a set of conventions and behavioral norms designed to minimize transaction costs.[63] This of course does not mean that collaborations always went smoothly and opportunistic acts could be ruled out entirely. But problems generally arose from differing interests and not because both parties had difficulties deciphering the guiding principles and worldviews of the other side. This is also not to say that the merchants' customary law could function completely without the protection of state and political authorities. When political orders became unstable, as described in the present study with regard to China and the interwar era, the existence of commercial networks was seriously threatened.

Political Economy and International Trading Companies

Although the field of global history is often characterized by efforts to overcome the nation-state paradigm, studies of the history of global trade have not led researchers to dismiss the importance of the nation. Indeed, the immense importance of the nation can often be better understood, or at least grasped in a different manner, from a global or transnational perspective. International trade relations have always been complicated by the fact that cross-border commodity and financial transactions could potentially conflict with the efforts of state governments to secure their borders and maintain their national sovereignty. The relationship between private economic players and state authorities has always been extremely contradictory and in a constant state of flux. Indeed, although the late nineteenth century witnessed the first emergence of a globally interconnected economy and imperial expansion, often leading it to be called the first era of globalization, this period in history was also characterized by a consolidation of national identities and state borders.[64] Not surprisingly, researchers like Ian Clark and Sebastian Conrad have expressed the view that globalization and territorialization are not antithetical trends, but instead should be seen as two sides of the same coin, and that a dialectical interdependency exists between the two concepts.[65]

During the nineteenth century, it was by and large the expansion efforts of imperial powers that paved the way for European companies to be able to do business in certain overseas markets. In their classic essay on the

"Imperialism of Free Trade," John Gallagher and Roland Robinson noted that the European powers had a preference for informal exertion of influence and strove to integrate non-European regions into the global economy dominated by Europe, yet without instituting formal colonial rule.[66] When this proved impossible, they often resorted to gunboat diplomacy to force reluctant nations to open their ports and allow Western merchants to establish trade ties,[67] as happened in China and Japan during the mid-nineteenth century. Colonial possessions like India were transformed with great effort to meet the needs of Western merchants, for example, by building roads and railroads, installing telegraph lines, tailoring agricultural production to the raw material requirements of European industry and instituting Western law.[68] Although these interventions often had serious consequences for the indigenous population, and can be rightly qualified as acts of economic exploitation, colonial rule remained an extremely fragile entity, as it constantly relied on the cooperation of native elites. The social and economic power structures in the colonial hinterland, which the Europeans had difficulty controlling, often led to the failure of the economic objectives of the colonial rulers. Furthermore, European merchants generally favored the intervention of the colonial power apparatus only to the extent that it served their interests and they reacted otherwise with indignation when state bureaucrats took it upon themselves to interfere in their business.

Even though European companies were able to benefit from the expansion efforts of imperial powers, the relationship between the realms of business and politics, even under capitalism, was far more contradictory than what is postulated by the world-systems theory or Marxist historical research.[69] Italian sociologist Giovanni Arrighi even argued that capitalism and state territoriality were two completely different modes of rule. Arrighi said that territoriality endeavors to control the land and the local population, whereas the control of capital is merely a means to an end. In other words, capitalism is primarily concerned with achieving the greatest possible mobility of capital, whereas controlling territories and people is, in his view, nothing more than a means of increasing returns for shareholders.[70] Likewise, David Fieldhouse challenges the conventional wisdom that multinational industrial companies could only be profitable in foreign markets if they received a state guaranteed monopoly status: "Exactly the opposite is generally true of the modern manufacturing multinationals. They are, by their nature, interested in freedom of trade outside their protected home base. They do not need physical control over their markets."[71] This phenomenon was even more pronounced for internationally active trading firms. As long as they did not own vast estates or large industrial plants—and many trading companies consciously refrained from such backward and forward integration—and instead focused on the international trading business, their interest in territorial matters was relatively limited. Moreover, as will be shown throughout the course of this work, they often used the transnational structures of their businesses to evade domestic and international efforts to control the trading sector.

Between the mid-nineteenth century and the late twentieth century, there were changing views on whether, and to what extent, international trade should be politically regulated. Whereas the decades following 1846, when Britain unilaterally abolished its key tariffs, were characterized by the spirit of free trade, this was followed by a period of increasing politicization of international trade from the 1880s onwards that intensified during the inter-war era and culminated in the economic crisis of the 1930s.[72] In a bid to protect their domestic economies, most states subsequently regulated the cross-border movement of goods and capital.[73] This trend intensified after 1945 with the outbreak of the Cold War and, more importantly, the decolonization movement, which led to the nationalization of companies in many commodity-producing countries and more control of foreign trade.[74] These political regulations were rescinded again with the end of the Cold War and the rise of neoliberal ideologies starting in the 1970s, resulting in an ever-growing liberalization of global trade.

While government policies on controlling global trade charted a highly erratic course, trading companies gradually underwent a consolidation process that focused first and foremost on the commodities business, in which new industrial production methods made economies of scale more and more important. Whereas up until the mid-nineteenth century countless small and medium-sized mercantile houses vied for control of the commodities trade, by the end of the twentieth century only roughly 50 internationally active trading companies controlled the global trade in products like cotton, coffee, sugar and grain. Firms like Cargill, Bunge & Born, Ralli, Louis Dreyfus and Swiss trading companies such as André and Volkart no longer focused on specific geographical regions, as they had done during the nineteenth century, but instead began to establish an increasingly global company structure, which explains why the literature refers to them as multinational traders.[75] Thanks to their powerful hold on the market, but even more so to their transnational organizational structures, these companies evolved to become modern leviathans—at least that is what they are called by Alfred Chandler and Bruce Mazlish—that were successfully able to fend off all political attempts to intervene in their business transactions.[76]

Corporate Culture and Micro-political Structures

Besides examining the context in which global trading companies operated, this study also aims to shed light on the nature of their internal structure. Because global trade is characterized by volatility and an asymmetrical information situation, trading firms required a high degree of internal stability to survive. An action-theoretical approach allows us to view these firms not simply as mysterious "black boxes," which mediate between buyers and sellers in various corners of the world, but rather as social entities.

Like all companies, trading firms consist of coalitions of collaborating individuals, each with their own interests. These "micro-political" structures can be interpreted as transaction costs for the company.[77] Particularly when it came to overseas trading, the vast distances involved often made it difficult for company owners to control their employees working in branch offices abroad. This asymmetrical information situation made the principal-agent problem a significant hurdle for trading firms.[78] In an attempt to limit opportunistic behavior to the greatest degree possible, trading companies in pre-modern times dealt with this conundrum at diverse trading centers around the world by frequently employing individuals who were committed to them through family, regional or confessional ties.[79]

The challenges that the owners of trading companies faced were compounded by the economic developments that took place during the second half of the nineteenth century, which Alfred Chandler described in his pioneering study "Scale and Scope."[80] Until the mid-nineteenth century, overseas trading was predominately pursued by small and medium-sized mercantile houses that offered a wide range of products, from jewelry and textiles, to sugar, spices and cotton. From the second half of the nineteenth century, these trading firms could no longer meet the needs of the growing industrial manufacturing sector. Commodities like cotton, silk, coffee and cocoa were henceforth imported by specialized companies that had to achieve economies of scale to remain competitive. To safeguard product quality, many trading companies established procurement agencies in the areas of cultivation along with sales organizations in the industrialized countries, giving major trading companies a customer base that went far beyond their own countries of origin. Since it required a great deal of capital to establish purchasing and sales agencies that would pave the way for the necessary increase in sales, from the late nineteenth century onwards the lion's share of the global trade in commodities was dominated by a handful of multinational companies, some of which had enormous turnovers. This consolidation process went hand-in-hand with increasingly advanced business practices. Trading companies were forced to institute control mechanisms to ensure product quality and they had to recognize changes in supply and demand as early as possible. What's more, they had to establish and maintain contacts with commercial and merchant banks to ensure a sufficient ongoing line of credit. Last but not least, they had to familiarize themselves with the functioning of the emerging commodity exchanges of the late nineteenth century so they could carry out operations in the futures market to safeguard their transactions against price fluctuations. Leading trading companies became highly complex entities with agencies and branches in diverse parts of the world and a large number of employees who often had very different linguistic, cultural, religious and national backgrounds. The job of running individual divisions of these companies was increasingly assumed by a professional management staff, which is a development that has unmistakable parallels with the evolution of modern industrial companies.[81]

Nevertheless, there was no transition from family capitalism to manager capitalism in the trading business. Because long-term investments were limited—in contrast to industrial large-scale enterprises—and daily operations could be financed with bank loans, most trading companies remained privately owned until well into the twentieth century. But the control mechanisms of traditional family capitalism were no longer sufficient to manage companies that often had thousands of employees on a number of different continents. In addition to relying on strict monitoring, which was facilitated by improved communications and means of transport, company owners established a corporate culture based on trust to prevent employees from engaging in speculative or fraudulent transactions. The many years of socialization experienced by the workforce played a key role here.[82] Employees could generally assume that they would be employed by the respective trading firm for the duration of their careers, not least of all because throughout the course of their professional life they had amassed enormous knowledge of the products carried by the company, along with the business practices of the relevant markets, all of which often made it extremely difficult for their employers to replace them.[83]

The fact that Volkart, like many other trading companies, remained family owned played a decisive role in the establishment of a corporate culture that was highly influenced by the ideals of an entrepreneurial family, and thus had a decidedly paternalistic quality to it.[84] Family enterprises operated as a rule according to long timescales and owners often took into account family and company traditions when making their decisions.[85] Various action-theoretical and cultural anthropological studies have also shown that economic players did not always allow themselves to be swayed by cost considerations, even in modern companies.[86] Their decisions often adhered to a bounded rationality that was path dependent to the extent that it was characterized by ideals and earlier decisions. Particularly in family enterprises—but certainly not limited to such environments—players often did not differentiate between a company-related economic rationality and a family-private rationality, as they should have done according to mainstream economic and sociological schools of thought. Max Weber, for example, was of the opinion that entrepreneurs in the "capitalist enterprise" allow themselves to be guided by the "the objective interests of rational management of a business," adding that this is by no means identical to their private or family interests that have an "affectual basis" and are characterized by "feelings of mutual solidarity." Hence, these private interests "stand in direct conflict with the rational . . . economically specialized organization of their environment."[87] However, surveys that place economic players at the heart of their analyses show that these players often do not orient their actions toward the specific logic of certain functionally differentiated social subsystems, but instead transcend these in their thoughts and actions. As will be shown in this study, the occasional big-hearted gestures of company owners toward their employees were not necessarily motivated by goal-oriented monetary motives. Instead, they were born out of a sense of obligation toward company traditions and thus characterized by a certain company-specific habitus.[88] This does not mean that the cultural concept of an entrepreneurial family, governed by feelings of mutual obligation, cannot be economically profitable. On the contrary, investing in long-term social relationships ensured mutual loyalty, thereby reducing internal transaction costs. Yet the corporate culture of these firms was far more than a corporate strategy to prevent opportunistic behavior on the part of employees. It was an integral part of the self-image of each individual player and represented a set of company-specific precepts used by all parties to guide their actions, at times consciously or unconsciously, at times in an effort to reach a consensus or foment conflict. Both owners and employees thus acted within the parameters of bounded forms of rationality made to fit the logic of their own interpretations of their surroundings. They relied upon inventories of self-evident, preconscious local or implicit knowledge, which characterized the culture of the company and its identity.[89]

Ideally, such a corporate culture operated in harmony with commercial activities, as was the case with Volkart and various other European trading firms. The company owners relied on informal rules, both with respect to their customers and their employees, and on business practices based on trust and long-term relationships. The question of whether this was a general characteristic of modern trading companies or whether, depending on the sector or geographical origin, other forms of corporate culture took shape cannot be answered within the scope of this study and will have to be clarified in future works.

Source Material

The main source of material for this work was the Volkart company archives, which were not open to the public until 2015 and could only be accessed with special permission (they were transferred to the Winterthur Municipal Archives after the completion of this study). This was the first time that all of the existing material in the company archives was examined within the context of an academic study. Although for reasons of space large amounts of material were destroyed after the company withdrew from the trading business in the late 1990s, by international standards the archives still contain an abundance of high-quality material, including letter books, correspondence files, minutes of meetings, statistics and printed matter spanning the entire history of the company, from the 1850s to the late twentieth century. The company placed no restrictions on the access or use of archival files.

Yet despite the relatively comprehensive available source material, there are a number of notable gaps. For instance, there remain only sporadic figures on the sales achieved by the company, often making it difficult to trace the quantitative development of the business. Furthermore, the majority of the archives concern either business activities on the Indian subcontinent or transactions via the headquarters in Winterthur. By contrast, the company archives contain far fewer records on a number of offices, namely the branches in Japan and China, along with subsidiaries in Latin America. As a consequence, local employment situations and the embedding of commercial activities in the respective business surroundings cannot be described in as much detail as would be desirable.

Much of the source material cited in the present volume was originally written in a German that reflects the stylistic conventions of Swiss usage throughout the years. In compiling this English-language edition, every effort has been made to preserve the register and tenor of the original texts in a translation that is readily understandable. Given the international nature of the Volkart company, it should also be noted that much of the source material was in fact originally written in English, but often by non-native speakers of the language, which explains the occasional odd choice of wording or atypical grammatical constructions in the source texts.

Since the source material is particularly sparse for the period after 1950 and for the firm's entry into the coffee business, a series of interviews were conducted, most notably with the former heads of the coffee division, Peter Zurschmiede and Paul Moeller. Likewise, during an archival visit to Central America, several interviews were undertaken with former employees and partners of the Volkart subsidiaries in Guatemala and Costa Rica or with the descendents of these individuals.[90]

In order to explore the economic and political contexts in the various countries in which Volkart conducted business, the author consulted an additional 23 public and private archives in seven countries. At the research library in Winterthur, the collections from the estates of Theodor, Georg and Werner Reinhart were examined, as were the collections of the Swiss Association of Transit and Global Trading Companies, which are housed in the Swiss Economic Archive in Basel. The following collections were examined at the Swiss Federal Archive in Bern: the collections of the Swiss Federal Department of Economic Affairs, of the Political Department and of the Swiss consulates in the countries in which Volkart was active. Likewise, the author visited the archives of diverse companies that cooperated with Volkart, including in Switzerland the archives of the companies of Rieter and Sulzer (both in Winterthur), Diethelm Keller Siber Hegner (Zurich), ABB (Baden), Nestlé (Vevey) and Novartis (Basel), as well as the archive of the Tata firm in Pune, India.

Fruitful sources of information for research into the company's transactions in India included the archives of the Asia, Pacific and Africa Collections in the British Library in London, in India the collections of the Maharashtra State Archives (Mumbai), the National Archives of India and the Nehru Memorial Library (both in New Delhi), and, regarding the company's trade in cotton in Germany, the Archive of the Bremen Cotton Exchange. Documents were consulted pertaining to trading companies that were involved in sectors similar to that of Volkart, most notably at the Guildhall Library (London), which houses the collections of Ralli Brothers and Wallace Brothers, and at the Baker Library of Harvard University (Cambridge, MA), which contains the collections of Neill Bros. & Co. and Stephen M. Weld and Co. The National Archives in London have extensive source material on how global trade was affected by the wartime economic measures enacted by Britain during World War I. Statistical data and source material on coffee exports from Central America were located in the archives of the Asociación Nacional del Café de Guatemala (Ciudad de Guatemala), the Instituto del Café de Costa Rica (San José) and the Archivo Nacional de Costa Rica (San José). Additional sources on the coffee trade were found in the Library of the International Coffee Organization and in the Special Collections of University College (both in London).

Printed sources were found primarily in the following specialized libraries: The Library of the Johann Jacobs Museum in Zurich on the history of coffee, the Library of the International Coffee Organization in London, the Library of the School of Oriental and African Studies in London, the Centre of South Asian Studies of the University of Cambridge, the Widener Library and the Baker Library of Harvard University, the Biblioteca Nacional de Costa Rica in San José and the Archivo General de Centro America in Ciudad de Guatemala. It should also be pointed out that most of the records used for this study stem from European and North American players. It will require additional studies to examine how the processes described in this book were experienced by Asian and Latin American merchants and peasants.

Preview

Based on the story of the Volkart company, the following chapters trace the social and cultural-historical foundations of global trade from the mid-nineteenth to the late twentieth centuries. The chapters are organized chronologically. It is only in Section II that the book makes a slight digression in the time sequence to shed light on the relationship between company owners and employees.

Section I of the book deals with the history of the company within the context of the European expansion between the mid-nineteenth century and the end of World War I. Chapter 1 focuses on the founding phase of the firm and shows that the two company founders acquired extensive commercial experience as employees of diverse trading companies, banking institutions and textile companies—and became intimately familiar with the Indian market—before they launched their own trading firm in 1851. Chapter 2 looks into how business practices changed in the trade between India and Europe thanks to advances in transport and communications starting in the 1860s that resulted in a major process of consolidation in the trading sector. In the late nineteenth century, Volkart rose to become one of the most important trading companies on the Indian subcontinent and, most notably, one of the leading exporters of raw cotton. Nonetheless, companies like Volkart continued to rely on close cooperation with Indian merchants to finance purchases and establish contacts with customers. Chapter 3 shows how sales in Europe were handled by local merchant companies that served as agents for Volkart in the various industrial districts. This chapter also sheds light on the key importance of contact with European banking institutions, which made it possible to finance the ever-growing volume of exports. Such business relationships were extremely stable, in large part because they were characterized by a great degree of interpersonal trust. Chapter 4 shows how the wartime measures instituted during World War I undermined the cultural foundations that, until then, were commonplace in global trade. The national origins of companies became an increasingly important criterion, which exerted pressure on the cosmopolitan orientation that had been adopted by many global trading companies.

Section II examines the company's inner workings. Chapter 5 explains why it was important that Volkart was a family firm in terms of the organization of the business. The emphasis here is on the role of family ownership in stabilizing the enterprise and maintaining business relationships with other companies. Chapter 6 outlines the measures undertaken by the company to counter the risk of opportunistic behavior by employees. Chapter 7 deals with the working conditions in colonial India. The opportunity to work in an exotic country was an important motive for many employees to take on a position with a trading firm abroad. The colonial situation led to various problems, however, such as difficulties relating to the ethnic mix of the workforce.

Section III examines the development of the corporate culture during the interwar era, with a special emphasis on the de-Europeanization of global trade. Chapter 8 describes the degree to which the business of importing commodities to Europe was influenced by rampant protectionism and the crisis-stricken economy during the interwar era. Chapter 9 shows that the increasing influence of Indian companies on agricultural policy led to improvements in the quality of cotton, which was something that the British had tried in vain to achieve during the previous decades. India's industrialization forced the company's owners to decide whether they should continue to limit their activities to trading commodities or instead invest in Indian industrial facilities. Chapter 10 depicts the influence that industrialization in East Asia had on the global cotton trade. During the 1930s, Volkart's involvement in the American cotton sector helped to make it one of the leading companies to export cotton to China and Japan, which shows the extent to which the cotton trade had achieved global dimensions during this period. Chapter 11 shows how Volkart sought to capitalize on Asia's industrialization by selling large quantities of European and American machinery to manufacturers in India, China and Japan.

Section IV demonstrates that the sector was characterized by two contrasting developments after 1945. First, decolonization and, starting with the economic crisis of the 1930s, the ever-growing influence of national governments on commodities exports meant that trade became increasingly regulated and politicized. Second, trading companies underwent a sweeping consolidation process, which explains why the global commodities trade was dominated by a handful of multinational firms toward the end of the twentieth century. Chapter 12 shows how Volkart was progressively forced out of South Asia after the end of colonial rule. Chapter 13 deals with how Volkart entered the coffee trade through its cotton exports from Brazil and, thanks to its global sales structure and the company's financial strength, became one of the world's leading coffee traders during the 1960s. Chapter 14 outlines the development of the cotton trade after 1945 and explains that the intervention of national governments in the sector was often beneficial for multinational companies because trading firms could ship enormous volumes on behalf of state-supported export organizations and cooperatives.

Notes

1 In the mid-1970s, Volkart achieved annual sales of 1.4 billion Swiss francs, making it the 14th largest company in Switzerland: *Schweizerische Handelszeitung*, 12 June 1975. For a general overview of the history of Swiss trading companies in the nineteenth and twentieth centuries, see Dejung, "Unbekannte Intermediäre," 2010.
2 Purtschert/Fischer-Tiné (eds.), *Colonial Switzerland*, 2015.
3 Roy, *Economic History of India*, 2011, 15ff.; Lubinski, "Global Trade and Indian Politics," 2015.
4 Osterhammel/Petersson, *Globalization*, 2005, 127.
5 Nonetheless, a number of individual studies on this topic have been written over the course of the past few years, most notably the following books and collections of articles: Reber, *British Mercantile Houses*, 1979; Chalmin, *Négociants et chargeurs*, 1985; Yonekawa/Yoshihara (eds.), *General Trading Companies*, 1987; Chapman, *Merchant Enterprise in Britain*, 1992; Jones (ed.), *The Multinational Traders*, 1998; Jones, *Merchants to Multinationals*, 2000; Jonker/Sluyterman, *At Home on the World Markets*, 2000; Sugiyama/Grove (eds.), *Commercial Networks in Modern Asia*, 2001; Gossler, *Société commerciale de l'Océanie*, 2006; Bähr/Lesczenski/Schmidtpott, *Winds of Change*, 2009; Machado, *Ocean of Trade*, 2014.
6 Jones, "Multinational Trading Companies," 1998, 1–2; Casson, "The Economic Analysis of Multinational Trading Companies," 1998, 22.
7 Although a corporate history that provides an overview of the company's development was published in 1990 (Rambousek/Vogt/Volkart, Volkart, 1990), the work was commissioned by Volkart and fails to meet academic standards. In addition to this book, there are a number of popular historical works that deal primarily with the founding of the company (e.g., Peter, *Salomon Volkart*, 1956) along with an essay by Sébastian Guex on the history of Swiss trading firms in the nineteenth and twentieth centuries (Guex, "The Development of Swiss Trading Companies," 1998), which is the only previously existing academic work

that touches on the topic of Volkart, although it is largely based on an analysis of the published company histories and is supported by very little original research.

8 For a similar approach, see Beckert, *Empire of Cotton*, 2014.

9 VA, Dossier 62: ex GR persönliches Archiv II, Verbesserungen im Geschäftsbetrieb und verschiedene Anregungen, 1896–1924: Graphische Darstellung unserer Organisation für den Ankauf und Verkauf indischer Produkte, Winterthur, December 1921. This chart was published in V. B. News, no. 3, August 1921, 10–11.

10 Schlögel, *Im Raume lesen wir die Zeit*, 2003, 95.

11 For more on the concept of commodity chains, see Gereffi/Korzeniewicz (ed.), *Commodity Chains and Global Capitalism*, 1994; Hughes/Reimer (ed.), *Geographies of Commodity Chains*, 2004.

12 Arndt, *Deutschlands Stellung in der Weltwirtschaft*, 1ff.

13 For more on the concept of embeddedness, see Granovetter, "Economic Action and Social Structure," 1985; Beckert/Diaz-Bone/Ganßmann (ed.), *Märkte als soziale Strukturen*, 2007; Dejung, "Einbettung," 2014. Berghoff, *Zwischen Kleinstadt und Weltmarkt*, 1997, has produced a pioneering study for the conceptualization of business history as social history.

14 For more on the notion of shifting between micro- and macro-perspectives, which was borrowed from the terminology of the film industry, see Kracauer, *Geschichte—vor den letzten Dingen*, 1973, 125–161; Pomata, "Close-Ups and Long-Shots", 1998, 114–115.

15 Pohl, *Aufbruch der Weltwirtschaft*, 1989; Foreman-Peck, *A History of the World Economy*, 1995; Fischer, *Expansion—Integration—Globalisierung*, Göttingen 1998; Tilly, *Globalisierung aus historischer Sicht*, 1999; Torp, "Weltwirtschaft vor dem Weltkrieg," 2004; Borchardt, "Globalisierung in historischer Perspektive," 2008.

16 For instance in Ott, "Kriegswirtschaft im 1. Weltkrieg," 1981; Cameron, *A Concise Economic History of the World*, 1989, 273–368; O'Brien, "The Great War," 1995; Hobsbawm, *The Age of Extremes*, 1994; Findlay/O'Rourke, *Power and Plenty*, 2007, 429ff.; Feinstein/Temin/Toniolo, *The World Economy Between the World Wars*, 2008, 7.

17 Bammatter, *Der schweizerische Transithandel*, 1958, 3–4; Chalmin, *Négociants et chargeurs*, 1985, 95–184.

18 Hicks, *Theory of Economic History*, 1969; Herrmann-Pillath, *Kritik der reinen Theorie*, 2001.

19 Weber, *Economy and Society*, 1978 [1922]; Giddens, *The Constitution of Society*, 1984.

20 Castells, "Materials of an Exploratory Theory," 2000.

21 Osterhammel/Petersson, *Globalization*, 2005, 22–23.

22 By linking cultural and economic historical perspectives, the present study examines economic processes with an approach that has been postulated in various manners in recent years: Carrier (ed.), *Meanings of the Market*, 1997; Haskell/ Teichgraeber III (ed.), *The Culture of the Market*, 1993; Siegenthaler, "Geschichte und Ökonomie nach der kulturalistischen Wende," 1999; Berghoff/ Vogel (ed.), *Wirtschaftsgeschichte als Kulturgeschichte*, 2004; Lee, *Commerce and Culture*, 2011.

23 Geertz, *The Interpretation of Cultures*, 1973, 3–30.

24 Weber, *Economy and Society*, 1978, 1.

25 Gorissen, *Der Preis des Vertrauens*, 2003; Berghoff, "Die Zähmung des entfesselten Prometheus?", 2004.

26 Fiedler, "Vertrauen ist gut," 2001; Guinnane, "Trust," 2005.

27 Jones, "The End of Nationality?", 2006, 164.

28 Cooper, "What Is the Concept of Globalization Good For?", 2001.

29 See, for example, Wilkins, *Maturing of Multinational Enterprise*, 1974; *Dunning, Multinational Enterprises and the Global Economy*, 1993; Bonin et. al. (ed.), *Transnational Companies*, 2002; Amatori/Jones (ed.), *Business History Around the World*, 2003; Chandler/Mazlish (ed.), *Leviathans*, 2005. An exception to the rule is Jones, *Merchants to Multinationals*, 2000.

30 For an overview of premodern trading companies, see Braudel, *Wheels of Commerce*, 1979; Carlos/Nicholas, "Giants of an Earlier Capitalism," 1988; Price, "What Did Merchants Do?", 1989; Subrahmanyam (ed.), *Merchant Networks*, 1990; Valentinitsch, "Ost- und Westindische Kompanien," 2001; Webster, "An Early Global Business", 2005; Pomeranz/Topik, *The World that Trade Created*, 2006; Häberlein/Jeggle (ed.), *Praktiken des Handels*, 2010.

31 Jones, *Multinational Trading Companies*, 1998, 1.

32 Chapman, *Merchant Enterprise in Britain*, 1992, 15; Dunning, *Multinational Enterprises and the Global Economy*, 1993.

33 Welter, *Die Exportgesellschaften*, 1915; Hauser-Dora, *Die wirtschaftlichen und handelspolitischen Beziehungen der Schweiz*, 1986; Bähr/Lesczenski/Schmidtpott, *Winds of Change*, 2009.

34 Engel, *Farben der Globalisierung*, 2009, 20–25.

35 For an overview of institutional economics, see Williamson, *The Economic Institutions of Capitalism*, 1985; Casson, "Institutional Economics and Business History," 1998; Richter/Furubotn, *Neue Institutionenökonomik*, 2003; Wischermann/Nieberding, *Die institutionelle Revolution*, 2004.

36 North, *Institutionen*, 1992, 4.

37 Coase, "The Nature of the Firm," 1937.

38 Jones, *Merchants to Multinationals*, 2000, 4.

39 Petersson, *Anarchie und Weltrecht*, 2009, 212–213.

40 Landa, *Trust, Ethnicity, and Identity*, 1994; Casson, "The Economic Analysis of Multinational Trading Companies," 1998; Casson, "An Economic Approach," 2003; Rothermund, "Globalgeschichte als Interaktionsgeschichte," 2007, 202.

41 McNeill, *The Rise of the West*, 1963.

42 Wallerstein, *The Modern World-System*, 1974–2011.

43 See for a critique of world-systems theory Torp, "Die Weltsystemtheorie Immanuel Wallersteins", 1998; Hack, "Auf der Suche nach der verlorenen Totalität", 2005; Conrad/Eckert, "Globalgeschichte", 2007, 16–17.

44 Pomeranz, *The Great Divergence*, 2000. For a critical evaluation of this approach, see O'Brien, "The Deconstruction of Myths", 2003; Darwin, *After Tamerlane*, 2007, 186–209; Kramper, "Warum Europa?", 2009.

45 Chaudhuri, *The Trading World of Asia*, 1978; Das Gupta, *Indian Merchants*, 1979; Das Gupta, *The World of the Indian Ocean Merchant*, 2001; Perlin, *The Invisible City*, 1993; Ray, "Asian Capital," 1995, 455–464; Bhattacharya/Dharampal-Frick/Gommans, "Spatial and Temporal Continuities," 2007, 91–95; Markovits, "Structure and Agency", 2007; Riello/Roy, *How India Clothed the World*, 2009.

46 Braudel, *La dynamique du capitalisme*, 1985; Braudel, *Wheels of Commerce*, 1982; Fischer, *Expansion—Integration—Globalisierung*, 1998, 37.

47 See Chapter 10.

48 Braudel, *La dynamique du capitalisme*, 1986.

49 Sugihara (ed.), *Japan, China, and the Growth of the Asian International Economy*, 2005; Akita/White (ed.), *The International Order of Asia*, 2010.

50 Braudel, *La dynamique du capitalisme*, 1985; Schulte Beerbühl/Vögele (eds.), *Spinning the Commercial Web*, 2004.

51 Manning, *Navigating World History*, 2003, 3; Bayly, *The Birth of the Modern World*, 2004, 475–476; Osterhammel/Petersson, *Globalization*, 2005, 14–27;

Conrad/Eckert. "Globalgeschichte," 2007; Rothermund, "Globalgeschichte als Interaktionsgeschichte," 2007.

52 Darwin, *After Tamerlane*, 2007, 330–331. The European hegemony has been primarily interpreted as a result of the Industrial Revolution: Rabb, "The Expansion of Europe", 1974, 675–689; Wong, "The Search for European Differences," 2002, 468–469.

53 See Chapter 2.

54 Randeria, "Geteilte Geschichte und verwobene Moderne," 1999.

55 Washbrook, "Law, State and Society," 1981; Bayly, *Rulers, Townsmen and Bazaars*, 1983; Ray, "Asian Capital," 1995.

56 Robertson, "Glocalization," 1995; Appadurai, *Modernity at Large*, 2000.

57 There has been a rekindled interest among historians in recent years for the spatial dimension: Osterhammel, "Die Wiederkehr des Raumes," 1998; Schlögel, *Im Raume lesen wir die Zeit*, 2003; Middell, "Der Spatial Turn," 2008.

58 Landes, *The Wealth and Poverty of Nations*, 1998; Clark, *A Farewell to Alms*, 2007. Of course, Max Weber presented similar arguments with his groundbreaking theory on Protestantism: Weber, *The Protestant Ethic*, 2001 [1930].

59 Goody, *The East in the West*, 1996.

60 Bayly, *Rulers, Townsmen and Bazaars*, 1983.

61 Teubner, "Global Bukowina," 1997.

62 For more on the importance of a shared standard of professional ethics for concluding collaborative agreements among merchants, see Braudel, *Wheels of Commerce*, 1982, 150ff.

63 North, *Institutionen*, 1992.

64 Maier, "Consigning the Twentieth Century," 2000.

65 Clark, *Globalization and Fragmentation*, 1997; Conrad, *Globalisation and the Nation*, 2010.

66 Gallagher/ Robinson, "The Imperialism of Free Trade," 1953.

67 For more on the importance of imperial power in establishing the global cotton trade during the nineteenth century, see Beckert, *Empire of Cotton*, 2014.

68 Mommsen/de Moor (ed.), *European Expansion and Law*, 1992.

69 For more on the view that states should primarily be seen as an expression of specific social power structures, thereby rendering the distinction between market and politics moot, see, for example, Wallerstein, *Historical Capitalism*, 1983; Robinson, *A Theory of Global Capitalism*, 2004, 97.

70 Arrighi, *The Long Twentieth Century*, 1994, 34. Similar arguments are presented by Holloway, "Reform des Staats," 1993, 21; Harvey, *The New Imperialism*, 2003, 26.

71 Fieldhouse, "A New Imperial System?", 1986, 237.

72 James, *The End of Globalization*, 2001, 10–25; Osterhammel/Petersson, *Globalization*, 2005, 70–106.

73 Reinhart/Rogoff, *This Time Is Different*, 2009, 248–274.

74 Chalmin, *Négociants et chargeurs*, 1985, 6; Amsden, *The Rise of "the Rest"*, 2001, 119.

75 Chalmin, "Problématique d'un contrôle", 1981, 28–29; Chalmin, "The Rise of International Commodity Trading Companies", 1987; Jones, "Multinational Trading Companies", 1998.

76 Chandler/Mazlish (ed.), *Leviathans*, 2005.

77 Welskopp, "Das institutionalisierte Misstrauen," 2000.

78 See Richter/Furubotn, *Neue Institutionenökonomik*, 2003, 163ff.

79 Chapman, *Merchant Enterprise in Britain*, 1992, 93; Greif, "Institutions and International Trade," 1992; Gorissen, "Der Preis des Vertrauens," 2003.

80 Chandler, *Scale and Scope*, 1990.

81 Chandler, *The Visible Hand*, 1977; Chandler, *Scale and Scope*, 2004 [1990].

82 Nieberding, "Unternehmerische Sinnkonstruktion," 2004.
83 Jones, *Merchants to Multinationals*, 2000.
84 Berghoff, "Unternehmenskultur und Herrschaftstechnik," 1997.
85 Sluyterman/Winkelman, "The Dutch Family Firm," 1993, 176.
86 Chapman/Buckley, "Markets, Transactions Costs, Economists and Social Anthropologists," 1997; Frey, *Not Just for the Money*, 1997; Yanagisako, *Producing Culture and Capital*, 2002, 5–6; Lubinski, *Familienunternehmen*, 2010, 16.
87 Weber, *Economy and Society*, 1978, 98 and 153.
88 For more on the concept of habitus as an operator that mediates between structures and practices, see Bourdieu, *Outline of a Theory of Practice*, 1977.
89 Wischermann/Borscheid/Ellerbrock, "Vorwort," 2000; Bonus, "Unternehmen in institutionenökonomischer Sicht," 2000, 26ff.; Wischermann, "Unternehmensgeschichte als Geschichte der Unternehmenskommunikation," 2000, 39–40; Berghoff, *Moderne Unternehmensgeschichte*, 2004, 55ff.; Welskopp, "Unternehmensgeschichte im internationalen Vergleich," 2004, 272–273; Maitte/Martini, "Introduction," 2009, 24.
90 These were not biographical interviews, but were instead primarily aimed at reconstructing the factual chronology and filling the gaps in the written archival records.

Part I
European Expansions

1   From Winterthur to Bombay
The Establishment of the Firm

In November 1844, Swiss merchant Salomon Volkart left the familiar surroundings of his native town of Niederglatt and traveled to India via Naples,
Smyrna, Constantinople and Cairo. The main objective of his expedition
was to seek out new markets for Swiss textile products in Naples, the Levant
and India.[1]

Volkart's journey to India is a striking example of the global market
orientation of the Swiss textile industry of the day. The high quality standards of proto-industrial textile production, early industrialization and
the small domestic market paved the way for Swiss companies to venture
abroad and increasingly market their goods on the world market from the
eighteenth century onwards. Since the protectionist economic policies of
many countries made large areas of the European market inaccessible to
the Swiss, they began to export their products on a large scale to North
and South America, and to the Levant.[2] From 1840 onwards, they also
made inroads into markets in Africa, India and Southeast Asia. By 1845,
roughly 40–50 percent of Swiss exports went to North and South America,
while 15–20 percent was shipped to Asia and the Middle East.[3] Switzerland was by no means unique in this respect. Recent studies have shown
that the success of the British textile industry rested largely on its ability to
export cotton products to West Africa and North and South America. This
is an indication that the market for cotton textiles had achieved increasingly global dimensions since the medieval period in Europe. Although the
bulk of the textiles purchased in Europe, Africa, the Middle East and East
Asia came from India until the eighteenth century, afterwards a growing
number of cotton products manufactured in European factories were sold
on the global market.[4]

Global Market Orientation and Market Information

The distinct orientation of the Swiss economy toward the global market
attracted attention in other European countries. During a fact-finding mission to Switzerland on behalf of the British government in the late 1830s,

John Bowring, a member of parliament, noted with astonishment the progress made by Swiss merchants and manufacturers:

> It could not but excite the attention of any reflecting person, that the manufactures of Switzerland—almost unobserved, and altogether unprotected—have been gradually, but triumphantly, forcing their way into all the markets of the world, however remote, or seemingly inaccessible.

He went on to note that Switzerland had no ports, nor did it produce the raw materials for its own industry, nor were its companies protected from foreign competition by tariffs or subsidies. In the eyes of this British observer, this made Switzerland a shining example of the virtues of a free trade policy.[5] Since Switzerland's geographical location as a landlocked country made shipping costs abroad relatively high, Swiss manufacturers specialized in high-quality products to minimize the impact of transport costs.[6] To determine which exports would be most marketable, Swiss manufacturers conducted intensive market surveys of the tastes, habits and incomes of their overseas customers. Starting in the 1830s, leading industrial firms began to employ their own representatives and travelers to acquire first-hand information on the latest fashionable colors and patterns.[7] In many cases, however, market information was gathered in the conventional manner by local merchants.[8] The vital nature of this information is revealed in a report filed by an inspector who visited Switzerland on behalf of the Belgian government in 1846 and was thoroughly impressed with the business acumen of Swiss manufacturers, who he viewed as far more savvy than their Belgian rivals:

> Unlike the Swiss, we don't know which goods can be sold in each locality, nor how the tastes of consumers vary from region to region due to climate and customs; we often work in a haphazard manner, as noted earlier.

To illustrate his point, he recounted a visit to the Winterthur company of Greuter & Rieter, which in the mid-1840s dispatched a draftsman to Sumatra to study the colors, patterns and scents of the sarongs there. The Winterthur textile printing works even copied certain irregularities perceived to be defects, as the women purchasing these textiles apparently viewed these as marks of quality.[9]

All of this indicates that Stanley Chapman is mistaken in his assumption that the overseas export business was an exceedingly speculative endeavor prior to the introduction of the telegraph, at least with regard to the Swiss textile industry.[10] Swiss producers and the merchants cooperating with them were intimately familiar with foreign markets and tailored their exports as best as possible to local requirements.[11] Salomon Volkart also conducted detailed market analyses during his journey to India. For instance, he visited a silk weaving mill in Poona and sent samples of the articles manufactured there to one of his employers in Europe, Swiss textile manufacturer Hüni & Fierz, in the hope "that you will manage to work in this area as well." He wrote that he was convinced that his extensive journey clear across India would sooner or later lead to interesting new fields of activity for his Swiss employer, adding:

> With your keen acumen, you have perhaps already guessed my ambition here, namely, after sounding out every locality there, to establish a type of export business with you that would be most lucrative if it could be run in an agency-like manner.[12]

These statements show that at this point in his career Salomon Volkart was already giving intensive thought to his prospects for the future. He had just turned 29 and had acquired extensive business qualifications. Salomon Volkart came from a respected family in the area around Zurich. Since children from rural regions were not allowed to attend city vocational schools, he was enrolled in an institution for farm boys in Zurich and went on to attend the Hüni Institute in Horgen, a respected private secondary school that provided the sons of up-and-coming rural families with training in commercial occupations. During his school days, he befriended Eduard Fierz, the brother of Johann Heinrich Fierz, who later commissioned Volkart to travel to India in the mid-1840s. In 1832, Volkart began an apprenticeship at Caspar Schulthess & Co. zum Rech, a distinguished financial institution in Zurich. Starting in 1844, he worked in Italy, first as a commercial clerk at the olive oil company of M. Croce in Genoa, and subsequently as a treasurer at the German firm of Stellinger & Co. in Naples. After the company headquarters was severely damaged in a catastrophic fire, Volkart returned to Switzerland. In September 1844, he went to Leipzig to visit Swiss merchant Hans Caspar Hirzel, who had made a fortune trading with South Asia and had made the journey to India himself twice during the 1820s.[13]

Hence, Salomon Volkart already had extensive business experience and excellent contacts in diverse European countries when he traveled to India in 1844–1845. During his stay in Bombay, he contacted Bernhard Rieter, a younger brother of Johann Heinrich and Johann Rudolf Rieter, the partners of the Greuter & Rieter cotton printing and dye works in Winterthur. Bernhard Rieter had been in Asia since 1843 to find a market for the products of Greuter & Rieter. During Volkart's stay in India, Rieter had an office on the premises of the German trading company Wattenbach & Co. in Calcutta, where Salomon Volkart visited him in late 1845.[14]

During his stay in Calcutta, Volkart may have discussed with Bernhard Rieter his plans to open a trading firm in Japan. Since nothing came of this project, he returned to Europe and tried to persuade Eduard Fierz to join him in establishing a trading company in Singapore. In addition to importing European goods to the region, this would have created an opportunity to gain a foothold in the Chinese market in the wake of the Treaty of Nan-king of August 1842, which marked the end of the First Opium War and forced China to open five ports to trade with Europe. Fierz declined the offer, however, because he was suffering from ill health and believed that the firm of Hüni & Fierz offered him more promising career prospects. This led Salomon Volkart to take a position with Greuter & Rieter in 1846. Acting on behalf of this Winterthur company, already in July of that same year he purchased in Venice a large consignment of glass beads that were destined for export to India. In 1848, he married Emma Sultzberger, the daughter of Winterthur town councilor and tax official Johann Heinrich Sultzberger.[15]

The Establishment of the Volkart Brothers Trading Company in 1851

In the summer of 1845, shortly after Salomon Volkart had arrived in Bombay, his younger brother Johann Georg Volkart had begun a commercial apprenticeship with Hüni & Fierz. He had received this post in part thanks to a recommendation by Salomon Volkart.[16] In February 1847, the younger brother left Switzerland and took a position in Bombay with Huschke, Wattenbach & Co, a joint venture established in the early 1840s by two German trading companies: Wattenbach & Co. operating in Calcutta, and Huschke & Co. in Bombay.[17] It appears that Johann Georg Volkart also received this job thanks to his older brother, who put in a good word for him. After only one year, Johann Georg Volkart was promoted to manager of the branch in Bombay. In 1849, the two partners Huschke and Wattenbach dissolved their joint company and opened separate offices in Bombay. Johann Georg Volkart worked for another year in the newly established branch of Wattenbach & Co. in Bombay before it was closed again.[18]

After Johann Georg Volkart returned to Switzerland, the two brothers founded on 1 February 1851 the "commission agency under the direction of Volkart Brothers," as it was described in the first partnership contract, with headquarters in Winterthur and Bombay. It was agreed in the contract that both brothers were equal partners in the company and would share in the profits and losses. It was determined that "Joh. Georg Volkart would relocate to Bombay as the managing director of the establishment there, while Salomon Volkart would continue to reside here and run the business in Europe."[19]

Thanks to their outstanding contacts to business associates, both in Switzerland and abroad, and their extensive business experience, the two brothers had every reason to expect that they could successfully position themselves in the trading sector between Europe and India. In the initial days following the establishment of their company, they sent a large number of offers to potential business partners in Germany, France, India and Switzerland. As references the two brothers listed two former employers, namely Wattenbach, Heilgers & Co. in Calcutta and the Zurich banking institution of Caspar Schulthess Erben, along with the trading company Hirzel & Co. (which belonged to Salomon Volkart's friend Hans Caspar Hirzel), the London-based shipping agency J. C. im Thurn & Co., the respected Winterthur trading firm Biedermann & Co. and the textile trading company and dye works J. Ziegler & Co. in Neftenbach, Switzerland (whose managing director was a son of Johann Heinrich Rieter, the partner of Salomon Volkart's former employer Greuter & Rieter).[20]

In the spring and summer of 1851, Salomon Volkart traveled to a number of towns and cities in Italy, Germany, Austria, France, Belgium, Britain and the Netherlands. The purpose of these business trips was to drum up commissions and find suitable local firms that could serve as agencies to represent the young company in various cities. This approach appears to have been quite successful. Indeed, the Volkart brothers soon had an agency network that covered a large number of Europe's major trading centers.[21] Meanwhile, Johann Georg Volkart returned to Bombay in early May, where J. C. Johnston, the sole employee of the burgeoning young firm, had already received the first shipments of European manufactured goods.[22]

Business was clearly thriving. Salomon Volkart wrote to his brother in Bombay to express his delight with the latest news of the progress made by the firm, and to impress upon him the necessity of following the example of fellow European merchants in India who "visited the bazaars and auction rooms on a daily basis to assess, in person, what continental articles could be of use in Bombay," adding that this was a far more dependable means of gauging the needs of the market than "the highly unreliable statements of the natives."[23]

The First Exports of Commodities from India

In addition to importing European goods to India, the brothers also endeavored to export Indian commodities to Europe.[24] In May 1851, Johann Georg Volkart sent an initial shipment of 70 bales of cotton to Europe to evaluate the trade as a potential avenue of business. For the next year and a half, the company's books contain no further entries for exports from India. It appears that the partners were striving to gain a stable foothold for importing European textiles and other consumer goods before venturing to export Indian goods abroad. The export of raw materials was a highly competitive sector because a considerable number of European and Indian trading companies had already established operations in Bombay. To make matters worse, the vast distances between Europe and the subcontinent meant that all trade with India was fraught with difficulties. Before the opening of the Suez Canal in November 1869, all large consignments of goods had to be shipped by sea around the Cape of Good Hope. The journey lasted three to four months. Passengers, mail and valuable small consignments were transported via the so-called Overland Route, opened in 1830, which made it possible to sail people and small packages to the port of Alexandria, then across the desert by horse-drawn carriage to the Gulf of Suez, and finally by ship to India. This route required roughly 30 days, meaning that it took at least two months to receive confirmation of orders and responses to written correspondence.[25] During the monsoon season, which lasted from June to September, stormy weather brought shipping to a standstill, sometimes for weeks on end, and the transport of goods within India was often rendered impossible.

This had serious ramifications for the sector. When European manufacturers ordered Indian commodities from a trading company, it was impossible for the supplier to provide exact information on the current price situation in India. The prospective buyers had to make do with more or less precise estimates of the anticipated price. Although price limits were generally established for orders, if the cost of Indian raw materials dropped sharply after the conclusion of a contract, manufacturers back in Europe could not benefit from additional orders because the lines of communication were too long for quick reactions. Export transactions on a commission basis that were conducted on behalf of merchants based in India also had their pitfalls. Trading companies generally had to pay huge advances as they vied to sign export contracts with leading Indian wholesalers and book cargo space as soon as possible for the passage to Europe. Such advances could amount to as much as 80 percent of the expected sales price.[26] These practices had the advantage for the clients that they could take part in the export business with very little capital and use their credit for the purchase of additional goods. As a result, the export of commodities from Bombay was a highly speculative enterprise.[27]

The difficulties associated with the Indian export business were undoubtedly the main reason why Volkart did not recommence shipments of cotton to Europe until October 1852. This transaction, which concerned a total of 256 bales of cotton, was conducted on behalf of the Winterthur textile company J. & A. Biedermann. Volkart subsequently increased both the quantity and frequency of its cotton shipments until they became a permanent fixture of its business model. In some cases, the cotton was ordered by European textile manufacturers and delivered to them directly. In other cases, the transactions were conducted on behalf of other trading companies that were located in Bombay and, in exchange for a 5 percent brokerage commission, the goods were shipped to London, where they were sold at auction. On behalf of Indian and European companies, Volkart also shipped products like fish oil, coconut fiber, black pepper and curry to Europe from 1853 onwards.[28]

Trade with the Indian subcontinent had undergone enormous changes since the middle of the eighteenth century. After the Treaty of Paris in 1763, virtually all trade between India and Europe was subject to the monopoly of the British East India Company. But the expansionist policies of the company exhausted its finances to the point that it was forced to petition the British government for support. This allowed the British crown to enjoy a growing degree of influence on the subcontinent. In 1833, the company lost all monopoly rights, but retained administrative control of large parts of India.[29] The dissolution of the trade monopoly soon paved the way for private trading firms to establish themselves on the subcontinent. Most of these companies were from Britain. Nevertheless, starting in the 1840s, there were at least a dozen trading companies in India that had German, French, Swiss or American partners.[30] Hence, there is no basis whatsoever to the opinion voiced in various summaries of Volkart's company history that the firm's establishment was only made possible by the repeal of the Navigation Acts in 1849.[31] The Navigation Acts, which stipulated that trade with British colonies could only be conducted with British ships, solely extended to the Atlantic and thus were limited to trade with the British colonies in North America and the Caribbean. Trade with the colonies in Asia was never hampered by legislation.[32] Even after India became a crown colony in 1858, foreign companies were able to continue to engage in trade. The British colonial government, which was fully committed to the principle of free trade, placed no obstacles in their way.

Starting in the late eighteenth century, Bombay was one of the leading trading ports on the West Coast of India, after it eclipsed Surat as the major port in the region.[33] Bombay was primarily used for the export of Indian raw cotton to Europe and China. In the year 1860, no less than 92 percent of all Indian cotton exports were shipped via Bombay. From the mid-nineteenth century, Bombay even surpassed Calcutta as the most important trading port on the subcontinent. Since neither the East India Company nor the many private trading companies that had established themselves in Bombay from the early nineteenth century had sufficient capital to pursue the high-risk Indian export business alone, and since they also lacked the necessary business ties and linguistic knowledge, Indian traders were able to secure a considerable share of the cotton exports from Bombay.

The Indian traders who worked as middlemen for the Europeans usually did not originate from the established Hindu merchant dynasties from Surat, who were in fact too successful on the domestic market to venture into the precarious export sector and accept limits to their independence by cooperating with European merchants. Instead, they provided deliveries of cotton and other commodities from the upcountry to the coast and made their capital available to the Europeans, who used this primarily to finance the export trade to China. Meanwhile, the overseas trade was increasingly pursued by ethnic communities such as the Armenians, Parsis, Khojas, Bohra and Konkani, who had only played a marginal role in the trading sector until the eighteenth century. These groups pursued export transactions on their own behalf, but also served as brokers or commission agents for the East India Company and private European trading firms. The Parsis were particularly successful. They began to export goods to Britain on their own account in the early nineteenth century and dominated the trade with China until the 1830s.

Since European merchants could use their connections to gain better access to cotton presses and transport insurance policies, and could acquire cheaper loans from British banks, they were able to drive the Parsis out of the opium trade with China from the 1830s onwards. While the opium trade was dominated by a number of large British trading companies like Jardine Matheson & Co., the export of raw cotton, which generated fewer profits, was primarily the domain of smaller export firms. This was a sector in which Indian merchants were still able to hold their ground until the late 1860s. Although 1849 was the first year in which more Indian raw cotton was used in Lancashire than in China, in 1851 Indian firms were responsible for roughly 55 percent of all cotton exports from Bombay to Liverpool. Of the 12 largest companies that shipped cotton from Bombay to Liverpool in 1861, seven had Indian owners. In fact, Indian companies controlled roughly two-thirds of all cotton exports to Liverpool at the time.[34]

The Business Practices of the Volkart Company

During the first years of its existence, the Volkart company conducted hardly any transactions on its own account, but instead focused on the less risky business of forwarding orders on a commission basis. In the mid-nineteenth century, this was the most common type of business in the trade between India and Europe.[35] Trading companies like Volkart received a fixed commission for their work, which generally amounted to 5 percent of the sales price. This type of business in the overseas trade was primarily pursued by companies with relatively little capital.[36] The first partnership contract signed by the Volkart brothers explicitly stipulated that transactions on one's own account were only permitted if both partners gave their consent.[37] This restriction was eased over the following years, and finally dropped entirely, but it is an indication of the cautious approach adopted by the newly founded company. The business prospered and during the first fiscal year of 1851–1852 Volkart reported profits of 4,400 rupees, or roughly 11,000 Swiss francs at the time, and the two partners each received half of this amount deposited onto their private accounts.[38]

A trading company's good reputation was vital in the commission business.[39] Thanks to Volkart's tireless efforts to fulfill contracts under any circumstances, which advanced to become its guiding principle, and the business acumen of the firm's founders, the company soon managed to carve out an excellent reputation in the business world. August F. Ammann, who began a commercial apprenticeship with Volkart in 1868 and later became a partner in the firm, felt that "good management and sound organization" were the reasons why the company's business developed so well and the firm refrained from the type of speculative transactions that drove many trading companies into bankruptcy at the time.[40]

From the mid-1850s, Volkart began to conclude so-called *conto à metà* agreements with other European trading companies for the export of cotton, coffee, coconut oil and seeds. With this type of contract, Volkart invested to a certain degree with its own capital in the exports, usually between 25 and 50 percent of the value of the goods. The profits were then divided up proportionally between the participating trading companies. Although Volkart suffered a loss in connection with some of these transactions, they appear to have been generally more lucrative than the export business on a fixed commission basis.[41] Indeed, the company was able to steadily improve its results over the first few years until it achieved record profits of 465,210 rupees during the 1856–1857 fiscal year. It was not until the early twentieth century that the company made similar profits, although this was achieved thanks to a much higher turnover and with the help of a much larger company structure.[42]

In view of the positive development of their business, the two Volkart brothers decided to expand the company.[43] In 1857, the firm opened two new branches, one in Cochin and one in the city of Colombo in Ceylon. The office in Cochin was charged primarily with overseeing the export of coconut oil, coconut fiber, coffee, spices, fish oil, cotton and tropical woods, while the office in Colombo was to focus primarily on the export of coffee and cotton from the city of Tinnevelly on the mainland. The new branches were intended to make it possible for Volkart to manage the exports directly on site and more effectively monitor the quality of the products.[44]

The high earnings that Volkart generated during the 1856–1857 season were the result of a number of exceedingly successful transactions that were conducted on its own account—an approach that, as mentioned earlier, was only rarely taken by the firm during the initial years.[45] Volkart greatly benefited from a boom in business out of Bombay after the company was established. Cotton exports from the city soared from 84,163 bales in 1851 to 770,914 bales just ten years later. This flourishing trade created fertile ground for small and medium-sized companies to become established in Bombay.[46]

The constant growth in the volume of business also fueled the demand for cargo space. Direct connections between the European continent and India did not exist until the late 1860s, forcing merchants to ship the vast majority of Indian commodities via England.[47] As sales began to grow, Volkart joined forces with a number of other Winterthur-based companies in 1853 to purchase their own ship, the *Präsident Furrer*. The company also purchased shares in two other ships that had been bought by companies in Winterthur.[48] In 1857, all three ships were sold again. It remains unclear whether this was in reaction to the economic crisis at the time or whether there were disagreements between the companies involved. At any rate, neither Volkart nor other companies based in Winterthur subsequently purchased or operated their own ships[49] and Volkart did not require such vessels for its trading business anyway. Since the company's three branches in India and Ceylon were by then moving large quantities of goods, from the late 1850s the trading firm was able to charter ships with cargo holds exclusively reserved for Volkart's freight.[50]

Rising sales and the opening of the new branches in Cochin and Colombo naturally led to an increase in the number of employees. When it was founded in 1851, the company only had a staff of five. In their small office in the heart of Winterthur, Salomon Volkart and his wife Emma managed the sales of imported commodities in Europe and handled the orders of European products destined for export to India. In Bombay, Johann Georg Volkart and his first employee, J. C. Johnston, ensured that European goods were sold at the bazaar and they concluded contracts for the export of Indian raw materials to Europe.[51] In the very first year of the company's existence, the first Indian was hired to work for the company. Cowasjee Jehangir Jussawala, a Parsi, became the head of the insurance department.[52] By the late 1850s, Volkart had developed into a medium-sized trading company with a growing number of employees. By 1859–1860, nine Europeans—in addition to Johann Georg Volkart—were working for the company in India: four in Bombay, two in Cochin and three in Colombo.[53] In Winterthur, Salomon Volkart began to hire employees and apprentices in 1857 because he and his wife could no longer handle the workload on their own.[54] In addition to diverse European employees, a large number of Indians were soon employed in various functions at the company. The source material does not, however, indicate just how many of them were employed by the firm during this early phase.

Collaboration with Indian Merchants

Due to the vast distances involved, a number of months often passed between the date the goods were shipped out and the moment when the seller received payment. Financing was thus of vital importance to the overseas trade. Up until the late 1860s, in addition to the client and the exporting trading company, a third party was always involved to provide the loans required for the deal. When customers from Europe ordered goods, they had to pay the trading company an advance that amounted to between 50 and 75 percent of the value of the goods. They also had to present a payment guarantee from a European bank.[55] Before the introduction of the telegraph, the actual price of the goods was not yet known at the moment a contract was concluded. European customers placed orders for a specific amount of money to purchase commodities like cotton, coconut fibers, coffee, spices and oils without knowing exactly how high the market price for these goods would be when they were ultimately purchased in India. The trading company merely promised to acquire the goods for the best possible price in exchange for a 5 percent commission. As for the quality of the goods, the trading company gave a guarantee that was, in the words of then Volkart employee August F. Ammann, "as simple as it was harmless." The trading company merely committed itself to delivering the goods, which had to meet the "fair average quality of the season."[56]

Up until the 1870s, when a trading company exported goods on commission on behalf of a local merchant based in India, the seller would, as a rule, receive an advance on the expected sales price. In the export trade out of Bombay, these advances—as previously mentioned—could amount to up to 80 percent of the value of the goods. Trading companies could only hope to win export contracts if they were prepared to pay such advances. Not surprisingly, a considerable share of Volkart's capital funds was tied up in advance payments, at least until the late 1860s.[57] But exporters often had too little capital to finance all advances by mobilizing their own reserves, so they borrowed money from an affluent Indian merchant who served as a banker, a so-called shroff.[58] Such Indian lenders were often bound by contract to an export company, in which case they were called guarantee brokers. Most guarantee brokers either belonged to the Parsis—a strictly separate ethnic group that originally immigrated from Persia, had primarily established itself in Bombay and was extremely successful in business matters—or they were members of Hindu trading castes or Muslim merchant families.[59] Volkart also had such a guarantee broker from July 1851 onwards. His name was Dossabhoy Bomanjee and he was a Parsi. Guarantee brokers served as both lenders and intermediaries for negotiating export transactions. Hence, they needed to have both sufficient assets and impeccable reputations within the local business community. After the trading companies had sold the goods in Europe, they had to pay back the shroffs and guarantee brokers who had provided the loans to pay for the advances.[60]

European trading companies also relied on indigenous guarantee brokers for import transactions. In return for a commission of 1.5 percent, the brokers guaranteed payment of the European consumer goods that were delivered by European trading companies to merchants at the bazaar, and they organized orders for future deliveries.[61] The importance of Indian merchants and their function as guarantee brokers and shroffs in the granting of credit shows that the economic success enjoyed by European merchants in Asia would have been unthinkable without the aid of existing efficient Asian trading and lending networks.[62] In fact, a number of trading companies— such as the precursor to the British firm of Wallace Bros, which rose to become one of the leading cotton exporters in Bombay during the 1860s— were in fact jointly established by British and Indian merchants.[63] Up until the mid-nineteenth century, Indian mercantile firms were often not only more financially sound, but also often viewed as more reliable than their European counterparts.[64] Throughout the late nineteenth century, many Europeans expressed a deep sense of appreciation for their Indian business partners, which stands in sharp contrast to the imperial racism that was prevalent at the time. August F. Ammann described the Indian traders that Volkart encountered during the 1870s in Karachi as "a class of men who would be an ornament to any commercial community in and out of India. They were honest, straightforward and reliable in their dealings with others and cautious, nay conservative, as regards their own affairs."[65]

In view of their key position as intermediaries, the brokers had to be absolutely reliable. In his reminiscences of his stay in India in the 1870s, Ammann described Naomull Panjanmull, the head broker of Volkart's Karachi branch, established in 1861, as an "honest man, wide awake and cautious." Panjanmull was a Hindu from the merchant caste of the Lohanas and, at the same time, served as the broker for the local branch of the Bank of Bombay. This gave the Volkart company valuable insights into the financial situations of the native merchants, since every exchange that the bank organized at the bazaar was handled by the broker. Ammann laconically recounted that "this knowledge was of great value to the firm." In addition to the head broker, a procurement broker worked at Volkart's Karachi branch. He received a small salary and a percentage of all purchases that he could negotiate. His job was to visit the local cotton merchants in the bazaar on a regular basis, acting on the instructions of the Volkart manager, who had previously informed him of the quantity, quality and price of the cotton that the company required. If the broker could not reach an agreement with the bazaar dealers, one or two of the leading cotton merchants were invited to Volkart's office for talks with the broker, the head broker and Volkart's maccadam. The maccadam, or head-man, was a respected Indian who took part in all negotiations between Volkart and the local merchants. At the end of their discussions, a special custom was observed. The broker and the bazaar traders would grip hands under the broker's scarf and exchange "mysterious signs," as Ammann put it, which effectively sealed the deal. Then the broker returned to the bazaar, where the other merchants would follow the lead of their colleagues and conclude the sales agreements with Volkart according to the agreed conditions.[66]

Ammann's account can be seen as evidence that markets were not only commercial structures, but also social entities in which transactions had to be embedded, sometimes by means of cultural customs such as the "mysterious" hand signals under the broker's scarf.[67] It is also clear that the exact meaning of this custom could not be deciphered by the Europeans who witnessed it. The cooperation between the trading company and the brokers was thus based on a relationship of mutual trust. This trust stemmed from the fact that the brokers possessed precisely those qualities that were the hallmarks of a reliable merchant in Europe.[68] In an article published in 1922 in Volkart's in-house magazine *V. B. News*, the qualities of a capable broker were described as follows:

> If a good financial standing . . . is a main factor, ability and qualities of character are no less important. Indeed, the success of the broker's work depends to a great extent on a shrewd business sense, a wide experience in the trade, good knowledge of the articles and the market conditions and last, but not least, sound judgment of character and ability to deal with all sorts and conditions of people. These qualifications

coupled with absolute integrity secure him the confidence and esteem of the dealers and his principals alike.[69]

The confidence of the Europeans in their Indian shroffs and brokers, however, was by no means unconditional. Volkart regularly made inquiries at local banking institutions concerning the financial situations and business practices of their Indian intermediaries.[70] In addition to such information, the legal institutions that the British introduced to India also played an important role. They gave the Europeans certain legal grounds to stand on when a supplier failed to meet his contractual obligations. Indeed, from a theoretical perspective, trust is not so much an explanatory means of illustrating the stability of business ties, but rather an *explanandum*, i.e., something that requires an explanation and is derived from an evaluation of the available information and the existence of possible sanctions, as has been pointed out by Timothy Guinnane.[71]

British Law and Business Risks

Starting in the mid-eighteenth century, the British endeavored to enforce British commercial law in India. As indicated by the first statutes of the East India Company in the presidency towns, all business disputes involving Hindus and Muslims were to be resolved with reference to their own respective existing laws. British mercantile law was only to be applied if all parties concerned agreed to accept it.[72] This arrangement worked out astonishingly well on a daily basis. Right from the beginning, Indian merchants relied on British courts, which were viewed as efficient and fair. What's more, there were apparently no major differences between British commercial law and general business practices on the subcontinent. Sir Lawrence Peel, the chief justice of Bengal, noted in 1845:

> I may observe . . . that the English law as to contracts . . . is so much in harmony with the Mahomedan and Hindoo laws as to Contracts that it very rarely happens in our courts . . . that any question arises on the law peculiar to those people in actions on contracts.

These similarities prompted the British to enact a new commercial code in 1855 that eliminated special regulations for certain ethnic groups.[73]

The British legal system offered Europeans a remedy if a business partner failed to fulfill his legal obligations,[74] as evidenced by an incident that occurred at the Cochin branch in the 1870s. Although the available source material renders it difficult to make specific statements, in the late 1860s it appears that Volkart managed to purchase Indian raw materials without making any advance payments, at least in Bombay and Karachi.[75] In Cochin and Colombo, however, it was still only possible to pursue export activities if a trading company was prepared to provide advances of between 50 and

75 percent of the anticipated sales value of the merchandise. These advances had to be transferred from the buyers in Europe to the trading company before it endeavored to procure the goods. In a booklet from 1873, Volkart informed its European customers that, for orders handled by its Cochin branch, the firm was solely liable for advance payments, but not for the actual fulfillment of the delivery contracts. At the same time, the company sought to placate its customers by emphasizing that "a non-delivery of the purchased merchandise has never occurred," as they only ordered from "solid and respectable merchants."[76]

This approach worked extremely well for many years and a large volume of trade was conducted via the Cochin branch. But in 1873 the risks associated with this system became manifest.[77] Volkart had been obliged to make all of its purchases in Cochin through a single supplier. Polikalagata Marakar, or Markar for short, was a Moplah[78] and seems to have been the only merchant in the area who could deliver the large quantities required by Volkart when a ship was anchored in the harbor and waiting to be loaded. The Cochin branch of Volkart had granted Markar cash advances for his purchases from local dealers. During the 1872–1873 season, the price of coffee in the local market suddenly plummeted, no doubt as a consequence of the economic crisis that erupted in the US in 1873 and soon spread to Europe, India and the Far East.[79] Markar, either because he had speculated on a price increase or had been left in the lurch by one of his suppliers, declared himself unable to meet the commitments stipulated in his contract with Volkart unless further advances were granted. The local manager of Volkart's Cochin branch, A. Spitteler, paid him another advance without asking the head office in Winterthur (India had been connected with Europe by a telegraph line since 1865).[80] This enraged Salomon Volkart who had been against paying advances for a long time and had repeatedly expressed his skepticism about conducting the entire business at Cochin through a single distributor.[81]

The local Volkart manager, Spitteler, was very intent on not disappointing the firm's Europeans customers. As a matter of fact, global trade was—and still is today—inherently volatile and reliability was imperative for the success of a merchant house like Volkart, which was anxious to forge and preserve a culture of mutual trust with its European customers, many of whom were extremely concerned about the commercial risks of the commodities business in nineteenth-century India. Not surprisingly, for many years Volkart had remained reluctant to draw attention to the fact that, in the event of a contract failure, the firm would be liable only for the advance payments, and not for any possible losses incurred by the purchaser from the non-delivery of the consignment.[82] Still, although the legal position was in its favor, the trading company did its best to maintain the trust of its continental buyers. In other words, Spitteler's decision to provide Markar with another advance to enable him to purchase the ordered merchandise was entirely in line with company policy. Nevertheless, Spitteler was dismissed due to the large losses that the company suffered. After his return to Europe, he sued Volkart, although he had previously reached an agreement with the firm. Volkart then paid him a large compensation to avoid a trial and the unwelcome publicity that would have ensued.[83]

In 1877, the Markar case was dealt with by the District Court of South Malabar, which ordered him to pay Volkart 392,990 rupees in compensation. When this sentence was confirmed by the Madras High Court one year later, Markar appealed to the Privy Council in London, which served as a higher level court for legal disputes in the British colonies from 1833 onwards,[84] but this appeal was also rejected in December 1880. Since Markar was bankrupt, his real estate was awarded as compensation to Volkart, but many of the premises had been neglected, were encumbered with mortgages or had already been sold. As a result, the income received by Volkart from the sale of Markar's property did not cover the considerable losses incurred by the company.[85] This example illustrates why trading companies could not entirely rely on formal institutions like the legal system, whose enforcement was usually time-consuming. In fact, the outcome of legal disputes was often extremely uncertain. Traders thus had to base their transactions largely on informal institutions, such as the good reputations of suppliers and customers, although formal institutions such as courts of law played a key role as a last resort to resolve conflicts.

Business in Cochin temporarily came to a halt after the Markar affair. In 1875, Georg G. Volkart, the son of Salomon Volkart, decided to embark on a tour of various trading centers along the Malabar Coast. This trip, on which Georg G. Volkart was accompanied by Ammann, was a revelation, and Volkart decided to open up an additional branch in Tellicherry, along with procurement agencies in the upcountry and along the coast.[86] Yet even at the new branch in Tellicherry goods could not be purchased without the help of indigenous middlemen. In 1886, Volkart established a factory in Tellicherry in which green coffee was prepared for transport to Europe. It proved highly difficult to buy a steady supply of coffee to operate the factory profitably, largely because Volkart refused to pay advances on future coffee deliveries, and the firm considered closing down the operation. Its long-term future was only assured when members of the Cooty family of Moplah merchants were employed as brokers. The sons of the family worked as purchasing agents in the backcountry during the season and became successful in supplying Volkart with sufficient volumes of coffee and other merchandise. This collaboration was so fruitful that it continued up until the 1960s.[87]

Notes

1 Peter, *Salomon Volkart*, 1956; Peyer, "Aus den Anfängen des schweizerischen Indienhandels," 1960; Anderegg, *Chronicle*, 1976, 26.
2 Weisz, "Zur Geschichte des europäischen Handels mit Indien," 1954/55; Peyer, *Von Handel und Bank*, 1968, 182–189; Pfister, "Entstehung des industriellen Unternehmertums," 1997, 15–16.

3 Weisz, *Die Zürcherische Exportindustrie*, 1936; Forster, *Die Baumwolle*, [approx. 1985], 48ff. and 58; Fischer, "Toggenburger Buntweberei auf dem Weltmarkt," 1990; Veyrassat, "1945–1990: Bilan des recherches," 1991; Veyrassat, *Réseaux d'affaires internationaux*, 1993.

4 David/Etemad, "Gibt es einen schweizerischen Imperialismus?", 1998, 20; Parthasarathi/Riello, "Introduction," 2009.

5 Bowring, *Report on the Commerce and Manufactures of Switzerland*, 1836.

6 Buchheim, *Industrielle Revolutionen*, 1994, 93.

7 Fischer, "Toggenburger Buntweberei auf dem Weltmarkt," 1990, 198.

8 Alder, *Jugenderinnerungen*, 1929, 76f.; Peter, *Salomon Volkart*, 1956.

9 Kindt, *Notes sur l'industrie*, 1847, 23–26.

10 Chapman, *Merchant Enterprise in Britain*, 1992, 163.

11 Veyrassat, *Négociants et Fabricants*, 1982, 39–40.

12 Peyer, "Aus den Anfängen des schweizerischen Indienhandels," 1960, 116.

13 Weisz, *Die Zürcherische Exportindustrie*, 1936, 209; Hürlimann, "Hans Caspar Hirzel"; Sigerist, *Schweizer in Asien*, 2001, 134–135; VA, Dossier 19, Winterthur II: 13. write-ups about the firm by VB and corrections thereto by JA.

14 Isler, *Winterthur in Wort und Bild*, 1895, 150.

15 Peter, *Salomon Volkart*, 1956, 52; Peyer, "Aus den Anfängen des schweizerischen Indienhandels," 1960, 117–118.; Anderegg, *Chronicle*, 1976, 28–29.

16 Peyer, "Aus den Anfängen des schweizerischen Indienhandels," 1960, 115.

17 Despite claims to the contrary made in various publications (e.g., Isler, *Winterthur in Wort und Bild*, 1895, 150; Reinhart, Gedenkschrift, 1926, 14; Peter, *Salomon Volkart*, 1956, 51), Salomon Volkart did not visit his brother during his trip to India.

18 Anderegg, Chronicle, 1976, 33ff.

19 Rambousek/Vogt/Volkart, *Volkart*, 1990, 71.

20 VA, Dossier 1, B) Die Teilhaber, 1) Salomon Volkart, excerpts from the first letter book, 3 February 1851–1811 November 1851: Winterthur (J.G.V.) to J.F. Wolff, Elberfeld, 8 February 1851.

21 VA, Dossier 1, B) Die Teilhaber, 1) Salomon Volkart, excerpts from the first letter book, 3 February 1851–1811 November 1851: Sal. Volkart to J.M. Grob, Calcutta, 3 July 1851; Anderegg, *Chronicle*, 1976, 45.

22 Anderegg, *Chronicle*, 1976, 39.

23 VA, Dossier 1, B) Die Teilhaber, 1) Salomon Volkart, excerpts from the first letter book, 3 February 1851–1811 November 1851: Winterthur (S.V.) to Bombay (J.G.V.), no date.

24 The terms 'import' and 'export' in the Volkart source material are both used from the perspective of the Indian branch offices. The delivery of European consumer goods to India thus qualifies as imports, while the shipping of Indian raw materials to Europe is viewed as exports. This terminology is also maintained throughout the book.

25 VA, Dossier 19, Winterthur II: 13. write-ups about the firm by VB and corrections thereto by JA; Anderegg, *Chronicle*, 1976, 8.

26 Anderegg, *Chronicle*, 1976, 48–52.

27 Vicziany, "Bombay Merchants and Structural Changes," 1979, 175ff.

28 VA, Dossier 3: Bombay I, 4. Table of Events 1851–1961/2; Anderegg, *Chronicle*, 1976, 46, 50ff.

29 Lawson, *East India Company*, 1993, Chapters 6–8.

30 Anderegg, *Chronicle*, 1976, 13.

31 An argument presented in Reinhart, *Gedenkschrift*, 1926, 24; Rambousek/Vogt/Volkart, *Volkart*, 1990, 69.

32 Schuyler, *The Fall of the Old Colonial System*, 1945, 96 and 109; Anderegg, *Chronicle*, 1976, 2.

33 Guha, *More About Parsi Seths*, 1982, 19ff.; Subramanian, "The Castle Revolution," 1987; Chandavarkar, *The Origins of Industrial Capitalism*, 1994, 21ff., 44–45 and 55–64; Dobbin, *Asian Entrepreneurial Minorities*, 1996, 75–108; Markovits, *Global World of Indian Merchants*, 2000, 14–15.
34 Vicziany, "Bombay Merchants and Structural Changes," 1979, 170.
35 Vizciany, "Bombay Merchants and Structural Changes," 1979, 174–179; Ammann, *Reminiscences*, 1921, 8–9.
36 Biedermann, *Lehrbuch des Überseehandels*, o. J., 13–15.
37 Anderegg, *Chronicle*, 1976, 65.
38 VA, Statistik der Gebrüder Volkart 1851–1914; Anderegg, *Chronicle*, 1976, 49.
39 Fischer, "Toggenburger Buntweberei auf dem Weltmarkt," 1990; Forster, *Die Baumwolle* [approx. 1985], 48ff.
40 Ammann, *Reminiscences*, 1921, 7.
41 Anderegg, *Chronicle*, 1976, 52.
42 VA, Statistik der Gebrüder Volkart 1851–1914.
43 There also appears to have been plans to open a branch in Batavia (today's Jakarta) in the mid-1850s, but this notion was scrapped because Volkart decided to focus on the development of its business in India: DA, Ca DI 32: Letter sent by Johannes Niederer, Batavia, to Salomon Volkart, Winterthur, 20 December 1854.
44 VA, Dossier 6: Colombo, 4. Table of Events; Dossier 7: Cochin, 2. Table of Events; Anderegg, *Chronicle*, 1976, 66.
45 Anderegg, *Chronicle*, 1976, 64.
46 Dholakia, *Futures Trading*, 1949, S. 9; Vicziany, "Bombay Merchants and Structural Changes," 1979; Royce, *The Crimean War*, 2001.
47 Anderegg, *Chronicle*, 1976, 47.
48 Ammann, *Reminiscences*, 1921, 11.
49 Anderegg, *Chronicle*, 1976, 58–64.
50 Ziegler, *Der Import ostindischer Baumwolle*, 1922, 16.
51 Anderegg, *Chronicle*, 1976, 38f.
52 VA, Dossier 3: Bombay I, 4. Table of Events 1851–1961/2; Dossier 24: I/P/C Terms of Local Staff II: Indianisation in P. & C.
53 Anderegg, *Chronicle*, 1976, 71.
54 VA, Dossier 18: Winterthur I, 1. Table of Events.
55 See Volkart Brothers, *Calculationstabellen*, 1873, 13, 43 and 81.
56 Ammann, *Reminiscences*, 1921, 9–10.
57 Anderegg, *Chronicle*, 1976, 51–52.
58 Vicziany, "Bombay Merchants and Structural Changes", 1979, 175–178.
59 Jones, *International Business*, 1987, 81; Bayly, *Rulers, Townsmen and Bazaars*, 1983, 31, 163 and 178–180.
60 Anderegg, *Chronicle*, 1976, 55–56.
61 Ray, "The Bazaar," 1988, 83.
62 Ray, "Asian Capital," 1995; Bayly, *Rulers, Townsmen and Bazaars*, 1983.
63 Pointon, *The Bombay Burman Trading Corporation*, 1964, 5; Pointon, *The Wallace Bothers* 1974, 1–4.
64 Anderegg, *Chronicle*, 1976, 57.
65 Ammann, *Reminiscences*, 1921, 59.
66 Ammann, *Reminiscences*, 58–60.
67 Granovetter, "Economic Action and Social Structure," 1985.
68 Bayly, *Rulers, Townsmen and Bazaars*, 1983. 6, 229 and 239–240.
69 V.B. News, No. 4, March 1922, 17.
70 VA, Dossier 26: Finance/Exchange 1887–1977, 3 Inland Financing—Shroffage Agreements: Karachi to Winterthur, 17 September 1931.
71 Guinnane, "Trust," 2005.
72 Remfry, *Commercial Law*, 1912, 3–4.

73 Rankin, *Background to Indian Law*, 1946, 90; for more on the adoption of British law by Indian merchants, see Smith, "Fortune and Failure," 1993.

74 Ammann, *Reminiscences*, 1921, 22.

75 Gebrüder Volkart, *Calculationstabellen*, 1873, 13 and 31ff.

76 Gebrüder Volkart, *Calculationstabellen*, 1873, 44.

77 Ammann, *Reminiscences*, 1921, 19.

78 The Moplahs are the oldest known community of Indian Muslims and have existed since the eighth century, when they were converted to Islam by Arab merchants.

79 Anderegg, *Chronicle*, 1976, 119.

80 Ammann, *Reminiscences*, 1921, 19–20.

81 VA, Dossier 1, B) Die Teilhaber, 1) Salomon Volkart, 3. Privat-Copierbuch 9 January 1867–1825 August 1870: Salomon Volkart to Noelke, Winterhur, 15 October 1869.

82 VA, Dossier 1: B) Die Teilhaber, 1) Salomon Volkart, 3. Privat-Copierbuch 9 January 1867–1825 August 1870: Sal. Volkart to Spitteler, acting BM Cochin, 22 July 1869.

83 VA, Dossier 7: Cochin, 4. The Marcar case 1870s.

84 Hamid, *A Chronicle of British Indian Legal History*, 1991, 139.

85 VA, Dossier 7: Cochin, 4. The Marcar case 1870s.

86 Ammann, *Reminiscences*, 1921, 31–34.

87 VA, Dossier 9: Tellicherry, 2. Table of Events; Anderegg, *Chronicle*, 1976, 146.

2 From the Indian Coast to the Hinterland

The Birth of a Large-Scale Enterprise

During the initial years of its existence, Volkart's activities hardly differed from the business practices that other mercantile houses had pursued for centuries. Working on a commission basis, they imported and exported a wide range of products, without limiting themselves to specific goods. But in the 1860s Volkart changed its course. Although the company continued to import large quantities of European consumer goods, the focus of its activities shifted increasingly toward the export of Indian commodities. Indian raw cotton remained an important commodity for a number of decades, although Volkart was no longer content to solely serve the traditional European market and expanded its operations in the late 1860s, opening up a branch in China and, from the 1890s, exporting cotton to Japan.[1] By the end of the nineteenth century, Volkart ranked among India's leading exporters of cotton. As will be shown in the following chapter, one of the driving forces behind this development was that in the mid-1860s Volkart started to acquire its own cotton presses and dispatch employees to the country's interior. This in turn was only possible thanks to diverse new advances in infrastructure. The establishment of telegraph communications between Europe and India, the construction of roads, railways and telegraph lines on the subcontinent and the opening of the Suez Canal led to a rash expansion of the trading business during the second half of the nineteenth century, similar to the development that Alfred Chandler described for manufacturing companies.[2]

The Impact of the American Civil War on the Subcontinent

In the late 1850s, British business circles and the British government started to explore ways to make the textile industry in Lancashire independent of American cotton imports. Deliveries of this vital commodity were threatened by growing tensions in the US between the industrial northern states and the largely agricultural southern states, which relied heavily on slave labor. In 1860, a British officer wrote the following text concerning the export of textile goods from Lancashire:

> [T]he extension, not to say the sustenance of this trade, is primarily dependent upon the supply of the raw material: upon this, the one

hundred millions of our capital, and the livelihood of near four millions of our countrymen is dependent, a matter so serious and of such magnitude, as to make the question one of the state. . . . . [T]he only manner in which [it] can be assured, is in the liberal encouragement of the cultivation in our colonies, and in brief to have as many sources of supply, to guard against a local failure.[3]

Just three years earlier, the British Cotton Supply Association had been established to help spur the cultivation of cotton in India and Egypt.[4] The outbreak of the American Civil War brought home the importance of finding alternative sources of this precious commodity. The naval blockade imposed by the northern states reduced US cotton deliveries to a trickle and choked supplies of US cotton to European spinning mills from 1861 onwards. To defuse the crisis, the British colonial government and British investors stepped up their efforts to promote the cultivation of cotton in India. They shipped large quantities of cottonseed to Bombay and pressed ahead with the construction of irrigation systems, paved roads and railway lines. During the 1860s, the colonial government also began to standardize the weights and measures used in the Indian trading business.[5] The establishment of a colonial cotton economy caused Indian agriculture to lose its self-sustaining character. Cultivators who had traditionally worked to meet the needs of the local rural economy were increasingly urged to plant cash crops for the world market, with priority given to the growing of cotton.[6]

Like many other established trading companies in India, Volkart also benefited from the outbreak of the American Civil War. When American cotton no longer reached Europe between 1861 and 1865, European demand for Indian cotton boomed, doubling the volume of cotton exports from the subcontinent, with most of the trade going through Bombay.[7] Prices for Indian cotton soared during the war to three times what they were prior to 1861,[8] while players in the cotton trade regularly achieved semi-annual returns of 30 to 40 percent. The Volkart company, which was one of more than 30 trading companies that were shipping cotton out of Bombay at the time, was able to increase its cotton exports out of Bombay from 56,000 bales in the 1859–1860 fiscal year to an average of 98,000 bales during the Civil War,[9] making it one of the leading exporters of Indian cotton to Europe.[10]

Arthur Crawford Travers, an English civil servant working as a policeman in Bombay at the time, described in his memoirs the massive speculative frenzy that gripped India during the American Civil War:

How many are alive still to remember those silver times?. . . . [W]hen the majority of citizens at Bombay were just as mad as the Ryots (cultivators) in the cotton districts, with their silver-tired wheels, . . . when there was a new Bank or a new 'Financial' almost every day . . . no one ever drank anything but champagne in those days.

The end of the Civil War caused the speculative bubble to burst: "[F]ortunes were . . . lost in a few days; when the fatal telegram came announcing the peace between the North and South American States, . . . all our houses of cards came tumbling down about our ears."[11] During the panic year of 1866, no fewer than 24 of Bombay's 31 banks failed.[12] Many trading companies, including a large number of Indian firms that had been active in the cotton export business during the boom years, were ruined by the sudden decline in cotton prices because they had placed a great deal of their capital in advances.[13]

By contrast, Volkart had been extremely cautious during the war and, to guard against payment default, had avoided paying large advances that were not covered by consignments of goods.[14] As a result, the company remained in the black, even after 1865, and managed to venture into new fields of business after the end of the Civil War. During the 1866–1867 and 1867–1868 seasons, for instance, when many companies in Bombay were forced to file for bankruptcy, Volkart Bombay reported annual profits of over 270,000 rupees, and thus earned more than what this branch office made per fiscal year during the entire Civil War.[15] These positive results were in part thanks to the vacuum left behind by the disappearance of many competitors who had gone bankrupt during the economic crisis of 1866. Profits were also buoyed by a major expansion in the requisite infrastructure for the trading business during the 1860s. In Bombay local authorities launched drainage projects, refurbished the financial district and enlarged the port facilities.[16] Furthermore, the construction of the Indian railways and the opening of telegraph lines, both on the subcontinent and between India and Europe, helped to revitalize exports and allowed trading firms to increase their sales.

Changes in Cotton Exports Due to the Introduction of the Telegraph

The news of the end of the American Civil War reached India via the recently opened telegraph line. Bombay was linked to Europe by telegraph for the first time in 1865, forcing the city's trading companies to fundamentally change their business practices in the export sector. Jakob Brack-Liechti, a senior official in the Volkart cotton division during the late nineteenth century, wrote in his memoirs in 1918 that conditions at the firm were "idyllic" before the advent of the telegraph.[17] European manufacturers would place orders with trading companies for a certain amount of rupees' worth of cotton or other commodities without knowing exactly how high the market price for these goods would be at the time of their purchase later in India.[18] In exchange for a 5 percent commission, the trading companies merely promised to acquire the goods for the best possible price and in accordance with the average quality for the seasonal harvest.[19] Although samples of the individual Indian cotton varieties were readily available at the Liverpool Cotton Exchange, they were generally already a few years old and therefore not indicative of the average quality of the *current* season. Purchasers also bore other market risks such as fluctuations in cargo and currency exchange rates.[20]

Market conditions changed abruptly with the introduction of telegraph communications. By 1870, the time required to transmit a message from Europe to Bombay had been reduced to just over six hours. This was a far cry from the first telegrams in the mid-1860s, which had taken an average of more than six days to reach their destination.[21] The telegraph made it much easier for buyers in Europe to compare the offers of diverse trading companies. Meanwhile, the trading firms had to work harder and harder to address their European customers' "increasingly strident" demands, which, according to Brack-Liechti, " 'were in line with the changed circumstances,' as the buyers put it."[22] The trading companies were forced to present their European buyers with offers that were no longer in rupees, but instead, as a rule, in pounds sterling. Buyers could review the various offers that they received and select the one that they found most attractive.[23] For their part, the trading companies could no longer separately bill the fees and commissions accrued in India and now had to integrate these costs into the sales price. Purchasers soon also refused to have anything to do with fluctuations in cargo and currency exchange rates.[24] This virtually brought to a grinding halt the relatively cumbersome practice of conducting transactions on a commission basis, in which merchants more or less blindly exported their goods to Europe in the hope that they could be sold at a profit. "Why, indeed", recalled Ammann,

> should intending buyers bind their hands by giving orders of which they could not foresee whether they would prove workable or not, when they could make sure of having the goods they were in need of by accepting the most tempting of the firm offers laid before them?[25]

The partners at Volkart were anything but delighted with this development, since the company now had to conduct all exports entirely on its own account. But since a growing number of competitors were embracing this new form of business, they eventually decided to give the system a chance. Over time, sales of Indian commodities according to price lists became the rule at Volkart, although initially only for cotton.[26] The establishment of telegraph communications meant that the prices of Indian raw materials increasingly approached global market levels. Moreover, this development bolstered the importance of the Winterthur headquarters, which henceforth exerted a greater degree of influence on daily operations.[27]

The Opening of the Suez Canal

Faster communications with Europe went hand-in-hand with improved means of transport. With the opening of the Suez Canal in 1869, Indian commodities bound for Europe no longer had to be shipped for months by sea around the Cape of Good Hope. This was a particularly favorable development for continental European ports. While the Suez Canal reduced the traveling distance from Bombay to London by more than 44 percent, from 12,275 to 7,220 miles, the distance for the journey to Marseille dropped by nearly 60 percent, and to Trieste it declined by even 65 percent.[28]

The opening of the Suez Canal also sparked a breakthrough for steamship trade with Asia. While it had been a logistical problem to supply the steamships with sufficient coal on their journey around the Cape of Good Hope, refueling was much easier on the Suez route. By contrast, sailing ships were unsuitable for the Suez route, as the merchant fleets often ran into windless conditions on the Red Sea.[29] Whereas practically no steamships traveled between Bombay and continental Europe before the opening of the Suez Canal, from the early 1890s onwards all transport from Bombay to Europe was done by steamship.[30] A wide range of technical innovations introduced during the 1850s and 1860s also drastically reduced steamship transport costs. This was the driving force behind a full 50 percent drop in freight rates between 1870 and 1910.[31] Moreover, steamships could be loaded within just a few days, while sailing vessels had loading times of up to five weeks. Since this meant that the cotton had to be stored in Bombay for shorter periods of time, export companies saved on storage fees and premiums for fire insurance. And since the journey via the canal was shorter and safer, premiums for marine insurance declined and there were fewer damages to goods during transport.[32] All of these changes reduced the amount of time required for the transport of goods on the route from Bombay to Britain from between three-and-half and five months to between one-and-a-half and two months. Steamships departing from Bombay now needed only roughly four weeks to reach ports in the Mediterranean.[33]

Since the Suez Canal did more to shorten the distance between India and the European continent than it did for the route between India and Britain, direct trade between the subcontinent and continental Europe became increasingly important. Before 1869, the transport of goods between Europe and South Asia was nearly completely dominated by British ships that were able to offer cheaper cargo rates than continental shipping companies.[34] As late as 1880, 80 percent of all ships that passed through the Suez Canal sailed under the British flag. By 1910, however, this number had fallen to 62 percent; 12 percent of the ships on the Suez route were German; French and Dutch ships each represented 5 percent of the traffic; and 4 percent belonged to shipping companies from the Austro-Hungarian Empire.[35] These changes had an enormous impact on the Indian cotton trade because continental textile mills were loyal customers of Indian cotton. They used spinning machines that were specially designed to process short-staple Indian varieties.[36] After the end of the American Civil War, their British competitors, however, preferred once again US cotton because it had a longer staple, i.e., longer fibers, making it more suitable for the production of the fine cloth that was woven in Lancashire.[37] Although the British colonial government went to great lengths to encourage the cultivation of long-staple American cotton instead of the short-staple Indian varieties, the British did not manage to push through a complete conversion to American varieties in the Indian cotton growing industry. There were a number of reasons for this. First, the American varieties grew slower than the varieties tradition-ally cultivated in India, and they produced lower yields.[38] Second, although the British succeeded in establishing Dharwar American in India during the 1840s, the seeds were constantly being mixed with an Indian cotton variety called *kumpta*, in part because the mixed seeds could be sold as the Ameri-can variety to obtain a higher price. Ultimately, none of the economic play-ers involved in the Indian cotton trade—neither European merchants nor Indian traders and peasants—saw why they should bother to adopt new cotton varieties when the traditional types of cotton were enjoying high demand in continental Europe and East Asia.[39] Since progress was slug-gish in making the switch to long-staple cotton in India, British spinning mills soon reverted to using US cotton after the end of the American Civil War.[40] By the end of the nineteenth century, of the over 2 million bales of cotton that were produced on average in India each year, only roughly 38,000 were shipped to Britain. By contrast, every year more than 600,000 bales of Indian cotton were exported to continental Europe and more than 460,000 were shipped to China and Japan. Nearly half of the indigenous cotton production, almost 910,000 bales, was processed in Indian spinning mills.[41] Since there was a large demand for Indian cotton on the European mainland, and particularly since the Suez Canal had reduced the distance to continental ports, direct exports to continental Europe increased sharply from 1869 onwards. The proportion of Indian cotton exports that were directly transported to the European continent without taking the circuitous route via Liverpool had risen to 60 percent by 1885, a remarkable increase considering that it represented less than 1 percent in 1866 and less than 11 percent between 1866 and 1870.[42]

The Volkart company, which was one of the few continental European export firms in India, began in 1869 to ship cotton and other commodities with continental European ships through the Suez Canal to mainland ports like Marseille, Trieste, Antwerp and Hamburg, making it the first company to regularly export large volumes from India to these destinations.[43] In Janu-ary 1870, not even two months after the opening of the canal, Salomon Volkart informed the managers of the Bombay branch that the company was thinking of "securing a number of steamboats to ring in the new era."[44] Starting in the late 1870s, diverse steamship lines were established for the transport between India and Europe, allowing trading companies to book the necessary cargo space for their commercial activities. It was now no lon-ger absolutely necessary to charter entire ships to transport goods and mer-chandise, which had been a regular practice until then.[45] The new steamship lines had to be represented by brokering agencies in key port cities and this job was often performed by local trading companies. In the early twentieth century, Volkart represented in India a wide range of companies, including the Hamburg America Line, the Deutsche Dampfschiffsgesellschaft Hansa, the Swedish East India Steamship Co., the Spanish Compania Transatlantica and the Italian Navigazione Generale Florio Rubbatino. During the course of the following decade, a number of other steamship lines sought to establish themselves in the freight business with India and the Far East.[46] Brokering shipping contracts was lucrative for trading companies because it guaranteed them a steady and relatively risk-free income that was a welcome addition to the volatile commodities trade. For the shipping lines it was profitable to be represented by trading companies like Volkart because these firms could guarantee a minimum booking rate through the export of goods like cotton, coffee, coconut fiber and spices.[47]

The Construction of Railway and Telegraph Lines in India

Connections improved not only between Bombay and India, but also within the subcontinent. In 1855, the first Indian telegraph lines were opened; one year later, the network already boasted an astonishing 4,250 miles of lines. Since the telegraph had served the British well during the Indian Rebellion of 1857, a major effort was launched to expand the network. By 1865, the telegraph network had grown to 17,500 miles, by 1900 this figure had soared to 52,910 miles and by 1947 there were no less than 117,190 miles of telegraph lines on the subcontinent.[48] Consequently, from the late 1860s onwards Indian cotton markets were connected with coastal cities, where the large trading companies had their branch offices, as well as with European cotton exchanges. European merchants stayed constantly abreast of the latest developments with the harvest. Furthermore, the government expanded the Indian postal system, which, in addition to colonial officials, was primarily used by merchants; and cotton traders used the postal system to send cotton samples from the areas of cultivation to the coast.[49]

Starting in 1850, the British pressed ahead with the construction of the Indian railway. Up until the mid-nineteenth century, Indian merchants had used ox carts and light sailboats to transport the cotton grown in the upcountry to Bombay, Karachi and Calcutta, where the goods could be loaded on ships and sent to Europe. The new railway lines made it possible to ship the cotton more quickly and securely to the coast. The first short railway line, connecting Bombay with Thane, was opened in 1853.[50] By 1860, a total of 850 miles of track had been laid in India. In the 1880s, the railway network extended over 10,000 miles and linked all major Indian cities. In the early twentieth century, India had the fourth-largest railway network in the world. By the end of the colonial era, it had grown to a length of 40,000 miles and virtually no corner of the country was farther than 20 miles from the nearest railway line. In addition, paved roads were built as supply lines to connect railway stations with inland markets. Large warehouses were built next to the stations to store the cotton until it could be loaded onto the trains. Thanks to the improved transport network, freight rates in 1930 had dropped to one-twentieth of the prices in 1850. It also goes without saying that the expansion of the railway network went hand-in-hand with a surge in the volume of freight that was transported by rail in India, rising from only 3.6 million tons in 1871 to 42.6 million tons of cargo in 1901 and 116 million tons by 1930. Since domestic trade was soon geared entirely to rail transport, large trading centers sprang up along the railway lines. This development spelled the end, however, for the precolonial trading towns and cities outside the service areas of the railway lines.[51]

Colonial Officials and the Quality of Indian Cotton

Construction of the Indian railway lines allowed trading firms like Volkart to expand into the hinterland (Figure 2.1), in some cases putting them in competition with smaller rivals that had entered the market after the opening of the telegraph line to Europe.[52] Instead of purchasing their raw cotton exclusively from middlemen at the bazaars of port cities like Bombay, Madras, Tellicherry and Karachi, the large export companies gradually established a network of procurement agencies in the interior of the country. This was something that European trading firms had repeatedly attempted since the early nineteenth century, but failed to accomplish due to poor transport routes and the difficulties of providing their agents in the back-country with sufficient cash to make purchases.[53]

The opening of procurement agencies made it possible for export firms to more effectively monitor the quality of the cotton. Up until the 1860s, cotton was only available to exporters in the bazaars of coastal cities, where the coveted fibers were offered for sale in bags or partially pressed bales. Such bales had to be carefully checked. According to Volkart employee Jakob Brack-Liechti, native merchants took advantage of the fact that buyers examining the partially pressed bales could not reach into the interior of the bales when assessing the overall quality of the goods.

> During the pressing process in the upcountry, the interior was often spiked with inferior goods and quality goods were only placed on the outer layers of the bales as far as the hand could reach. The full extent of the fraud could only be determined when the bales were opened in the steam presses.

Fraudsters also often attempted to exchange the bales selected by European trading companies for export with bales of lower quality goods or spinning mill waste.

> These *bad* bales were then shipped back home at the expense of the European, while the bales with the quality goods were shipped to

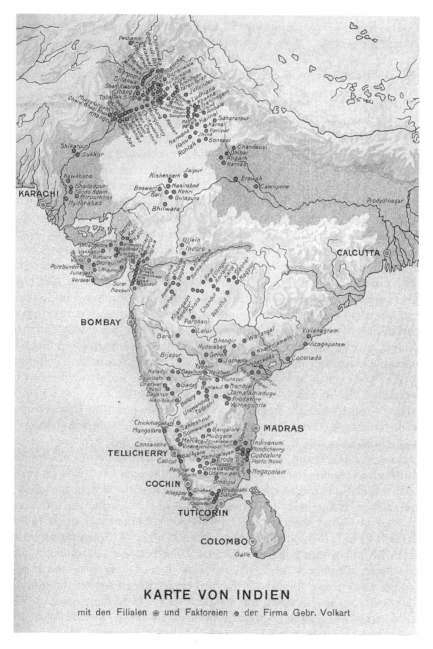

Figure 2.1 Map published by Volkart with the branches and buying agencies in India and Ceylon (from: Reinhart, Gedenkschrift, 1926, 36a)

Europe on consignment at the expense of the native under his (prepared) brand name. The loss was incurred by the European shipper, who had no explanation for this disappointment, and the native pocketed the profits.[54]

Brack-Liechti's account clearly reveals the difficulties of purchasing cotton in India, even for highly specialized trading companies.

The frequent manipulations and contaminations of Indian cotton had a negative impact on the price: "The European manufacturer, taught by long experience, has ceased to expect a pure article, and therefore never gives the price which he otherwise would for cotton of the same quality," wrote J. Forbes Royle, an expert in cotton-related issues for the British India Office, in a report filed in 1851. Several observers blamed the situation on the European merchants in Bombay and alleged that they went ahead with purchases even though the majority of the Indian cotton was soiled or that high-quality cotton had been mixed with cotton of a lesser quality. Royle vehemently opposed this view and cited a letter, sent by the Bombay Chamber of Commerce to the administration of the Bombay Presidency in 1841, which pointed out how difficult it was for merchants in Bombay to establish direct contacts with peasants in the backcountry. The Bombay businessmen went on to say that most of the approximately 20 European cotton export firms in the city employed no more than two staff members, which, in their opinion, was hardly enough to handle local transactions, not to mention undertake excursions into the backcountry. "The merchants here, therefore, are . . . wholly dependent on the cotton to be found in Bombay, whatever be its quality," the Bombay merchants stated in their letter.[55]

The British repeatedly attempted to improve the purity of Indian cotton by introducing legal regulations. In 1829, they passed the first law designed to curb the amount of impurities in cotton, but it failed to improve the situation.[56] The passing of another law in 1851 also failed to achieve the desired effect. Following the outbreak of the American Civil War, however, the manipulations increased to such a degree that the British launched a new attempt and passed the Cotton Fraud Act in 1863. But the law never achieved its desired effect because, still reeling from the shock of the Indian Mutiny of 1857, the colonial government was wary of provoking any conflict with Indian merchants or peasants.[57] Furthermore, the Bombay and Manchester Chambers of Commerce were against it because the Indian colonial government imposed a duty on every bale of cotton the officials examined, thus jeopardizing the competitiveness of Indian cotton on the world market.[58] Likewise, merchants argued that as long as East Asian and continental European spinners were willing to purchase the cotton, government interference was undesirable. For instance, Gaddum & Co., one of the leading cotton exporters in the country, resisted a government order to clean various bales of cotton in 1874 and claimed that the soiled condition posed no problem because the firm took this into account by paying a lower price. Paying a higher price for cleaned cotton had already been tested, the firm argued, with the results being "that although the dirty cotton readily found a market, we were quite unable to sell the cleaned cotton at a fair price and eventually had to sell it at a very heavy loss."[59]

The resistance of European trading companies was a source of constant frustration for the British colonial government. In 1869, an inspector employed by the Bombay Cotton Department complained of "the extreme sensitiveness generally exhibited by the European and Native cotton exporters to our interference with their cotton, which is permitted only on sufferance, not as a matter of right."[60] Instead of relying upon the colonial bureaucracy, merchants generally sought to resolve conflicts within the business community. For example, during the 1875–1876 season Volkart purchased fraudulent bales of cotton from an Indian middleman. Colonial officials hoped that the company would help them take legal action against the Indian merchant, but were severely disappointed when they learned that Volkart had reached an out-of-court settlement with the Indian merchant and there would be no criminal prosecution.[61] After years of this futile tug-of-war between the colonial bureaucracy and the business community, the Cotton Fraud Act was ultimately suspended in 1882 and problems associated with manipulated cotton remained endemic until well into the twentieth century.[62]

Differences between the Indian and American Cotton Industries

The colonial cotton laws failed due to the particularities of the colonial situation and the structure of nineteenth-century Indian agriculture. Whereas commodities such as tea and coffee were produced on large plantations whose European owners were in direct contact with exporters, and thus unable to risk selling adulterated merchandise, the cotton trade was far more fragmented.[63] Indian cotton was cultivated by *ryots*, petty farmers who planted cotton in addition to other crops and were rarely able to harvest more than one or two bales from their land. Because they lacked capital, they had to sell their crops long before the harvest to local moneylenders who resold them later. The moneylenders, however, were not wealthy enough to do business without obtaining credit from traders in large inland towns, who in turn often acted as agents for wealthy Indian merchants from Bombay and other coastal cities. Up until the 1870s, Indian cotton thus passed through a number of hands before it finally reached the coast, where it was shipped to Europe and China. The *ryot* who sold his cotton in advance received no reward for high quality and suffered no penalty for poor quality. He was simply obliged to provide a certain quantity of cotton to the moneylender from whom he had received an advance. The same was true for the other dealers in the inland trade. And since cotton was generally sold by weight, each owner was tempted to water it down by adding to the bales dirt, seed or lower quality cotton. Finally, because all cotton was equally adulterated before reaching the coast, the European and Indian merchants who exported it to Europe and East Asia had no choice but to accept it, regardless of its quality.[64] It needs to be emphasized that European merchants were not the only ones who had to contend with these difficulties. Indian export firms also suffered from the situation. The low quality standard of Indian cotton was not, as one British observer stressed in the early 1860s, a problem that had arisen due to differences between Europeans and natives, but instead resulted from the diverging interests of export companies and merchants from the interior.[65]

As mentioned earlier, British trade regulations proved to be highly effective formal institutions to govern transactions between European traders and affluent Indian merchants, since both groups had a solid education and similar mercantile cultures.[66] But they were not a suitable means of regulating transactions between peasants, indigenous middlemen and large export companies in the interior of the country, nor did they safeguard the quality of cotton in Indian upcountry markets. British civil servants and European merchants thus pinned their hopes on Bombay business circles being able to organize a system of quality control of their own. Such a system had been established in the American cotton trade in the mid-1870s, after European merchants had complained about adulteration and contamination of cotton deliveries on a scale that was comparable to what occurred in India. In contrast to the situation in India, the pressure of European merchants—who had threatened to boycott deliveries from port cities that did not address the problem—had been strong enough for controls to be implemented on every bale of cotton shipped from ports in the American South. The American system differed from the one implemented under the Cotton Fraud Act in India by dispensing with any legislative sanction or government agency; the bylaws and constitutions of the various American cotton exchanges had to be consistent solely with the laws of the US and the federal state in question.[67] Measures were introduced on the authority of the cotton exchanges alone, which appointed supervisors, levied fees and sanctioned fraudulent sellers.[68]

Salomon Volkart appears to have had such a system in mind when he penned a letter to the Bombay office in 1870:

> The simplest and most reliable solution for all parties involved would be if you managed on site to establish a type of association, which would endeavor to provide assessments of the shipped cotton that would be as close as possible to those made in Liverpool. . . . We see no reason why, as long as the cotton inspectors go about their duties with care, the Bombay assessments should not enjoy the same reputation and the same level of recognition as those in Liverpool.

It appears, though, that he was not particularly optimistic about the ability of the Bombay cotton market to introduce such quality controls:

> If these efforts should come to nothing on site, we take comfort in knowing that you shall be called upon to purchase the lion's share of the cotton in the interior, where you will have a better opportunity and greater sense of certitude in making your selection.[69]

There were several reasons why a control system like that in the US did not take root on the subcontinent, despite the similarities between the structure of the cotton trade in the American South and in India. As in India, many American tenants—former slaves freed after the end of the Civil War and poor white farmers who had migrated from the East Coast—were heavily in debt to merchants from the country's interior and local shop owners and thus lived in constant fear of dispossession.[70] As in India, until the late nineteenth century trading in the American interior was also characterized by a chain of commission agents who shipped the raw cotton to Europe from ports like New Orleans and Galveston and to textile mills in the industrialized North. It was not until the 1880s—more or less at the same time that European trading companies began to open buying agencies in the Indian backcountry—that American merchant houses such as Alexander Sprunt and Son managed to gain control of the supply chain linking the cotton fields with factories by establishing brokerage offices, cotton gins, presses and warehouses.[71]

Despite these parallels, the establishment of agrarian capitalism had been successful in the US, whereas it failed in India, not least because capitalist entrepreneurs did not have to deal with the same local mercantile structures in America as on the subcontinent, which was mired in centuries-old commercial structures. Aside from making comments on the climate, which was virtually unbearable for Europeans, and the poor transport network, a British cotton inspector in the late 1860s explicitly emphasized the entrenched nature of Indian traditions:

> The trade was entirely in the hands of the local dealers, and it was in their interest to keep out outsiders. . . . The weights, which differed in every market, were alone sufficient to baffle a stranger; and the constant holidays and consequent stoppages in the work, and the passive resistance which had to be encountered at every step, were quite enough to wear out even a very energetic European.[72]

Such problems were unknown in the US.

Moreover, American cotton was cultivated for consumption on the global market. Plantations in the US were generally much bigger than the cotton fields in India, which were all cultivated by small farmers. This made cotton from India far less uniform when it was pressed into bales for export, and it was far more difficult to punish fraudsters. A British cotton inspector made the following remark in 1864:

> Unlike the cotton bales from the Southern States of America, which can, in cases of fraud, be traced by certain marks to the very plantation where the cotton was grown and packed, Indian packages are made of contributions from a number of small cultivators. . . . All *pressed* bales can be traced to the place only where they were compressed for shipment.[73]

While some Indian cultivators could produce no more than half a bale of cotton per year, the average American cotton farm achieved an annual harvest of ten bales and hardly any farm in the US harvested fewer than three bales per year; in fact, a number of large US cotton farms were even able to obtain yields of several hundred bales. Regulations in the US were also easier to enforce than in India, where cultivators were extremely apprehensive of the colonial government's attempts to intervene, where corruption was rampant and where British officials continuously had to keep an eye on the political situation and could not afford to aggravate the Indian business community.[74]

One could say that the cotton industry in India suffered from the idiosyncrasies of the colonial situation, in which there was no cultural consensus and no basic sense of trust.[75] Meanwhile, the needs of merchants and textile mills in the American cotton industry could be met thanks to the transition to a capitalist economy, something that was not possible for many years in colonial India.

The Opening of Upcountry Buying Agencies

For the reasons listed above, up until the 1870s neither Bombay business circles nor the colonial bureaucracy were able to ensure a consistent level of quality for Indian cotton. Leading European trading companies achieved a major breakthrough on this front, however, when they established buying agencies in the upcountry after the Indian railway was opened. During the American Civil War, Volkart sent employees to interior markets for the first time to purchase large quantities of cotton. Due to the expansion of the transport and communication infrastructure, it became increasingly important for trading firms to achieve economies of scale and maintain standard qualities for cotton. In the late 1860s, this prompted Volkart to set up three cotton presses in the hinterland of Bombay and Tuticorin. The presses were intended to make it easier for Volkart to purchase and export cotton from the growing districts. Likewise, in March 1870 Volkart's Bombay branch dispatched one of its employees to Khamgaon to purchase cotton for the company. Khamgaon was a small city in Berar Province that had been built virtually overnight in the wake of the transformation of the Indian cotton industry between 1867 and 1869. The town quickly became the largest cotton market in Asia and the entire British Empire. As many as 100,000 bales of cotton, worth an estimated 1 million pounds sterling, were shipped by rail from here to Bombay every year.[76] Volkart was highly successful in its bid to station a buying agent in this newly built cotton city, as Salomon Volkart noted in a letter to Bombay:

> If you have dispatched yet another staff member from your office to the interior, you have our wholehearted support. . . . The attempt with the young Cowasjee in Khamgaon teaches us the necessity of having our own cotton procurement specialists in the interior.[77]

In 1872, in addition to the purchasing opportunities afforded by the new presses, three additional buying agencies were opened in the country's interior.[78] By the 1920s, Volkart had established some 100 agencies on the subcontinent,[79] which—although they were also responsible for purchasing commodities like coconut fiber, coffee and spices—primarily purchased raw cotton. The procurement agencies were usually located near the *mandi* (collection centers) along the railway lines where the cotton was stored that had been brought in from the surrounding villages by ox cart.[80] This network made Volkart, along with the Greek-British trading firm Ralli Bros., one of the main buyers of Indian cotton in virtually every *mandi*. Whereas Ralli primarily hired Greek procurement agents, Volkart had, in addition to Europeans and Americans, a large number of Indians as purchasing agents in the interior of the country.[81]

Volkart's buying agents in the interior of the country were urged at the beginning of the rainy season to submit weekly reports to Winterthur on the weather, planting, crop conditions and growth, and to regularly send product samples to Bombay to provide ongoing documentation of the quality of the harvest (Figure 2.2).[82] The information that Volkart gathered from its buying agencies throughout the subcontinent gave the company a huge advantage in the highly competitive cotton business. Yet this also clearly reflects the immense efforts that were required to become successful in the international cotton trade in the late nineteenth century. In view of the required investments and stiff competition, it would have been extremely difficult, if not impossible, even for a large trading company like Volkart to establish a comparably dense procurement network in other cotton growing areas like Egypt, Brazil and the US. It was not until the 1930s that Volkart was able to gain a foothold for purchasing cotton in the US, and not until the 1940s that the company had made inroads into Brazil, although this expansion was only made possible by collaborations with local companies.[83]

In the upcountry, the company purchased what was known as *kappas*, in other words, cotton that still contained the seeds. In order to prepare this product for export, Volkart and other large export companies pooled their resources and invested in cotton gins and steam presses in the interior of

Figure 2.2 Volkart's cotton sampling room in Bombay, 1941, with samples from the various brokerage agencies (Fotomuseum Winterthur, Volkart Collection, CD 1, Bombay Album 1941)

the country. By the late 1860s, hand presses were used in the backcountry to compress cotton into partially pressed bales that were transported to the coast, where they were opened and inspected. Then high-pressure steam presses were used to pack the cotton into fully pressed bales. This was necessary because partially pressed bales took up too much cargo space, which is why shipping lines refused to accept them for destinations like Europe and East Asia. Likewise, in a bid to make better use of its transport capacity, the Peninsular Railway Co. began to raise its freight rates for partially pressed bales during the 1869–1870 season. The savings and transport costs made it worthwhile for exporters to invest in steam presses, and full pressing became standard in the upcountry from the 1870s onwards. The gins and presses primarily benefited the export business of the European trading companies, which controlled the majority of the new facilities, allowing them to gain virtually total control over the cotton sector in the hinterland (Figure 2.3). Although several Indian merchants used the gins and presses as a financial investment, their share in such ventures did not extend beyond an interest in collecting dividends. Moreover, at the turn of the century large Japanese trading companies established their own procurement agencies in India after Japan had become the most important sales market for Indian raw cotton in the late 1890s.[84]

In 1873, Volkart consolidated the three existing presses in the company's ownership under the banner of Volkart's United Press Co. Ltd. (VUP). This

Figure 2.3 Industrialization changed not only textile production in the industrial-ized countries, but also the way commodities were prepared for export in producing countries: cotton press owned by Volkart in Amraoti in the late nineteenth century (Fotomuseum Winterthur, Volkart Collection, CD 3: Jakob Brack Collection)

newly established company started out with a capital of 450,000 rupees. The majority of the shares were purchased by Indian investors and Volkart only had a minority interest in the firm. Up until the beginning of the twen-tieth century, VUP built four more presses and set up the first cotton gins. By 1926, VUP had 12 presses and eight gins on the entire subcontinent. At no point in time right up until the 1920s did Volkart have more than 30 percent of the shares, yet the Swiss actually controlled VUP because they managed the company.[85]

Gins and presses were an important part of Volkart's purchasing organi-zation, since they allowed the company to buy large quantities of cotton in the backcountry and more effectively screen the merchandise.[86] The buy-ing agents were urged to meticulously inspect the quality of the cotton on offer and, in particular, to check the calibration and adjustment of the scales used in the interior of the country to ensure that they were consistently accurate.[87] In the 1870s, Volkart established certain standardized types of cotton, classified according to their uniform color, length of staple and firm-ness. Salomon Volkart wrote a letter to the Bombay office in 1870:

If you manage to establish certain types in Oomra [the Oomrawutnee cotton district] and stick to these, this would be of great importance to our business. The qualities must have certain characteristics and always be consistent, so our customers will know at all times what type of cotton to expect.[88]

Selections were made in accordance with the classification system of the Liverpool Cotton Exchange. Volkart called these types of cotton "Bombay grades"[89] and European textile manufacturers soon recognized them as the standards for Indian cotton. Volkart thus managed to "establish a V.B. brand[90] that commanded extra high prices from buyers," as it said in a letter sent by the Winterthur headquarters in 1922.[91] The introduction of standardized types of cotton was not only essential for offering textile mills consistent grades of merchandise, but also to safeguard against fluctuating prices for transactions on the futures market of the Liverpool Cotton Exchange.[92]

Indian Moneylenders and the Colonial Cotton Economy

As mentioned previously, one of the main reasons why the British colonial government commissioned the construction of railway lines, telegraph stations and roads was that it wanted to make the subcontinent into a producer of commodities for the textile mills of Lancashire.[93] In the eyes of many Europeans, this was not an act of economic exploitation, but rather an important step for India on the road toward modernization and for industrial development on the subcontinent.[94] The following statement by John Chapman, one of the leading proponents of the construction of the Great Indian Peninsular Railway, reveals just how convinced the British were that Western institutions and infrastructural projects in India would usher in a surge in development like the one in Europe. Chapman said in 1848 that many British merchants would see the construction of the Indian railway "as nothing more than an extension of their own line from Manchester to Liverpool."[95]

The British were also firmly convinced that construction of modern infrastructural facilities would lead to the disappearance of the multitudes of middlemen and ultimately lay the cornerstone for a modern cotton market. At first, it actually looked as if they would achieve their objectives. In 1868, the British trading firm of W. Nichol & Co. informed the colonial government's cotton commissioner, C. F. Forbes, that the construction of the railway line to Bombay had greatly improved the quality of cotton in Berar. The trading company was confident that Dharwar would undergo the same development if they were

> blessed with Railway communication with the Coast. . . . The Ryots would be brought into direct communication with the agent of the Bombay purchasers, and would speedily see that it was to his advantage to bring his Cotton to market well cleaned and of good quality.[96]

A few years later, J.K. Bythell, chairman of the Bombay Chamber of Commerce, was pleased to note that at inland cotton markets like Khamgaon and Oomrawutnee "every morning during the season . . . a very large number of the ryots bargain directly with the European buyer and discuss as keenly and acutely as anyone the latest news from Liverpool as given by Reuters daily in these markets."[97] Likewise, in a price booklet that Volkart distributed to its customers in 1873, the company wrote that it was highly optimistic that the railway lines would eliminate the Indian intermediaries in the cotton trade:

> The establishment of our own buying agencies and especially the steam presses under our management in the main growing districts allows us to conclude our purchases of cotton in a more favorable manner than in the past. Direct buying from cultivators namely makes it possible for us to avoid the traditional interventions of native cotton traders and ensure that we purchase genuine, unadulterated quality right from the source.[98]

In contrast to what is maintained in the company publication cited here, Volkart and other trading companies rarely purchased cotton directly from cultivators in the cotton districts, but instead continued to rely on local intermediaries.[99] Many of these were local traders or moderately wealthy peasants who borrowed money from prosperous Indian businessmen from the cities to act as *sowkars* (rural moneylenders) and grant loans to the *ryots*. The *sowkars* were better placed than urban lenders to assess the solvency of the *ryots* since they had more extensive agricultural knowledge, were familiar with local conditions and—thanks to their deep roots in village communities—were in a better position to collect debts.[100]

The establishment of an export-oriented agricultural system fundamentally altered the relationship between peasants and rural moneylenders. The *sowkars* had provided agricultural credits for many centuries. However, during the pre-colonial period—and in the princely states during colonial times—local authorities had introduced a series of measures to curb their profiteering, including regulations that obliged the *sowkars* to sustain peasant families when they ran out of food and to provide these farmers with seed to plant the next harvest. As David Hardiman has indicated, the colonial cotton economy, based on free-market ideology, severed such age-old social ties in the Indian backcountry and upset the "moral economy" of the villages. As a result, famines and grain riots became far more common in areas that fell under the direct control of the British Crown after 1858 than during the precolonial period, and such unrest also occurred more frequently in the Indian princely states during the colonial period.[101]

Another example of how the British altered the rural microcosm was the introduction of land rights by the colonial administration. Although the *ryots* were provided with land title deeds, they were not considered outright owners, but rather merely tenants of the state who could be ousted from their holdings if they failed to pay the land tax introduced by the British. This was a radical departure from the precolonial system, in which the state was not considered to have any general rights to dispossess peasant proprietors.[102] To make matters worse for the peasants, the land tax was based on the average prices of raw materials over the previous decade, with no reductions granted for crop failures or sudden downturns on the world market. The new system also brought about an additional change in the relationship between peasants and *sowkars*. In addition to borrowing money to purchase seed and agricultural equipment, the peasants had to take out loans to pay their land taxes. They obtained the required credit by selling their crops to the *sowkars* in advance at a fixed price, often even before they were sown. For their loans, the moneylenders demanded interest rates that often exceeded 30 percent a year. If the cultivators failed to deliver the stipulated amount of cotton after harvest, which was not unlikely because of the perpetual menace of drought, they had to take out another loan. This of course increased their dependency on the *sowkars*. As a result, the vast majority of cultivators were deeply in debt, with moneylenders controlling up to 80 percent of the cotton crop in the villages.[103]

The loans by the moneylenders offered two advantages to the colonial state. First, they allowed the peasants to pay their taxes, which provided the state with urgently needed revenues. Second, they ensured that the peasants would keep working in the fields, where they could continue to produce for the export of cash crops (Figure 2.4). The downside of this system was that the strong position of the moneylenders in the villages and the permanent indebtedness of the peasants nullified all attempts to improve the quality of Indian cotton. The cultivators had no reason to reap cotton carefully because the crop was already in the possession of the moneylenders. Often it was left on the ground for several days before being gathered. By contrast, the grain that the peasants cultivated for their own use, and which was still in their possession, was always harvested with great care.[104]

Throughout the colonial period, British officials lamented the indebtedness of the peasants, who were, according to a British observer in 1861, "little better than slaves to the money lending class."[105] Yet in condemning the *sowkars* for their purported extortion, the British failed to grasp the deeper causes of the problem, especially the fact that the colonial state was unable to provide farmers with alternative forms of agricultural credit.[106] State-sponsored cotton cooperatives that provided farmers with capital to finance cultivation were not established in India until the 1920s, and not until Indian entrepreneurs were able to exert greater influence on the agricultural policies of British India.[107] In the nineteenth and early twentieth centuries, however, the British relied upon Indian merchants to use their capital to finance the cultivation of cotton. The idea of the subcontinent as a paradise for indigenous moneylenders, whose chokehold on the peasants was responsible for the poor state of Indian cotton, thus represents a

Figure 2.4 Indian peasants transporting bags of cotton by oxen to an inland market in the late nineteenth century (Fotomuseum Winterthur, Volkart Collection, CD 3: Jakob Brack Collection)

Western projection, as Neil Charlesworth has argued. This notion fails to take into account the considerable risks incurred by the *sowkars*, such as the permanent risk of a bad harvest due to the failure of the monsoon or the risk of drastic price fluctuations on the world market.[108] This was particularly problematic for the *sowkars* because they lacked sufficient funds to pay the advances to peasants out of pocket and instead had to take out loans from wealthy merchants in the big cities. Consequently, it is unlikely that the moneylenders could make substantial profits in the villages, in contrast to those taken in by European trading companies and a thin layer of upper-class urban Indian merchants.[109]

Furthermore, the colonial legal administration helped the *sowkars* to keep their debtors in check. The trade regulations introduced by the British were primarily aimed at protecting the investments of lenders. Such legislation was appropriate for transactions between equals, but when it came to commercial exchanges between peasants—who were generally illiterate—and shrewd lenders, the latter were clearly at an advantage. Lenders rarely took indebted peasants to court, though. Instead, they were chiefly interested in gaining greater access to the harvest. They had no interest in taking over the farmland because it produced little in the way of profits and they lacked the labor to till the fields. The threat of summoning a delinquent borrower before a colonial court was usually enough to coerce peasants into meeting their lenders' demands.[110]

European Merchants and Indian Intermediaries

Even after European trading companies opened procurement agencies in the interior of the country starting in the 1860s, the *sowkars* continued to play a central role in the lending of money for agricultural production. Initially, European exporters tried to circumvent the moneylenders and purchase directly from the peasants. But the *sowkars* enjoyed such a strong position in the villages that they could counter these efforts with a strategy of non-cooperation, which made it significantly more difficult for the Europeans to conduct their business transactions and ultimately forced them to cooperate with the rural moneylenders.[111] Although the Europeans had managed by the 1870s to assert control over the thousands of miles between the *mandis* in the Indian backcountry and the textile manufacturing districts in Europe, they were unable to exert the desired influence on the first 10 or 20 miles between the cotton fields and the Indian inland markets. In that sense, historians Dietmar Rothermund and Laxman Satya are only partially correct in their view that European merchants were able to utilize Indian agriculture during the colonial era as an immense plantation, the major difference being that the traders did not have to worry about the livelihoods of the peasants because these cultivators grew enough food to be self-sufficient.[112] Plantation owners were usually relatively successful at monitoring the quality of the commodities produced in their fields, yet due to the social and economic conditions in the Indian upcountry, the Europeans failed to accomplish precisely this objective throughout the entire colonial era.

This was not a serious problem for European trading companies, however. Cooperating with local lenders generally allowed export companies like Volkart to avoid paying advances to suppliers. In fact, starting in the late 1860s Volkart made a policy of never granting loans to suppliers or customers, but instead insisted upon immediate payment upon delivery of the goods, or at least required the client to produce a payment guarantee from a bank or broker.[113] Even if the company occasionally made an exception, it generally succeeded in asserting this business principle. It was not until after World War I that Volkart was forced to sell cotton on credit to manufacturers in Germany and East Asia. And it was not until after 1945 that Volkart returned to the practice of paying advances for the purchase of commodities.[114]

On the subcontinent Volkart was able to make use of the intermediary role of affluent merchants who served as a link between rural growers and the European export firms that were oriented toward the global market.[115] Numerous economic historians argue that loans for agricultural exports came from the large export companies from the 1860s onwards.[116] But this is an erroneous assumption.[117] Trading companies at the time lacked the resources to raise the amounts of money that would have been necessary to finance cotton cultivation and they could not afford to have their money immobilized in agricultural loans for months on end. It was bad enough that the commodities that they purchased in India had to be shipped for months before they could finally be sold in Europe or East Asia. Because trading firms generally exported goods on their own account from the 1860s onwards, they did not receive the proceeds for their shipments until the merchandise reached its port of destination and was received by the textile mills. In the meantime, trading companies relied upon their own capital and short-term bank loans to stay afloat.[118] To make matters worse, the risks of agricultural loans are traditionally very high because pests and weather conditions can ruin a harvest and plummeting global market prices can render it impossible for cultivators to repay what they owe to banks and lenders.[119] Trading companies lacked the necessary resources to collect payments from recalcitrant debtors in the Indian hinterland. It was therefore far more economical for them to delegate this risk to local moneylenders.

In addition to the moneylenders, who generally served as intermediaries and supplied the exporters with cotton, European trading companies also worked hand-in-hand with Indian financiers or shroffs. One of the main challenges faced by European merchants since the early nineteenth century had been supplying their buying agents in the interior of the country with sufficient hard currency.[120] Indian cultivators and shopkeepers refused to accept bank notes or *hundis*—the common bill of exchange in the Indian bazaar economy—and often only accepted silver coins. Up until the 1920s, many towns in the interior of the country had no banks that could have supplied European procurement agents with sufficient cash. Volkart occasionally shipped silver coins in ironclad chests to the procurement agencies, and each shipment was accompanied by two trustworthy employees. But in most cases the company relied on the help of a shroff to pay for its purchases. Whereas the *sowkars* provided long-term agricultural credits to the farmers and had no contractual ties with the export firms, the shroffs were bound by contract.[121] The shroffs had to pay local intermediaries in cash for their deliveries of commodities when they were instructed to do so by Volkart's agents. Volkart undertook to reimburse the shroffs for these expenditures when they presented proof of payment at the buying agencies. The shroffs received a certain percentage of the amount due as a commission for their work. It was only in exceptional cases that Volkart granted the shroffs an advance so that they could pay indigenous middlemen.[122] But these were merely extremely short-term loans and the local buying agents were responsible for "ensuring that our money is used immediately to pay for *our* purchases, and that the merchants immediately get receipts from the diverse out-stations."[123]

The lack of regular commercial banks at many trading venues in the interior of the country was not seen as a disadvantage for many years, not least because the shroffage system allowed European trading companies to embed their transactions in local business structures. For instance, a Volkart instruction manual from 1912 made note of the following advantages to this way of doing business:

> Besides a Bank will be no help to us in other branches of our business whilst an influential Shroff is able to and may do a good deal to influence dealers in our favour and thus facilitate our business in general.[124]

The disadvantages of the system became clear to Volkart during the interwar era, as reflected in a letter sent from Karachi to the headquarters in Winterthur in 1931:

> It is no easy task these days to locate financially strong and absolutely reliable shroffs. A man might be very rich one day and on the verge of bankruptcy six months later. Hence, it is totally impossible to judge the financial standing of an Indian beyond any given year.

This prompted Volkart to consider making more arrangements with banks to finance its purchases.[125] Even though the source material does not indicate exactly when the company began to work together with Indian commercial banks, it is clear that the company had already been doing business with the Presidency Banks of Bombay and Madras for quite some time when these financial institutions merged with the Imperial Bank of India in 1921. The Imperial Bank of India had branches throughout the entire subcontinent, making it an extremely valuable partner for financing the firm's purchases. However, since this financial institution was rather inflexible when it came to granting credit, Volkart switched to the Chartered Bank in the 1930s. Over the long term, Volkart gradually moved from the traditional form of financing purchases with shroffs to a modern form of funding using commercial banks. But even during the early 1930s this transition was not yet complete and the firm still depended to some degree on shroffage arrangements with Indian merchants.[126]

Despite the vertical integration of procurement by establishing agencies in the interior of the country, export companies still relied on the close cooperation of Indian merchants (Figure 2.5). As late as 1922—in other words, half a century after the establishment of the first buying agencies—an article printed in a Volkart in-house newspaper highlighted the important function fulfilled by Indian brokers:

> Anybody who is acquainted with business life in India knows by experience what an important part the broker plays therein. The Broker . . . is so to speak the central figure, around which the daily business is transacted, the connecting link between the European firm and the dealers.[127]

In the early 1930s, in reaction to increasingly intense competition from Indian export firms, company officials at Volkart headquarters in Winterthur

Figure 2.5 Seth Sobhraj Chetumal: guarantee broker for Volkart in Karachi, 1899 (Fotomuseum Winterthur, Volkart Collection, CD 4, individual towns in India, Karachi)

considered the option of no longer employing a house broker in Bombay and instead making purchases on the local cotton market through a loose collaboration with reputable bazaar brokers.[128] This proposal was rejected by Volkart Bombay, however, in large part because independent brokers would

only display a fraction of the loyalty that we can count on with a house broker arrangement such as we currently have. We have to give this old

Indian institution some measure of credit in this regard, even if it is no longer consistent with our modern conceptions.[129]

The loyalty of the brokers to the company was also important because they played a key role as a source of information. For instance, a letter written in 1939 by the branch in Madras pointed out that it was not strictly necessary to join the local chamber of commerce "to find out what the competition was up to because we have the brokers to keep us informed on this."[130]

Family Businesses and the Stabilization of Relationships Based on Trust

Because the collaboration with Indian middlemen could only be legally safeguarded to a certain extent, these business relationships were fundamentally based on mutual trust. Local intermediaries were especially important to the Europeans who, as foreigners, enjoyed relatively little social capital on the subcontinent and lived in constant fear that they would be deceived by customers and suppliers. O. Haefliger, a Volkart purchasing agent in Lyallpur, gave the following testimony to the Indian Cotton Committee in 1918:

> I find that, in matters of trade, the Punjab is in a state little short of anarchy, so much so that, the one element so very important and so highly esteemed in European business life, trust, is entirely out of place here.[131]

This gap in confidence was filled by cooperating with Indian brokers and shroffs.

In some cases, Volkart worked for a number of decades with Indian trading companies that assumed the shroffage for a specific area.[132] It was a similar story with its cooperation with brokers. "Sometimes these posts are handed down from father to son as a sort of inherited tradition," according to an article in *V.B. News* from the year 1922, "and the fact that generations of the same family have been acting for us in this capacity bears testimony to the good spirit prevailing between the firm and the brokers."[133] Even if this statement is to be taken with a grain of salt, the fact that members of a merchant family worked for Volkart as brokers and shroffs over a number of generations is a clear indication that the company endeavored to embed its transactions in previously existing trade networks and their business culture.

The family is revered in traditional Indian society—and this remains true to this day. The reputation of a family firm was therefore of key importance to the social standing of the members of this family.[134] As C. A. Bayly has noted, it was unthinkable for Indian merchants to view their companies separately from their families, if for no other reason than the fact that in most Indian languages there was no specific term for a company that was not family-owned. Economic decisions always had to be made with regard to their social impact on the members of the merchant family in question. During particularly successful business years, merchant families would make lavish donations to charities and support religious festivals and rituals. This enhanced the prestige of their families and strengthened social networks that could prove essential in the throes of a business crisis. In that sense, the Indian merchant enterprise had a dual function; it was both a profit-maximizing venture and an entity in which social ties, which were established on the strength of honor and respectability, came together and promoted the business success of the family-owned firm.[135] By employing the members of certain merchant families as brokers or shroffs for a number of decades, Volkart used these dynamics to establish a relationship based on trust with their Indian intermediaries, which helped to stabilize the trading firm's business collaborations.

As mentioned earlier, the trading firm did not have unlimited confidence in its brokers and shroffs, but instead kept abreast of their financial situations by consulting local banks on a regular basis. Likewise, in the event of any irregularities, Volkart could always rely on the legal institutions that had been established by the British.[136] Furthermore, the firm's employees not only had to take English language courses for a number of years, but also complete an intensive "study of the indigenous languages" to allow them to "express themselves fluently in overseas countries without the aid of an interpreter," as then partner Georg Reinhart wrote in the jubilee publication celebrating the company's 75th anniversary in 1926.[137] When employees passed the tests that certified their basic level of proficiency in Hindi, Tamil, Malayalam, Singhalese or Kanare, they received a bonus and were urged to take additional courses.[138] Based on the limited available source material, it is no longer possible to determine exactly when employees were urged to learn the local languages, but the records do show that August F. Ammann had no such linguistic knowledge when he arrived in India in 1874 and did not learn Hindi until he was in Cochin and Karachi.[139] So it is very possible that the requirement to learn the native languages was made in connection with the country's expansion into the Indian backcountry.

The Emergence of Large-scale Enterprises in the Global Cotton Trade of the Late Nineteenth Century

As trading companies began to conduct more transactions on their own account after the introduction of the telegraph, new solutions had to be found to finance the export trade. Starting in the 1860s, textile mills no longer paid advances on their orders, but instead issued payment only after the goods had been delivered to the port of destination. This put a halt to the business of exporting commodities on a commission basis on behalf of Indian merchants, which also meant that exports could no longer be financed by Indian guarantee brokers and shroffs. Up until 1870, Volkart had used a Parsi merchant as a guarantee broker who made credits available for the export of cotton and other commodities. But the company encountered a number of situations in which the guarantee broker stood in the way of transactions because he was far too cautious in his selection of Indian business partners, or he conveyed a false sense of security that induced Volkart to engage in business dealings that the firm would have otherwise turned down. Moreover, the guarantee broker went to court on a number of occasions to escape his responsibility for business transactions that he had assured were with reliable suppliers. Switching to another guarantee broker was not an option because prosperous Indian merchants no longer had any interest in acting as intermediaries for Indian trading firms for the simple reason that they could make more money trading on their own account. Volkart thus decided to change its approach in the 1870–1871 season and run its export business in Bombay without the help of a guarantee broker. To finance exports and safeguard the company's liquidity, Volkart increasingly made use of loans from British commercial banks and continental European financial institutions.[140]

During the second half of the nineteenth century, Volkart established an extensive procurement organization in India and, back in Europe, a growing network of sales agencies that were responsible for selling Indian raw materials to European manufacturers, with Indian cotton as the company's leading export commodity. The Indian merchants who had controlled a considerable share of the export trade to Europe until the mid-1860s could not keep pace with the sweeping innovations of the day, primarily in the cotton trade. The Indians lacked the requisite business connections to negotiate the same advantageous credit conditions with European commercial banks as their rivals from Europe, or to safeguard their transactions on the futures market of the European cotton exchanges. They were also incapable of organizing a similarly effective sales organization in the main European industrial regions that would have allowed them to come into direct contact with European manufacturers. The changes in the overseas trading sector that were driven by advances in transport and communications sparked a major shift in global trade and the export trade to Europe fell completely into the hands of European trading companies from the 1870s onwards.[141] Indian merchants, who until then had controlled a substantial share of the exports to China and Europe, were pushed out of the cotton export business and forced to find new investment opportunities for their capital. Many of them subsequently began to invest in newly established cotton mills on the subcontinent or they granted loans for the domestic trading sector and agricultural production.[142]

But even after the mid-nineteenth century trade with India was by no means firmly in European hands. Although Indian merchants played a secondary role in the cotton export sector, they still controlled a large segment of the market in the trade of other goods between India and the rest of Asia and the African continent.[143] In the early twentieth century, the Indians staged a comeback when Patel Brothers started exporting cotton to Europe. Even if Patel only had a turnover of nearly 40,000 bales per year, which paled in comparison to the amount sold by Volkart and Ralli, this showed that Indian companies were definitely capable of winning back the share of the market that they had lost in the late nineteenth century.[144] In the 1930s, several Indian companies were again active in the cotton export business to Europe and Japan, although their sales remained far below those of the large European and Japanese trading firms.[145] Starting in the 1890s, however, the Europeans faced stiff competition from Japanese trading companies and, from 1897, Japan remained the main buyer of Indian cotton for five decades. The export business to Japan was almost entirely controlled by Japanese trading firms that were also highly successful in exporting Indian cotton to Europe during the years following World War I.[146]

Shorter transport times and the advent of the telegraph reduced the price difference between Europe and India in the export trade, which in turn reduced the profit margins that trading companies could achieve. Profits could now only be made if purchasing prices and transport costs were kept as low as possible. Given the key importance of economies of scale in this development, a large-scale consolidation process took place in the sector during the 1870s, forcing an ever-growing number of small and medium-sized exporters out of the business. Whereas in 1861 the largest cotton exporter in Bombay, Richard Stewart and Co., shipped 66,000 bales to Liverpool, in 1875 the newly established company of Gaddum and Co. sent more than 100,000 bales to Liverpool, which amounted to 20 percent of all cotton exports from Bombay to Europe (Table 2.1).[147]

By the 1870s, Volkart had become the fourth-largest exporter of Indian cotton to Europe. In 1888, the company opened an additional office in Madras, primarily for the export of cotton from southern India. In the years 1889–1895, Volkart was the third largest cotton exporter from Bombay to Europe after Ralli Bros. and Gaddum Bythell & Co. Whereas Volkart usually shipped out roughly 100,000 bales during these years, which amounted to between 5 and 10 percent of all exports to Europe, during the 1882–1883 season Gaddum Bythell exported more than 232,000 bales from Bombay to Europe, and more than 244,000 bales in 1889–1890.[148] These large turnovers went hand-in-hand with an extreme aversion to risk because, given the huge volumes of trade involved, speculative activities could have easily caused trading companies to go bankrupt in the event of a crisis. Instead, they focused on shipping increasingly large quantities of cotton with small profit margins.[149]

Volkart was able to increase its sales even further during the twentieth century. In 1922–1923, the company exported to Europe some 175,000 bales out of Bombay and around 350,000 bales from throughout India. The second-largest exporter during this year was Ralli with more than 150,000 bales from Bombay and around 315,000 from throughout India.[150] Moreover, with sales of 244 million Swiss francs, the cotton trade accounted

Table 2.1 Cotton exports out of Bombay during the 1882–1883 season for shipments between 1 July 1882 and 30 June 1883 (only shipments to Europe were taken into account). Figures in 44-pound bales.

		To Continent direct & via London	Liverpool	Total
1.	Gaddum & Co.	168,151	64,451	232,602
2.	Killick Nixon & Co.	115,944	31,665	147,609
3.	Ralli Bros.	84,634	36,483	121,120
4.	Volkart Bros.	107,467	500	107,967
5.	Cassels & Co.	54,861	18,300	73,161
6.	Lyon & Co.	30,599	29,794	60,393
7.	Glade & Co.	39,634	6,743	46,377
8.	Spinner & Co.	40,365	4,638	45,003
9.	Blascheck & Co.	40,361	4,451	44,812
10.	Sanquet & Co.	41,425	2,250	43,375
11.	G. Lockhart & Co.	35,208	600	35,808
12.	T. H. Moore & Co.	18,525	8,886	27,411
13.	Lang Moir & Co.	21,851	5,235	27,086
14.	Harvey & Sabapathy	21,674	4,691	26,383
15.	J. C. Bushby & Co.	10,030	15,723	25,753
16.	Wallace & Co.	4,100	19,205	23,305
17.	John Marshall	3,705	10,748	14,453
–	25 sundry European firms	43,398	32,809	76,207
–	Natives	6,685	108,110	114,795
–	Transshipment of other ports	28,845	———	28,845
		917,138	405,282	1,322,420

(Source: VA, Dossier 3: Bombay I, 9. Cotton Statistics)

for roughly two-thirds of Volkart's turnover that year.[151] In addition to its exports to Europe, Volkart and Ralli also shipped commodities to Japan and China. During the 1925–1926 season, the two firms each exported more than 40,000 bales from Bombay to East Asia.[152] There are unfortunately no available statistics that would shed light on the importance of exports to China and Japan for European trading companies during the late nineteenth and early twentieth centuries. There are also very few figures that would allow for a comparison of the sales of European trading companies in India and those of rival firms that were active in other cotton growing regions. It can be generally said, though, that Volkart ranked among the world's top cotton companies in the late nineteenth century and had become a market leader in the shipping of the most important agricultural export commodity in the world.[153] The highest turnovers at the time appear to have been achieved by US trading companies. Between 1889 and 1891, for instance, Alexander Sprunt and Son shipped an annual average of nearly 94,000 bales and, during the first decade of the twentieth century, between 300,000 and 400,000 bales. Another cotton merchant, Anderson Clayton, sold 2.087 million bales between 1925 and 1928, and 2.288 million bales between 1936 and 1938.[154] Likewise, large Japanese trading companies like the Japan Cotton Trading Company and Toyo Menkwa Kaisha achieved enormous turnovers and exported in 1925–1926 around 489,000 and 436,000 bales of Indian raw cotton, respectively, to Japan, China and Europe.[155]

Volkart's business also boomed from a financial perspective. The four branches in Bombay, Colombo, Cochin and Karachi achieved aggregate profits of over 3 million rupees by 1875, which amounted to more than 9 million Swiss francs.[156] The company also benefited from the extremely low taxes for European companies on the subcontinent, which were not introduced in British India until 1860 and initially amounted to just 4 percent of net income. The corporate tax rate was even reduced to 2.6 percent after 1886.[157] This made colonial India's export-oriented cotton trade a highly lucrative business, primarily for European trading companies, commercial banks and wealthy Indian merchants. Indian peasants, however, could hardly shield themselves from the risks of declining global market prices and failed harvests. They received no assistance during the colonial era from state-supported institutions like agricultural cooperatives, nor did they draw on subsidies. Hence, they could hardly make a profit from the expansion of the Indian cotton economy and instead mostly eked out a living in dire poverty.[158] This was not so much a consequence of colonial rule, but rather a circumstance that they shared with millions of peasants around the world who cultivated their fields to produce commodities for the capitalist economy from the nineteenth century onwards.

Notes

1 Anderegg, Chronicle, 1976, 113 and 195; for more on the expansion of Volkart into East Asia, see Chapter 10.
2 Chandler, *Scale and Scope*, 2004 [1990].
3 Mann, *The Cotton Trade of India*, 1860, 3–4.
4 Satya, *Cotton and Famine in Berar*, 1997, 52.
5 Harnetty, *Imperialism and Free Trade*, 1972, 36–58; Satya, *Cotton and Famine in Berar*, 1997, 160; Beckert, "Emancipation and Empire," 2004, 1411ff.
6 Satya, *Cotton and Famine in Berar*, 1997. During the late nineteenth century, a similar development took place in other colonial possessions, for example, in Africa. For more on this, see Isaacman, *Cotton Is the Mother of Poverty*, 1996; Engdahl, *The Exchange of Cotton*, 1999; Beckert, "From Tuskegee to Togo," 2005; Robins, "The Black Man's Crop," 2009; Zimmerman, *Alabama in Africa*, 2010.
7 Beckert, "Emancipation and Empire," 2004, 1415.
8 Anderegg, *Chronicle*, 1976, 87.
9 VA, Dossier 3: Bombay I, 4. Table of Events 1851–1961/2.
10 Vizciany, "Bombay Merchants and Structural Changes," 1979, 167.
11 Crawford, *Reminiscences of an Indian Police Official*, 1894, 242–244.
12 VA, Dossier 3: Bombay I, 4. Table of Events 1851–1961/2.
13 Vizciany, "Bombay Merchants and Structural Changes," 1979, 187–188.
14 Anderegg, *Chronicle*, 1976, 90.
15 VA, Statistik der Gebrüder Volkart 1851–1914.
16 Anderegg, *Chronicle*, 1976, 88.

17 VA, Weisse Schachtel: Jakob Brack-Liechti, *Einige Betrachtungen über den indischen B'wollmarkt aus älterer Zeit*, 23 February 1918, 3.
18 Ammann, *Reminiscences*, 1921, 9–10.
19 VA, Weisse Schachtel: Jakob Brack-Liechti, *Einige Betrachtungen über den indischen B'wollmarkt aus älterer Zeit*, 23 February 1918, 5.
20 Ammann, *Reminiscences*, 1921, 8–9.
21 Headrick, *The Tentacles of Progress*, 1988, 100–101. For the history of telegraph communications in India, see Mann, "Telekommunikation in Britisch-Indien," 2009.
22 VA, Weisse Schachtel: Jakob Brack-Liechti, *Einige Betrachtungen über den indischen B'wollmarkt aus älterer Zeit*, 23 February 1918, 3–4.
23 Ammann, *Reminiscences*, 1921, 10.
24 VA, Weisse Schachtel: Jakob Brack-Liechti, *Einige Betrachtungen über den indischen B'wollmarkt aus älterer Zeit*, 23 February 1918, 3–5.
25 Ammann, *Reminiscences*, 1921, 10.
26 Ammann, *Reminiscences*, 1921, 10.
27 VA, Dossier 1: B) Die Teilhaber, 1) Salomon Volkart, 3. Privat-Copierbuch 9 January 1867–1825 August 1870: Winterthur to Bombay, 27 May 1870.
28 Ziegler, *Der Import ostindischer Baumwolle*, 1922, 13; Headrick, *The Tentacles of Progress*, 1988, 26.
29 Ziegler, *Der Import ostindischer Baumwolle*, 1922, 14.
30 Harley, "The Shift from Sailing Ships to Steamships," 1971, 222ff.
31 Headrick, *The Tentacles of Progress*, 1988, 20–26.
32 Vicziany, "Bombay Merchants and Structural Changes," 1979, 182.
33 Anderegg, *Chronicle*, 1976, 114–115.
34 VA, Dossier 13: London/Liverpool (VB + Woods&Thorburn) / Bremen: 2. Table of Events.
35 Chapman, *Merchant Enterprise in Britain*, 1992, 5.
36 Harnetty, *Imperialism and Free Trade*, 1972, 93.
37 Ellison, *A Hand-Book of the Cotton Trade*, 1858, 39.
38 Brit Lib, IOR/L/E/7/1143, Commerce and Revenue Department, 1922, File 4982: W. H. Himbury, Cotton Growing in India, Report to the British Cotton Growing Association, Manchester, 3 April 1923.
39 Jean Rutz, Agent Volkart Bros., "Guntur (28.2.18)," *Indian Cotton Committee, Minutes of Evidence*, 5 (1920), 19; Harnetty, *Imperialism and Free Trade*, 1972, 83–93.
40 Ellison, *A Hand-Book of the Cotton Trade*, 1858, 39.
41 Bombay Chamber of Commerce, *Report for the Year 1908*, 135.
42 VA, Weisse Schachtel: Jakob Brack-Liechti, *Einige Betrachtungen über den indischen B'wollmarkt aus älterer Zeit*, 23 February 1918, 4.
43 VA, Dossier 19: Winterthur II, 13. Write-ups about the firm by VB and corrections thereto by JA.
44 VA, Dossier 1, B) die Teilhaber, 1) Salomon Volkart, 3. Privat-Copierbuch 9 January 1867–1825 August 1870: 14 January 1870, Winterthur to Bombay.
45 Ziegler, *Der Import ostindischer Baumwolle*, 1922, 16–17.
46 Anderegg, *Chronicle*, 1976, 202–201.
47 Frech, *Baumwolle, Stahl und Stolpersteine*, 2001, 57–58.
48 Headrick, *The Tentacles of Progress*, 1988, 121–122.
49 Satya, *Cotton and Famine in Berar*, 1997, 152–153.
50 Headrick, *The Tentacles of Progress*, 1988, 62.
51 Rothermund, *Government, Landlord, and Peasant in India*, 1978, 17; Tomlinson, *The Economy of Modern India*, 1993, 55–56; Satya, *Cotton and Famine in Berar*, 1997, 144–145 and 179.

52 Jones, *International Business*, 1987, 106–111.
53 Bayly, *Rulers, Townsmen and Bazaars*, 1983, 249–245.
54 VA, Weisse Schachtel: Jakob Brack-Liechti, *Einige Betrachtungen über den indischen B'wollmarkt aus älterer Zeit*, 23 February 1918, 7–12.
55 Royle. *Culture and Commerce*, 1851, 60–61.
56 Harnetty, *Imperialism and Free Trade*, 1972, 102.
57 To read about the not uncommon peasant revolts in colonial India, see Stokes, *The Peasant and the Raj*, 1978; Guha, *The Agrarian Economy*, 1985.
58 Harnetty, *Imperialism and Free Trade*, 1972, 104–107
59 MSA, Revenue Department, 1874, Vol. 26, No. 658: Cotton—Complaint made by Messers. Gaddum & Co. against the Cotton Inspector at Dhollera for seizing eight bales of cotton of low quality purchased by them: Letter from Messrs. Gaddum & Co., Bombay, to the Chief Secretary to Government, Revenue Department, Bombay, 25 February 1874.
60 MSA, Revenue Department, 1869, Vol. 8, No. 90: Cotton—Report on the working of the Cotton Fraud Department for 1868–1869, Appendix H: J.H. Merritt, Inspector of Cotton, Bombay, to G.F. Forbes, Esq., Officiating Inspector-in-Chief, Cotton Department, Bombay, 28 May 1869.
61 MSA, Revenue Department, 1876, Vol. 29, No. 15: Cotton—Administration Report of the Cotton Department for 1874–1875 & 1875–1876: Administration Report of the Cotton Department for the year 1875–1876, 14.
62 Harnetty, *Imperialism and Free Trade*, 1972, 102–122; MacAra, *Trade Stability*, 1925, 204–206.
63 Watson, *Report on Cotton Gins*, 1879, 162.
64 Smith, *The Cotton Trade of India*, 1863, 12, 21–22, 28; Harnetty, *Imperialism and Free Trade*, 1972, 101–102; Rothermund, *Government, Landlord, and Peasant in India*, 1978.
65 Smith. *The Cotton Trade of India*, 1863, 56.
66 Bayly, *Rulers, Townsmen and Bazaars*, 1983, 31ff., 239ff. Also see Chapter 1.
67 Cox, *Department Bulletin*, 1926, 25.
68 Watson, *Report on Cotton Gins*, 1879, 163.
69 VA, Dossier 1, B) die Teilhaber, 1) Salomon Volkart, Privat-Copierbuch 9 January 1867–1825 August 1870: 7 July 1870, Winterthur to Bombay.
70 Reidy, *From Slavery to Agrarian Capitalism*, 1992, 222–247; Osterhammel, *Die Verwandlung der Welt*, 2009, 997.
71 Killick, "The Transformation of Cotton Marketing," 1981, 146–153.
72 Rivett-Carnac, *Report of the Cotton Department*, Bombay, 1869, 131–132.
73 MSA, Revenue Department, 1865, Vol. 9: Report by A.W. Hughes, Esq., Inspector of Cotton for Scind, dated 12 December 1864, 103.
74 Garside, *Cotton Goes to Market*, 1935, 35; Watson, *Report on Cotton Gins*, 1879, 159ff.; Pearse, *The Cotton Industry of India*, 1930, 31.
75 Osterhammel, "Symbolpolitik und imperiale Integration", 2004, 401.
76 Satya, *Cotton and Famine in Berar*, 1997, 173
77 VA, Dossier 1, B) die Teilhaber, 1) Salomon Volkart, 3. Privat-Copierbuch 9 January 1867–1825 August 1870: Winterthur to Bombay, 17 March 1870.
78 Anderegg, *Chronicle*, 1976, 108–109.
79 VA, Dossier 3: Bombay I, 4. Table of Events 1851–1961/2.
80 Rivett-Carnac, *Report of the Cotton Department*, 1869, 134.
81 Ray, "The Bazaar", 1988, 286.
82 VA, Dossier 64: Geschäftsordnung 1915/1921 mit Nachträgen bis 1940 / Upcountry Bookkeeping Instructions 1912–1926 / Upcountry Instructions 1952: General Regulations and Instructions for the Use of Volkart Brothers Upcountry Agencies, Winterthur 1912, 21–27.

83 Rambousek/Vogt/Volkart, *Volkart*, 1990, 102–104 and 162; see Chapters 10 and 13.

84 Naoto, "Upcountry Purchase Activities," 2001, 205ff.; Satya, *Cotton and Famine in Berar*, 1997, 171; Vicziany, "Bombay Merchants and Structural Changes," 1979, 181–184; Ray, *The Bazaar*, 1988, 286. For more on the export of Indian cotton to Japan, see Chapter 10.

85 VA, Dossier 10: VUP (Volkart United Press Comp.), 1. The Tinnevelly Press Co. Ltd. / The Comrawattee Press Co. Ltd. / The Bhownuggar Press Co. Ltd.

86 VA, Dossier 20: VB Organisation 1952/53: Aide-mémoire on some principles of the cotton business, 18, March 1953.

87 VA, Dossier 64: Geschäftsordnung 1915/1921 mit Nachträgen bis 1940 / Upcountry Bookkeeping Instructions 1912–1926 / Upcountry Instructions 1952: General Regulations and Instructions for the Use of Volkart Brothers Upcountry Agencies. Winterthur 1912, 13.

88 VA, Dossier 1, B) die Teilhaber, 1) Salomon Volkart, 3. Privat-Copierbuch 9 January 1867–1825 August 1870: 22 December 1870 Winterthur to Bombay.

89 Gebrüder Volkart, *Calculationstabellen*, 1873, 14.

90 V.B. is the abbreviation for Volkart Brothers.

91 VA, Dossier 13: London/Liverpool (VB + Woods&Thorburn) / Bremen: Bremen (incl. Hamburg office), 3. Correspondence: Winterthur to Bremen, 9 June 1922.

92 Vicziany, "Bombay Merchants and Structural Changes," 1979, 181.

93 For more on the importance of infrastructural projects for colonial rule, see, for example: van Laak, *Imperiale Infrastruktur*, 2004.

94 Headrick, *The Tools of Empire*, 1981, 181–188.

95 As quoted by Thorner, *Investment in Empire*, 1950, 96.

96 MSA, Revenue Department, 1868, Vol. 4, No. 844: Cotton—Cotton cultivation and trade in the Southern Maratha Country: Letter of W. Nichol and Co. to C.F. Forbes, Cotton Commissioner, Bombay, 29 July 1868.

97 MSA, Revenue Department, 1874, Vol. 27, No. 351: Cotton—Opinion of Officer of Cotton Dept. in reference of the statement made by the Bombay Chamber of Commerce on the present state of the Mofussil cotton trade: Letter from J.K. Bythell, chairman of the Bombay Chamber of Commerce, Bombay, to the Chief Secretary to Government, Revenue Department, Bombay, 11 March 1874.

98 Gebrüder Volkart, *Calculationstabellen*, 1873, 11.

99 Dantwala, *Marketing of Raw Cotton*, 1937, 31. See also Mr. N. P. Dantra, Agent, Messrs. "Volkart Bros., Nagpur, 13 November 1917", *Indian Cotton Committee, Minutes of Evidence 5* (1920), 20.

100 Chandavarkar, *The Origins of Industrial Capitalism*, 1994, 50; Dantwala, *Marketing of Raw Cotton*, 1937, 114–116; Satya, *Cotton and Famine in Berar*, 1997, 205ff.; Guha, "The Agrarian Economy," 1985, 71 and 146.

101 Hardiman, "Usury, Dearth and Famine," 1996.

102 Von Albertini, *Europäische Kolonialherrschaft*, 1976, 37–45; Hardiman, "Usury, Dearth and Famine in Western India," 1996, 125.

103 Rothermund, *Government, Landlord, and Peasant in India*, 1978, 17; Charlesworth, *Peasants and Imperial Rule*, 1985, 83; Satya, *Cotton and Famine in Berar*, 1997, 208–228.

104 Satya, *Cotton and Famine in Berar*, 1997, 241. Satya interprets this negligence during the cotton harvest as a subtle form of peasant resistance in accordance with the theories of Scott, *Weapons of the Weak*, 1985.

105 Smith, *The Cotton Trade of India*, 1863, 20.

106 This contrasted sharply with Europe and Britain, where the state went to great lengths during the nineteenth century to provide credits for cultivators and small businesses: Buchheim, *Industrielle Revolutionen*, 1994, 149–151.

107 NML, Manuscript Section, Purshotamdas Thakurdas Papers, File No. 6; Dantwala, *Marketing of Raw Cotton*, 1937, 116–117 and 124. This topic is dealt with in greater detail in Chapter 9.

108 See Charlesworth, *Peasants and Imperial Rule*, 1985, 83–84 and 89.

109 Dantwala, *Marketing of Raw Cotton*, 1937, 33; Satya, *Cotton and Famine in Berar*, 1997, 197.

110 Rothermund, *Government, Landlord, and Peasant in India*, 1978, 17; Rothermund, "Currencies, Taxes and Credit," 2002, 15–18; Charlesworth, *Peasants and Imperial Rule*, 1985, 103; Satya, *Cotton and Famine in Berar*, 1997, 208–209.

111 Satya, *Cotton and Famine in Berar*, 1997, 242.

112 Satya, *Cotton and Famine in Berar*, 1997, 208–228; Rothermund, *Government, Landlord, and Peasant in India*, 1978, 17.

113 VA, Dossier 1, B) die Teilhaber, 1) Salomon Volkart, 3. Privat-Copierbuch 9 January 1867–1825 August 1870: 22 July 1869, Sal. Volkart to Spitteler, acting BM Cochin; Gebrüder Volkart, *Calculationstabellen*, 1873, 13 and 31ff.; VA, Dossier 14: Japan: Winterthur to Osaka, copies to Bombay, Karachi, Tuticorin, 10 April 1918 (Diktat von E. Müller-Renner).

114 For more on this topic, see Chapters 8, 10 and 12–14.

115 Ray, "The Bazaar," 1988. A similar mutual dependency existed already in the early nineteenth century between Indian moneylenders and the British East India Company: Siddiqi, "Some Aspects of Indian Business," 1987, 79. This can be interpreted as an indication that European and Asian capitalists had similar interests during the colonial era and complemented each other in their activities: Austin/Sugihara, "Local Suppliers of Credit," 1993, 18.

116 Tomlinson, *The Economy of Modern India*, 1993, 68; Satya, *Cotton and Famine in Berar*, 1997, 126–127; Beckert, "Emancipation and Empire," 2004, 1425.

117 Indian Cotton Committee, *Minutes of Evidence, Volume IV*, 1920, 45–46, 60 and 107; Indian Cotton Committee, *Minutes of Evidence, Volume V*, 1920, 63.

118 See Chapter 3.

119 See Charlesworth, *Peasants and Imperial Rule*, 1985, 83–89.

120 Bayly, *Rulers, Townsmen and Bazaars*, 1983, 254.

121 VA, Dossier 64: Geschäftsordnung 1915/1921 mit Nachträgen bis 1940 / Upcountry Bookkeeping Instructions 1912–1926 / Upcountry Instructions 1952: General Regulations and Instructions for the Use of Volkart Brothers Upcountry Agencies, Winterthur 1912, 21–27; VA, Dossier 26: Finance/Exchange 1887–1977, 3 Inland financing—shroffage agreements, for the search of a shroff in the Karachi branch.

122 VA, Dossier 26: Finance/Exchange 1887–1977, 3. Inland Financing—Shroffage Agreements: Shroffage Agreement between the Firm of Messrs. Volkart Bros. and the Firm of Messrs. Tulsidas Meghraj, 19 November 1928.

123 VA, Dossier 26: Finance/Exchange 1887–1977, 3 Inland financing—shroffage agreements: Karachi to Winterthur, 19 April 1923.

124 VA, Dossier 64: Geschäftsordnung 1915/1921 mit Nachträgen bis 1940 / Upcountry Bookkeeping Instructions 1912–1926 / Upcountry Instructions 1952: General Regulations and Instructions for the Use of Volkart Brothers Upcountry Agencies, Winterthur 1912, 25.

125 VA, Dossier 26: Finance/Exchange 1887–1977, 3 Inland financing—shroffage agreements: Karachi to Winterthur, 17 September 1931.

126 VA, Dossier 26: Finance/Exchange 1887–1977, 3 Inland financing—shroffage agreements.

127 V.B. News, No. 4, 1922, 17.

128 VA, Dossier 3: Bombay I, 6. Bombay house brokers: conference of 20 May 32.

129 VA, Dossier 3: Bombay I, 6. Bombay house brokers: Bombay to Winterthur, 28 June 1932.

130 VA, Dossier 12: Tuticorin / Madras, Madras, 8. Miscellaneous information: Madras to Winterthur, 9 May 1939. Ralli also used its brokers in Calcutta in the 1880s to gain market information. Nevertheless, the company realized that "the news received from them is not very reliable, as it emanates from the bazaar and often comes from interested sources" (Ralli Brothers' Calcutta Handbook. Volume II. Articles. Calcutta, September 1888, 26).

131 O. Haefliger, "Agent, Messrs". Volkart Bros., "Lyallpur (12 and 13 January 18)", *Indian Cotton Committee, Minutes of Evidence, Volume IV*, 1920, 79.

132 VA, Dossier 26: Finance/Exchange 1887–1977, 3. Inland Financing—Shroffage Agreements: Karachi to Winterthur, 23 August 1928

133 V.B. News, No. 4, March 1922, 17.

134 Dutta, *Family Business in India*, 1998; Colli/Rose, "Family Firms in Comparative Perspective," 2003, 351.

135 Bayly, *Rulers, Townsmen and Bazaars*, 1983, 239 and 375–381.

136 See Chapter 1.

137 Reinhart, *Gedenkschrift*, 1926, 77.

138 V.B. News, No. 2, April 1921, 13–14.

139 Ammann, *Reminiscences*, 1921, 21.

140 Anderegg, *Chronicle*, 1976, 56–57. This topic is dealt with in greater detail in Chapter 3.

141 Vicziany, "Bombay Merchants and Structural Changes," 1979; Ray, "The Bazaar," 281–286.

142 Chandavarkar, *The Origins of Industrial Capitalism*, 1994, 45–52.

143 Markovits, The *Global World of Indian Merchants*, 2000, 15.

144 V.B. News, No. 9, December 1923, 16; VA, Dossier 30: Patel Cotton Comp., Patel/Volkart Cotton Merger, Volkart Bombay Pvt. Ltd. 1961.

145 VA, Dossier 3, 9: Cotton Statistics: Cotton Exports from India to all Destinations. Season 1935/36.

146 VA, Dossier 3: Bombay I, 4. Table of Events 1851–1961/2; Naoto, "Upcountry Purchase Activities," 2001, 199–213. This topic is dealt with in greater detail in Chapter 10.

147 Vicziany, "Bombay Merchants and Structural Changes," 1979, 167ff., 181.

148 Anderegg, *Chronicle*, 1976, 150, 174–175 and 756–757.

149 For instance, in a company history of Ralli it was noted that, in addition to strictly maintaining contracts, the trading firm's operations were guided by the principle of achieving large turnovers with small profit margins: "Ralli were not in favour of large percentage profits—they look for small profits which are multiplied by the big turnover" (GL, Records of Ralli Bros.: Leoni M. Calvocoressi, *The House of Ralli Brothers*, 1952).

150 V.B. News, No. 9, December 1923, 14 and 16.

151 VA, Dossier 61: ex GR persönliches Archiv I, Graphische Tabellen: Verhältnis von Stammkapital zu Gewinn und Verlust.

152 Contractor, *A Handbook of Indian Cotton*, 1928, 38–39.

153 Prior to World War I, the volume of international trade annually exceeded 12 million bales of cotton worth approx. $750 million. The annual value of exports of other commodities was much lower and amounted to some $590 million for sugar, $550 million for wheat, $500 million for meat products, $325 million for wool and $125 million for silk: Wheeler, *International Trade in Cotton*, 1925, 1.

154 Killick, "The Transformation of Cotton Marketing," 1981; Killick, "Response to the Comment."

155 Contractor, *A Handbook of Indian Cotton*, 1928, 38–39.

156 Anderegg, *Chronicle*, 1976, S. 130; VA, Statistik der Gebrüder Volkart 1851–1914.
157 VA, Dossier 28: Notes on Taxation in India, 1. Indian taxation laws—notes thereon; 2. Notes on taxation practices applicable to VB.
158 Rothermund, *Government, Landlord, and Peasant in India*, 1978, 16–17; Satya, *Cotton and Famine in Berar*, 1997, 208–228.

3 Banks, Commodity Exchanges and Agencies

The Organization of Sales in Europe

Starting in the 1850s, Volkart maintained sales agencies run by local merchants in several European cities. By the mid-1920s, the sales network for Indian commodities included nearly 150 agencies in 18 European countries. There were also individual agencies in Argentina, Canada, the US and on the African continent, as well as subsidiaries in China and Japan.[1] One of the main differences between the European sales network and the procurement network in India was that Volkart was able to enter into cooperations in Europe with independent mercantile firms that were only occasionally inspected by employees of the company. By contrast, procurement in India had to be completely integrated into the company and constantly supervised by its own staff. This difference mainly had to do with the fact that selling a commodity like cotton was a transaction that was far easier for a trading firm to monitor than the process of procurement. As described in the previous chapter, procurement largely revolved around making proper selections, whereas precisely defined quality standards came into play during sales. The agents in the various European cities received price lists for the commodities carried by Volkart and they presented these lists to the company's customers. Due to large price fluctuations, these lists were regularly updated, sometimes several times a day. As soon as a sale was agreed, the staff at the Winterthur headquarters would send instructions to the relevant branches in India. In some instances, the sales contracts only became effective when the Indian branches had confirmed that they could supply the merchandise at the agreed price, while at other times the trading firm had to bear the risk of a change in price during the interim.[2]

The greatest sales-related problem for the trading firm was that it had to ensure that customers met their payment obligations. This explains why prior to World War I Volkart's general company policy was to deny any deferment of payment. The company insisted that its customers pay in cash for the delivered goods immediately upon receipt, or that they issue a bill of exchange that was covered by a bank guarantee. The then head of the company's cotton division, Ernst Müller-Renner, defended this practice in 1918 by stating that we have no intention of compounding the enormous risks of the purchase in India with capital risk on this side and in every corner of the globe and a capital risk would be incurred . . . for issuing the [sales] documents without immediate payment in cash or a prime banker's acceptance.[3]

Despite the relative ease of conducting sales in Europe, it was essential to select the right agents. They had to have excellent contacts to local manufacturers and the trading company relied upon them to regularly visit their assigned customers. When a trading company had found a suitable agent for a given district, this usually led to a collaboration that lasted for decades and in which the emotional boundaries between the company and the agent became blurred at times. For instance, in 1923 the Volkart employee magazine published a tribute to Edouard Valette, who had represented the firm in Marseille for nearly three decades. The text praised Mr. Valette at length, including the following highly personal description:

[D]uring our long and intimate association with him we have come to look upon him almost as belonging to us. On one of Mr. Werner Reinhart's last visits to Marseille, Mr. Valette led him into the office, saying in a simple and touching manner: 'This is Volkart's office.' These few words express more than anything else his great devotion and affection for our firm, and the development of our business in Marseille was in a large measure due to his spirit, his fostering care and his unwavering energy.[4]

Establishing a Sales Network in Europe

The business conditions for selling raw cotton varied from region to region. At the beginning of the twentieth century, Volkart was able to use its agents to establish direct contact with textile mills in diverse sales regions, yet in cities like Rouen and Liverpool it was forced to sell the cotton to local intermediaries who in turn supplied the manufacturers with raw materials. In Rouen, for example, the local trading companies had shares in the cotton mills and could afford to grant grace periods for payment of 60 or even 90 days, which was, as a matter of principle, entirely out of the question for Volkart at the time. It was a similar story in Lancashire. Müller-Renner had this to say about the situation:

The Liverpool brokers who are located directly in the district can offer the Lancashire spinning mills favorable terms of payment, cajole them and flatter them. We cannot do this. . . . We have realized that it is impossible for us in Oldham to enjoy the same benefits as those who hold the contacts and have the wherewithal and take the requisite financial steps. We simply must accept that we have to sell to the Liverpool brokers.[5]

The local network of brokers and textile manufacturers in Lancashire was one of the reasons that Volkart was never able to gain a firm foothold in Britain. Another important reason why Volkart only achieved modest sales results in Lancashire was that the British textile manufacturers preferred long-staple American cotton over the short-staple Indian varieties.[6] From the late 1890s and during the first decades of the twentieth century, rarely more than 5 percent of Indian cotton was exported to Britain and the majority of the harvest was spun into cloth in continental Europe, East Asia and India.[7] This meant that the trade with British textile mills was of only marginal interest to Volkart. For instance, of the 107,967 bales of cotton that Volkart shipped out of Bombay in 1882–1883, only 500 went to Liverpool and the rest were sold on the continent.[8] It was only just prior to the outbreak of World War I, when Volkart managed to recruit an employee of the prestigious Ellison & Co. to work as a brokering agent, that the Swiss trading company was finally able to secure a larger share of the cotton business in Liverpool.[9] By the late 1920s, Volkart was regularly selling more than 20,000 bales of cotton in Britain every year via several different agents, but sales in the British Isles still lagged far behind the results achieved on the continent.[10]

The second half of the nineteenth century was an exceedingly propitious time to enter the cotton trade. Between 1848 and 1873, the economy was booming throughout most of Europe.[11] After the Panic of 1873 had subsided, economic growth continued virtually unabated until the outbreak of World War I. The textile industry was one of the main drivers of this growth. For instance, cotton weaving mill production in Germany increased by tenfold.[12] As a result of this global economic boom, the volume of worldwide trade grew by a factor of ten between 1850 and 1913.[13]

Despite these favorable economic conditions, the companies involved in the cotton trade engaged in a bitter rivalry. By offering lower prices and more attractive terms of payment, they constantly endeavored to edge out the competition and win over new customers for their own types of cotton. Trading companies regularly dispatched representatives to the major hubs of the European textile industry to study the markets. In 1913, cotton division head Erich Müller-Renner and Werner Reinhart, who had become a partner and authorized signatory in the firm the previous year, visited Germany's industrial Ruhr region to find out why sales in this part of Germany were so much lower than elsewhere. The two men noted that most of the textile mills were struggling to stay afloat in the highly competitive industry, which led manufacturers to make compromises on quality to maintain low prices. Ralli Bros., Volkart's main rival in the Indian cotton trade, made a big concession to the German textile manufacturers when it agreed to waive the necessity of a payment guarantee issued by a London bank and instead began to accept promissory notes from buyers. In doing so, the trading firm granted the purchasing companies a deferment of payment of up to 90 days. This meant that the trading firm bore the credit risk during the interim.

Selling goods in exchange for promissory notes was a practice that Volkart categorically ruled out prior to 1914. Ralli deliberately assumed this financial risk in a bid to squeeze out its main competitor.

Reinhart and Müller-Renner pinpointed an additional problem in Germany, namely that the Volkart agency in Mönchengladbach failed to make the grade. Although the agents there were respectable men, the Volkart envoys noted that it was not enough to be "a highly respectable individual, you also have to be tough and tenacious if you intend to do business in such a rough-and-tumble industry." Since its own representatives were too reserved, the textile manufacturers had the mistaken impression that Volkart was not competitive.

> Then we pulled out the Indian export statistics, which had been compiled in detail by the Bombay office, and demonstrated how our shipments compared to those of the competition, usually much to the astonishment of the individuals concerned, who often apparently had the impression that we were less important than the Bombay Co. and Gaddum, thanks to the modest disposition of our representatives and the loud demeanor of Möller & Bey.[14]

This example shows that even markets in Europe were highly intertwined with social networks. It is also an indication that the principal–agent problem concerned the sales agents as well. Since the key connection between Volkart and its customers was its network of local agencies, their way of working was regularly monitored by company representatives. In 1911, for instance, a Volkart inspector noted that the types of cotton presented to textile mills by the company's agent in Belgium were much more unsightly than the goods offered by Ralli. The reason for this was that the Volkart agent had stored some of the samples in his attic.[15] The firm could also take countermeasures if it realized that its agent was overly complacent and could not be bothered to visit the textile mills.[16] Or they could redistribute the representative areas if certain customers had personal differences with regard to the agents appointed by Volkart.[17]

Feedback from Buyers

The sales representatives sent by Volkart also met with key customers on these inspection tours to gather feedback on how their firm's cotton was received by manufacturers. By establishing standardized types of cotton, companies like Volkart had taken a roughly defined commodity and turned it into a proprietary product that could be selectively marketed.[18] Some textile manufacturers even swore by the types of cotton sold by Volkart. After visiting a cotton mill in Tourcoing, France, a Volkart employee reported to the headquarters in Winterthur: "These friends process no bales of Indian cotton that do not come from us and don't even look at the prices of the competition."[19] Volkart representatives occasionally acted as consultants and advised textile manufacturers how to select the most suitable types of cotton. One staff member reported that a spinning mill owner in Rouen was looking for a type of cotton with somewhat longer fibers: "I suggested he try the T.116, which is undoubtedly suitable."[20]

The spinning mills also provided Volkart with feedback on how its own types of cotton compared with those of the competition. During a trip through northern Italy, Volkart inspectors noted that the company's Type 56 was too yellowish for the textile mills, which is why many preferred Type 67 from Ralli. A Volkart staff member wrote: "I have heard songs of praise about this T 67 (Gruber & Co. also swear by it), so it would be advisable for us to attempt to create an equivalent type to allow us to compete more effectively."[21] Furthermore, during a visit to the Ruhr region, local textile manufacturers showed Werner Reinhart and Ernst Müller-Renner a type of cotton by Ralli that they had never seen before. The description of this new type in their reports clearly reflects the importance of having an intimate knowledge of the product in the highly competitive trading business, and how vital it was to have a precise selection of goods in the manufacturing countries:

> We immediately saw that this was hand-ginned Rajputana. But the merchandise is not as coarse as a Beawar, but rather softer like a Jaypore, i.e., with the character of a Type 6, only purer. This brings us back to the earlier observation that Ralli is shipping a Bengal that appears to be a blend of machine-ginned and hand-ginned cotton, and perhaps comes from Bilara. . . . Ralli must be working in a district that has a particularly white variety of cotton, which is very pure, and yet not categorically coarse.[22]

Marketing and Media Campaigns

Aside from visits by their agents and representatives, companies like Volkart used various forms of media to make contact with their customers. Since the late nineteenth century, Volkart had regularly published "cotton bulletins" and "situation reports" in which the company kept its customers up to date on the harvests in several growing countries, on the expansion of the textile industry, on political developments in various parts of the world and on the global inventory of cotton and anticipated price movements.[23] These reports, which resembled the articles published by all major cotton trading companies, primarily aimed to enhance the loyalty of the textile mills as customers of the firm.[24] This appears to have been highly successful. Following an inspection tour through northern France in 1924, a Volkart employee remarked that the company not only had an outstanding position in the market there, but that its bulletins were widely read and respected by local textile manufacturers.[25]

One problem for Volkart was that many European textile manufacturers did not have a particularly high opinion of Indian cotton because of its relatively short fibers and high levels of impurities. Not only British but also many continental European textile mills preferred higher quality American varieties, even though they were more expensive.[26] Many European textile manufacturers were also unaware that it could be worthwhile to blend cheaper Indian cotton with American varieties to reduce costs. A Volkart employee on a visit to St. Petersburg shortly before World War I noted that the art of blending various varieties of cotton was relatively unknown in Russia at the time. The manager of a local textile mill thought that it was impossible to mix American cotton with Russian or Indian cotton because the latter two varieties had shorter fibers.[27]

In 1917, this led Volkart to conduct a written survey of several Indian spinning mills to find out why these manufacturers could make a higher quality of thread from Indian cotton than their European rivals.[28] Although the company received relatively few responses because many Indians were reluctant to divulge their business secrets to the European competition, the spinning mills that responded said that they spun together several varieties of cotton and altered the blend to meet diverse climatic conditions. Moreover, they used extra brushes and combs to remove dirt, leaves and dust from the cotton.[29] European textile mills reacted very positively to the brochure that Volkart published with the survey results from India. In a letter from the headquarters in Winterthur, it was noted that the European textile manufacturers had informed the company that, thanks to the advice from Volkart, they had

> now learned how to spin in Germany and Austria, and that before the war they would have never believed it possible to make thread from such a hodgepodge, . . . and that they would extract considerably more from Indian cotton than they had in the past, where they would have only thought it possible to produce no. 20 thread from the best American varieties.[30]

Thanks to such bulletins, along with the regular visits of agents and representatives to textile manufacturers, trading companies like Volkart helped to create a European market for Indian cotton. But they were not always successful. A textile manufacturer from Normandy said in 1920 that his firm was producing special towels for which he felt that American cotton was better suited than Indian varieties. He said that he had conducted a number of trials with Indian cotton, but was dissatisfied with the results and complained that "the Indian varieties are not as absorbent as the American ones and thus do not produce the quality that is the hallmark of this company."[31] And the manager of a Viennese spinning mill said in 1923 that he wanted to have nothing more to do with Indian cotton, adding that he had given up trying to master the tricks of this variety and would prefer to stick with American cotton, which, in his opinion, was easier to work with.[32]

The Function of the Winterthur Headquarters

Coordinating purchases in India and sales in industrialized countries demanded a sophisticated organization, particularly in view of the growing complexity of the business, and this went hand-in-hand with a rising need for office space. The headquarters in Winterthur, which after 1851 was located on the second floor of the home of Salomon and Emma Volkart in the heart of Winterthur, soon proved to be too small and the office was relocated on a number of occasions until the company moved to the top floor of the main building of the Bank in Winterthur in 1879. In 1905, the headquarters was transferred to a new building in Turnerstrasse, across the street from the Winterthur train station. When this structure also proved to be too small, Volkart moved a few blocks away to St. Georgenplatz, where it built a large office building with a monumental curved facade that was to house the company from 1928 until it withdrew from the trading business in the 1990s.[33]

The Winterthur office had a dual function. First, it served as the company headquarters, in which all major decisions were made. This appears to have been the case right from the moment of its establishment, although Johann Georg Volkart in Bombay was an equal partner, at least in principle.[34] Second, the office in Winterthur served the function of a general representative for the European continent and Britain.[35] The growth of the company saw an increase not only in the workforce, but also in the specialization of individual staff members. In 1924, for example, of the nearly 300 Europeans who worked for Volkart as commercial clerks, more than 40 were in Winterthur. Furthermore, Volkart headquarters employed several office assistants and maintenance staff members (in the various branches in Asia the company also had an additional 2,200 indigenous employees, who received a monthly salary, and some 2,800 day laborers). The staff members in Winterthur were employed in 15 departments (Table 3.1).

Thanks to the increasing diversification of the company's transactions, individual department heads wielded considerable authority within the firm, particularly the director of the important cotton division, who in many ways was just as influential as the partners in the company. Like other large trading companies in the late nineteenth century, Volkart established an employee structure that had much in common with the managerial capitalism that Alfred Chandler identified as a characteristic of modern industrial firms.[36] At the same time, the company increasingly moved toward a centralized decision-making process. For example, from the 1880s onwards new employees were only hired in Winterthur, whereas previously the branch offices had made their staff selections independently.[37] This centralization took place against the background of constantly growing sales and the increasing specialization of the trading business, but it was also made possible by rapid advances in transport and communications technologies. The telegraph in particular made it much easier for the headquarters to

Table 3.1 Departments at the Volkart head office in Winterthur, 1924

Dept. 1	Office of senior management and human resources
Dept. 2	Insurance
Dept. 3	Cash, billing and information
Dept. 4	Raw cotton
Dept. 5	Peanuts, sesame seeds, poppy seeds, castor oil seeds, cotton seeds, Niger seeds, ajwain seeds, dill seeds, fennel seeds, coriander seeds, millet, rapeseed, linseed and caoutchouc
Dept. 6	Nux vomica, senna, yellowroot, graphite, cardamom, cocoa, cinnamon, tea and cocculus indicus
Dept. 7	Hides, essential oils, tamarinds, raw silk waste
Dept. 8	Sugar, paper, matchsticks, Turkey red, metals, aniline dyes, chemicals, perfumeries, spirits, piece goods, woolens, cement, timepieces, silks, lace, embroidery, soaps and metal goods
Dept. 9	Machines, turbines and trucks
Dept. 10	Coprah, coconut oil, oil cake, ginger, desiccated coconuts, sandalwood, sandalwood oil, exotic woods, fish oil, steamship agencies and cargo business
Dept. 11	Coffee, pepper, cashew nuts and palmyra fibers
Dept. 12	Coir yarn, coir and bristle fiber
Dept. 13	Office material administration
Dept. 14	Accounting
Dept. 15	Sales outlet for Switzerland

(Source: VA, Dossier 64: Geschäftsordnung 1915/1921 mit Nachträgen bis 1940 / Upcountry Bookkeeping Instructions 1912–1926 / Upcountry Instructions 1952: Geschäftsordnung, version from 15 February 1925; V.B. News, no. 1, November 1920, 11–15)

closely monitor the decisions made by the branch offices. This shows that new means of communications always have an influence on social power structures.[38]

Winterthur enjoyed a more favorable location as a control center for coordinating Volkart's transactions than was apparent at first glance, despite the company's rhetoric to the contrary. In 1892, for instance, the firm asserted in a letter written to the Swiss Federal Department of Trade and Justice that it was purely coincidental—following the marriage of Salomon Volkart to a woman from Winterthur—that the city of Winterthur

> was selected as the home of the company's European operations. That this transpired is often seen as a grave disadvantage in view of the current situation because . . . frequently enough the vast distances from global markets have been painfully damaging to our business.[39]

This complaint was included in a letter to the Swiss government in which Volkart requested permission to keep its name after the departure of the company's founders. As will be explained in greater detail later in the book, an amendment to the Swiss corporate code had called into question the legitimacy of the Volkart Brothers name. But the fact of the matter was that Winterthur was an outstanding central location for the firm's business. The main European sales regions for Indian cotton were in northern France, Belgium, the Ruhr region, Switzerland, northern Italy and the areas surrounding Vienna and Prague. Geographically speaking, Winterthur was at the very heart of the continental European textile industry.

In addition to its highly favorable location, Winterthur had a long tradition as a center of commerce. When Napoleon enacted the Continental Blockade in 1806 and placed an embargo on importing British goods to continental Europe, it led to a massive boom for the Swiss textile industry, which became one of the leading producers in Europe during the early nineteenth century, second only to Lancashire. Companies in Winterthur were among the prime beneficiaries of the elimination of British competing products. Switzerland's first mechanical spinning mill was established by Johann Rudolf Sulzer on the outskirts of Winterthur in 1803. In 1812, the J. J. Rieter & Cie. company opened the town's first large-scale spinning mill with 4,000 spindles. In the 1830s, Rieter began to produce spinning mill machines and went on to become a worldwide leader in the manufacture of embroidery and spooling machines and looms.[40] Winterthur companies were also highly active in the business of exporting Swiss-made fabrics. The Winterthur textile printing works of Greuter & Rieter sold their products to customers as far away as India, Southeast Asia, Japan and North and South America,[41] and Salomon Volkart worked for years as a sales agent for this company before establishing his own firm.[42] What's more, the Société maritime pour le commerce avec les Indes orientales began exporting printed fabric from Switzerland to India in 1787; this firm, in addition to merchants from France and western Switzerland, included several Winterthur firms on its roster of shareholders. Business flourished and the company, which changed its name to Société maritime Suisse after the French Revolution, was able to open branch offices in Calcutta, Pondicherry and Madras. After France declared war on Britain in 1793, the British seized the Indian branches of the Société maritime Suisse along with three ships and their cargo as spoils of war, forcing the company to declare bankruptcy in 1795.[43] In the late eighteenth century, merchants from Winterthur became the main importers of raw cotton to German-speaking Switzerland after this sector had been dominated primarily by companies from Basel.[44]

During the nineteenth century, Volkart was by far the largest trading company in Winterthur. Its main rival in town was Geilinger & Blum, an internationally significant company in its own right that changed its name in 1889 to Paul Reinhart & Co., after the name of the main owner. Geilinger & Blum/Paul Reinhart had a global network that included subsidiaries in Le Havre and Alexandria, and the firm maintained close business ties with the key US cotton-trading company of McFadden & Bros. in Philadelphia.[45] A range of contacts existed between Geilinger & Blum/ Paul Reinhart and Volkart. In the late 1870s, Theodor Reinhart, son of the owner of Geilinger & Blum, married Salomon Volkart's daughter Lilly and shortly thereafter became a partner at Volkart.[46] This did not lead to a closer collaboration between the two companies, though, which only maintained relatively loose business contacts. For instance, on a number of occasions Geilinger & Blum/Paul Reinhart served as a representative of Volkart in southern Germany and Switzerland from the 1850s onwards, and in the 1930s Volkart sold Egyptian raw cotton for Paul Reinhart to customers in India and the US. In the 1920s, both companies invested in a cotton import company in Italy, but this joint venture was rather brief and the Italian firm had to be liquidated a few years later.[47]

The Importance of the London Branch

Even though Winterthur had evolved to become an important hub of the continental European cotton industry during the nineteenth century, it was essential for Volkart to have its own branch in London, which was the center of global trade at the time. Already during the 1850s, Volkart had established contacts with several London-based merchants who acted as agents for the company there. In 1869, Rudolph Ahlers—who had worked for the company in India and had been made a partner in 1863—opened his own firm in London, which subsequently became Volkart's most important representative in the British capital. After Ahlers resigned due to poor health in 1875, his company was transformed into a regular Volkart branch that was henceforth involved in a wide range of business areas. The Volkart Brothers London Agency sold Indian products like cotton, coffee and coconut oil in Britain, supplied British coal and Russian oil to the British navy, served as an agent for several shipping lines and from the 1890s shipped metal from continental Europe to India and Ceylon. Most importantly, Volkart's London branch was able to ensure that the company maintained vital contacts to British commercial banks, insurance companies and shipping lines.[48]

Between 1893 and 1940, the London branch was also the nominal headquarters of Volkart, primarily for legal reasons. The Swiss corporate code of 1881, known as the Swiss Code of Obligations, required that a company's name reflect its actual ownership structure. As there were no longer *brothers* at Volkart Brothers after the death of Johann Georg Volkart in 1861, the Swiss authorities demanded that the name be changed. In a letter dated November 1892 and addressed to the Swiss Department of Trade and Justice, the company argued strongly that an exception be made in this particular case. The Volkart partners asserted, for example, that "the name of our company means more today than the mere title reflecting an arbitrary family relationship." It just so happens

> that the three oldest and most noteworthy companies in East India's import and export trade in Bombay all contain the name 'Brothers' (the largest Greek firm, Ralli Brothers; the largest English firm, Wallace Brothers; and Volkart Brothers) and that in the local market a great deal of superstition and partiality is attached to these three old

cornerstones of the Bombay trade. Please excuse this digression, but we have to reckon with such things out in the field and if we suddenly go by another name, and our invoices and other written documents to the natives are signed differently, it will cause a sense of uneasiness that can be detrimental to us for quite some time and put an end, once and for all, to our prestige in belonging to the above-mentioned venerable triad.[49]

This assertion was not entirely correct. In 1886, Wallace Brothers had renamed its subsidiary for the export of Indian cotton Bombay Co. and apparently not suffered any major commercial disadvantage as a result.[50] The arguments presented by Volkart were also somewhat exaggerated. Indeed, the merchants in India would have had far fewer difficulties with a name change than the company suggested in its letter to the Swiss authorities. Nevertheless, the efforts to retain the name of the company, and the willingness to relocate the headquarters to London should its request be turned down, show that the partners at Volkart viewed the corporate name as a cultural capital that they were unwilling to simply relinquish.

In response, the Swiss Department of Trade and Justice expressed its deep appreciation for the difficulties and inconveniences associated with a name change for Volkart, but insisted that it was bound by current legislation and the partners would simply have to change the name of their company. Otherwise they "would have no option but to relocate the focal point of their business operation to a foreign country . . . and accordingly turn their Winterthur establishment into a branch office."[51] This is precisely what the partners ended up doing. Effective 1 January 1893, the London office was declared the company's nominal headquarters. Volkart's Winterthur headquarters was transformed on paper into a branch office.[52] Volkart's London office assumed a coordinating function within the company, especially in the many instances when Indian branches directly arranged transactions with London without involving the Winterthur office. An exception to this rule was the cotton trade, which was coordinated in Winterthur.[53] In general, however, Winterthur remained the actual headquarters of the company. All important decisions with regard to company policy were made there and the partners still had their offices in Winterthur. It was not until 1940, when the Swiss corporate code was amended and the outbreak of World War II radically changed the company's situation, that Volkart decided to transfer its headquarters back to Switzerland.[54]

The Influence of the Rupee Devaluation on Trade with India

In the late 1870s, several continental European countries switched from the silver to the gold standard. This meant that diverse national currencies could be exchanged at a fixed rate for gold at any time and it had a major impact on Volkart's business. The gold standard was introduced in

Britain in the early nineteenth century. Since Britain subsequently rose to become the leading global trading nation and London gained the title of the world's premier financial center, the gold standard was adopted by all Western industrialized nations by the end of the nineteenth century.[55] But in 1876 the price of silver began to fall in relation to the price of gold. Much of the world's silver subsequently flowed to India, which absorbed 84 percent of the global silver production in 1877. Since the amount of money circulating in India rose by roughly one-third between 1877 and 1893, the silver rupee dropped sharply in value against European currencies. This made European imports to the subcontinent more expensive, but devaluation of the rupee was a boon to Indian exporters because it rendered Indian commodities relatively inexpensive for European buyers.[56]

Despite this positive development for trading firms, rupee devaluation created new challenges for companies like Volkart that not only exported Indian commodities, but also imported European consumer goods and industrial products to India. To prevent Volkart from accumulating a balance in rupees, whose value was constantly sliding, the Indian branches were instructed to take the rupees received from the sale of import products and immediately exchange them for British pounds in a bid to avoid the risk of losses from declining foreign exchange rates.[57] In the late 1880s, a number of Volkart employees still appear to have had some difficulties with this practice. Top executives at the Winterthur headquarters thus had to write to their managers in India in 1888 to remind them that currency speculation was strictly forbidden, as this practice would only lead to losses for the company over the long term and "these deviations could easily lead to the greatest of 'confusions' in the 'exchange statements.' " Furthermore, they had to give detailed instructions to their employees in India on how they were to make their exchange statements, in other words, the correct way to offset the proceeds from the sales of imports and the costs of exports to Europe in the branch offices' internal accounting system.[58] The fact that even highly qualified merchants who worked for Volkart in India were not always completely aware of how to deal with these accounting details is yet another indication of the increasing complexity of the modern trading business.

Demand for Credit and Bank Connections

Up until the 1870s, European buyers had to include with all orders a bank guarantee for the anticipated price. When the commission business dried up after the construction of the telegraph line between India and Europe, the trading companies on the subcontinent began to conduct export transactions on their own account and it became common practice for buyers to pay for their goods upon delivery.[59] This sparked a change in financing practices. Up until the 1860s, moneylenders and Indian merchants acting as guarantee brokers had paid advances for commodity exports. But since this type of financing had proven to be increasingly cumbersome, in the late 1860s Volkart started to finance its exports with loans from European banks.[60] This allowed the company, along with other large European trading firms, to benefit from the boom in the European banking system and, above all, from the emergence of specialized commercial banks that had evolved from prosperous trading companies and, starting in the 1820s, had stopped trading in goods and started granting loans to other trading companies. Following the introduction of the telegraph, which triggered an enormous boost in overseas trade, there was a rapid increase in the volume of credit from leading commercial banks like Baring Bros. and Frederick Huth & Co.[61]

Every week, Volkart's Indian branches required several hundred thousand pounds sterling to purchase the commodities traded by the company. The money had to be transferred to the more than 100 buying agencies that Volkart had throughout the entire subcontinent. This was comparatively easy when the buying agency was located in a town in the interior of the country that had a bank, or in which the Indian treasury had a branch office. However, such bank subsidiaries and branch offices of the treasury were not established in many backcountry towns until the 1920s. When no financial institutions existed in the area, the Volkart purchasing agents sold bills of exchange to local banks or shroffs, who could then redeem these documents later at a Volkart branch office on the coast for a full reimbursement. The Indian branches of Volkart obtained their funds by issuing sight drafts to a London commercial bank. Starting in the 1880s, Volkart primarily relied on the services of the commercial Bank of Glyn, Mills & Co. to finance its purchases in India. In the mid-1920s, the Volkart branches annually drew bills of exchange worth 18 million pounds sterling upon Glyn, Mills & Co. The Volkart branch in London had to make sure that these bills of exchange were settled in a timely manner. Since revenues from the sales of commodities generally arrived months later, Volkart had to use bank loans to pay off the bills of exchange presented by Glyn, Mills & Co. Volkart raised these funds through unsecured loans from Swiss banks and by mortgaging goods in the company's warehouses to various European banks. As the season progressed, an increasing amount of revenues flowed in from the sale of commodities and the cash requirements of the company's Indian branches diminished, gradually allowing Volkart to pay back the loans.[62]

Thanks to its outstanding contacts to financial institutions in Switzerland and England, from 1870 onwards Volkart was able to conduct its transactions without requiring any further loans from Indian merchants. This resulted in a centralization of its business activities, both inside and outside the company. Starting in the mid-1880s, the financing of commercial transactions was exclusively organized by the Winterthur headquarters through its branch in London, and no longer carried out independently by the branches in India.[63] For many years, British commercial banks granted credit according to extremely restrictive policies, which were only eased during the 1920s when they realized, according to a Volkart employee, that it was practically impossible to conclude and rapidly process the sheer number of business transactions generated by global trade on a daily basis when they narrow-mindedly insisted, based on their old-fashioned methods, on first receiving the goods, or the documents representing them, for every penny that they loaned.

Despite their initial skepticism, in 1923 British banks eased these restrictions and showed an increasing willingness to grant loans with warehoused or already shipped cotton as collateral.[64] This allowed Volkart to extend its credit line with the 28 London banks used by the company from 1 million to 2.5 million pounds between 1920 and 1926.[65] According to Volkart's own assessment, this was thanks to "the excellent personal relationships between our London management and the banks" and the fact that the London banks were well aware of Volkart's "financial strength and solid and loyal management."[66] Furthermore, because the City of London was the center of the global exchange of goods, the majority of the shipping documents, checks and invoices issued by Volkart went through the hands of the London bankers. In the eyes of Volkart employees in London, this was extremely important for the company's business, as witnessed by a letter sent from London in 1926: "[C]onstant contact with the banks creates a feeling of being known, which lends itself to concessions and special treatment at times, which can only be to our advantage."[67] Nevertheless, it was the company's own financial strength that allowed Volkart to obtain such generous loans from the banks in the first place. The successful development of the business in the late nineteenth and early twentieth centuries had fueled robust growth, leading to a tenfold increase in the firm's equity, which had soared from 3.5 million Swiss francs in 1875 to 35 million in 1922 (Table 3.2).

In order to ensure sufficient liquid funds to cover the bills of exchange, Volkart required long-term lines of credit, and since many British banks during the 1920s still refused to grant loans unless they were secured by

Table 3.2 Company equity (capital stock, in Swiss francs), 1875–1922

1 July 1875	3,500,000
1 July 1879	4,000,000
1 July 1880	4,200,000
1 July 1883	6,000,000
1 July 1894	7,200,000
1 July 1898	5,200,000
1 July 1904	8,000,000
1 July 1906	10,000,000
18 January 1919	19,000,000
1 July 1919	21,000,000
1 July 1922	35,000,000

(Source: VA, Dossier 61: ex GR persönliches Archiv I, Allerlei geschäftliche Informationen, Statistiken etc.)

warehouse inventories as collateral, Volkart had to raise money elsewhere. When Volkart launched its business in the mid-nineteenth century, the Swiss banking system was still in its infancy and Winterthur still lacked an effective financial institution. To remedy this situation, Winterthur merchants and industrialists established the Bank in Winterthur in 1862. Salomon Volkart was a founding member of the bank and served as a member of the supervisory board for many years. The bank had close connections to other European financial centers and focused mainly on financing import and export activities, primarily the import of raw cotton. Between 1902 and 1911, the Bank in Winterthur annually covered bills of exchange amounting to between 24 and 42 million Swiss francs. Of the more than 100,000 bales of cotton that were imported to Europe with the help of loans from the Bank in Winterthur during this period, roughly one-quarter to one-third came from India[68] and a considerable amount was shipped by Volkart. Hence, through its involvement in establishing the Bank in Winterthur, which merged with the Toggenburger Bank in 1912 to form the Union Bank of Switzerland (UBS), Volkart played an active role in ensuring that it could raise the capital required for its own import and export business.

Swiss banks subsequently became extremely important for Volkart because they granted large unsecured loans to the company.[69] In an internal paper from 1926, a staff member in Volkart's finance department voiced the opinion that Swiss banks were simply indispensable for the company:

> A connection like UBS, that is prepared to finance any transaction under reasonable conditions when the V.B. name stands behind it, . . . that puts us on the same level as major banks in all its quotations and has freely increased our open credit to 6 million [Swiss francs], . . . such a connection deserves to be cultivated.[70]

The magnanimity of the Swiss banks doubtlessly stemmed above all from the trust and confidence that had been painstakingly built up over many years of successful business contacts, yet it was also based on the multitude of close personal connections between the banks and the trading company. Not only did Salomon Volkart serve for many years on the supervisory board of the Bank in Winterthur, but his son-in-law, Theodor Reinhart, was a long-standing member of the board of directors of the Swiss National Bank.[71]

The company largely owed its success to the efforts of Salomon Volkart who managed to win the support of both British and European banks to finance the firm's commercial transactions.[72] The trading company deliberately used banks from various countries so it could benefit from short-term fluctuations in interest rates and avoid being too dependent on the development of the financial market in any one particular country. Moreover, "there was no individual country that had sufficient credit to meet all of [the company's] needs," as a staff member of the Volkart finance department remarked in 1925.[73] In the mid-1920s, Volkart relied on the services of no less than 12 Swiss banks and some 70 additional banks in half a dozen countries. Volkart always presented its current annual balance sheets to the Swiss and English banks as proof of its creditworthiness.[74]

Cotton Exchanges and the Advent of Futures Trading

One problem for cotton trading companies was that it was often only after a number of months that their goods could be sold to a spinning mill, or rather that they habitually sold cotton that in many cases was not yet in their possession and sometimes had not even been harvested. Since the cotton trading companies had extremely large turnovers, an adverse change in prices could lead to huge losses and even bankruptcy. To shield themselves from these risks, trading companies needed a market where they could sell their goods or purchase options on deliveries of cotton at any time. The futures market fulfilled all of these needs.[75] In the 1860s, trading firms started to safeguard their transactions with forward contracts. Whenever they purchased a certain amount of cotton for which they did not have an immediate buyer, they went to a cotton exchange and sold a futures contract that obliged them to deliver a certain quantity of cotton on a specific date. When they actually found a spinning mill to purchase the cotton, they bought back the futures contract. Hence, when a trading company sold a futures contract, it did not actually intend to deliver the cotton to the buyer of the contract. The futures contract was merely a means of hedging against a drop in prices. Conversely, when a trading company committed itself to supplying a textile mill with a certain quantity of cotton on a specific date, yet did not have the merchandise in its possession, it would purchase a futures contract that would give it the option of receiving the corresponding quantity of cotton on the date specified in the contract. Buying and selling cotton on the spot market, in which commodities were traded for immediate delivery, was thus balanced out by an opposite operation on the futures market. This method worked because the prices of spot cotton and cotton on the futures market fluctuated in a more or less similar manner. When the value of the cotton declined between the purchase and the sale, the profits from futures trading balanced out, at least to some extent, the losses incurred with spot cotton. Hedging operations on the futures market thus allowed trading companies to mitigate the risks from changing prices.

But hedging did not provide complete protection against price fluctuations, not least of all because intense competition in the sector did not allow trading companies to safeguard all of their transactions through futures contracts. Likewise, they repeatedly engaged in speculative transactions in the hopes of earning profits that would give them an edge on the competition.[76] Another problem was that although spot cotton and futures always followed the same general trends, the prices on both markets never evolved in a perfectly parallel manner. There was always a certain discrepancy between the price for spot cotton and the price that was paid on the futures market for cotton contracts. This difference was known as the basis. When a trading company used hedging to safeguard its transactions, its profits—or losses—resulted from the difference between the basis at the time of purchase and the basis at the time of sale. The company thus had to make sure that the basis at the time of sale was larger than at the time of purchase. In other words, the trading company had to earn more from its transactions on the futures market than it lost in trading in spot cotton or, conversely, it had to earn more in trading with spot cotton than it lost in its operations on the futures market.

Safeguarding commercial transactions through futures contracts demanded a great deal of business acumen. Even in the late nineteenth century, many merchants remained extremely skeptical of this commercial innovation and viewed futures transactions as pure speculation that was beneath the dignity of a reputable mercantile house.[77] It was only with time that the futures market became a widely accepted aspect of the international cotton trading sector.[78] Consequently, a growing number of banks only granted credit on the condition that the trading companies used hedging to safeguard most of their transactions.

Hedging dates back to the 1860s and was developed in Liverpool out of the forward sales that had become common during the American Civil War. When the naval blockade by the Northern states put a halt to the export of American cotton to Europe, it sparked a firestorm of speculation in Indian cotton, and by 1863 cotton prices were three to four times higher than before the war. At the time, many merchants had begun to engage in forward sales, meaning that they sold the cotton to the spinning mills at a point in time in which the merchandise had not yet arrived in the port of destination. After the end of the Civil War, prices declined again when American cotton returned to the market, but the forward sales continued. Importers feared that the surplus of cotton would cause prices to fall even further in the future and were thus more than willing to sell the cotton to speculators who were hoping for a price increase and prepared to buy the merchandise before it had even arrived in Liverpool. Such transactions were long frowned upon by many established merchants. In a letter to the Bombay branch office, Salomon Volkart commented on the news that the British trading company of Finlay Clarke & Co. had incurred heavy losses from the forward sale of 20,000 bales of cotton: "Serves them right, after all, the fraud and deception of this type of deal is simply too great and discourages real and healthy business transactions."[79] Despite the skepticism and the inherent risks involved, forward sales remained a common practice in the global commodities trade. This eventually led to the establishment of a bona fide futures market on the Liverpool Cotton Exchange, a development that was fueled by the construction of a telegraph line between Britain and the US in 1866. The telegraph made it possible for merchants to obtain up-to-date information on the global supply and demand of this coveted commodity. This further exacerbated the business risks involved as the price of cotton became increasingly volatile, making it an absolute necessity to use futures to safeguard transactions.

There is a fundamental difference between forward sales and futures. With futures transactions the merchandise is rarely actually delivered. Usually a futures contract is repurchased by the trading company before the delivery is due because the agreement is primarily a means of hedging against any possible losses from sales of cotton. By contrast, a forward contract is fulfilled with the delivery of the agreed amount of cotton. Both business practices have in common that they rely upon a high degree of standardization for the merchandise in question. As a result, the Liverpool Cotton Association established nine classes of cotton that differed in terms of the length of their fibers, their fineness, color, purity, tensile strength and smoothness.[80] Futures contracts were always concluded on the basis of the middling quality grade. When the cotton delivered on a forward sale turned out to be of a higher or lower quality, the price was adjusted accordingly.

The cotton standards that were established in the cotton exchanges served as the basis for the types of cotton that were developed by the leading big trading companies in the late nineteenth century. Since the establishment of consistently uniform standard types was only possible with large turnovers and an efficient sales organization in the manufacturing countries, this development accelerated the process of forcing smaller firms out of the trading business. Starting in the 1870s, Volkart was able to offer spinning mills certain types of cotton whose quality had been defined in relation to the standard types of the Liverpool Cotton Exchange (Figure 3.1).[81] This standardization allowed companies like Volkart to safeguard their sales with futures transactions on the cotton exchanges.

The commodities exchanges had the added advantage that they opened up the possibility for the trading companies to raise capital quickly and easily through sales of futures contracts.[82] Furthermore, they were important for the commodities trade because they established arbitration courts that convened if there were differences of opinion with regard to the quality and price of cotton deliveries.[83] The decisions of the arbitration courts were binding and the parties to the conflict were not allowed to take the dispute to an ordinary court. The former president of the Bremen Cotton Exchange, A. W. Cramer, had this to say about the process:

> It has proven to be a great blessing for all those involved that differences of opinion between the relevant parties are not to be resolved in a long and costly trial, but instead are subject to an immediate settlement through the convening of an arbitration court under the auspices of the cotton exchange.[84]

This allowed the players in the community of the worldwide cotton trade to establish globally valid rules of business without depending on international trade agreements, and it is yet another indication of the

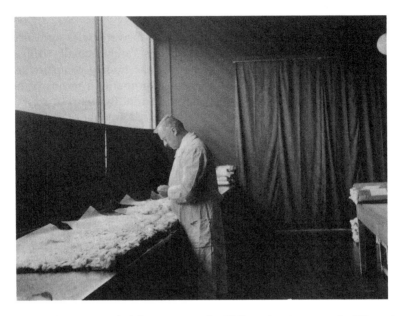

Figure 3.1 Cotton sample laboratory at the Volkart headquarters in Winterthur, where the company's standardized types of cotton were inspected to ensure consistent quality (photo presumably taken during the 1930s) (Fotomuseum Winterthur, Volkart Collection, CD 3, Volkart Winterthur)

ability of merchants to self-organize their commercial transactions on a global level.[85]

Cargo Insurance

Another risk in the overseas trade was that goods could be lost or damaged during transport. This made it necessary for the cargo to be insured at all times. In the years following the establishment of the company, shipments were generally insured by the Agrippina Insurance Co., a German firm that was represented by Volkart in Bombay from 1851 onwards.[86] After 1863, Volkart insured practically all shipments of goods to and from India and Ceylon with the newly established Swiss Lloyd in Winterthur,[87] which had been founded by several Winterthur entrepreneurs. Salomon Volkart served for years as vice president of the insurance company. The establishment of Swiss Lloyd, which was founded almost at the same time as the Bank in Winterthur, is further proof of the determination with which Winterthur entrepreneurs in the 1860s forged the necessary infrastructure for their import and export activities.[88] In 1865, Swiss Lloyd joined forces with the Basel Transport Insurance Company and the Helvetia Insurance Company to form the Swiss Marine Insurance Corporation in London. This soon became the largest transport insurance company on the European continent. Unfortunately, it encountered a crisis in 1883 and had to be liquidated in 1884.[89] Volkart subsequently used diverse Swiss, English and American insurance companies,[90] although most shipments of goods were insured with Lloyd's of London.[91]

Even when insuring the goods appeared to be a relatively straightforward matter on paper, in practice it was often a source of frustration for trading companies.[92] Erich Müller-Renner wrote about an incident in India in which the untimely expiration of an insurance policy nearly resulted in huge losses. At the time, Müller-Renner had decided that, in view of the extremely short span of time in which a certain consignment of cotton would be uninsured, it was not necessary to renew the policy, even though company regulations would have required him to do so. The following day, he came to the conclusion that it would in fact be reckless to risk hundreds of thousands of francs' worth of cotton for such minor savings in insurance premiums, so he paid the fees to renew the fire insurance. Shortly thereafter, the cotton warehouse burnt to the ground and Müller-Renner swore that he would henceforth scrupulously adhere to the regulations imposed by company executives.[93]

It was also often unclear at what point in time the goods had to be insured by the buyers. By the early twentieth century, the sector had introduced detailed insurance policies for maritime transport that precisely stipulated at what point in time and under what circumstances the owner of the ship was liable for damages in transit, in what situations the trading company that had organized the export was liable, and when the owner of the goods was responsible for insuring them.[94] To reduce conflicts to a minimum, companies like Volkart had a vested interest in seeing to it that their customers fully insured their consignments of goods. Yet this was not always the case. In a circular letter from 1907, the company wrote "despite our repeated warnings admonishing caution with regard to coverage of shipments at sea, some buyers still have entirely inadequate insurance policies." According to Volkart's sales contracts, the insurance was the buyer's responsibility from the moment that the goods left dry land. Many insurance contracts only went into effect when the transport documents had been signed in the port of shipment by the captain or the shipping agent. These policies were extremely problematic because the steamship in question could have been at sea for days before the papers were signed. If the goods were damaged before the papers were signed, the damages were the buyer's responsibility.[95]

Customer Loyalty and Generating Trust

No matter how crystal clear sales contracts, insurance agreements and stock exchange regulations may have been on paper, it was always possible that one of the parties did not understand the terms of the agreements, or at least professed not to understand them.[96] Moreover, arbitration procedures and legal disputes could be extremely protracted and arduous, and elaborate formal regulations were a fairly ineffective means of averting unpleasant surprises. In an effort to address these concerns, in 1896 Volkart's Winterthur headquarters instructed the company's branch offices only to send shipments on financially solid steamship lines to reduce the risk of the captain selling some of the cargo to repair damages to the ship or to pay for the vessel's passage through the Suez Canal.[97] Trading companies like Volkart worked diligently to avoid such problems with their customers and suppliers, and to base their transactions on informal institutions, for example, by doing as much business as possible with textile mills, shipping lines and insurance companies that had a solid reputation and close ties with the company.[98] An internal manual from the 1950s, for instance, commented on the transport insurance companies that were indispensable for the trading business:

> The underlying principle in insurance is that of good faith. This is . . . the only basis on which a contract of insurance can rest and give full satisfaction to both parties. . . . The long association of V.B. with several of our underwriters has brought about a state of mutual trust which is an essential part of the foundation on which a satisfactory insurance couverture can be built up.[99]

For its part, Volkart did everything in its power to meet its contractual obligations.[100] The company saw this as a cornerstone of its success. Georg Reinhart, who became a partner at Volkart in 1904, wrote in the jubilee publication celebrating the company's 75th anniversary in 1926:

> One of the key factors behind the success of our company lies in the reliable service to our customers. . . . Consequently, our deliveries are rightly known throughout the entire world for their reliability." Reinhart went on to say that "a commercial organization is based . . . not only on the spatial configuration of its purchasing and sales apparatus, . . . but just as much, if not more so, on intangible factors.[101]

His father had made similar comments a number of years earlier. In a speech before the Winterthur Commercial Association in 1913, Theodor Reinhart said that "good faith" had to be "absolutely reliable" because it was "linked to the perception of the business relationship with the merchant and thus above all to his credit with his customers and the banks."[102]

Striving to meet high standards of reliability and contract compliance thus served the function of an informal institution because they helped to reduce the business risks of buyers. The trading company hoped that such practices would win the long-term loyalty of its customers. A top official at Volkart had this to say on the topic in 1960:

> An overseas company has a relatively small circle of buyers in any given country. It does not have to address the public the way a manufacturing

company must. . . . The relationships to its buyers are maintained through personal contact, careful and prompt fulfillment of sales contracts and objective advice and information on market trends for its customers. These are the best advertisements in the overseas trade, along with prompt handling and fair settlements of complaints.

Furthermore:

> The overseas trade is a business based on trust. People buy and sell goods that they only see afterwards. It is recommended to stick with reliable suppliers that one knows from experience and, based on earlier transactions, can rely upon to fulfill their obligations with diligence.[103]

Conversely, it could also be worthwhile for a trading company to make an effort to be accommodating when differences of opinion arose with customers. Such conduct had not so much to do with generosity, but rather was viewed as an investment in long-term business relationships. During the 1930s, for example, when an Indian coffee farmer was unable to pay back an advance, the Winterthur headquarters urged the Tellicherry branch office not to put too much pressure on the debtor because Volkart could "not in hard times abandon old customers on whom we have earned money for years . . . without damaging our name and running the risk of losing these connections forever."[104] Likewise, in September 1939 Volkart management said that it was convinced that the company should generously fulfill all pending sales contracts, even if the company was not legally bound to do so due to the outbreak of war:

> The excellent relationships to our customers that in many cases have taken years of painstaking work to achieve must never be threatened by an action stemming from a split-second decision; instead, old contracts are to be fulfilled with future business opportunities in mind.[105]

This attitude was apparently not shared by all branch offices. Several local managers appeared to be more interested in the possibility of earning short-term profits than in maintaining long-term business relationships. As a result, in April 1940 the headquarters admonished the branch offices of the company as follows:

> It is with great concern that we have noticed of late a tendency in some quarters of our firm to deviate from the principles of business morality and business manners which up to now have made the reputation of V.B. . . . Confidence, i.e. reliability in one's dealings, is 99% of the capital of a firm and any infringement of these principles must prove terminal in the long run. A breach of confidence is therefore about the worst offence that any merchant can commit.[106]

It goes without saying that such a customer orientation was not respected by all globally active trading companies.[107] But Volkart was not an isolated case, either. Ralli also appears to have followed similar business principles, as illustrated by a text published in 1951 on how the staff was expected to treat the company's customers:

> [I]t is recorded in a Staff Instruction Book of 1881 that our fulfilment of moral obligation under a contract is more important than the letter of contract. Later, but nevertheless almost sixty years ago, a newly appointed departmental manager, when receiving his first instructions from the senior partner, was told to remember that his first consideration in all his dealings must always be the honour of the house.[108]

An event in 1914 shows that it was roundly condemned in these circles when another company terminated this long-time relationship built on trust in the event of a crisis. For decades, Volkart had maintained a close connection with the Schweizerische Kreditanstalt (the forerunner of Credit Suisse), which, according to Werner Reinhart, who was a partner from 1912 onwards,

> made a great deal of money on us and once even said that we should maintain exclusive ties with the institution, assuring us that it would open its purse strings for us in an emergency. When the war broke out, the bank was the first to put the thumbscrews on us.

Reinhart then cited the Commercial Bank of Basel as an opposite example, stating that this financial institution had

> documented the value that they placed on their connection to us by immediately sending their director, a man named Müller, to Winterthur, where he not only gave us a line of credit but offered to greatly facilitate matters for us in our hour of need. As a result, we immediately paid off our debts and closed our account at the Kreditanstalt and did not open it again until many years later when the bank management 'prostrated itself before us' and begged us to come back. From then on, we did an increasing amount of business with the Commercial Bank of Basel.[109]

This shows once again that global trade—which from the end of the nineteenth century onwards had become a highly complex and dynamic affair with futures transactions, standardized types of commodities and specialized lending and insurance institutions—was highly influenced by social relationships, and that the degree of mutual trust was often a decisive factor that determined whether business connections were made and maintained. Informal institutions were thus by no means rendered obsolete by the advent of formal institutions in the overseas trade. Indeed, they remained an essential element of business transactions and were a key prerequisite for the implementation of formal institutions.

Notes

1 Rambousek/Vogt/Volkart, *Volkart*, 1990, 81
2 Ziegler, *Der Import ostindischer Baumwolle*, 1922, 54–55.
3 VA, Dossier 14: Japan: Winterthur to Osaka, copies to Bombay, Karachi, Tuticorin, 10 April 1918 (Diktat von E. Müller-Renner).
4 V.B. News, No. 9, December 1923, 22.
5 VA, Dossier 14: Japan: Winterthur to Osaka, copies to Bombay, Karachi, Tuticorin, 10 April 1918 (Diktat von E. Müller-Renner).
6 Ellison, *A Hand-Book of the Cotton Trade*, 1858, 37ff.
7 Bombay Chamber of Commerce, *Reports*, 1898–1931.
8 Anderegg, *Chronicle*, 1976, 756a.
9 VA, Dossier 14: Japan: Winterthur to Osaka, copies to Bombay, Karachi, Tuticorin, 10 April 1918 (Diktat von E. Müller-Renner).
10 VA, Dossier 62: ex GR persönliches Archiv II, Personelle und organisatorische Probleme, Wirtschaftlichkeitsrechnungen 1918–1932: Baumwoll-Umsatz-Ziffern 1925/26–1928/29.
11 Wehler, *Deutsche Gesellschaftsgeschichte*, 1995, 66–67.
12 Fischer, "Bergbau, Industrie und Handwerk," 1976, 535 and 553.
13 Osterhammel/Petersson, *Globalization*, 2005, 76–86; Torp, "Weltwirtschaft vor dem Weltkrieg," 2004.
14 VA, Dossier 56: (PR) Reiseberichte, M. Gladbach: Winterthur an Bombay, Karachi, Tuticorin, 27. Oktober 1913, Rapport über die Tournée der Herren W. Reinhart und E. Müller in Rheinpreussen, Bremen, Enschede etc. vom 16.–24. Oktober.
15 VA, Dossier 56: (PR) Reiseberichte, Gent: E. Bruin, Lille, to Winterthur, 17 January 1911.
16 VA, Dossier 56: (PR) Reiseberichte, Rouen: M. Weber, Belfort to Winterthur, 17 September 1920.
17 VA, Dossier 56: (PR) Reiseberichte, Rouen: M. Weber, Lure, to Winterthur, 18 September 1920.
18 For more on the cultural-anthropological-oriented research on commodification, in which "things" can be transformed into goods, see Appadurai, Introduction, 1986.
19 VA, Dossier 56: (PR) Reiseberichte, Tourcoing: M. Weber, Tourcoing, to Winterthur, 18 November 1924.
20 VA, Dossier 56: (PR) Reiseberichte, Rouen: Winterthur, le 28 Mai 1930, Rapport sur la visite du Rayon Rouen.
21 VA, Dossier 56: (PR) Reiseberichte, Genova: R. Cedraschi auf Besuch bei Arpe & Pratolongo, Genova to Winterthur, 11 January 1915.
22 VA, Dossier 56: (PR) Reiseberichte, M. Gladbach: Winterthur to Bombay, Karachi, Tuticorin, 27 October 1913, Rapport über die Tournée der Herren W. Reinhart und E. Müller in Rheinpreussen, Bremen, Enschede etc. vom 16.–24. Oktober.
23 VA, Dossier 39: Baumwollstatistiken J. Brack 1884–1907; Gebrüder Volkart, *Situationsberichte*, 1921–1925.
24 See, for example: BL, RBA.9 N413: Neill Bros. & Co.'s Cotton Circular.
25 VA, Dossier 56: (PR) Reiseberichte, Rouen: M. Weber, Remiremont to Winterthur, 25 March 1924.
26 See Chapter 2 for a more detailed analysis.

27 VA, Dossier 56: (PR) Reiseberichte, St. Petersburg: St. Petersburg to Winterthur, 10 June 1914.

28 VA, Dossier 59: PR-Privatarchiv: Notizen / Briefe / Personelles etc. Neuenhofer—Cotton Corr. 1917–1925—Volkart Brothers, questionnaire, no place or date.

29 VA, Dossier 59: PR-Privatarchiv: Notizen / Briefe / Personelles etc. Neuenhofer—Cotton Corr. 1917–1925—Bombay to Winterthur, 24 August 1917.

30 VA, Dossier 59: PR-Privatarchiv: Notizen / Briefe / Personelles etc. Neuenhofer—Cotton Corr. 1917–1925—Winterthur an Neuenhofer, Zurich, 5 February 1918.

31 VA, Dossier 56: (PR) Reiseberichte, Rouen: M. Weber, Epinal à Winterthur, le 21 Septembre 1920.

32 VA, Dossier 56: (PR) Reiseberichte, Wien: Wiener Besuch durch die Herren Werner Reinhart und Müller-Renner in der Woche vom 25. September—1. Oktober, Winterthur, 3 October 1923.

33 Anderegg, *Chronicle*, 1976, 128–129, 226–227 and 312.

34 It is no longer possible to determine conclusively whether this had to do with the fact that Salomon Volkart, as the older brother, had more extensive business experience, or that Winterthur was in close proximity to the customers in Europe.

35 Ammann, *Reminiscences*, 1921, 8.

36 Chandler, *Scale and Scope*, 2004 [1990]. For more details on this topic, see Chapters 5 and 6.

37 Anderegg, *Chronicle*, 1976, 131.

38 For more on this, see Allen, *Lost Geographies of Power*, 2003, 137. It is essential to take into account, though, that up until the early twentieth century telegrams were very expensive. Volkart's telegram bill for the traffic between London and India in 1881–1882 amounted to an astonishing 30,008 Swiss francs. The costs of sending telegrams steadily declined thereafter: in 1900–1901 to 15,457 and in 1911–1912 to 13,513 francs: VA, Statistik der Gebrüder Volkart 1851–1914.

39 VA, Dossier 18: Winterthur I: 3 Nominal transfer of HO to LONDON from Winterthur: Gebr. Volkart an das Schweiz. Handels & Justiz Departement, Bern, 29 November 1892.

40 Weisz, *Die Zürcherische Exportindustrie*, 1936, 193–200; Forster, *Die Baumwolle*, [approx. 1985], 48–58; Sulzer, "Vom Baumwollzentrum zur Maschinenindustrie," 1995.

41 Kindt, "Notes sur l'industrie et le commerce," 1847, 25.

42 See Chapter 1.

43 Weisz, "Zur Geschichte des europäischen Handels mit Indien," 1954–1955.

44 Ganz, *Winterthur*, 1960, 128; Lendenmann, "Die wirtschaftliche Entwicklung," 1996, 138; Sulzer, "Vom Baumwollzentrum zur Maschinenindustrie," 1995, 14–15.

45 Hauser/Fehr, *Die Familie Reinhart*, 1922, 159–192.

46 Anderegg, *Chronicle*, 1976, 137–138.

47 VA, Dossier 1, B) Die Teilhaber, 1) Salomon Volkart, 3. Privat-Copierbuch: 9 January 1867–1825 August 1870: 23 April 1871, Sal. Volkart to Hr. Scheuermann; Anderegg, *Chronicle*, 1976, 379, 442 and 462–463.

48 VA, Dossier 13: London/Liverpool (VB + Woods&Thorburn) / Bremen, V.B. London: 2. Table of Events.

49 VA, Dossier 18: Winterthur I: 3 Nominal transfer of HO to LONDON from Winterthur: Gebr. Volkart an das Schweiz. Handels & Justiz Departement, Bern, 29 November 1892.

50 GL, Records of Wallace Brothers & Co. (Holdings) Ltd.: Ms 40076: Wallace Brothers private letters, Vol. 1 1885–1893: Wallace Brothers, London, to Busk & Jevons, New York, 24 September 1886.

51 VA, Dossier 18: Winterthur I: 3 Nominal transfer of HO to LONDON from Winterthur: Schweizerisches Handels- und Justiz Departement, Bern, to Gebrüder Volkart, Winterthur, 14 December 1892.

52 Schweizerisches Handelsamtsblatt, Freitag, 13. Januar 1893.
53 VA, Dossier 13: London/Liverpool (VB + Woods&Thorburn) / Bremen, V.B. London, 3. P.R. Note on London of 21.5.1958 and circular No. 117 of 3 August 1956 on changes in the London set up: formation of Volkart Brothers (UK) Ltd.: memo by Peter Reinhart, 21 May 1958.
54 See Chapter 8.
55 Cassis, *Les Capitales du Capital*, 2005, 100–112.
56 Rothermund, *Government, Landlord, and Peasant in India*, 1978, 20–21; Foreman-Peck, *A History of the World Economy*, 1995, 158ff.
57 VA, Dossier 15, The Far Eastern Organisation, I. Shanghai (incl. Tientsin etc.), 3. Correspondence: Winterthur to Shanghai, 28 April 1933.
58 VA, Dossier 26: Finance/Exchange 1887–1977: Circular-Schreiben an alle unsere Häuser, Winterthur, 27 July 1888.
59 Ammann, *Reminiscences*, 1921, 9–10; VA, Weisse Schachtel: V.B. Finanzen, Auszahlungs-Systeme, December 1926, 1.
60 Anderegg, *Chronicle*, 1976, 56.
61 Chapman, *The Rise of Merchant Banking*, 1984, 17, 34–44, 114 and 139.
62 VA, Weisse Schachtel, Unser Finanzsystem. (approx. 1925), 4, 7–10; V.B. Finanzen, Auszahlungs-Systeme, Dezember 1926, 1–7; V.B. Finanzen. Deckung der Verbindlichkeiten. March 1927, 3, 9, 13–17. During this period in history, the commodities trade was financed almost entirely by issuing bills of exchange, leading the author of a "Compendium of the Entire Commercial Sector" published in 1914 to surmise: "The bill of exchange plays a role in the exchange and circulation of goods that is nearly as important as that of the steam engine" (Maier-Rothschild, *Handbuch der gesamten Handelswissenschaften*, 1914, 479).
63 Ammann, *Reminiscences*, 1921, 4.
64 VA, Weisse Schachtel: Unsere Banken (March 1926), 8ff.
65 VA, Weisse Schachtel: V.B. Finanzen. Ressourcen. (October 1926), 4.
66 VA, Weisse Schachtel: Unsere Banken (March 1926), 8ff.
67 VA, Weisse Schachtel: Unsere Banken. Zu Londons Brief vom 12. März 1926.
68 Wetter, *Die Bank in Winterthur*, 1914, 6–7, 15–16, 135–138.
69 VA, Weisse Schachtel: Unsere Banken (March 1926), S. 4; V.B. Finanzen. Auszahlungs-Systeme. Dezember 1926, 3. For more on the apparently widespread aversion of British banks to the granting of long-term loans to trading companies, see Jones, *Merchants to Multinationals*, 2000, 229.
70 VA, Weisse Schachtel: Unsere Banken (March 1926), 4. This confirms Fritz Mangold's view that Swiss bank loans played an important role in the success of Swiss trading companies: Mangold, *75 Jahre Basler Transport-Versicherungs-Gesellschaft*, 1940, 16–17.
71 Rambousek/Vogt/Volkart, *Volkart*, 1990, 48.
72 VA, Dossier 26: Finance/Exchange 1887–1977, 1 general notes about financing business.
73 VA, Weisse Schachtel: Unser Finanzsystem. (approx. 1925), 9.
74 In addition to three large Swiss banks—the Swiss Bank Corporation, the Union Bank of Switzerland and the Swiss Credit Institution—the following banks were among Volkart's key financial institutions: Lloyds Bank, Midland Bank, British Italian Bank Corporation, Banque Belge pour l'Etranger, Guaranty Trust Company of New York, Union Discount Company of London, Reeves, Withburn & Co and the Imperial Bank of India: VA, Weisse Schachtel: Unser Finanzsystem. (ca. 1925), 8; Unsere Banken. Zu Londons Brief vom 12 March 1926; V.B. Finanzen. Ressourcen. (October 1926), 4; V.B. Finanzen, Deckung der Verbindlichkeiten. March 1927, 1.
75 Unless noted otherwise, the following remarks on the development of the futures market are based on: Garside, *Cotton Goes to Market*, 1935, 133, 144ff., 157ff.,

207–274, 316, 335–341; Dantwala, *Marketing of Raw Cotton*, 1937, 153 and 167–168; Hall, "The Liverpool Cotton Market," 1999.

76 Ziegler, *Der Import ostindischer Baumwolle*, 1922, 56; Ferguson, *The Ascent of Money*, 2008, 226.

77 Heine, *Die Baumwolle*, 1908, 214–215.

78 For example, for many years the owners of the American cotton trading company Sprunt remained extremely skeptical toward futures transactions and categorically banned such practices in their partnership contract of 1886. It was not until the price of cotton steadily rose during the early twentieth century that they realized that futures transactions could be worthwhile, but they strictly differentiated between speculative dealings on the futures market and futures contracts designed to safeguard transactions with cotton that was physically present: Killick, "The Transformation of Cotton Marketing," 1981, 157.

79 VA, Dossier 1, B) die Teilhaber, 1) Salomon Volkart, 3. Privat-Copierbuch 9 January 1867–1825 August 1870: Sal. Volkart to Noelke, Bombay 20 January 1870.

80 Ratzka-Ernst, *Welthandelsartikel und ihre Preise*, [approx. 1910], 161–162.

81 Gebrüder Volkart, *Calculationstabellen*, 1873, 14.

82 Williams, *The Economic Function of Futures Markets*, 1986, 230

83 O Haefliger, Agent, Messrs. Volkart Bros., "Lyallpur (12–13 January 1918)", in Indian Cotton Committee, *Minutes of Evidence, Volume IV*, 1920, 84; Garside, *Cotton Goes to Market*, 1935, 158–165. For more on the techniques of the cotton trade in the diverse European trading centers during the early twentieth century, see Oppel, "Der Handel mit Rohbaumwolle," 1908; Nicklisch, "Zur Technik des Baumwollhandels," 1909; Barre, "Zur Technik des Baumwollhandels," 1909; Schmidt, "Die Geschäfte in Baumwolle zu Le Havre," 1910–1912.

84 Quoted by Schildknecht, *Bremer Baumwollbörse*, 1999, 20–21.

85 For more on this topic, see Vec, *Recht und Normierung*, 2006; Petersson, *Anarchie und Weltrecht*, 2009.

86 VA, Dossier 3: Bombay I, 4. Table of Events 1851–1961/2; Anderegg, *Chronicle*, 1976, 46, 50ff.

87 VA, Dossier 18: Winterthur I, 1 Table of Events.

88 Already in 1970, Swiss historian Herbert Lüthy voiced the opinion that it was during the early modern period that the initial manifestations of a capitalist economy—cotton printing, equity trading, stock exchanges and a modern banking system—arose for the most part from the economic ties between the European and non-European spheres: Lüthy, "Die Kolonisation und die Einheit der Geschichte," 1991 [1970], 226. The example of Winterthur illustrates that such ties can also be documented for the Industrial Age. This apparently confirms C. A. Bayly's claim that the "birth of the modern world" during the nineteenth century was largely a result of global interrelationships: Bayly, *The Birth of the Modern World*, 2004.

89 Wetter, *Die Bank in Winterthur*, 1914, 37–38 and 135; Mangold, *75 Jahre Basler Transport-Versicherungs-Gesellschaft*, 1940, 25.

90 Such as Helvetia Insurance, the Swiss National Insurance Company, the American Aetna Insurance Company and the British Union Insurance Society of Canton: VA, Dossier 36: „Insurance" Notes etc. I seit 1888; Dossier 37: „Insurance" Notes etc. since 1920.

91 VA, Dossier 13: London/Liverpool (VB + Woods&Thorburn) / Bremen, 8. Banking & Insurance connections (Glyn Mills and Durtnell Fowler and others).

92 Ammann, *Reminiscences*, 1921, 9–10.

93 VA, Dossier 18: Winterthur I, 1 Table of Events: Letter from Winterthur to Bombay, written by E. Mueller-Renner, 24 May 1920. For more on the problems faced by European insurance companies due to their rudimentary knowledge

of fire hazards in Indian cities, see Zwierlein, *Der gezähmte Prometheus*, 2011, 337–350. It was therefore wiser for European insurance companies to establish contacts with well-established European companies in India—like Volkart— that had intimate knowledge of the conditions on the ground.

94 Ziegler, *Der Import ostindischer Baumwolle*, 1922, 19–23.

95 VA, Dossier 36: „Insurance" Notes etc. I seit 1888: B8 / Rundschreiben See-Assekuranz, Winterthur, 10 August 1907.

96 For example, the American cotton trading company Stephen M. Weld & Co. had a long standing dispute with a spinning mill that had complained about the quality of a shipment of raw cotton. But the spinning mill had not registered its complaint at the time of delivery, as it should have done in accordance with the regulations of the New York Cotton Exchange, but instead at a much later date, which was why Weld rightly refused to take back the shipment: BL: Mss. 761, Stephen M. Weld and Company Collection (Records, 1883–1931), Box 67, Papers 1883–1914: Answer to 'Statement of Claim' of the Pacific Mills against Stephen M. Weld & Co.

97 VA, Dossier 36: „Insurance" Notes etc. I seit 1888, B12: Winterthur an alle Häuser, 14 February 1896.

98 VA, Dossier 12: Tuticorin / Madras, 5. The Sri Ranga Vilas Case 1931–1938: Winterthur to Tuticorin, 6 February 1934.

99 VA, Dossier 20: VB Organisation 1952/53: V.B. Business and Insurance (no date).

100 VA, Dossier 1, B) die Teilhaber, 1) Salomon Volkart, 3. Privat-Copierbuch 9 January 1867–1825 August 1870: 22.7.1869 Sal. Volkart to Spitteler, acting BM Cochin; Dossier 2: Die Teilhaber II: Letter No. 70022–70020.11.42, Peter Reinhart (New York) to P. Scherer; Dossier 50: Engineering /Voltas Schriften, Dokumente etc.: *Volkart Brothers Engineering News* (1936–1940), Vol. 1, Nr. 1, January 1936.

101 Reinhart, *Gedenkschrift*, 1926, 75–76

102 Theodor Reinhart, "Rede gehalten am 50-jährigen Jubiläum des Kaufmännischen Vereins Winterthur am 30. November 1913," in *Reinhart, Ausgewählte Schriften*, 1920, 86–89.

103 VA, Dossier 48: Artikel/Abhandlungen/Gedichte/Briefe etc. von ehemaligen Mitarbeitern: O. Kappeler, Ueberseehandel, 23 November 1965.

104 VA, Dossier 9: Tellicherry, 9. General correspondence: Winterthur to Tellicherry, 9 April 1932.

105 VA, Konferenz-Protokolle 6 September 1939–1931 May 1940: Besprechung mit Herrn Peter Reinhart, 16 September 1939.

106 VA, Dossier 18: Winterthur I, 1 Table of Events: Vevey to all Branches and Associated Companies, 12 April 1940.

107 For instance, this practice seems to have been less common in the US. In any case, following the transfer of a number of former employees of the American Cotton Cooperative Association (ACCA) to Volkart, there was considerable friction when the partners at Volkart realized that the ACCA staff was focusing less on customers' concerns than on optimizing short-term profits: VA, Dossier 44, VBH Guidelines 1970–1983, written by Peter Reinhart. This topic is dealt with in greater detail in Chapter 14.

108 Ralli Brothers *Limited*, 1951, 9. To prove this claim, a company history of Ralli cites an example from World War I. At the time, the company was supplying the British government in India with goods. Since the products had become heavier due to the high humidity, at the end of the war Ralli found that its warehouses had a surplus of merchandise worth 300,000 pounds. These goods were refunded to the government although it was of the opinion that all contractual obligations for the agreed deliveries had been fulfilled. It took a great

deal of persuasion on the part of Ralli company officials to convince the British civil servants that the goods actually belonged to the government: GL: Records of Ralli Bros., Ms. 23836: Historical material on the company, 1902–1952: Leoni M. Calvocoressi, *The House of Ralli Brothers*, 1952.

109 VA, Dossier 9: Tellicherry, 9. General correspondence: Werner Reinhart zu diesem Brief von Herr Fenner, approx. April 1932 (no date).

4 "We are a Swiss firm, thank God!"

World War I and the Meaning of National Origins

The outbreak of World War I posed an existential threat to globally active trading companies. It brought to an abrupt halt the flow of goods and finances that had given world trade continuous and unprecedented growth for decades. Due to the global interdependencies of trade at the time, the conflict between 1914 and 1918 was a worldwide economic war that soon developed to become an unparalleled, relentless military struggle for the control of raw materials. This war of attrition was waged not only to achieve military victory, but also to weaken the national economies of the enemy. The Entente introduced blockade policies that were calculated to strangle Germany's foreign trade, causing companies like Volkart to lose access to lucrative sales markets in Germany and Austria. In February 1915, Germany responded to these blockade measures by launching a campaign of ruthless submarine attacks.[1]

Research to date on the impact of the economic war between 1914 and 1918 has focused primarily on the macro-perspective of the diverse economies and the wartime economic decisions of individual national governments. Far less attention has been given to describing the war from the micro-perspective of individual companies.[2] Such an approach reveals that wartime economic measures not only interrupted the worldwide flow of goods and capital, but also shook the cultural foundations of global trade. By seeking to identify the political loyalties of international companies, the warring countries had a long-term impact on the national identities of such firms. During the eventful second half of the nineteenth century, their national affiliations had only been of secondary importance. This was even true after the 1880s, when many continental European countries reverted to protectionist economic policies,[3] but it soon changed after the outbreak of hostilities in 1914. The parties to the conflict spared no effort in pinning national labels on goods and economic players, despite—or perhaps precisely because—their multinational character made it virtually impossible to categorize them according to a specific national orientation.[4] In this respect, the war fueled the politicization of the global economy, a trend that had begun with the recurrence of protectionism on the European continent in the late nineteenth century and culminated in the abolition of free trade after the Great Depression and the emergence of autarky policies in the 1930s.[5] Since most of the firm's operations were on the territory of the British Empire, it became a matter of economic survival for Volkart to ensure that British officials did not classify it as an enemy company, since Volkart's contacts to the British business world were of vital importance. This just goes to show that even in times of war the rationales of companies need not necessarily match with those of the bureaucracies of their home countries.

The Outbreak of War and the Collapse of Global Trade

After the outbreak of the conflict, global trade came to a complete standstill for a number of months. The cotton exchanges in New York and Liverpool were shut down in August 1914 and did not reopen until November.[6] To make matters worse, companies that were active in the territories controlled by the Entente could no longer fulfill orders to the countries of the Central Powers. This left Volkart with nearly 127,000 bales of undeliverable cotton worth over 1 million pounds, most of which had been ordered by customers in Austria and Germany.[7] It was, however, possible to sell the majority of this cotton in Britain over the following months. Yet 15 months after the outbreak of the war, Volkart was still in possession of more than 21,000 bales of cotton that had been destined for the Central Powers and could only gradually be sold.[8] The restraints on the sale of this inventory of cotton were an alarming development for the firm because at the outbreak of the war the banks had blocked all of its accounts and withdrawn all credit, forcing the company to the brink of insolvency.[9] German and Austrian spinning mills had repeatedly contacted Volkart during the initial months of the war and suggested that the cotton deliveries could be shipped via neutral ports like Venice, Genoa and Rotterdam, and secretly sent from there to Germany or Austria. Volkart categorically rejected such proposals because they would have constituted a violation of British war regulations. Whenever the company shipped cotton from India, it always had to specify the buyer who was destined to receive the goods. If British inspection officials had discovered that Volkart had used subterfuge to make deliveries to cotton mills in enemy countries, it could have resulted in the liquidation of its business branches within the British Empire. "It is not a matter of good or bad will, but of an absolutely dire predicament," the company informed a German cotton mill in April 1915, adding: "We can hardly believe that you seriously expect us to put the existence of our firm at risk for 1,100 bales of cotton."[10]

Another problem was the disruption of the lines of communication. Intense censorship of postal and telegram correspondence meant that many letters were delayed extensively by the authorities and telegrams could no longer be encrypted, a development that was especially problematic for companies operating internationally, as they relied upon maintaining strict confidentiality concerning their offers and prices. "We have been thrown back to the times of our forefathers who had to make do without telegram correspondence at a time when the Indian mail took four weeks," as a Volkart employee informed the owner of a German cotton mill in November 1914.[11]

Despite these difficulties, this was a very profitable era for Volkart because the company was able to capitalize on the soaring prices of commodities during the war.[12] Another positive development for Volkart was that World War I resulted in a decentralization of global trade. The loss of European exports led to an upswing in the industrialization of Asia and, particularly in Japan and India, an increase in the consumption of cotton.[13] During the war, Japan replaced India as the main supplier of cotton yarn and textiles for the Chinese market and brought cheap import goods to the Indian market. Volkart was able to benefit from this boom by securing a share of the imports of Indian cotton to Japan while, at the same time, supplying Indian trading companies with Japanese consumer goods. The Indian textile industry also boomed due to the loss of European import goods during World War I, and Volkart was able to capitalize on this as well. Instead of shipping the purchased raw cotton to Europe, the company could sell it directly on the subcontinent.[14] Although Volkart's sales declined during the war, the firm nevertheless made millions during the conflict. Even during the difficult first year of the war, the nominal net profit in 1915 was 1.8 million Swiss francs.[15] All in all, the war years were similarly successful for the company as the lucrative prewar years.[16]

Trade Bans and Blacklists

Immediately following the outbreak of the war, the British government banned companies in the Empire from having contact with firms in the countries of the Central Powers. Nonetheless, the British were initially highly reluctant to take further measures because free trade was viewed as the foundation of their economic policy.[17] The business community and the government were of the opinion that further limitations on economic freedom would have a negative impact on the British economy. Accordingly, the government declared in 1914 that it was "business as usual," and even allowed British subsidiaries of German companies like Daimler Benz and Siemens to continue to operate. The economic war initially only sought to put a stop to the flow of goods to and from enemy countries.[18]

In late 1914, it became clear that the war would last longer than initially presumed. This prompted calls for further war economy measures, partly in reaction to a significant increase in the amount of goods imported to neutral countries like the Netherlands, Switzerland and the Scandinavian countries following the outbreak of the war. The Allies suspected that the Central Powers were supplied with goods via these countries. In December 1915, Britain enacted legislation that placed further restrictions on trade.[19] In addition to prohibiting direct trade with the Central Powers, the new law brought companies in neutral countries under the control of Allied war economy measures. The British Navy began to seize consignments of goods on neutral ships whenever they suspected that they could be destined for enemy countries.[20] Not only were these measures in violation of standing international agreements, such as The Hague Conventions of 1899 and 1907 and the Paris Declaration Respecting Maritime Law of 1856, but they also fundamentally changed the previously widely accepted balance between politics and economics.[21]

In December 1915, the British government was authorized to place companies in neutral countries on a blacklist if they were suspected of maintaining contact with enemy countries or sympathizing with the Central Powers. Companies were also blacklisted if they had German or Austrian employees or there was reason to believe that they were controlled by German or Austrian owners. Since it was difficult to unravel the complex ownership structures of companies and their political sympathies, and the actual destinations of consignments of goods could only be determined with great effort, the measures could only be implemented with great difficulty. Shipments of goods were often held up because port authorities were uncertain of the precise application of the war regulations, or because they stumbled across documents in German that led them to summarily conclude that the shipments were destined for enemy territory.[22]

Although Volkart was able to earn profits throughout the war years, the war economy measures of the Allies put the company in a highly precarious position. A violation of the Trading with the Enemy Act would have undoubtedly entailed the liquidation of all branches of the firm on the territory of the British Empire, and this would have included all company divisions with the exception of the Winterthur parent company and the brokering agency in Osaka. The introduction of martial law significantly undermined the legal situation of Swiss companies doing business within the British sphere of influence. "The martial law in force throughout the British colonies means that accusations can be levied against our Indian companies at any time," as the company proclaimed in a letter to its German customers in 1914. Officials at Volkart's company headquarters went on to emphasize that "it is now no longer the plaintiffs who have to prove the charges, as is normally the case, but the defendant who has to prove his innocence, and the penalties are enormous."[23]

In response to this pressure, the company scrupulously respected British military regulations throughout the entire war. Nevertheless, shipments of cotton were often seized by the British and Volkart had to prove during protracted negotiations that the deliveries were not destined for customers in the countries of the Central Powers.[24] Moreover, the company had to fear that the British would become suspicious of the traditionally good connections that the firm had maintained to German and Austrian textile companies before the war and the fact that it had German personnel on its payroll.[25] Not surprisingly, Volkart made every effort to demonstrate its willingness to cooperate with British officials. Relatively minor transgressions were often enough to land a company on the blacklist. In December 1915, for example, the Swiss company Siber Hegner, which had branches in Kobe and Yokohama, found itself placed on the blacklist by the British.[26] In a letter to the company headquarters in Zurich, the Yokohama branch had requested a shipment of 200 vials of German perfume. Since this clearly violated British war regulations, it was suggested that the perfume be repackaged and declared as a Swiss product. Unfortunately, the letter fell into the hands of British officials, and although Siber Hegner in Zurich made it patently clear in its reply letter to Japan that the firm had to abide by the regulations and had no intention of dealing in German products, the request alone was enough to induce the British to ban all business contacts with the Swiss company. It was not until a number of months later, after Siber Hegner had apologized to British authorities and assured them that it would fully comply with the trade restrictions of the Allies, that the company was allowed to resume its business dealings.[27]

In view of the stringent trade restrictions, Volkart found itself in an extremely delicate situation in the summer of 1915 when British censors intercepted the letters of two employees who had made negative comments about the Entente.[28] Volkart immediately fired the two employees and emphatically admonished all personnel that they should *"strictly avoid discussions concerning the war, political issues and all related topics."*[29] As a result of this incident, the Volkart branch in Colombo was searched by British officials. Since most of the documents were written in German, they were carted off for closer examination and not returned until a number of days later. The British had not found anything suspicious.[30] The headquarters in Winterthur subsequently asked the personnel at the Colombo branch to remain calm and even welcomed the course of action taken by the authorities in Ceylon:

> Although we quite understand how disheartening it must have been for you to be innocently suspected, we on the other side can only welcome the steps which the Ceylon Government deemed necessary towards our firm, as we have nothing to hide neither there nor here nor in any other of our branches before the eyes of the British Officials. . . . We only hope that the result of this examination of our records and books will now do away with any suspicion which so unjustly has been held against our firm.[31]

The wartime difficulties encountered by the Basel Trading Company, a trading firm founded by missionaries from Basel in 1859, illustrate just how dangerous it could be for Swiss companies when they aroused suspicions that they were secretly cooperating with German firms.[32] Shortly after the outbreak of the war, the company ran into problems because its textile and brickmaking business in India was thought to contravene the Trading with the Enemy Act. Furthermore, its high percentage of German personnel and the fact that a share of its capital was in German hands aroused the suspicions of the Indian government. From 1916 onwards, the Basel Trading Company was under British control and at risk of being liquidated.[33] The company approached the Swiss consul in Bombay, who unsuccessfully attempted to prevent the liquidation of the firm. In 1919, the Indian holdings and properties of the Basel Trading Company were confiscated, a measure that was apparently illegal even under British law. At any rate, the company received compensation from the British government in 1952, but the Basel Trading Company never returned to India.[34]

Due to the often arbitrary decisions of British authorities, Swiss trading companies had to rely on their good connections to the British business community. This is reflected, for instance, by the Diethelm trading firm, one-third of which was Dutch-owned and two-thirds of which was in Swiss ownership. A Diethelm branch in Siam stood under the protection of the German consulate in Bangkok until shortly before the war. All ties to Germany were cut in 1914, but the British suspected that the company was continuing to trade secretly with its customers in Germany, which resulted in Diethelm being placed on the list of enemy firms. It was not until the Chartered Bank in London confirmed to the British government that Diethelm was a long-standing and cherished customer that the name of the trading company was removed from the list in September 1915.[35]

It was a similar story with Volkart a few months later. In August 1916, the firm was informed by Ellison & Co., a British trading company that represented Volkart in Liverpool, that the Swiss enterprise would henceforth only be allowed to conduct business under the supervision of the British Board of Trade. Volkart and Ellison were of the opinion that these difficulties stemmed from the actions of a British rival company, which had endeavored to tarnish Volkart's reputation among the British authorities as an elegant means of disposing of a competitor. After exchanging a flurry of letters with British authorities, and after presenting them with proof that the company had always followed regulations, Volkart was finally granted permission to conduct business without British supervision.[36]

Classifying Economic Players by their National Origins

With the outbreak of World War I, a company's nationality suddenly took on great importance. Classifying economic players by their national origins was a development that went hand-in-hand with the transition of World War I from an intergovernmental military conflict to a global economic war. For individual companies, this process stood in stark contrast to the prewar situation. Up until 1914, the nationality of a company was, at most, of secondary importance. This was also true after the turn of the century, when protectionist movements in continental Europe increasingly gained in strength and global trade began to undergo a process of politicization.

Yet pinning down the national identity of internationally active companies was by no means a simple matter. As Geoffrey Jones has pointed out, depending on one's point of view—be it the national origins of the company founders, the nationality of the shareholders, the location of the headquarters or the company's geographical field of activity—such companies could legitimately be ascribed entirely different nationalities.[37] Attempts by the warring parties to force these companies into a national mold often stood in stark contrast to the business operations and self-perceptions of these firms.

Likewise, determining the nationality of a company like Volkart was more difficult than one might suspect. Although the shareholders were Swiss and the de facto headquarters were in Winterthur, the main offices had been nominally in London since 1892 and most of the company's business transactions were handled outside Switzerland.[38] Accordingly, in a letter written in 1892, the owners of Volkart concluded that "our company is primarily a foreign entity and is actually viewed in London and India as British."[39] And, as recently as 1939, company officials noted in an internal memo that it was not unproblematic "that we conduct international business transactions, with huge interests in a wide range of countries, and yet we are not even sure which nationality our company may or must claim." Ironically, a possible future war was cited to illustrate the problematic nature of the company's hybrid identity:

> Just imagine . . . if hostilities were to erupt between Switzerland and Britain, this would raise once again the question of which nationality our company professes. The problem is . . . particularly difficult for us . . . because we cannot assume the position that in Switzerland we are a Swiss company and in Britain we are a British company.[40]

Classifying internationally active trading companies according to their nationality was made even more difficult by the fact that their employees often came from a wide range of countries. Even companies from neutral countries risked being placed on the Allies' blacklist if they had German or Austrian employees, and Volkart was no exception. Up until the summer of 1914, many leading company positions in London were occupied by employees from Germany. In the words of Georg Reinhart, the outbreak of war brought about "a radical change . . ., by which all Germans were interned and had to resign from their positions."[41] Furthermore, many of the British employees were inducted into the army, causing the London branch to lose over half of its qualified personnel at a time when it had to operate more or less without instructions from the main office in Winterthur.[42]

The nationality question remained virulent throughout the entire war. In 1917, the Business Registration Act came into effect, a law that required foreign companies to identify the names and nationalities of their owners on all business documents.[43] At Volkart headquarters in Winterthur, company officials felt that such a self-declaration of nationality would be an ideal way of dispelling the recurring doubts about the firm's origins.[44] This led to a heated exchange of letters over the question of how the company letterhead should look in the future. The company headquarters in Winterthur favored placing the following message on every business letter: "Volkart Brothers . . . Partners: Theodor Reinhart, George Reinhart, Werner Reinhart, Oscar Reinhart, Swiss Firm established 1851."[45] But a number of branches in India disagreed. They felt that, after the names of the partners, the letterhead should explicitly state: "nationality and origin: Swiss." This approach was justified with reference to the problems experienced by the Basel Trading Company, which had been placed under British control despite its Swiss origins.[46] But the company headquarters in Switzerland ultimately prevailed with its design of the letterhead. Henceforth, every business letter listed the names of the partners along with the affirmation that Volkart was a "Swiss Firm established 1851."[47]

The nationality debate was further fueled by the rivalry between British companies and firms from neutral countries. In India, for example, British entrepreneurs suspected that firms from neutral countries enjoyed an advantage because their employees, in contrast to those in British companies, did not have to be inducted into the military. In March 1917, the Indian Chamber of Commerce urged the Indian government to pass a law stipulating that foreign companies could only do business in India if they had an annually renewable license. Within this context, companies were classified as "foreign" if less than 75 percent of their capital was in British hands. Fortunately for Volkart and other Swiss companies doing business on the subcontinent, the Indian government rejected this proposal, stating that it was not in India's interest to place restrictions on all non-British companies.[48]

Establishing Swiss Consulates in Asia

By insisting that internationally active companies clearly declare their national origins, on a symbolic level the war economy measures resulted in closer ties between these firms and their countries of origin. When it came to Swiss trading companies that were active in Asia, on a structural level this also resulted in closer ties with the Swiss nation. One of the most pressing problems that Swiss entrepreneurs faced in Asia at the beginning of the war was the lack of consular representation by their home country in this region. At the beginning of the war, Switzerland only had diplomatic representations in Manila (from 1862), Jakarta (1863) and Yokohama (1866); by contrast, no Swiss consulate existed in India. As early as 1885, Volkart had asked the Swiss Federal Council how consular protection could be provided to the branches on the subcontinent in the event of a war. The Federal Council wrote in its response that Swiss companies that were active in countries without Swiss representation were free to choose the nations under which they intended to seek consular protection. Since 1871, Switzerland had concluded agreements with Germany and the US that would allow these countries to represent Swiss citizens in the event of a crisis. Volkart subsequently decided to place its Indian branches under the consular tutelage of the US, as it was feared that representation by Germany could lead to problems if war were to erupt in Europe.[49]

With the beginning of the war in 1914, it became clear that Switzerland also required its own diplomatic representations in Asia, a realization that led to the opening of a number of Swiss consulates: in Bombay in 1915, in Colombo, Singapore and Medan (on Sumatra) in 1917, in Shanghai and Canton in 1921, in Madras, Calcutta and Bangkok in 1922 and in Saigon in 1926. In Bombay, Colombo and Madras the heads of the relevant Volkart branches were appointed to the position of Swiss consul by the Swiss Federal Council. It was by no means unusual for merchants to serve as honorary consuls; in fact, it was a typical feature of Swiss foreign policy. At the outbreak of World War I, Switzerland only had 11 embassies abroad. On top of this, Switzerland had a network of honorary consulates that had often been established at the behest of Swiss citizens abroad. Yet with 115 honorary and six professional consulates, Switzerland had far fewer representations abroad than other European countries of a similar size.[50] Since the consulates were generally run by local merchants, the trading companies took on something of a para-state function.[51]

The awarding of consular posts was not linked to an individual's nationality. Starting in the mid-nineteenth century, for instance, the heads of diverse Volkart branches on the subcontinent had served as consuls for Belgium, the Netherlands, Sweden, Norway and Germany.[52] The outbreak of war in 1914 meant that Volkart managers in India also began to take an interest in posts as Swiss consuls and their ambitions were actively supported by the headquarters in Winterthur. One might wonder why a trading company like Volkart was prepared to allow its managers to assume responsibility for voluntary consular activities.[53] Despite the considerable time commitments associated with such positions, they were an excellent business investment. When a company manager was awarded the position of Swiss consul, it gave the company direct access to political decision-makers abroad in the event of political crises.

On 14 May 1915, the manager of Volkart's Bombay branch, Karl Ringger, was appointed Swiss consul for India by the Swiss Federal Council. In a letter dated 19 May 1915, the main office in Winterthur congratulated Ringger on his new position and expressed its firm belief "that, in view of the many Swiss citizens residing there and the flourishing trade between the two countries, a Swiss consul in Bombay will prove to be useful."[54] The interest of the company in placing its managers in consulate positions became clearly evident in the summer of 1915 when Swiss merchants in Colombo brought up the question of a consulate on Ceylon. When the top Volkart manager in Colombo, a man named Steiger, heard that another merchant had used the petition of the Swiss trading companies in the city as a springboard to launch his own bid for the position of consul, he turned to

Karl Ringger in Bombay. Steiger found that it was outright presumptuous for an official from another trading firm to aspire to the highly respected position of consul:

> Needless to say, I was of the opinion that, in view of the 60-year presence of our firm in Ceylon, the selection—subject to the approval of Volkart Bros. in Winterthur, of course—would and should fall upon a member of our company.[55]

Ringger subsequently informed his superiors at Volkart Winterthur of the incident and they personally approached the relevant federal authorities in Bern. In their response to Ringger, Volkart Winterthur expressed its hope that, "in considering the establishment of an independent consulate in Colombo, the authorities in Switzerland would take into consideration our firm, which is the oldest Swiss company in the country, for the appointment of the consul,"[56] which was, in fact, exactly what happened in 1917.[57]

Swiss merchants also applied for the position of honorary consul in other regions of the subcontinent. In December 1915, Swiss merchant Victor Zollikofer, who had business dealings in Burma, wrote an urgent letter to the newly appointed Swiss consul in Bombay. Zollikofer had heard rumors that there were plans to intern citizens of neutral countries in Burma, which, in his opinion, "would, of course, spell the end of our company."[58] He was particularly afraid that British businessmen could "spread malicious lies about him" that could lead to his internment. Zollikofer asserted in a second letter to the Swiss consul in late January 1916 that he knew with certainty "that much of this has to do with maneuvers by the competition."[59] He solicited not only the support of the Swiss consul, but also his personal recommendation for a consulate position. To avoid internment and the bankruptcy that this would entail, Zollikofer asked the consul directly if it was possible, in his capacity as "acting Swiss Consul", to delegate similar authority to him or, if it was not in his power to do so, to submit such a proposal along with a personal recommendation to the Federal Council in Switzerland.[60]

Since the Federal Council did not initially show an interest in Zollikofer's offer, he sent another letter to Bombay in the summer of 1917, in which he requested that he be appointed Swiss consulate for Burma, a position that he argued was necessary to protect Swiss citizens there because,

> since the outbreak of the war, we Swiss have suffered terribly from British . . . prejudices against German-sounding names that are indiscriminately condemned as either German or, at least, German-friendly. This state of affairs is likely to continue for many years and it would be a very welcome development if we could combat this scourge through the establishment of a consulate.[61]

Zollikofer's proposal was rejected by the Swiss Federal Council, which said that since very few Swiss lived in Burma it saw no need to establish a consulate there.[62] Nevertheless, his efforts clearly show that there were economic reasons why Swiss merchants on the subcontinent aspired to such diplomatic appointments during the war.

Toward the end of the war, Volkart also hoped that it could benefit from Karl Ringger's dual capacity as an employee of the company and Swiss consul. In 1917, the Volkart branch in Karachi was banned from any further trading in hides,[63] which prompted the company to ask the Swiss embassy in London to intervene on its behalf. The company noted that its Karachi operation was founded in 1861, making it one of the oldest trading companies in the region. Volkart also pointed out that the firm had always been Swiss, had never possessed German or Austrian capital, and had never had branch offices in Germany or Austria:

> The sympathies of our firm are entirely pro-British and this is also well known in enemy countries where our firm has broken off all relations on the outbreak of war. . . . It would therefore seem to us as a hardship that under these circumstances our firm should be treated in the nature of a 'hostile concern' and be excluded from a trade now under control, in which we would no doubt be participating to a large extent if it were not under control.[64]

In this situation, it was advantageous for Volkart that the Swiss consul in Bombay was an employee of the firm. In the summer of 1917, the main office in Winterthur asked Consul Ringger to intervene in the matter,[65] but his efforts proved fruitless. In January 1918, the Indian government informed him that it had examined the request submitted by Volkart's Karachi office to be allowed to resume trading in hides, but that, at the current point in time, it saw no means of changing the existing regulation.[66]

After the War

Due to the difficulties that the world economy and world trade encountered after the war, historians often voice the opinion that the years between 1918 and 1939 were a phase of deglobalization that followed on the heels of the first era of globalization between the beginning of the nineteenth century and 1914.[67] However, on the level of individual companies, it is certainly not true that firms after 1918 merely restricted their activities to within their respective national borders. On the contrary, despite the growing trend toward protectionism at the time, many companies intensified their foreign investments during the interwar era and used subsidiaries to penetrate foreign markets.[68] As will be shown in greater detail in the third section of this book, this also applied to Volkart. In the early 1920s, the company embarked on an ambitious expansion campaign and established in rapid succession new subsidiaries and branches in Asia, the US and Europe. This made Volkart a global player during a particularly dramatic period for the world economy.[69]

Oddly enough, this geographic expansion of the company's business activities went hand-in-hand with a greater emphasis on its national origins, which was a direct consequence of its experiences during World War I. In an internal memo, Georg Reinhart wrote in 1939: "We are a *Swiss firm* (thank God!) and we intend to remain one." Whereas Volkart had employed a large number of foreign personnel before the war, after 1918 it endeavored primarily to hire "Swiss of tried and tested character and with political views that harmonize with our own" to serve in managerial positions. "Only such individuals," Reinhart added,

> can we expect to act fully and completely out of patriotism for our company in all situations in foreign countries. British, Americans, Germans and Japanese can all find themselves in situations where their patriotism conflicts with their responsibilities to the firm.[70]

This business policy was consistent with the efforts of many Swiss companies that dispensed with their foreign shareholders and supervisory board members during the interwar years and instead embraced their *Swissness*.[71] Indeed, globalization and fragmentation in accordance with the notion of national identity are not mutually exclusive, but rather often mutually dependent and dialectically intertwined.[72] Stressing the company's Swiss origins and giving preference to hiring Swiss employees proved to be advantageous during World War II, as Georg Reinhart noted with satisfaction in 1944:

> Following our experiences during the last world war, I have striven to ensure that the offices of our company recruit as many Swiss as possible. Compliance with this policy has meant that at the outbreak of the current war we have lost none of our people through internment and that our company has never once been suspected of not being a purely Swiss firm.

Although Volkart employed a number of German and Japanese staff members in Bremen and Osaka, the business of the overall company remained unaffected by this situation because the branches in Germany and Japan were formally independent companies and the remaining branches had broken off all contact with them after the outbreak of the war.[73]

Notes

1 Hardach, *Der Erste Weltkrieg*, 1973; Offer, *The First World War*, 1989; Ferguson, *The Pity of War*, 1999, 248–281; Ullmann, "Kriegswirtschaft," 2003, 220–232; Broadberry/Harrison, *The Economics of World War I*, 2005; "Frey, Trade, Ships, and the Neutrality of the Netherlands," 1997.
2 Exceptions are Rossfeld/Straumann (eds.), *Der vergessene Wirtschaftskrieg*, 2008; Smith, Tennent and Mollan (eds.), *The Impact of the First World War*, 2016.

3 For more on the politicization of international trade after the 1880s, see Oster-hammel/Petersson, *Globalization*, 2005, 29 and 88–89. The argument that European governments before 1914 showed little interest in the nationalities of companies is also put forward by Jones, *Multinationals and Global Capitalism*, 2005, 282.

4 Jones, "The End of Nationality?", 2006, 152–158.

5 James, *The End of Globalization*.

6 Engdahl, *The Exchange of Cotton*, 1999, 194.

7 VA, Dossier 61: ex GR persönliches Archiv I, Allerlei geschäftliche Informationen, Statistiken etc.: In eternal memory of a critical episode.

8 Anderegg, *Chronicle*, 1976, 245ff.

9 Reinhart, *Aus meinem Leben*, 1931, 155–156.

10 VA, Dossier 42: Rechtliches, Cotton Business Germany 1st World War: Winterthur to Mech. Baumwoll-Spinnerei & Weberei, Augsburg, 23 April 1915.

11 VA, Dossier 42: Rechtliches, Cotton Business Germany 1st World War: Gebrüder Volkart, Winterthur, to J.H. Reitz, Chemnitz, 18 November 1914.

12 Engdahl, *The Exchange of Cotton*, 1999, 45; Anderegg, *Chronicle*, 1976, 251. The price increases were driven in part by a significantly reduced global output. In 1916–1918, roughly one-third less cotton was grown than in 1914–1915: Economic Associates, *World Cotton Position Chart*, 1934.

13 Koenig, *Der Baumwollweltmarkt*, 1919, 38ff.; Hardach, *Der Erste Weltkrieg*, 1973, 278ff.

14 Anderegg, *Chronicle*, 1976, 251–255.

15 VA: Dossier 61: ex GR persönliches Archiv I: Graphische Tabellen: Verhältnis von Stammkapital zu Gewinn und Verlust.

16 VA: Dossier 61: ex GR persönliches Archiv I: Graphische Tabellen: Verhältnis von Stammkapital zu Gewinn und Verlust.

17 Howe, *Free Trade and Liberal England*, 1997; Trentman, "National Identity," 2002; Soutou, *L'or et le sang*, 1985, 196–203.

18 McDermott, "Trading with the Enemy," 1997.

19 McDermott, "Trading with the Enemy," 1997.

20 Siney, *The Allied Blockade of Germany*, 1957, 61–74; Schildknecht, *Bremer Baumwollbörse*, 1999, 24; Dehne, "From 'Business as Usual' to a More Global War," 2005.

21 Schmidt, *Der Wirtschaftskrieg und die Neutralen*, 1918, 13.

22 Dejung/Zangger, "British Wartime Protectionism," 191 and 200.

23 VA, Dossier 42: Rechtliches, Cotton Business Germany 1st World War: Gebrüder Volkart, Winterthur, to Herrmann Brass, Brünn, 7 October 1914.

24 NA, CO 323/675: Foreign Office, General, vol. 26, 15 Aug.—7 Sept. 1915: 219: General Malta to Foreign Office, 23 Aug 15; 239–242: Aug. Thoele, Volkart Brothers, London, to the Swiss Legation, London, 6 August 1915; 244–246: Aug. Thoele, Volkart Brothers, London, to the Swiss Legation, London, 11 August 1915; CO 323/676: Foreign Office, General, vol. 27, 8 Sept.—30 Sept. 1915: 534–537: Aug. Thoele, Volkart Brothers, London, to the Under Secretary of State, Foreign Office, 16 September 1915; CO 323/679: Foreign Office, General, vol. 30, 20 Nov—31 Dec. 1915: 582–583: Foreign Office to the Under Secretary of State, Colonial Office, 24 December 1915; CO 323/713: Foreign Office, General, vol. 18, 22 June—31 July 1916: Foreign Office to The Under-Secretary of State, Colonial Office, 25 July 1916.

25 VA, Dossier 6: Colombo, 14: Two notes on VOLKART Colombo, compiled in 1918 by VOLKART Colombo in 1925 by P. De Abrew.

26 See, for example, BAR, E 2200.110 (Bombay), Akz. Nr. 1, Schachtel 1, Paket 1: Moll, Schütte & Co., Calcutta, to K. Ringger, Consul for Switzerland, Bombay, 13 December 1915.

27 Bartu, *The Fan Tree Company*, 2005, 82–83.
28 NA, FO 383/73: Prisoners, Germany Files 100091–105459, 1915: The Queens House, Colombo, to A. Bonar Law, M.P., 2 July 1915; FO 383/109: Prisoners, Miscellaneous (General) Files 51445–98039, 1915: India Office to the Under Secretary of State, Foreign Office, 24 July 1915; VA, Dossier 6: Colombo, 4. Table of Events.
29 VA, Dossier 18: Winterthur I, 1. Table of Events: Bombay, Zirkular, 22 October 1915.
30 VA, Dossier 6: Colombo, 4. Table of Events.
31 VA, Dossier 6: Colombo, 5. correspondence relating to produce & notes on taxation: Winterthur to Colombo, 31 August 1915.
32 Wanner, *Die Basler Handelsgesellschaft*, 1959, 32 and 253–292.
33 BAR, E 2200.110 (Bombay), Akz. Nr. 1, Schachtel 1, Paket 1: A. Eidenbenz, General Agent, Basel Mission Industrials, Calicut, to the Chief Secretary to the Government of Madras, 28 September 1915.
34 Wanner, *Die Basler Handelsgesellschaft*, 1959, 376–421.
35 Bartu, *The Fan Tree Company*, 2005, 83.
36 VA, Dossier 13, London/Liverpool (VOLKART + Woods&Thorburn)/Bremen: 2. Table of Events; Anderegg, *Chronicle*, 1976, 248.
37 Jones, "The End of Nationality?", 2006.
38 See Chapter 3 for the reasons behind moving the main office to London and for more on the geographical radius of the business activities in Europe.
39 VA, Dossier 18: Winterthur I, 3. Nominal transfer of HO to LONDON from Winterthur, Gebr. Volkart to the Schweiz. Handels & Justiz Departement, Bern, 29 November 1892.
40 VA, Dossier 19: Winterthur II, Umschlag "Dokumente in Zusammenhang mit Transfer VOLKART Head Office: nach London 1893 / nach Winterthur 1940": Memorandum from 10 December 1939, advantages and disadvantages of our current form of business.
41 Reinhart, *Aus meinem Leben*, 1931, 55.
42 Anderegg, *Chronicle*, 1976, 257–258.
43 Anderegg, *Chronicle*, 1976, 250.
44 VA, Dossier 13: London/Liverpool (VOLKART + Woods&Thorburn)/Bremen, 7. Proclamations during First World War: Winterthur to London, 30 January 1917.
45 The partners' names have been anglicized to a certain degree in the letterhead (George, Oscar) in an apparent attempt to appear less Germanic and avoid being classified as an enemy firm.
46 VA, Dossier 18: Winterthur I, 1. Table of Events—1917: Transcript of the relevant letter, no place and date.
47 VA, Dossier 13: London/Liverpool (VOLKART + Woods&Thorburn)/Bremen, 7. Proclamations during First World War: Winterthur to London, 23 April 1917.
48 Anderegg, *Chronicle*, 1976, 249.
49 BAR, E2, 1477: Correspondence between Volkart and the Eidgenössisches Politisches Departement, 25 April/27 April/1 May 1885.
50 At the time, Belgium had 562 honorary and 34 professional consulates, Denmark 500 and 16, Greece more than 310 and 20, the Netherlands 613 and 20, Norway 636 and 21, Portugal 496 and 33, Sweden 612 and 24, Spain 751 and 98: Rohner, *Die Schweizer Wirtschaftsvertretungen*, 1944, 21.
51 Altermatt, *Zwei Jahrhunderte Schweizer Auslandvertretungen*, 1990. For more on the influence of the Swiss economy on foreign policy, also see Siegenthaler, "Die Bedeutung des Aussenhandels," 1982, and Heinrich Wachter, "Die Handelsbeziehungen der Schweiz und der Schweizerische Transithandel," *Neue Zürcher Zeitung*, 5 October 1935.

52 VA, Dossier 1: Die Teilhaber I, A) Die Familie der Gründer, Johann Georg Volkart; Dossier 6: Colombo, 3. European staff lists; Dossier 8: Karachi, 1. Management.

53 Jean Frei, the manager of the Volkart branch in Madras, stated that he spent two to three hours a day on consulate-related activities: BAR, E 2200.110 (Bombay), Akz. Nr. 1, Dossier No. 1, Avril 1924 à Février 1925: Gebrüder Volkart, Winterthur, an das Eidgenössische Politische Departement, Abteilung für Auswärtiges, Bern, 1 April 1924.

54 BAR, E 2200.110 (Bombay), Akz. Nr. 1, Schachtel 1, Paket 1: Volkart Brothers, Winterthur, to K. Ringger, Bombay, 19 May 1915.

55 BAR, E 2200.110 (Bombay), Akz. Nr. 1, Schachtel 1, Paket 1: Steiger, Volkart Brothers, Colombo, to Ringger, Bombay, 17 July 1915.

56 BAR, E 2200.110 (Bombay), Akz. Nr. 1, Schachtel 1, Paket 1: Volkart Brothers, Winterthur, K. Ringger, Bombay, 24 August 1915.

57 BAR, E 2200.110 (Bombay), Akz. Nr. 1, Schachtel 1, Paket 13; Anderegg, *Chronicle*, 259.

58 BAR, E 2200.110 (Bombay), Akz. Nr. 1, Schachtel 1, Paket 1: Victor Zollikofer, V. Zollikofer & Co., Rangoon, to K. Ringger, Schweizer Konsul, Bombay, 20 December 1915.

59 BAR, E 2200.110 (Bombay), Akz. Nr. 1, Schachtel 1, Paket 4: Victor Zollikofer, V. Zollikofer & Co., Rangoon, to K. Ringger, Schweizer Konsul, Bombay, 24 January 1916.

60 BAR, E 2200.110 (Bombay), Akz. Nr. 1, Schachtel 1, Paket 1: Victor Zollikofer, V. Zollikofer & Co., Rangoon, to K. Ringger, Schweizer Konsul, Bombay, 20 December 1915.

61 BAR, E 2200.110 (Bombay), Akz. Nr. 1, Schachtel 1, Paket 6: Viktor Zollikofer, Zollikofer & Co., Rangoon to K. Ringger, Schweizerisches Konsulat, Bombay, 31 July 1917.

62 BAR, E 2200.110 (Bombay), Akz. Nr. 1, Schachtel 9, Swiss Consulate Rangoon: Schweizerischer Generalkonsul, Bombay, to the Konsulardienst des Eidg. Politischen Departements, Bern, 5 July 1928.

63 BAR, E 2200.110 (Bombay), Akz. Nr. 1, Schachtel 1, Paket 2: Volkart Brothers, London, to Swiss Legation, London, 12 July 1917.

64 BAR, E 2200.110 (Bombay), Akz. Nr. 1, Schachtel 1, Paket 2: Volkart Brothers, London, to Swiss Legation, London, 12 July 1917.

65 BAR, E 2200.110 (Bombay), Akz. Nr. 1, Schachtel 1, Paket 2: Gebrüder Volkart, Winterthur, to the Schweizerische Konsulat, Bombay, 19 September 1917.

66 BAR, E 2200.110 (Bombay) Akz. Nr. 1, Schachtel 1, Paket 3: Government of India, Indian Munitions Board, Delhi, to the Consul of Switzerland, Bombay, 2 January 1918.

67 For instance in Hobsbawm, *The Age of Extremes*, 1994; O'Brien, "The Great War," 1995, 252–263; Torp, "Weltwirtschaft vor dem Weltkrieg," 2004.

68 Jones, "The End of Nationality?", 164.

69 Rambousek/Vogt/Volkart, *Volkart*, 1990, 81–86.

70 VA, Dossier 62: ex GR persönliches Archiv II, The Family Code of the House of Mitsui, Japan, aufgestellt im siebzehnten Jahrhundert und mein Kommentar dazu vom 10./11. November 1939, 19–21.

71 Lüpold, "Wirtschaftskrieg, Aktienrecht und Corporate Governance," 2008.

72 Clark, *Globalization and Fragmentation*, 1997; Conrad, *Globalisation and the Nation*, 2010.

73 VA, Dossier 63: ex GR persönliches Archiv III, Richtlinien für unsere Geschäftstätigkeit, memorandum by GR, 28 April 1944.

Part II
Looking Behind the Scenes

5   The Owner Family

Family businesses have become an increasingly important focus of business and economic history in recent years. For a long time, these disciplines were highly influenced by the Chandlerian theory that family enterprises were a hallmark of preindustrial corporate organization and that, since the late nineteenth century, economic life has been determined by joint-stock companies run by managers.[1] This theory does not hold true across the board for all manufacturing companies; even today a number of leading industrial companies can be qualified as family businesses.[2] The theory is even less applicable to the trading sector, where a significantly large number of leading companies still remain in the ownership of families.[3] This was also the case with Volkart, where most partners came from the Winterthur mercantile families of Volkart and Reinhart. Aside from being the owners, they also ran the company, making Volkart more than just a mere mover of goods, but rather a social entity that was shaped by an owner family.[4]

Family Companies in Global Trade

The large number of family-owned trading companies reflects the economic particularities of this sector. From the 1870s onwards, family-owned enterprises were often replaced by joint-stock companies in the industrial sector because family-based networks were no longer capable of providing industrial firms with the necessary financial resources. It was above all capital markets and a modern banking system that provided the funding for investments in the industrial sector.[5] Trading firms on the other hand required far less long-term investments. Although the borrowing needs of the trading sector also soared during this period in history because low margins made economies of scale increasingly important, trading firms were not obliged to issue stock to raise outside capital, but instead could finance their massive turnovers by taking out short-term bank loans and pledging their inventories as securities.[6]

Furthermore, generating confidence and securing continuity have always played a key role in the global trading sector. According to Mark Casson, family companies are a type of business that has proven to be particularly effective in an environment characterized by extreme fluctuations and not entirely secured ownership rights.[7] No wonder family firms have been so widespread in the trading sector—and remain so today. As Harold James noted, the advantage of family businesses was that they were associated with a specific group of individuals, which ensured a certain degree of continuity in business relations and reduced transaction costs.[8] Even though many trading companies took on the form of joint-stock companies starting in the early twentieth century, their shares often remained in the possession of the founding families and were not publicly traded.[9] This made sense to the extent that the trading sector was highly volatile and reliant upon extreme discretion. Shareholders who reconsidered their portfolio strategies in times of crisis would have only created unnecessary turmoil within the company.[10] By contrast, the owner families were prepared to invest their capital over the long term—out of a sense of loyalty to the traditions of the family and because they intended to pass on the company to the next generation.[11] From the end of the nineteenth century, however, many large trading companies had developed certain attributes that, according to Alfred Chandler and Jürgen Kocka, are characteristic of modern companies. For instance, management took on greater importance because the owner families were no longer capable of monitoring work processes that had become ever more complex.[12] A similar transition can be observed at Volkart, as the business expanded toward the end of the nineteenth century from a medium-sized trading company—in which management, partnerships and family affiliations went hand-in-hand—to a large enterprise that, although it continued to be controlled by the owner family, was now largely run by a professional management team. Modern trading companies thus adopted an organizational structure that Chandler called an entrepreneurial enterprise. This is a form of business characterized by a hybrid between a traditional family firm and business practices shaped by management.[13]

Family firms have been described by many researchers as an overlapping of two different social systems, namely families and commercial enterprises.[14] This is in line with the long-standing prevailing view in sociology, economics and business history that the family is a counterpart to the market, since it is primarily characterized by tradition and the principle of solidarity. By contrast, in the "iron cage" of capitalism (Max Weber) the only thing that allegedly counted was rationalization aimed to enhance speed and precision and maximize short-term profits.[15] Strictly separating both spheres, however, is not entirely satisfactory for an analysis of family companies because the economic actors do not strictly observe the functional logic of specific social subsystems as they go about their daily business, but instead transgress the limits of this system time and again. In her study of German family firms, Christina Lubinski noted that when owners made decisions they hardly ever differentiated between economic and familial rationality. Moreover, these decisions were not always made based on economic considerations, but instead often adhered to a bounded rationality engendered on the basis of ideals, earlier decisions and future expectations.[16]

Family and business traditions play a key role, particularly in companies in which the owner family exerts a great amount of influence on business strategies, which results in a high degree of path dependence for all business decisions. This prompted anthropologist Sylvia Junko Yanagisako to study family businesses based on a cultural theory of economic action "that treats all social action—including capital accumulation, firm expansion and diversification—as constituted by both deliberate, rational calculation and by sentiments and desires: in other words, as cultural practices."[17] Viewed from this perspective, the family is also an economic entity while the company appears to be a social entity that is highly influenced by traditions and emotions. As will be shown here, it was precisely this combination of family and entrepreneurial spheres that paved the way for a family firm like Volkart to become such a reliable and effective intermediary in the global trading sector and allowed it, along with other trading companies that were often also family owned, to maintain lasting business relationships.

From a Family Firm to a Large-scale Enterprise

When the company was founded, Volkart was primarily a family affair. Working from the main office in Winterthur, Salomon Volkart was in charge of exports of European consumer goods to India and dealt with sales of Indian commodities in Europe. He was initially assisted by his wife, Emma, who handled some of the office work. Salomon's brother Johann Georg supervised the sales of European imports in Bombay and endeavored to secure export orders for Indian raw materials. Although the company had two employees in Bombay right from the first year, the responsibility for the business lay entirely with the two brothers[18] who had decided to establish a general partnership, a typical form of business for trading companies at the time, which meant that they were jointly liable with their private assets for any losses incurred by the company. Volkart thus had a business structure that was very similar to that of other trading companies during the premodern period. In most cases, family members who were also partners in the firm were sent to marketplaces overseas to ensure that business transactions were handled appropriately.[19] Since family affiliations were apparently well suited to reducing transaction costs in the risky overseas trading sector, there were many instances in which clerks and accountants married into the firm and became partners.[20] This allowed the owners of the company to kill two birds with one stone: They settled the matter of the line of succession for their business, which was a virulent problem in family firms, and they ensured that their daughters married men who were befitting of their station in life and could ensure a financially secure existence. Private and business interests overlapped to a large degree in such cases.

With the expansion of the business and the opening of new branches in diverse South Asian port cities, it became clear that the two Volkart brothers could no longer manage the company alone.[21] In the 1850s and 1860s, three employees were made partners. Nonetheless, they only invested a nominal amount of capital and exerted hardly any influence on the course of the company. In 1857, after opening the branches in Cochin and Colombo, Henry L. Brodbeck, who had been employed at the Volkart branch in Bombay since 1852, was made partner and appointed as the manager of the business in India. Shortly thereafter, Johann Georg Volkart, whose poor health had forced him to spend extensive periods of time in Europe between 1854 and 1856, returned to Winterthur, but his plans of retiring in Switzerland were dashed. Brodbeck died in 1859 and Johann Georg Volkart had to return to India to resume management of the business there. In 1861, shortly before he could leave India for a second time, Johann Georg Volkart died at the age of 36. Two years later, in 1863, Salomon Volkart made the head of the branch office in Colombo, Rudolph Ahlers, a partner in the firm. The remaining company founder decided to take this step because the firm would have been without leadership in the event of his death, and probably because he had greater confidence in the abilities of a partner—rather than a mere employee—to manage the business in India and Ceylon. This was most likely the reason why Salomon Volkart made another employee from India a partner in the firm when Ahlers returned to Europe in 1866. The new partner, Albert E. Denso, was the head of the Karachi branch office, but this partnership did not last long and Denso had to leave India for personal reasons in 1868. Accordingly, he resigned his position as partner in the overall company in 1869, but retained a stake in the Karachi branch until 1871.

The other partners during the first decades of the company's existence usually had family ties to the Volkarts. In 1871, another member of the founding family was made partner, namely Salomon Volkart's nephew, Johann G. Sigg, who had worked for the firm in India for a number of years and, from 1865 onwards, was the right hand of the company founder in Winterthur.[22] In 1875, Salomon Volkart's son Georg Gottfried Volkart became a partner in the company. He had been trained in Winterthur and London to work in his father's company and had spent a number of months in India and Ceylon in 1875. During the same year, Theodor Reinhart also joined the firm. After receiving a doctorate in law, Reinhart had worked until 1874 for Geilinger & Blum, the trading company of his father, Johann Caspar Reinhart, in Le Havre, London, New York and New Orleans. In 1876, he married Lilly Volkart, a daughter of Salomon Volkart. In 1879, he was made partner. Sigg resigned his partnership in the firm that very same year and established his own trading company, which was also involved in the import and export business between India and Europe. In 1880, August F. Ammann, who had been an employee at Volkart since 1868, was made partner, and one year later he married Emma Volkart, another daughter of Salomon Volkart (Table 5.1). Hence, his partnership was fortified by the

Table 5.1 Family tree of the Volkart and Reinhart families

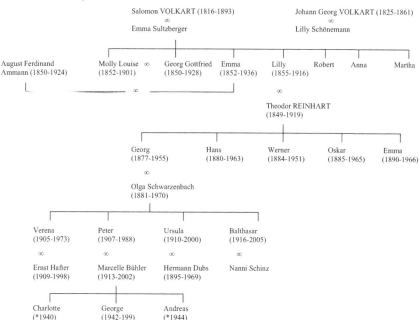

(Sources: VA, Dossier 1, A) Die Familie und ihre Gründer; Dossier 2: Die Teilhaber II; Rambousek/Vogt/Volkart, Volkart 1990, S. 46; www.winterthur-glossar.ch)

bond of the family, a bond that had already previously existed. Indeed, in 1876 Georg Gottfried Volkart had married Molly Luise Ammann, the sister of August F. Ammann,[23] and already back in 1867 Lilly Schönemann, the widow of Johann Georg Volkart, had wed in her second marriage Gottfried Ferdinand Ammann, August F. Ammann's father.[24] The company's equity amounted to 3.5 million Swiss francs in 1875 and, only a few years later, in 1883, had risen to 6 million Swiss francs. Salomon Volkart had a share of 2.5 million, Georg Gottfried Volkart 1.5 million and Theodor Reinhart and August F. Ammann each had 1 million.[25]

There was only one other occasion, after the resignation of August F. Ammann, that an employee of the firm who was not related to the Volkart or Reinhart families was made a partner, namely in 1894, when Jakob Steiner-Prior, a man who had worked for Volkart in India since the 1860s, became a member of the company's inner circle.[26] Steiner-Prior resigned from the company's board of directors in 1912, the same year that Georg Gottfried Volkart, the son of Salomon Volkart, also stepped down as partner. Since Johann Georg Volkart died in 1861 without producing children, and the sons of Georg Gottfried Volkart died at an early age, henceforth none of the partners bore the name of the company founders and the firm was now completely in the possession of the Reinhart family.[27]

A Hybrid of a Family Firm and a Manager-run Company

In contrast to the initial decades after the establishment of the firm, when an increasing number of employees were made partners, there was a clear division between partners and managers from the late nineteenth century onwards. Thanks to improved means of transport and communication, the owners of the company no longer needed to have a partner permanently stationed in India to keep an eye on the business. The partners could limit their direct involvement in the branches to occasional inspection tours. After World War I, the partners also played less and less of a direct role in everyday business activities in Europe. Until then, it had been common for them to visit their key clients on a regular basis. But due to the increased volume of business, from 1920 onwards these visits were primarily carried out by leading executives of the company.[28]

Even though managers could no longer hope to be made partners— Theodor Reinhart had made it clear that the firm should only accept family members as partners[29]—they were nevertheless important for the further development of Volkart and in some cases even occupied key positions. The growth of the company had made it impossible for the owner family to manage the business without the help of highly qualified employees. For instance, Ernst Müller-Renner, who was in charge of the cotton division from 1895 onwards and had the general power of representation for all branches of the company, was largely responsible for the successful development of the cotton business.[30] His outstanding position within the company is also reflected by the fact that he was the only non-partner who was honored with a personal portrait in the anniversary publication of 1926, which symbolically placed him on the same level as the company owners.[31] His ties with the partners also extended beyond mere business matters. For example, Georg Reinhart was the godfather of Müller-Renner's daughter.[32]

Since the heads of the individual departments had become indispensable for the commercial success of the business, they and the partners together formed the senior management of the company. The last word on strategic decisions, however, was reserved for the Partners' Conference,[33] which meant that the strategic management of the company remained firmly in the hands of the owner family. Nevertheless, Volkart was no longer a family firm in the traditional sense. In the late nineteenth century, the company had become a large enterprise, whose organization was a hybrid of a family firm and a company run by managers.[34] Volkart thus adopted a business structure that was essentially a hallmark of modern trading companies.[35]

Continuity in the Male Hereditary Line and the Allure of Art

A fundamental problem faced by family firms was the process of succession.[36] In 1921, Georg Reinhart (Figure 5.1) stated in his last will and

Figure 5.1 Theodor Reinhart (sitting, 2nd from left), his wife, Lilly, née Volkart, and their four sons (back row, from left to right) Oskar, Georg, Werner and Hans, along with the couple's daughter, Emma (VA, Dossier 101: Photos Partners)

testament that he hoped that his sons Peter and Balthasar, who were four and 13 years old at the time, would carry on the traditions and manage the firm as a family business in its fourth generation, adding: "It is my hope that my sons also have this sense of responsibility . . . for the achievements of our fathers, which they have bequeathed upon us so that we may dutifully carry on with their work."[37] This quote shows that family companies at the time primarily saw themselves as an intergenerational male fellowship. Daughters and wives were never considered as possible candidates to manage the company. The wives and daughters of company owners, but also the sons who played no part in managing the firm, were relegated to the margins of the family business community.[38]

In contrast to other family firms, Volkart never had a problem finding partners from the family circle. There were always a number of sons who were prepared to take over the reins of the business from their fathers. But this was not necessarily an easy decision for the next generation, as witnessed by the fact that Georg Reinhart and his three brothers had relatively little interest in the mercantile profession. For them it was not so much a matter of the dichotomy between family and company spheres, but rather a conflict between the allure of individual life goals and the demands of the family business. Georg Reinhart wrote in his memoirs that he toyed extensively with the idea of becoming a painter, but he noted that his father,

Theodor Reinhart, was able to convince him "to seize upon the secure employment in the paternal business and only pursue my artistic inclinations to paint and draw as an amateur during my leisure hours." Yet for many years Georg Reinhart was plagued with doubt over whether he had perhaps given in too hastily.[39] Like his brothers and his father, throughout his life Georg Reinhart maintained close contact to artists and writers who he also supported financially.[40]

Georg Reinhart's brother Werner, who was an active partner and helped to steer the course of the company for nearly 40 years, would have also greatly preferred to focus on artistic pursuits. At a memorial event held in honor of Werner Reinhart in 1951, a leading company official said that the commercial profession "did not . . . match with the desires and disposition" of the deceased, "but he saw it as a binding obligation to the work and accomplishments of his grandparents and parents."[41] Werner Reinhart also patronized artists and particularly musicians throughout his life. His villa, which after his death was bequeathed to the Winterthur Music Conservatory, was regularly sought out by writers like Charles Ferdinand Ramuz, Hermann Hesse and Rainer Maria Rilke, composers like Igor Stravinsky, Othmar Schoeck and Arthur Honegger, and pianist Clara Haskil.[42]

Oskar Reinhart, the youngest son of Theodor Reinhart, became an active partner at Volkart in 1912. He resigned from this function in 1924, but remained a silent partner until 1940. Afterwards, he patronized the arts and devoted himself above all to his art collection, which after his death in 1965 was bestowed to the Swiss Confederation and today, as the Oskar Reinhart Collection 'Am Römerholz,' ranks among the most important private collections in the world. Finally, Hans Reinhart, who, after Georg, was the second oldest son of Theodor Reinhart, never worked for the family business. He was a poet, dramatist and journalist who used his share of the inheritance from his father as an endowment in 1957 to create the Hans-Reinhart-Ring, the most prestigious Swiss theater award.[43] The close connection between art and commerce reveals that the sons of Theodor Reinhart did not have the stereotypical one-dimensional business personalities of many other entrepreneurs of the day,[44] but were instead complex individuals torn by inner conflicts, almost on par with the inner strife experienced by the members of the fictitious patrician merchant family in Thomas Mann's famous novel "Buddenbrooks." Indeed, they were true representatives of contemporary bourgeois values, including a fascination for the arts, and often had to put their personal interests on hold as they bowed to the imperatives of business and commerce.[45]

Although a number of family members were somewhat reluctant to embrace the mercantile profession, their strong connections to the family business ultimately motivated them to work in the firm. When one of the partners' sons showed an interest in the trade, he was diligently prepared for his future career at the company. After completing his obligatory schooling, he would first work as an apprentice at the main office in Winterthur. This was usually followed by further training at the Volkart office in London and briefer stints with companies owned by friends of the family, usually bankers and freight forwarders, before the training was completed with a longer assignment at an Asian branch of the company. This allowed the up-and-coming partners to familiarize themselves with the basics of accounting and the features of the products traded by Volkart. Likewise, it gave them an opportunity to meet the staff in the various branches and become acquainted with customers and business associates before they joined the ranks of the managers of the company.[46]

Since the sons of the company owners were made partners after their education and training, it was in the firm's interest that the partners married women who would be a credit to the company. This was not a formal policy, but unofficially there was a certain amount of pressure to keep the firm's best interests in mind when choosing a spouse.[47] It was certainly no coincidence that the sons of Volkart partners generally married daughters of highly respected families and quite a few marriages were sealed among the families of local merchants. This began with the marriage between Salomon Volkart and Emma Sultzberger, who was the daughter of a Winterthur merchant and city councilor, and continued with the flurry of matrimonies described above between members of the Volkart, Ammann and Reinhart families.[48] Even the 1904 marriage between Georg Reinhart and Olga Schwarzenbach, the daughter of a successful Swiss silk trader, was unquestionably befitting of his social status. That notwithstanding, Reinhart had to submit to a lengthy "interrogation" by Robert Schwarzenbach senior before the critical father gave his blessing to the marriage.[49] The marriages between the children of these diverse mercantile dynasties did not, however, mean that the respective companies subsequently cooperated with each other or intensified their business relations. For instance, Geilinger & Blum had been representing the Volkart trading company since the 1850s in southern Germany and Switzerland,[50] but there is no indication that ties between the two firms changed as a result of the nuptial alliance between Theodor Reinhart and Lilly Volkart. Moreover, the Volkart and Schwarzenbach companies never did business with each other despite the wedlock of Georg Reinhart and Olga Schwarzenbach. This indicates that these marriages were not strategic moves aimed at safeguarding business relationships, as was still common among mercantile families until the mid-nineteenth century, but instead primarily served the purpose of ensuring the continuity of the owner family.[51]

No Harmony despite Blood Ties

The model of the family firm by no means meant that harmony prevailed among the owners.[52] Intense bouts of wrangling frequently erupted among senior members of the company. Georg Reinhart, for instance, recounted in his memoirs the first disagreements between his father Theodor Reinhart and his uncle Georg Gottfried Volkart. This nearly led to the dissolution of the partnership, which would have entailed the liquidation of the company and replaced it with two rival firms. The partners managed to avoid a rupture, yet the disagreements only came to an end when Georg Gottfried Volkart retired to private life in 1908.[53] As such disputes between partners were a constant menace for general partnerships, it was enshrined in the company's articles of association that no partner, acting alone, could demand the liquidation of the firm.[54]

The atmosphere in the company continued to be marred by tension after Georg Gottfried Volkart's retirement. Georg Reinhart acknowledged that he and his brothers had not always lived up to the creed of the family business "to deal with one another in close friendship and with kindness" and he deplored the disputes that "had often strained the relationship between my brothers and me."[55] His relationship to his brother Werner, with whom he managed the company from 1924 onwards, was fraught with tension for many years. Their first major disagreement concerned the closing of the Singapore branch, which had been opened in 1924 and remained deep in the red for years. It was not until Georg Reinhart told his brother in 1929 that he had been suffering from a nervous heart disorder for years as a result of these tensions and begged him to reconsider his position, if not for objective reasons, then at least for humane reasons, that Werner Reinhart finally relented and the branch was closed in early 1930.[56]

Despite these conflicts, Georg Reinhart advocated the convention that only family members could become partners by arguing that "whenever differences of opinion arise, blood ties are a safeguard against public dispute."[57] An important advantage of confining the partnership to family members was, in his eyes, that the continuity of the firm could be guaranteed even in times of crisis:

> Despite momentary differences of opinion, . . . consideration for the honor of the common family name constitutes a strong bond that unites the partners in times of difficulty. By contrast, with outside elements there is always the danger that they will commit acts for the sake of personal or momentary gain that we, who have been connected to the firm for many generations, would reject out of hand.[58]

Evolutionary Growth and Controlling the Employees

In accordance with evolutionary economics, a company's decisions can be significantly influenced by its form of organization.[59] Hence, if a company is in the hands of a specific family that manages its affairs, this can have an impact on the firm's strategy.[60] Georg Reinhart had the same point of view: "The major guidelines of a long-term business policy in a family firm like our own are based on a tradition and should be altered according to an evolutionary path and after cautious, tentative attempts,"[61] as he wrote in 1939. In his last will and testament written 15 years earlier, he had requested that his presumed successor at the firm exercise great caution when making any changes to the company's organization:

> Our company is a living organism, like a tree that . . . would suffer terribly if it were removed from its element or extensive operations were performed on its trunk. Changes to the structure of our business organization . . . should thus only be made when circumstances force us to take action, . . . and not by adopting a revolutionary course or acting according to theoretical or abstract ideas.[62]

The metaphor from nature used here shows that Georg Reinhart saw the company directors not as omnipotent titans of industry, but rather as stewards of an organic entity that demanded respect and consideration. By contrast, his brother Werner urged a far more aggressive business strategy. During the interwar years, this led to a protracted dispute between the two brothers over the course that the trading firm should adopt. Toward the end of the 1920s, Georg Reinhart firmly maintained that the firm had expanded too quickly during the boom in world trade between 1915 and 1925. During this period, Volkart had established new branches and subsidiaries in Osaka, Shanghai, Bremen, New York, Calcutta and Singapore, along with a department for machine imports in India. This policy of rapid expansion stands in stark contradiction to Mark Casson's assertion that family firms tend to expand slowly during economic booms, which allows them to benefit from their cautious strategy during times of crisis.[63] As global trade was increasingly engulfed by the crisis from the mid-1920s onwards, Volkart lost millions every year. Georg Reinhart blamed his brother Werner for the company's critical situation in the late 1920s, accusing him of ignoring his "repeated . . . warnings" against continuing to maintain unprofitable branch offices and called for a "fundamental decision . . . to simplify and scale down our organization." The problem was that the two brothers could not agree on the goal of their business activities. For Georg Reinhart, though, there was no doubt that profit was the key to doing business:

> The company is a means of *making a living*. We are not working *pour la gloire*. We would rather be in second or third place in terms of our sales of a given article if we can make a decent profit than to be in first place with losses.

He more or less directly accused his brother of megalomania: "I ask you time and time again to keep in mind that *we are working to earn money* and not to pretend that we are the lords of the manor."[64]

His guiding principle that it was necessary to focus on the core business led Georg Reinhart to conclude that, since Volkart was a family firm, the owner family and the company represented two closely intertwined entities. In his view, the drawback with enterprises that became too large was that the partners could no longer keep track of all in-company developments.[65] He noted that business trips or military duty would make it increasingly likely that one of the two brothers would have to run the business alone, which meant that the firm had to be organized so it could be managed without exceeding the capacity of a single partner.[66] Due to the principal-agent problem, Reinhart said that it was imperative that the decision-making process be centralized at the headquarters to place it within the partners' sphere of influence. He felt that this was an important step to prevent the disintegration of the branches and subsidiaries that were scattered across a number of continents:

> It is very tempting for branch heads and directors of subsidiaries to break away from the parent company and pursue their own business objectives. This leads to what my father called a *satrap economy*, and it has been the downfall of many a large firm. The centralization of the *nervus rerum* at the headquarters is an important means of maintaining control . . . of the threads of the organization.[67]

Family and Business Culture

As late as the 1960s, Volkart was run as a general partnership in which the partners were jointly liable with their private assets for any losses incurred by the company. This ownership structure was largely responsible for the firm's rather conservative business practices. Moreover, it gave clients and suppliers confidence in the integrity of the company. The family traditions of the trading firm were held up both within the company and in its communications to the outside world as a symbol of its reliability and solid business practices.

The cornerstone of the company's self-image was the memory of its founders. Yet although Salomon Volkart was honored in all portrayals as the progenitor of the company and in the jubilee publication of 1926 was presented as "the founder" of the firm, Johann Georg Volkart assumed a far more humble position in the in-company traditions and was only referred to in passing in the abovementioned text celebrating the 75th anniversary of the firm.[68]

The Indian employees of Volkart's Khamgaon buying agency also staged their own commemoration of the event in 1926 with a group photo that symbolically placed Salomon Volkart as a father figure at the center (Figure 5.2).[69] This preference for the older of the two brothers stemmed from the fact that Salomon Volkart was the father-in-law of Theodor Reinhart, which made him the forefather of all members of the Reinhart family who managed the company during the twentieth century. Johann Georg Volkart, on the other hand, who died without producing any offspring, had no direct bloodline to subsequent company owners. What's more, many employees and partners in later years were familiar with Salomon Volkart

KHAMGAON

Figure 5.2 Employees of the buying agency in Khamgaon on the occasion of the celebration of the company's 75th anniversary, with a photograph of Salomon Volkart at the center (from: V.B. News, no. 14, June 1926, 19)

from his time as the undisputed head of the company and as a cofounder of such leading firms as the Bank in Winterthur, Swiss Lloyd, the Hypothekar-bank Winterthur and the Schweizerische Lokomotiv- und Maschinenfabrik (SLM).[70] Johann Georg Volkart, who until his early death primarily worked in Bombay, left far fewer traces in the business world.

Despite the unequally weighted contribution of the two brothers to the success of the company, which was replaced in later years by a far more balanced portrayal, there is no doubt that the memory of the company founders is often held up as proof of the spirit of solidarity within the trading firm. Peter Reinhart, for instance, said the following in a speech marking the company's centennial anniversary in 1951:

> The generations before us have laid a solid foundation for current business and already many decades ago given the firm a *name* that I, although it is not even worth a symbolic franc on the balance sheet, without the least bit of hesitation would call our *greatest* asset. . . . It goes without saying that in the future it must remain our top priority to maintain this name, come what may.[71]

Worldwide Inter-family Networks

The illustrious history of the Volkart company was not only used to present itself to the outside world, but also to influence the way business transactions were to be conducted. The company had always made it a rule that contracts were to be strictly respected.[72] In 1942, this guiding principle was directly linked to the company's family tradition under the title WHAT WE STAND FOR:

> Firms like Volkart Brothers with an honorable family tradition of several generations, do not stoop to shady transactions or treat a contract obligation as if it were a scrap of paper. They feel that they have an ideal to live up to—and they prosper, because their clients instinctively respect them. . . . The better the reputation for service, the greater employment stability and success will result, for satisfied customers mean steady jobs.[73]

This refers to a key characteristic of the global trade in commodities. Although—or perhaps because—this was a highly competitive sector, honesty and fairness to other merchants were important business principles, primarily because there were only a relatively small number of market players and unsavory business practices would have been exposed, sooner or later, and ruined their reputations. From the late nineteenth century onwards, a select group of large trading companies generally controlled the export of certain raw materials from certain parts of the globe. The buyers of these traded commodities also consisted of a relatively small number of industrial companies. Other players included banks, insurance firms and shipping companies that provided the financing and infrastructure for the global trade in goods. All of these companies often maintained business ties that went back decades and the owners and top officials of the firms involved in the trade often knew each other personally.[74]

Volkart, of course, was by far not the only trading company that went out of its way to meet the needs of its customers, and credibility and establishing a loyal clientele ranked among most important assets of a trading company, but such business principles were not to be taken for granted, either, and it appears that they tended to be pursued more in Europe than in the US. For instance, after Volkart hired a number of former employees of the American Cotton Cooperative Association in the 1930s, it turned out that the American managers paid less attention to customer preferences than was usually the case at Volkart and instead focused more on price fluctuations. This led to a good deal of tension with the American branches of the company.[75] Likewise, a number of British trading firms that established offices in the US during the 1920s learned the hard way that their rather cautious business culture was not very compatible with the dynamic business practices in the US,[76] where people had a fundamentally different notion of what a company should be. In Europe a company was seen as not just an economic organization, but also a social entity. It would appear that the connection between family and company that was typical of family firms and the embedding of this type of family enterprise in its social surroundings were much stronger in Europe than it was in the US.[77]

At Volkart the abovementioned close business relationships were often nurtured for decades and the fact that many of the companies concerned were family owned had a stabilizing function. In addition to maintaining business ties for a number of generations with Indian mercantile firms that worked for Volkart on the subcontinent as brokers or shroffs, the trading company also employed independent merchants as representatives in diverse European trading cities.[78] The extent to which family traditions had a stabilizing influence is reflected, for example, in the ties between Volkart and the Valette mercantile firm based in Marseille. From the late nineteenth century onwards, Edouard Valette worked for a number of decades as a representative of Volkart in southern France.[79] The close relationship between the two firms was what motivated Volkart to rescue Gabriel Valette, a descendent of Edouard Valette, with a generous loan of 3,000 Swiss francs when the French merchant was on the brink of bankruptcy after World War II.[80] Economic considerations were not explicitly mentioned when the board of directors discussed the bailout. It appears that the partners took it more or less for granted that a company like Volkart would rush to the aid of a long-term business partner who had run into difficulties through no fault of his own. This gesture of solidarity ultimately had a positive impact on Volkart's business activities because it allowed Valette to get back on his feet again and remain a loyal broker for the trading firm in Marseille.[81]

When Volkart began to expand its operations to Latin America in the 1930s, the company did so by cooperating with local export firms like Prado Chaves in Brazil, Peter Schoenfeld and Juan Waelti in Guatemala and Café Capris in Costa Rica. All of these merchant firms were family owned.[82] What from a macro-economic perspective appears as a global commodity market in which thousands of tons of raw cotton and coffee are exchanged annually turns out to be a dense network of family firms around the globe when examined at the micro level. With reference to the stability of family connections in the global economy, Harold James argued that the "DNA chains are the real chains that bind the capitalist economy," adding that the "information gains achieved over time by expanding networks of relationships provided a social capital that complemented financial capital, contributing to efficiency by reducing transaction costs."[83]

Transformation to a Joint-stock Company

As the company continued to grow and its business became increasingly complex, the model of a family-managed general partnership began to reach its limits. But most of the partners were highly skeptical about transforming the firm into a joint-stock company. Although Werner Reinhart had toyed with the idea of making Volkart a stock corporation in the early 1920s, his brother Georg Reinhart was fiercely determined to maintain the model of the general partnership because he found that a joint-stock company was a "cumbersome and impersonal apparatus."[84]

In behind-the-scenes discussions after 1945, Volkart executives gave serious consideration, for the first time ever, to relinquishing the model of a purely family-owned company and allowing foreign capital to be invested in the company. Peter Reinhart, the son of Georg Reinhart and a partner since 1934, said in 1950 that by continuing to focus exclusively on the raw materials business Volkart might be missing out on lucrative diversification opportunities.[85] Shortly thereafter, Peter Reinhart fundamentally questioned the model of a purely family-owned business in which ownership and management of the company were solely in the hands of the family. In his words,

> a more detailed study . . . leads me more or less to the conclusion . . . that having ownership and management as a single entity is not necessarily advantageous. In fact, . . . one does not take greater care of one's own capital than of foreign capital, quite the contrary, and the fact that we primarily risk our own capital when making decisions actually often leads to decisions . . . that we would reject . . . if we were accountable to a third party.

He went on to say that, if capital ownership and management were separated, "then the current heated debate in our company over whether, and to what extent, the Indian business should be reduced would not take place at all . . . or would be influenced by other factors."[86]

These quotes show that the misgivings that many economists have expressed about family firms—i.e., that their histories steeped in tradition caused them to cling too long to outdated structures—were also shared by the very entrepreneurs who had to grapple with these issues. But before this entrepreneurial reorientation could be adopted, Volkart was overtaken to a certain extent by events in South Asia. After the end of the colonial era, the company was forced to transform its branches in India, Pakistan and Ceylon into independent subsidiaries, in which local businessmen had large shares and eventually acquired a majority holding.[87] Volkart subsequently intensified its expansion into the US and Mexican markets, where the company became a major player in the cotton business. Moreover, it established a coffee export organization in Brazil and soon acquired holdings in coffee trading companies in Guatemala and Costa Rica.[88] The old model based on a general partnership was no longer suited to managing this increasingly complex corporate entity. Hence, a new company, Gebrüder Volkart AG, was founded in 1964 to manage the business at the headquarters in Winterthur, and this was followed shortly thereafter by the establishment of two additional firms, Gebrüder Volkart Holding AG and Inpaco AG, which controlled the subsidiaries and holdings in other companies. The capital of the holding was increased between 1966 and 1977 from 12 to 45 million Swiss francs. Shares in the new companies were not floated on the stock exchange, however, but remained in the possession of the Reinhart family.[89] By adopting this restructuring of its business, Volkart was taking its cue from other Swiss trading companies. According to a survey conducted in the mid-1950s on behalf of the Swiss Association of Transit and Global Trading Companies, 35 of the 48 surveyed Swiss trading firms were joint-stock companies, while 15 of these had been run previously as general partnerships or sole proprietorships. Shares of the companies concerned were not traded on the stock exchange, but instead owned by a small number of partners. In a cultural sense, these companies also differed markedly from industrial firms: "In accordance with the character of the transit trade, which is closely tied to specific individuals, personal aspects outweigh institutional ones," said Emil Gsell, a professor at the Handelshochschule St. Gallen and the author of the study, "which explains why we don't have such a pronounced managerial society here as in other companies of a similar size."[90]

In 1973, Volkart introduced a new management structure that for the first time allowed individuals from outside the Reinhart family to assume top-flight positions at the company.[91] Up until then, the partners had always had the last word on managing the company. Before that, executive employees had been involved in practically all important decisions, but it was not until 1973 that their management role in the upper echelons of the firm received formal approval.

Leaving the Trading Business

The year 1981 marked the first time in the history of Volkart that it came to a power struggle over control of the company. Following Peter Reinhart's resignation as chairman of the board, his son Andreas Reinhart issued an ultimatum to the executive board and demanded that he be allowed to take the helm of the company within the next two years. Following the ensuing confrontation, Andreas Reinhart had to leave the firm.[92] In 1984, after the dust had settled, Andreas Reinhart returned to his family's firm as a member of the board and a little over a year later acquired a majority holding from his uncle Balthasar.[93] Under Andreas Reinhart the company soon diversified its operations and made inroads into investment banking and financial services.[94] In the coffee sector, Volkart embarked on a massive expansion course that made it the second-largest firm in the trading of green coffee. However, after the company suffered a number of severe losses, Reinhart decided to sell the coffee division in 1989.[95] A few years later, he withdrew entirely from active business dealings. He ended the activities in the financial sector and in 1999 sold the cotton division, which was the last remnant of the traditional company.[96]

This closed the final chapter of Volkart's history as a trading company. The company was henceforth only active in the real estate sector and in promoting ecological and socially sustainable projects. The end of the Volkart family firm does not, however, mean that the company completely disappeared from sight. Business continued under a new name and new owners, but under the guiding hand of the previous management. Volcafé, the former Volkart coffee division, remained one of the leading traders of coffee in the world, even after it was sold off. And the cotton division lived on in the newly established Volcot company and in the traditional Winterthur cotton trading firm of Paul Reinhart AG, which had also remained a purely family-owned company since its establishment.

Notes

1 Chandler, *The Visible Hand*, 1977; *Scale and Scope*, 2004 [1990].
2 Jones/Rose, "Family Capitalism", 1993; Colli, *The History of Family Business*, 2003; James, *Family Capitalism*, 2006; Landes, *Die Macht der Familie*, 2006.
3 Due to the extremely fragmentary literature on trading companies, it is currently not possible to pinpoint the exact number of such companies.
4 Schäfer, *Familienunternehmen und Unternehmerfamilien*, 2007, 15.
5 Chandler, *Scale and Scope*, 2004 [1990]; Kocka, *Unternehmer in der deutschen Industrialisierung*, 1975; Kocka, "Familie, Unternehmer und Kapitalismus," 1982.
6 See Chapter 3.
7 Casson, "The Family Firm," 2000, 204.
8 James, *Family Capitalism*, 2006, 5–6.
9 For example, Diethelm, 1907, Ralli, 1941.
10 Interview with Peter Zurschmiede, 2008.
11 Sluyterman/Winkelman, "The Dutch Family Firm," 1993, 176.
12 Chandler, *Scale and Scope*, 2004 [1990]; Kocka, *Unternehmer in der deutschen Industrialisierung*, 1975; Kocka, "Familie, Unternehmer und Kapitalismus," 1982.
13 Chandler, *Visible Hand*, 8–9. Similar developments can also be observed in many industrial family companies: Sluyterman/Winkelman, "The Dutch Family Firm," 1993, 176; Epple, "Gebr. Stollwercks Aufstieg zum Multinational," 2007.
14 Tagiuri/Davis, "Bivalent Attributes of the Family Firm," 1996; Simon/Wimmer/Groth, *Mehr-Generationen-Familienunternehmen*, 2005, 17 and 162.
15 Weber, *Die protestantische Ethik*, 1920 [2006]. For a critique of this notion, see Carrier, "Introduction," 1997, 18.
16 Lubinski, *Familienunternehmen*, 2010.
17 Yanagisako, *Producing Culture and Capital*, 2002, 21. This approach fits in very well with Max Weber's theory of action, although it requires leaving aside Weber's overriding distinction between economic and noneconomic goals of social action: Weber, *Wirtschaft und Gesellschaft*, 1972 [1922], 1.
18 See Chapter 1.
19 Killick, "The Cotton Operations of Alexander Brown and Sons," 1977, 169–170; Markovits, The *Global World of Indian Merchants*, 2000; Gorißen, "Der Preis des Vertrauens," 2003.
20 Gorißen, "Der Preis des Vertrauens," 2003, 97.
21 For the evolution of the partnerships at Volkart during the 1870s, see Anderegg, *Chronicle*, 1976, 65, 70, 78–85; VA, Dossier 1, B) Die Teilhaber.
22 Anderegg, *Chronicle*, 1976, 104–105.
23 Anderegg, *Chronicle*, 1976, 137–140.

24 VA, Dossier 1, A) Die Familie und ihre Gründer; Dossier 2, Die Teilhaber II: August Julius Ferdinand Ammann, Partner 1880–1894.

25 The profits were divided among the four partners as follows: Salomon Volkart 25%, Georg Gottfried Volkart 30%, Theodor Reinhart and August F. Ammann each 22.5%: Anderegg, *Chronicle*, 1976, 141.

26 Anderegg, *Chronicle*, 1976, 192–193.

27 Rambousek/Vogt/Volkart, *Volkart*, 1990, 80.

28 VA, Protokolle der Dienstag Konferenzen vom 8. Juni 1920—Okt. 1928: Konferenz vom 28. September 1920.

29 VA, Dossier 62: ex GR persönliches Archiv II, The Family Code of the House of Mitsui, Japan, aufgestellt im siebzehnten Jahrhundert und mein Kommentar dazu vom 10./11. November 1939, 3.

30 V.B. News, no. 14, June 1926, 31.

31 Reinhart, *Gedenkschrift*, 1926, 23.

32 Reinhart, *Aus meinem Leben*, 1931, 47.

33 VA, Partners' Conference (4. Juni 1946–1931. August 1956): Konferenz vom 4. Juni 1946.

34 For a similar development among Dutch industrial companies like Shell, Unilever and Philips, see Sluyterman/Winkelman, "The Dutch Family Firm," 1993, 176.

35 Jones, *Merchants to Multinationals*, 2000, 195–196.

36 Berghoff, "Unternehmenskultur und Herrschaftstechnik". 1997.

37 VA, Dossier 62: ex GR persönliches Archiv II, Geschäftliches Testament mit Beilagen 1921–1925, GR, Geschäftliches Testament, 22 April 1921.

38 Schäfer, *Familienunternehmen und Unternehmerfamilien*, 2007, 162 and 225.

39 Reinhart, *Aus meinem Leben*, 1931, 36–37.

40 One of the artists patronized by Theodor Reinhart was the painter Karl Hofer who was widely traveled and undertook two trips to India, where he met with Georg, Werner and Oskar Reinhart: Hofer, *Erinnerungen eines Malers*, 1953. One of the most prominent artists supported by Georg Reinhart was Hermann Hesse; see Hesse, *Der schwarze König*, 1956.

41 Wachter, *Nachruf im Namen der Arbeitsgemeinschaft der Firma Gebrüder Volkart*, [1951].

42 Rambousek/Vogt/Volkart, *Volkart*, 1990, 49 and 53–54.

43 Rambousek/Vogt/Volkart, *Volkart*, 1990, 55.

44 Lesczenski, *August Thyssen*, 2008.

45 Hettling/Hoffmann, "Der bürgerliche Wertehimmel," 1997. For more on the cultural horizon of businessmen at the time, see Berghoff, "Vermögenseliten in Deutschland und England", 1995

46 SSW, Nachlass Theodor Reinhart, Ms Sch 84, letters from A–G. Reinhart to Theodor Reinhart)/56: Georg Reinhart to Theodor Reinhart, 1894–1911 and Ms Sch 84, letter from A–G. Reinhart to Theodor Reinhart)/ 60: Georg Reinhart to Theodor Reinhart, 1899–1901; Nachlass Werner Reinhart, Dep MK 397/5: Werner Reinhart to Theodor and Lilly Reinhart-Volkart.

47 VA, Dossier 62: ex GR persönliches Archiv II, The Family Code of the House of Mitsui, Japan, aufgestellt im siebzehnten Jahrhundert und mein Kommentar dazu vom 10./11. November 1939, 5; Reinhart, *Aus meinem Leben*, 63.

48 VA, Dossier 2: Die Teilhaber II.

49 Reinhart, *Aus meinem Leben*, 1931, 85ff.

50 VA, Dossier 1: B) Die Teilhaber, 1) Salomon Volkart, 3. Privat-Copierbuch: 9.1.1867–1825.8.1870: 23.4.1871 Sal. Volkart to Hr. Scheuermann.

51 James, Family Capitalism, 2006, 14–15.

52 Claude Markovits has made a similar observation for Indian family firms: Markovits, The *Global World of Indian Merchants*, 2000, 261.

53 Reinhart, *Aus meinem Leben*, 1931, 76–77

54 VA, Dossier 62: ex GR persönliches Archiv II, The Family Code of the House of Mitsui, Japan, aufgestellt im siebzehnten Jahrhundert und mein Kommentar dazu vom 10./11. November 1939, 6–7.

55 VA, Dossier 62: ex GR persönliches Archiv II, The Family Code of the House of Mitsui, Japan, aufgestellt im siebzehnten Jahrhundert und mein Kommentar dazu vom 10./11. November 1939, 2.

56 VA, Dossier 63: ex GR persönliches Archiv III, Mappe: Aufgabe des Rubbergeschäftes und Liquidation von Singapore 1929, letter from Georg Reinhart to Werner Reinhart, 9 September 1929, and memo from GR, 12 September 29, 9:30 a.m.

57 VA, Dossier 62: ex GR persönliches Archiv II, The Family Code of the House of Mitsui, Japan, aufgestellt im siebzehnten Jahrhundert und mein Kommentar dazu vom 10./11. November 1939, 3.

58 VA, Dossier 62: ex GR persönliches Archiv II, Geschäftliches Testament mit Beilagen 1921–1925, GR, Geschäftliches Testament (last will and testament), 22 April 1921

59 Nelson, "Evolutionary Theorising about Economic Change," 1994.

60 Colli, *The History of Family Business*, 2003, 24.

61 VA, Dossier 62: ex GR persönliches Archiv II, The Family Code of the House of Mitsui, Japan, aufgestellt im siebzehnten Jahrhundert und mein Kommentar dazu vom 10./11. November 1939, 17.

62 VA, Dossier 62: ex GR persönliches Archiv II, Geschäftliches Testament mit Beilagen 1921–1925, GR, Gedanken zum Societätsvertrag der Firma, 5 December 1924.

63 Casson, "The Family Firm," 2000, 202. Also see Colli, *The History of Family Business*, 2003, 15.

64 VA, Dossier 63: ex GR persönliches Archiv III, Mappe: Aufgabe des Rubbergeschäftes und Liquidation von Singapore 1929, GR, Memorandum I, 23 July 1929, 14–15 and 17–18.

65 VA, Dossier 62: ex GR persönliches Archiv II, The Family Code of the House of Mitsui, Japan, aufgestellt im siebzehnten Jahrhundert und mein Kommentar dazu vom 10./11. November 1939, 12–13.

66 VA, Dossier 62: ex GR persönliches Archiv II, The Family Code of the House of Mitsui, Japan, aufgestellt im siebzehnten Jahrhundert und mein Kommentar dazu vom 10./11. November 1939, 14.

67 VA, Dossier 62: ex GR persönliches Archiv II, The Family Code of the House of Mitsui, Japan, aufgestellt im siebzehnten Jahrhundert und mein Kommentar dazu vom 10./11. November 1939, 8–9.

68 Reinhart, *Gedenkschrift*, 1926, 13ff.

69 V.B. News, no. 14, June 1926, 19. See Chapter 6 for more on the concept of the corporate family.

70 Isler, *Winterthur in Wort und Bild*, 1895, 152.

71 Reinhart, "Rede zur Hundertjahrfeier, o.J". [1951], 14.

72 VA, Dossier 1, B) Die Teilhaber, 1) Salomon Volkart, 3. Privat-Copierbuch 9.1.1867–1825.8.1870: 22.7.1869 Sal. Volkart to Spitteler, acting BM Cochin.

73 VA, Dossier 12: Tuticorin / Madras, 9. V.B. News issued by Madras in 1942–1943, vol. 1, no. 2, October 1942. This passage was printed almost verbatim in an article printed in 1936 in *Volkart Brothers Engineering News*: VA, Dossier 50: Engineering/Voltas Schriften, Dokumente etc.: *Volkart Brothers Engineering News* (1936–1940), vol. 1, nr. 1, January 1936, 2.

74 Reinhart, "Rede zur Hundertjahrfeier," [1951], 14.

75 VA, Dossier 44, VBH Guidelines 1970–1983: Peter Reinhart, Cotton and other Commodity Operations and Discretions, 21 May 1970. See also Chapter 14.

76 Jones, *Merchants to Multinationals*, 2000, 216.

77 Colli, *The History of Family Business*, 2003, 41ff.
78 For more on this, see Chapters 2 and 3 of this book.
79 V.B. News, no. 9, December 1923, 22.
80 VA, Konferenz-Protokolle 4. Juli 1947–1928. Juni 1949: Konferenz vom 6. Oktober 1947.
81 SSW, Nachlass Georg Reinhart, Ms GR 32/102: Gabriel Valette, Marseille, to Georg Reinhart, Winterthur, 20 December 1951.
82 See Chapter 13.
83 James, "Family Capitalism," 2006, 2 and 14–15.
84 VA, Dossier 62: ex GR persönliches Archiv II, Geschäftliches Testament mit Beilagen 1921–1925, GR, Geschäftliches Testament, 22 April, 1921
85 VA, Dossier 18: Winterthur I, 1 Table of Events: Notiz von Peter Reinhart, 1950.
86 VA, Dossier 20: VB Organisation 1952/53—Peter Reinhart, Ueberlegungen zur Frage der Gesellschaftsform, 29.4.52.
87 See Chapter 12.
88 See Chapter 13.
89 VA, Dossier 18: Winterthur I, 1 Table of Events: Bekanntmachung vom Oktober 1964, Winterthur; Rambousek/Vogt/Volkart, Volkart, 1990, 171.
90 WA, Handschriften (HS) 421: Verband schweizerischer Transit- und Welthandelsfirmen, Basel, F6: Korrespondenz und zwei Entwürfe, betr. die Enquête über den Transithandel, durchgeführt von Prof. Dr. Gsell an der Handelshochschule in St. Gallen, 1953–1958: Der schweizerische Transithandel. Ergebnisse der Enquête 1954, June 1955, 2–3.
91 Rambousek/Vogt/Volkart, *Volkart*, 1990, 171.
92 Weltwoche, 21 April 1994; Cash, 11 January 2002.
93 VA, Dossier 45: Betriebsmitteilungen 1965–1986, Volkart Brothers Ltd. Betriebsmitteilungen 1978–1986: Betriebsmitteilung, 27 March 1984; Betriebsmitteilung, 4 November 1985.
94 *NZZ am Sonntag*, 27 April 2008; Reinhart, "Nachwort," 1990, 200.
95 *Schweizerische Handelszeitung*, 10 April 1986; *Tages-Anzeiger*, 9 May 1989; *Weltwoche*, 29 April 1989; *Weltwoche*, 9 September 1999. See also Chapter 13.
96 *Der Landbote*, 22 November 2006.

6 Keeping Everyone in the Fold
The Employees and
the Corporate Family

In early 1936, senior officials at Volkart headquarters in Winterthur made an unpleasant discovery when it emerged that a European employee in Bombay had "committed fraud." In a subsequent letter to Bombay, they criticized the naivety of the management there, which apparently thought that the integrity of the employee was, in their words, "beyond all doubt to such a degree" that it "could feel justified in paying no heed . . . to all the signals and warnings." Senior management in Winterthur reflected on how it could avoid such incidents in the future and came to the following conclusion:

> This entire episode shows that it is not enough to monitor the books and check the math. Instead, . . . [we need to engender] an atmosphere of trust among management and personnel . . . that makes it considerably more difficult, if not impossible, for employees, as well as their bosses, to conceal disloyal behavior.[1]

The case of the fraudulent employee in Bombay was no isolated incident. In fact, it shed light on a fundamental problem faced by the Volkart trading firm, which, like all companies, was not a homogenous entity, but rather consisted of coalitions of collaborating individuals with highly diverse interests. From an institutional economics perspective, these "micropolitical" circumstances can be interpreted as transaction costs for the company.[2] The enormous distances between the parent company and its overseas branches often made it particularly difficult for the partners to keep tabs on their employees abroad. This made the principal-agent problem a major challenge for trading firms. Especially when trading companies reduced their usage costs of the market by shifting certain transactions into the company, the resulting growing complexity of the firm generated new, in-company transaction costs.[3]

In principle all companies encountered such problems. In contrast to manufacturing companies, in which many work processes could be standardized and easily monitored by company owners, trading firms were unable to establish set routines for key individual tasks like making selections, negotiating prices and establishing contacts with clients. Moreover, although trading firms had highly centralized organizational structures, they relied heavily on the individual decisions and judgments of their employees during daily business activities. In a bid to maintain control of the situation, the partners instituted a series of measures to curb opportunistic behavior by their employees. For instance, the branches had to submit regular financial statements to the headquarters and were regularly inspected by representatives from the main office or the company owners in person. In addition to regulations and economic incentives, establishing a trust-based corporate culture was viewed as a possible means of tackling fraudulent behavior by employees, as shown by the opening quote of this chapter. Of course, a substantial amount of the social and cultural capital of trading companies rested on their specific business structures, which were characterized by both the large distances between principals and agents (branch managers) as well as the specific competencies of employees, and this presumably made them far more inclined to embrace a consensus-oriented corporate culture than industrial manufacturers.[4]

Companies are far more than organizations that are solely devoted to maximizing profits. They are also social collectives that provide a sense of purpose and identity for many of those involved.[5] Company traditions play an important role in decision-making, particularly in family-controlled firms, and this indicates a certain path dependency. A potential conflict exists between diverse economic interests, such as those of shareholders and employees, and a shared set of basic values that serve as a code of conduct in many companies. Hence, a company can be interpreted as a cooperative and confrontational field of activity that, even in its economic core functions, is inconceivable without an overarching cultural framework.[6] As will be shown in this chapter, the concept of a family enterprise, based on the example of the Volkart company, was an—ultimately successful—attempt to create a cultural code for the mutual dependencies of employers and employees. Although this concept had pronounced paternalistic traits, it also allowed employees to assert their own needs.

Problems with Employees in the Early Phase of the Company

After the company rode a wave of success during the American Civil War, Salomon Volkart, who ran the trading firm more or less single-handedly after his brother's death, complained repeatedly of frictions with his employees in South Asia during the late 1860s and early 1870s. This largely had to do with the growing need for more personnel as the company expanded its activities. In 1860, only nine European employees were working in the branches in India and Ceylon, which soon proved to be hardly enough staff to keep pace with burgeoning sales and the rapid establishment of new agencies.[7] However, there were only a limited number of reliable candidates for employment available in Europe who were familiar with the intricacies of the Indian trade. Up until the 1870s, Volkart recruited new employees primarily in India and Ceylon. Many of these were Germans, who were culturally close to the Swiss, while others were Europeans born in Asia, so-called Eurasians, whose working methods were often not to the taste of the company founder.[8] To rectify the situation, the headquarters in Winterthur soon launched a training program for apprentices who, after three years, were transferred to India or Ceylon. From the 1880s onwards, new European employees were, as a rule, only hired in Winterthur, which was yet another sign of the increasing centralization of decision-making within the company.[9]

Monitoring overseas employees was hampered by the enormous distances between the company's far-flung outposts, rendering it extremely difficult for management to ensure that staff were adhering to guidelines and creating a constant source of exasperation, primarily with the branches in Colombo, Cochin and Karachi, which were plagued by losses. Salomon Volkart considered closing these branches on a number of occasions.[10] In his opinion, the heads of the branches were primarily to blame for the poor results because they did not follow his instructions. In the summer of 1869, for instance, Volkart issued a reprimand for sloppy management to A. Spitteler, who worked for the firm in Cochin and was involved in managing the Colombo branch, which had assumed the management and financing of a number of coffee plantations in Ceylon and incurred large losses. Volkart blamed Spitteler for the plantation deal, which "not only produced no earnings, but caused us considerable damage." It turns out that Spitteler miscalculated the amount of green coffee that was required to produce a hundredweight of dried and cleaned coffee beans.

> I don't know how you drew such an unfortunate conclusion and it is beyond my comprehension how you, based on this very assumption, could have ventured to continue to operate throughout the entire season without hitting upon the very obvious idea of conducting a small-scale test. . . . This is completely mystifying to me and a failure on your part that deserves a sharp rebuke.

What also annoyed Salomon Volkart was the fact that his staff in Colombo had only gradually informed him of the reasons behind the ill-fated business deal. In fact, he was positively outraged over errors made in Colombo "that all of us here had to alleviate with the greatest of effort, . . . and which left us red in the face with embarrassment." For instance, the Colombo branch was a full year behind in its bookkeeping: "What irresponsible negligence! No wonder such blatant mistakes like this occurred."[11]

The lamentable state of the various branches was a constant threat to the existence of the company. It was also problematic that local managers received a share of the profits that they produced—in the 1870s, it was 10 or 20 percent of the annual results of their branches—while any losses were completely absorbed by the parent company and thus came out of the partners' pockets.[12] Circumstances did not improve until Johann G. Sigg (1871) and Georg Gottfried Volkart (1875) became partners in the firm and Theodor Reinhart, who was an exceedingly competent merchant, joined the company in 1875 and was likewise made partner in 1879. Reinhart traveled to India and Ceylon in 1877–1878 on an inspection tour. To his dismay, he discovered that all European employees in Colombo were doing deals on the side, in direct violation of the express ban by the company management and without its knowledge. In their defense, the staff members argued that the cost of living in Colombo was much higher than in other places in South Asia, and that this made it impossible for them to accumulate savings that they could fall back on following their return to Europe.

Reinhart had to admit that the employees had a point. In a letter to the headquarters in Winterthur, he wrote that the salaries of the Europeans at Volkart in Colombo were too low "to encourage them to work from six in the morning till six in the evening in the Indian climate." He went on to say that if profits at the branch did not increase dramatically, the branch manager, for instance, would not even be able to amass enough wealth to allow him to "be able to earn enough interest . . . to maintain a living for himself and a small family later in Europe if he did not engage in speculation to earn money on the side here." In Reinhart's opinion, the main consideration for the company was

> that we . . . can benefit from the collected experience of a manager . . . and to do so we must earn their loyalty and offer them a future, otherwise they will view the position as a stopgap solution until something better comes along and feel that their interests are not sufficiently aligned with our own.[13]

Reinhart's report resulted in a wage increase for the employees. It was also made clear to them that the company would, as a matter of principle, no longer tolerate the staff doing business deals on their own behalf, although in the 1860s and 1870s the partners had given various employees permission to conduct such transactions.[14]

Inspections and Regulations

Aside from raising the wages of employees in India, Theodor Reinhart introduced a wide range of organizational reforms.[15] Since Reinhart had noted during his visits to India and Ceylon that many employees had difficulties with accounting, from the late 1870s onwards the branches were regularly visited by inspectors to ensure that the books were in order and instructions from headquarters were followed. Furthermore, the managers of the individual branches had to send statistical reports and balance sheets to Winterthur on a regular basis so company owners were kept up to date on the performance of the business. Individual employees found the reforms extremely irritating, but they eventually had to accept them.[16]

The partners, however, were not content to make do with dispatching inspectors and passing regulations. They regularly visited the branches to form their own opinions of the employees and the way the local agencies were organized. Werner Reinhart echoed this notion in a letter that he wrote during an inspection tour of the branches in India: "I have once again come to the conclusion that even such a short 'inspection' on site as I have performed here provides incomparably more insights into matters than extensive correspondence and personnel reports could ever do."[17] During a visit to the Karachi branch in 1923, he even engaged in intensive discussions with the staff and with businessmen in the city's clubs to assess which employees should be entrusted with managing Volkart Karachi in the future.[18]

Business contacts with other companies and banks gave the partners at Volkart important clues about possible misconduct by the trading firm's employees. For instance, in 1932 a member of the board of directors of the Swiss Bank Corporation confided in Georg Reinhart, who was a member of the bank's advisory board at the time, that an employee at Volkart Bombay had accumulated a sizable debt with the bank. The employee had apparently lost money from private stock market deals that had gone sour. Although the employee was making regular installments to pay off the debt (and was in fact completely debt-free again by 1937), such speculative deals amounted to a breach of contract, and since there was a risk that an indebted employee might misappropriate funds, after receiving the tipoff Georg Reinhart gave concrete consideration to "possibly replacing" the staff member in question.[19]

Lifelong Employment and Social Benefits

The long-term employment conditions largely contributed to the employees' loyalty to the company. Until the 1950s, employees were hired for limited periods of time, but the first five-year contract was always followed by additional four-year contracts[20] and employees could always count on their contracts being renewed if they diligently performed their duties. Many employees continued to work for Volkart throughout their entire professional lives. Europeans working for the company in India were usually employed at the company headquarters after their return to Europe. Such long-standing working relationships were also common at other trading companies. This should come as no surprise since the employees' expertise— their knowledge of products, business practices and local conditions— was vital to the success of a trading firm. This knowledge was the company's cultural capital and was inseparably linked to the individual employees.[21]

In an internal memo written in 1939, Georg Reinhart also referred to a further advantage of long-term employment conditions, namely the positive socialization of the employees: "Whenever possible, it is recommended to train junior staff ourselves, as this gives us a better idea of their *character traits* and we can mold these traits to a certain degree." To gain the loyalty of the employees, it was essential that the company always treated them fairly. Georg Reinhart put it this way:

> When dismissing older individuals who have not reached retirement age, the company has consistently compensated them in a liberal manner, and even treated fallible employees with generosity. The firm owes its prestige in large part to the *humane* and liberal treatment that it grants its employees.[22]

These were not empty words. During the second half of the 1920s, Volkart suffered heavy losses due to the crisis in world trade. Nevertheless, even during these loss-making years, the partners paid their employees a bonus, even though these bonuses had originally been conceived as a profit-sharing measure. This money could only be dispersed because the company had decided to forgo all write-offs and returns on capital that the partners had invested in the company. What's more, the partners contributed hundreds of thousands of Swiss francs from their private fortunes to pay the bonuses. But instead of asking the employees to be thankful for this measure, the partners apologized in a circular letter in 1926 for the fact that the poor business results did not allow for the same bonuses as during boom times. The partners appealed to the employees that they needed to think like businessmen in the current situation, and not as mere wage earners:

> We hope that each and every employee feels like an actual partner in the business, sharing in the results, but also in the efforts and concerns and the constructive work. We hope to engender a genuine feeling of community with our employees.[23]

In an internal letter addressing this issue, Georg Reinhart specifically pointed to the difference between partners who, like the Reinhart brothers, managed their own company and shareholders who merely invested their capital in a firm that was organized as a joint-stock company. Aside from their financial investments, he said that the shareholders had no connection to the company and the employees who worked for it. But the Volkart partners had an entirely different approach:

> In our company, the 'investors' view their employees as their *collaborators* and, in turn, also hope to be viewed by them as their *collaborators*. In my opinion, this collaboration can engender a feeling of mutual trust and solidarity, even in difficult times, . . . that a joint-stock company cannot expect to the same degree.[24]

It is remarkable that in his letter, which was solely directed to the members of the board, Georg Reinhart did not once rationalize this generosity with economic arguments, such as the notion that it would be expedient for the company to ensure the long-term loyalty of highly qualified employees with such measures. Instead, it appears that the partners saw themselves as bound to an unwritten law that served as a guideline for how a family firm like Volkart should treat its employees.

Social benefits within the company were gradually expanded during the first half of the twentieth century. In 1916, Volkart instituted for its European and indigenous employees in India and Ceylon a staff provident fund with equal contributions made by the company and employees. In 1919, a similar pension fund was established for employees in Switzerland, in 1938 for employees in Germany, in 1942 for the workforce in the US and in 1948 for staff members in Britain.[25] These pension funds were doubtlessly introduced by the partners at Volkart to stabilize the relationship between the company and its employees and to win the long-term loyalty of highly qualified personnel. But the establishment of the Swiss pension fund was also driven by entirely banal tax-related motives. From 1916 onwards, corporate profits in Switzerland that were invested in in-company pension funds were exempt from taxation. The corresponding law was originally intended as a social policy measure to balance out the introduction of the war profit tax, but it remained in force after 1918 as a tax measure in support of occupational pensions. As a result, numerous companies established company foundations for retirement plans or concluded group policies with life insurance companies.[26]

Rhetorical Means of Forging a Sense of Community

The sense of solidarity between employees and the company was not forged with social benefits and long-term employment conditions alone. Rhetorical means were also used in an effort to foster the notion of the company as a large community. In a speech to the employees of the Winterthur headquarters in January 1919, Theodor Reinhart said that the company owed its success "not least to the tight-meshed union of head and limbs and the outstanding esprit de corps throughout the ranks." In order to keep pace with stiff competition, he said it was essential that every member of the company "see himself more as a 'servant of the firm' than as an advocate of his individual interests or, if you will, as a soldier rather than a soldier of fortune." Speaking on behalf of the partners, he asked the younger members of the firm to bear in mind "that you belong to an elite corps of the merchants of the global wholesale trade" and as such

> it is a noble and fine duty of honor for each and every one of you, and especially for those who serve the firm in distant lands, far from the

eyes of your bosses or superiors, to remain impeccable before your own conscience and in the eyes of others.[27]

The notion of service to a company resurfaced a number of years later in a speech by the head of Volkart's Bombay branch to commemorate the firm's 75th anniversary. The manager asked the rhetorical question of what motivates people to devote themselves to a company's success and answered it as follows:

> In an organization like the Firm of Volkart Brothers the spirit of service, the guiding ideal must never be lost sight of . . . its aim must be to accumulate the means wherewith to render ever greater service to the peoples in the four corners of the earth. . . . Only if we admit, if we recognize the truth in the saying that 'man does not live by bread alone'—that is by money alone— . . . can we hope in the fullness of our time to look back upon work well done.[28]

These appeals were more than just mere rhetoric. They were an expression of the company's self-image, i.e., that a company's main purpose could not be to generate the highest possible profit, but rather that the goal was to provide a service to its customers. It should be noted that it was only after 1918 that the Volkart partners used such rhetorical methods to enhance the company's team spirit. Indeed, in the wake of the business expansion after World War I, it was no longer a matter of course that individual members of the firm knew each other on a personal basis, and this meant that direct contact had to be replaced by in-house media like *V.B. News*, an elaborately designed employee magazine that first appeared in 1920. This publication aimed to "forge a team spirit that connects our employees across three regions of the globe," to quote a passage from the anniversary issue of 1926. In the editorial of the first issue, the purpose of the publication was described as follows:

> Contact is the basis of good understanding and good understanding is the basis of friendship and where friendship guides the promotion of mutual interests, the success cannot be wanting. . . . [T]he first number of 'The V. B. News' goes out into the world to assure our friends in branch offices, agencies and sub-agencies of the interest we take in their work and their recreation and in their well-being in general.[29]

Employees wrote detailed articles about their experiences during their vacation trips through the Indian backcountry and gave descriptions of the idiosyncrasies of Japanese culture. *V.B. News* also served as a means of informing employees of new business developments along with changes in personnel and service anniversaries. Regular articles were published on the work of individual branches, such as the fine points of the trade in coconut products on the Malabar Coast, the intricacies of the American cotton trade and common practices revolving around machine imports to East Asia. Some articles introduced important European agents or Indian brokers, and on a number of occasions employees had an opportunity to read about the financial sector or find out more about maritime transport. The magazine included photos of the workforce that featured the staff of the individual branches, in which the company hierarchy was typically symbolized by placing the managers at the center of the photos, either seated or standing, and grouping their subordinates around them.[30] *V.B. News* was thus an attempt to engender a feeling of connectedness with the company that could no longer be maintained through face-to-face contact due to the enormous distances between the individual branches.

Metaphorical images to describe the firm frequently appeared in in-company publications from the 1920s onwards and were particularly profound in the speeches given to mark diverse company anniversaries. When Volkart celebrated its 75th year of existence, Georg Reinhart gave voice to his conviction that the main purpose of such commemorations was to convey the "good spirit, this collective will . . . that usually operates as a hidden force below the surface," adding that

> we are thus joined today by thousands of people of virtually every race, nationality and religion throughout the world in celebration of the sense of community that we share under a unifying flag, which bears the initials V.B. Japanese, Chinese, Malays, Indians, Parsis, Swiss, Germans, Englishmen and Americans today feel more than ever that they are part of an organism that extends across the globe and that, regardless of state borders and national rivalries, lives its own life and embodies its own laws.

He then took his listeners on a mental journey from the branches in Japan and China to the agencies in Singapore, India and Ceylon, followed by a visit to the Winterthur headquarters and onward to the branches in Bremen, Hamburg, Liverpool and New York to draw the audience's attention once again to the worldwide organization of the trading firm.[31]

Reinhart's speech was referred to 25 years later by a top official at Volkart's Bombay branch as he gave an address to mark the firm's 100th anniversary. He pointed out that the company had expanded even further in the meantime and now had established numerous branches in the US to purchase cotton:

> It is now five o'clock Indian standard time. While our friends in Japan may already be thinking of going home, on the other side of the world, in California, Mr. Hurschler, whom many of you will remember, and his staff, are still fast asleep. We might, therefore, say that the sun does not set on Volkart Brothers.[32]

This employee also compared the trading firm to an organism and implied that all parts of the company were interconnected and could not survive without each other. And yet the firm

> has the advantage over the human body of constant rejuvenation, pro-
> vided the people who make up the firm are willing to keep it alive. They
> take over from their predecessors, they hand over to their successors
> after working and improving and enlarging.[33]

A metaphor from nature with similar implications was also used by Peter Reinhart to mark the company's anniversary in 1951. He confessed that the image of the tree with which his father had once compared the company had always depressed him because every tree is destined to die one day. If this metaphor were true, he said, then today customers would have to do business with a young company, and not with an old one like Volkart. "But fortunately the comparison is simply inaccurate. The company cannot be compared to a tree, but instead is analogous to a forest. . . . Who talks about an 'old forest'?" He argued that a forest continuously renews itself and, barring a natural disaster or falling victim to the foolishness of a ruthlessly exploitive authority, it can thrive for centuries.[34]

The Metaphor of a Corporate Family

All of these metaphors underscored the longevity, vibrancy and sense of community that characterized the Volkart firm. This also particularly applies to the metaphor of a corporate family, which was regularly used by the partners and employees to describe their relationship to the company. When Werner Reinhart died in August 1951, Heinrich Wachter, who had been a leading figure at Volkart for many years, expressed his condolences to the family of the deceased in a speech that he gave at the church funeral service in Winterthur. "But," he added,

> you are not the only ones who have suffered a terrible loss. There exists
> a second family that also feels an overwhelming sense of heartfelt grief.
> I am thinking of the vast working community of the Volkart Brothers
> firm, from our young apprentices and interns to our employees, depart-
> ment heads and agents, and including the staff of the overseas branches
> all over the world and our numerous representatives abroad, right up to
> the closest aides and colleagues of our deceased principal.[35]

This statement shows that the employees' close ties were not limited to the company, but also extended to the owners, which is hardly surprising as the business, which remained a family firm, was virtually identical with the partners. Harold James argues that the personal contact between company owners and employees is a major advantage of family enterprises. It stands

to reason that when companies are associated with a specific group of individuals, it guarantees employees a high degree of continuity and enhances
their ties to the business.[36] This was clearly recognized as an advantage by
the partners at Volkart. In an internal exposé written in 1923, Georg Reinhart said that the

> fact that we are a purely family-run business gives our employees the
> secure feeling that the company capital will stay put and that they are
> not working for partners who one fine day will decide to withdraw their
> money from the firm because they think they have earned enough.[37]

The personal connection to the company also remained strong when
employees were dispatched by the headquarters in Winterthur to work in
branch offices on remote continents. This was partly because all of the European employees knew the partners on a personal basis, since all hirings of
Europeans were made in Winterthur from the 1880s onwards. But it should
also be noted that the owner family constituted an important element in
the company's symbolic self-portrayal. Beyond the importance of whoever
happened to be at the helm of the company at any point in time, the former
partners, particularly the two company founders, played a key role here.
Their portraits were a regular feature of in-house publications, such as com-
memorative volumes and company magazines.[38] Likewise, photos of the
partners and the company founders often adorned the walls of individual
branch offices, in a sense allowing these esteemed individuals to look over
the shoulders of employees as they worked (Figure 6.1).

One example of the extensive close-knit relationships maintained among
the partners and their top managers is that Georg Reinhart became the godfather of the daughter of Ernst Müller-Renner, who headed the cotton division at Volkart.[39] But close personal contact also played an important role in
relations with the workforce, as reflected in a speech given by a long-standing
employee at a memorial ceremony for the late Georg Reinhart in 1955:

> It was always a pleasure to speak with Mr. Georg Reinhart about busi-
> ness problems, . . . and every encounter with him renewed the comfort-
> ing awareness that a distinguished-minded executive stood at the helm
> of our company. Indeed, he succeeded in spurring each individual to
> work to their full capacity, for the good of the company and the satis-
> faction of its workforce.

The employee ended his address with the following comment:

> For all of us who have had the honor and good fortune to work in our
> company for many years under the judicious leadership of Mr. Georg
> Reinhart, he was and shall always remain a fine example of a sensitive,
> noble man, a benevolent principal and a model employer.[40]

Figure 6.1 Robert Scherer, co-manager of the Bombay Volkart branch in 1941. A picture of Salomon Volkart hangs on the left-hand wall (VA, Dossier 104: Photos Bombay, Bombay 1941)

On the occasion of the 100th anniversary, the same employee had already commented on the social attitude of the partners, which he illustrated by pointing out that they always handed out bonuses at the end of the year:

> And how happy we are every year, with Christmas just around the corner and in accordance with good old traditions, to be called one by one, from the oldest agent to the youngest apprentice, into Mr. Georg Reinhart's office, where the four partners have gathered, and many of us with our hearts beating somewhat faster, . . . to receive from their hands the wonderful New Year's bonuses.[41]

This description shows that the relationship between employees and partners was not purely of a business nature. It is no coincidence that the partners personally distributed the special bonuses to the employees shortly before Christmas, the family festival *par excellence*, and that they received it with racing hearts like little children, all of which reflects that this relationship largely took its cue from the symbolic family order.

It goes without saying that these formal speeches at public events like memorial services and company anniversaries followed the convention that no one was allowed to say anything negative about their superiors or the company. Nevertheless, they were far more than a staged rendition of a polished corporate self-image. Instead, they reflected the partners' thoroughly accommodating attitude toward their employees, such as during the crisis in the late 1920s. Furthermore, reminiscing over the generosity of former company owners could also be interpreted as an appeal to the current partners to continue to respect this tradition in the future.

Marriage Proposals

The "Volkart spirit"[42] that was frequently invoked in in-company publications had clear paternalistic tendencies, as witnessed by the father-son relationship between company owners and employees. For instance, one long-standing employee made reference to the "fatherly, wise and often humorous advice" that Theodor Reinhart gave to "the greenhorns who were leaving for India."[43] However, the company also carried a great deal of weight when it came to the question of when and whether its employees were allowed to marry. Even if it was not explicitly mentioned in the work contracts, there was an unwritten law that employees who were sent overseas were not able to marry until the second contract, in other words at the age of 28. If they wanted to marry earlier, the partners expected the employees to ask for their permission. It was even common for them to present their future spouses to the partners in Winterthur.[44]

This tight control over marriages stemmed from the company owners' firm conviction that the family circumstances of their employees had a direct influence on their ability to work and on the firm's public reputation. In a speech given by Peter Reinhart to mark the company's anniversary in 1951, he extended explicit greetings to the wives of the employees and added that the partners knew all too well

> how much the company owes to the direct and indirect cheerful and patient support with which you, ladies, regularly encourage your husbands and spur them on to new deeds when they occasionally come home from work feeling glum and upset.[45]

The fear of the partners that a relationship that was deemed disreputable could have a negative impact on the company's business is reflected in the following episode from the 1920s. Georg Reinhart was extremely concerned that the behavior of the wife of the head of Volkart's Shanghai branch could damage the company's reputation in China. He was upset not only about the woman's apparent shady past, but also about her current behavior, which, according to Reinhart, was the reason why the head of the branch "did not keep company with the right circles in Shanghai." According to Reinhart, a young Swiss man was unabashedly playing the role of manfriend to the wife of the Volkart manager. To make matters worse, a Volkart employee who had earlier lived for a time with the Shanghai boss had allegedly also had carnal relations with the man's wife. Reinhart suspected—wrongly, as it turned out—that these tawdry circumstances were the reason why Volkart had not been granted the Chinese concession for Swiss electrical engineering firm Brown, Boveri & Cie.[46] It was therefore decided that the Shanghai branch could not remain under the same management. But since the manager in question had done nothing wrong, he could not be dismissed. Hence, the partners at Volkart opted to wait until his contract expired and then simply not renew it.[47] Sure enough, the Shanghai branch received a new manager four years later.[48]

It was only in exceptional cases that the conduct of an employee's wife posed such a problem for the company's business. Yet even under normal circumstances the climatic stresses in Asia and the personal adjustments that were necessary to adapt to a foreign culture were so immense that the attitude of an employee's wife could have a decisive influence on whether or not he felt at home in Asia. Not surprisingly, Werner Reinhart noted with great satisfaction during a visit to Karachi that the wife of an employee was "delighted with India" and that she "copes well with everything and knows how to navigate social circles with great skill." He also observed that another employee's wife, who received no support from her husband in settling in, had to contend with far greater difficulties: "She has reportedly already complained to the older Swiss at our company that she doesn't like it at all out here and that she is bored." Reinhart drew a direct connection between these private circumstances and the company's business success: "I am addressing these questions because the home of a manager also plays a certain role for the branch office."[49]

When it came to the establishment of a paternalistic corporate culture, Volkart was by far not an isolated case. Other firms, such as industrial manufacturing companies, maintained similar corporate cultures far into the twentieth century.[50] But Volkart is a rare example of a globally active large-scale enterprise that managed to maintain this symbolic order, in large part thanks to the fact that the company remained family owned throughout its entire history and members of the owner family constantly took part in managing the firm. Another likely reason for this was that, despite its prodigious sales, the trading company only employed a relatively small number of European staff members, most of whom were personally acquainted with the partners and, in a certain sense, formed the inner circle of the corporate family. In 1924, Volkart employed only 150 Europeans, but it had a far greater number of non-Europeans on the payroll, including more than 2,200 workers who received monthly salaries and another 2,800 day laborers.[51] This non-European workforce represented the outer circle of the corporate family. Most of them never met the partners in person and, at most, only had a symbolic connection to them.

Blackmail, Attempted Fraud and Speculative Activities

To what extent did Volkart actually succeed in using controls, regulations, moral appeals and cultural ideals to prevent employees from damaging the company by engaging in speculative activities and embezzlement? Judging by the company's own version of events, it was relatively successful. For instance, on the occasion of the company's anniversary in 1951 a long-standing employee thanked the partners on behalf of his colleagues:

> I would like to extend my very special thanks to you for something that cannot be expressed in money: for the wonderful spirit of trust throughout our company, and for the gracious and heartfelt treatment that we have always enjoyed from you.[52]

But the actual state of affairs within the company was not always so harmonious. Fraud, speculation and attempted blackmail by employees could not be completely averted. In the early 1930s, for example, the company realized that ten years earlier the manager of the New York branch had cost the company more than $40,000 by engaging in unauthorized stock market speculation—a belated discovery that does not exactly speak in favor of the in-house control mechanisms instituted by the partners.[53] At any rate, Georg Reinhart said:

> The firm runs the risk of being damaged in a similar manner . . . through unauthorized speculation by dishonest employees in the future unless ways and means are found of preventing such unauthorized transactions. The possibilities of suffering losses are theoretically unlimited and could, in a worst-case scenario, lead to the loss of all of our company assets.[54]

Another difficulty facing management was that, as a trading firm, Volkart was bound to discretion in its business dealings, and this made it highly vulnerable. The company was especially exposed when disgruntled employees left the firm because they could use their knowledge to blackmail their former employers. This is exactly what happened when Spitteler, the former manager of the Cochin branch, sued the company in the 1870s after he was dismissed for incurring major losses.[55] Salomon Volkart eventually paid a settlement to prevent "an open trial that would give the public insights into the innermost confidential aspects of the Cochin business," as Georg Gottfried Volkart wrote in a letter in 1874.[56]

All of these examples show that Volkart was highly successful in developing a system to control its employees and maintain a sense of community that was stabilized by excellent social benefits and the ideals of the corporate family.[57] Nonetheless, opportunism posed a constant menace, as the conflict of interest between employees and owners continued to exist and the asymmetrical information situation of its employees stationed on the other side of the globe made it impossible for the owners to completely control their workforce.

Notes

1 VA, Dossier 24: I/P/C Terms of Local Staff, IV. Branches: General staff terms/ Unions, 9: Winterthur to Bombay, 30 May 1936.

2 Berghoff, *Moderne Unternehmensgeschichte*, 2004, 55ff.; Welskopp, Das institutionalisierte Misstrauen, 2000.

3 Coase, "The Nature of the Firm," 1937.

4 Jones, *British Multinational Banking*, 1993, 49; Jones, *Merchants to Multinationals*, 2000, 213–216. Also see Nicberding, "Unternehmerische Sinnkonstruktion," 2004.

5 Chapman/Buckley, "Markets, Transaction Costs, Economists and Social Anthropologists," 1997 239.

6 Welskopp, "Unternehmensgeschichte im internationalen Vergleich," 2004, 273.

7 Anderegg, *Chronicle*, 1976, 71.

8 VA, Dossier 1: B) die Teilhaber, 3. Privat-Copierbuch 9.1.1867–1825.8.1870: Sal. Volkart to Spitteler, Cochin, 9. 9. 1869.

9 See Chapter 3.

10 VA, Dossier 1, B) die Teilhaber, 3. Privat-Copierbuch 9.1.1867–1825.8.1870: 2.7.1867, Sal. Volkart to Chevalier in Cochin.

11 VA, Dossier 1, B) die Teilhaber, 3. Privat-Copierbuch 9.1.1867–1825.8.1870: 22.7.1869, Sal. Volkart to Spitteler, acting BM Cochin.

12 Anderegg, *Chronicle*, 1976, 105.

13 VA, Dossier 2: Die Teilhaber II, Theodor Reinhart: Dr. Th. Reinhart, Winterthur to Colombo, 20 December 1877.

14 Anderegg, *Chronicle*, 1976, 155–156.

15 VA, Dossier 2: Die Teilhaber II, Theodor Reinhart.

16 VA, Dossier 18: Winterthur I, 2 Functions of the HO (Winterthur); Anderegg, *Chronicle*, 1976, 173.

17 VA, Privates von Hr. Werner Reinhart, Karachi (Management-Wechsel) 1923 (Nov.): WR, an Bord S/S Movehaw to Volkart Winterthur, 5 Nov 1923. See also VA, Rapporte von Herrn Georg Reinhart anlässlich seiner Inspektionsreise nach Indien etc. im Jahre 1923.

18 VA, Privates von Hr. Werner Reinhart, Karachi (Management-Wechsel) 1923 (Nov.): WR, an Bord S/S Movehaw to Volkart Winterthur, 5 Nov 1923; WR, Karachi, 1 November 1923 to Herrn Gebr. Volkart Winterthur.

19 VA, Dossier 61: ex GR persönliches Archiv I, Schwarze Schafe: C. Huggenberg, Direktion der Schweizerischen Bankgesellschaft to Georg Reinhart, Mitglied des Verwaltungsrates der Schweizerischen Bankgesellschaft, Winterthur, 3 March 1932; Georg Reinhart to Werner Reinhart, 11 February 1932.

20 VA, Dossier 25: I/P/C Terms of European Staff: Circular to all Employees on Home Agreement, Winterthur, 15 June 1954.

21 Jones, *Merchants to Multinationals*, 2000, 213–215. Employees at Ralli also enjoyed long careers at the trading firm: GL, Records of Ralli Bros., Ms. 23836: Historical material on the company, 1902–1952: Leoni M. Calvocoressi, *The House of Ralli Brothers*, 1952.

22 VA, Dossier 62: ex GR persönliches Archiv II, The Family Code of the House of Mitsui, Japan, aufgestellt im siebzehnten Jahrhundert und mein Kommentar dazu vom 10./11. November 1939, 10–11.

23 VA, Dossier 62: ex GR persönliches Archiv II, Zur Frage Tantièmen vs. Bonus 1917–1933: Rundschreiben an unsere Mitarbeiter, Winterthur, 23 December 1926, strictly confidential.

24 Dossier 62: ex GR persönliches Archiv II, Zur Frage Tantièmen vs. Bonus 1917–1933: Georg Reinhart, Zu Herrn Häfligers Exposé über "Bonus versus Beteiligung," 4 March 1929.

25 Rambousek/Vogt/Volkart, *Volkart*, 1990, 181.
26 Lengwiler, "Drei-Säulen-Konzept," 2003, 34; Leimgruber, *Solidarity Without the State*, 2008, 64–82.
27 SSW, Nachlass Theodor Reinhart: Ms Sch 79/20: Article in the *Neues Winterthurer Tagblatt*, 1 October 1928, on the new headquarters building Volkart Bros.: Excerpt from a speech by Theodor Reinhart to Winterthur employees on 2 January 1919.
28 V.B. News, No. 14, June 1926, 6.
29 V. B. News, No. 1, November 1920, 1.
30 For more on the link between photographic visualization and company disciplining, see Lüdkte, "Gesichter der Belegschaft," 1994.
31 Reinhart, *Aus meinem Leben*, 1931, 301–305.
32 VA, Dossier 48: Artikel/Abhandlungen/Gedichte/Briefe etc. von ehemaligen Mitarbeitern: R.H. Schuepp, Ansprache anlässlich des 100-Jahr-Jubiläums in Bombay, 1 February 1951.
33 VA, Dossier 48: Artikel/Abhandlungen/Gedichte/Briefe etc. von ehemaligen Mitarbeitern: R.H. Schuepp, Ansprache anlässlich des 100-Jahr-Jubiläums in Bombay, 1 February 1951.
34 Reinhart, "Rede zur Hundertjahrfeier" [1951], 12–13.
35 Wachter, "Nachruf im Namen der Arbeitsgemeinschaft der Firma Gebrüder Volkart," [Winterthur 1951].
36 James, "Family Capitalism," 2005, 5–6.
37 VA, Dossier 62: ex GR persönliches Archiv II, Zur Frage Tantièmen vs. Bonus 1917–1933: Zur Frage der Gewinnbeteiligung von Managers und Angestellten. Abschrift eines von Herrn Georg Reinhart am 8. November 1923 verfassten Exposés, 11.
38 Volkart is not unique in this respect. The metaphor of the corporate family was also frequently used by other trading firms: Guex, "The development of Swiss trading companies," 1998, 158.
39 Reinhart, *Aus meinem Leben*, 1931, 47.
40 Weber, "Rede gehalten am 16. September 1955," 1956.
41 Weber, "Rede" [Winterthur 1951], 25–26.
42 Rambousek/Vogt/Volkart, *Volkart*, 1990, 177–187.
43 VA, Dossier 48: Artikel/Abhandlungen/Gedichte/Briefe etc. von ehemaligen Mitarbeitern—Walter Fenner, Erinnerungen, January 1977.
44 Rambousek/Vogt/Volkart, *Volkart*, 1990, 183.
45 Reinhart, "Rede zur Hundertjahrfeier" [1951], 10.
46 The sources in the archives of BBC successor ABB show that the reason BBC chose a Chinese company to represent it actually had nothing to do with the reputation of the manager's wife, but was simply because Volkart was too unfamiliar with the industrial situation in China: ArABB, B.1.2.3.23.6: Letter written by J. Elink Schuurman from Kobe to Brown, Boveri & Cie., Baden, 29 November 1922.
47 VA, reports by Mr. Georg Reinhart on the occasion of his inspection tour of India etc. in the year 1923: GR, Osaka, to Winterthur, 29 May 1923.
48 Rambousek/Vogt/Volkart, *Volkart*, 1990, 230.
49 VA, Privates von Hr. Werner Reinhart, Karachi (Management-Wechsel) 1929 (Nov.): WR, Karachi, 1 November 1923 to Herrn Gebr. Volkart Winterthur.
50 Berghoff, "Unternehmenskultur und Herrschaftstechnik," 1997.
51 VA, Dossier 64: Geschäftsordnung 1915/1921 mit Nachträgen bis 1940 / Upcountry Bookkeeping Instructions 1912–1926 / Upcountry Instructions 1952: Geschäftsordnung, 15.2.1925.—During this period, Ralli employed a similar number of people. From 1931 to 1938, Ralli employed between 2,700

and 3,500 people: GL, Records of Ralli Bros., Ms. 23834: Report to the Chairman of Ralli Brothers Limited, 12 April 1939, 2.

52 Weber, "Rede" [Winterthur 1951], 26.

53 VA, Dossier 61: ex GR persönliches Archiv I, Dossier über die grossen Verluste, die uns Max Greeven als Leiter von New York eingebrockt hat: Bericht von Hürlimann, New York in Sachen Max Greeven, 4 May 1932

54 VA, Dossier 61: ex GR persönliches Archiv I, Dossier über die grossen Verluste, die uns Max Greeven als Leiter von New York eingebrockt hat: Handschriftliche Notiz von Georg Reinhart, 14 May 1932

55 For more on the circumstances of this dispute, see Chapter 1.

56 VA, Dossier 1, B) die Teilhaber, Später aufgetauchte Briefe: G.G. Volkart, Bombay 29 December 1874 to Cochin.

57 The owners of chocolate manufacturer Gebr. Stollwerck used a very similar mixture of controlling and paternalism in a bid to maintain a tight hold on the employees of their multinational family company: Epple, "Gebr. Stollwercks Aufstieg zum Multinational," 2007.

7 Working in Colonial India

The opportunity to work in exotic countries was a major motivating factor for many Europeans to seek employment at Volkart.[1] Writing in his memoirs, August F. Ammann described his delight upon learning in 1874 that he would be dispatched to Asia: "[M]y heart's desire was gratified and I was allowed to proceed to India in the service of the firm." When his ship later entered the port of Bombay and he saw the city's impressive panorama, he described the experience as follows: "I had a first glimpse of the land of my dreams, the wonderland India."[2] In his speech to mark the company's anniversary in 1926, Georg Reinhart also made reference to a "certain romanticism . . . that has always been associated with coming into contact with distant lands" and that every employee of the firm had felt on at least one occasion, "if only when exotic spices and fragrances told them for the very first time of their faraway origins."[3]

But what was the encounter with India really like for employees? Apparently they had widely divergent reactions. For some European merchants the subcontinent did in fact offer an opportunity to enjoy a certain colonial romanticism and experience exotic adventures. Ammann wrote extensively in his memoirs of hunting tigers, elephants and crocodiles, and recounted unpleasant encounters with snakes and scorpions, along with his attempts at winning the friendship of a moody little monkey in Cochin.[4] Aside from statistics and serious business essays, the employee magazine *V.B. News* also regularly featured so-called "monkey stories" in which staff members described their weekend excursions to the backcountry and their encounters with the Indian animal world.[5]

However, for many employees India was by no means the paradise of their dreams, in large part due to the rigors of the subtropical climate. Papers and documents had to be kept in steel cabinets to avoid being consumed by ants or destroyed by the high humidity.[6] The climatic conditions were also physically taxing. The trials and tribulations experienced by many Europeans are vividly reflected in a poem written by a Volkart employee in 1926:

> Balmy fragrances fill the breeze,
> with dried fish and rancid cheese;

Roaming about, sweaty and tattered,
a former man, completely shattered.

His noble face, once so fair,
has turned gray under his disheveled hair,
and with a tinge of curry and rice
blue-black rings have formed around his eyes.

His spindly legs are sheathed in a loose pantaloon
that oddly resembles a hot-air balloon,
and swarms of mosquitoes stab into his skin
and suck the red juice that pulses therein.

Who is this wretch, this unfortunate creature?
And what, pray tell, is his most prominent feature?
A man who has endured all manner of injury,
a European in India, a picture of misery.[7]

In view of the tenor of these lines, it is hardly surprising that this employee, who was sent to India in 1926 at the age of 22, had already left the company by 1927.[8] He was not the only one to throw in the towel. Although many Volkart employees remained with the firm for decades, others disappeared from the payrolls after only a brief stint. Their reasons for leaving the company cannot be reconstructed based on the available sources. While a number of employees presumably proved to be unsuited for the commercial sector, others saw better prospects in establishing their own trading companies. Still others had to return to Europe for health reasons because they could not cope with the subtropical climate and poor sanitary conditions. Various members of the firm, including the two partners Johann Georg Volkart and Henry L. Bodbeck, died while working in India.[9]

To minimize the risk of employees contracting tropical diseases, Volkart issued a manual during the 1920s that recommended staff members receive vaccinations against smallpox, typhus and cholera.[10] Employees in the interior of the country were additionally advised to avoid being bitten by rabid dogs.[11] Volkart also gave its employees leaflets with hygienic guidelines in which they were warned against consuming raw milk, unboiled water and fruit.[12]

Volkart and Daily Colonial Life

Since Volkart employees on the subcontinent came in close contact with Indian society, both in business and private life, the company's branches can be described as a "contact zone," a concept developed by Mary Louise Pratt that emphasizes the interactive dimension of imperial encounters in which individuals are often forced to resort to improvisation.[13] Within the scope of

Volkart's business activities, relations between Europeans and Indians were in a constant state of flux and plagued by ambiguity. As the Indian independence movement increasingly clamored for the British to withdraw from the country from the 1920s onwards, Volkart officials faced a particular dilemma. As Swiss citizens, they undoubtedly harbored sympathies for the demands for political independence and condemned the frequent racist attitudes of many Europeans toward the indigenous population. Yet they also realized that Volkart largely owed its business success to British colonial rule, and there were those in the company who had negative things to say about Mahatma Gandhi and the boycotts of British goods that he initiated. Accordingly, Volkart decided to take a very Swiss approach and endeavored to maintain a neutral attitude toward the political tensions on the subcontinent.[14] An instruction manual from the 1920s exhorted all employees to be aware

> that they, as members of a non-British firm in India, benefited from the hospitality that the government of the country had shown them with such magnanimity. Natural tact would thus dictate that, when dealing with the British, we refrain from all dismissive criticism of the British administration in India.[15]

Despite this ambivalent political attitude, Volkart employees were an integral part of the colonial system on a sociocultural level (Figure 7.1). It was perfectly normal for employees in India to have indigenous servants who, if required, would accompany them on trips.[16] The painter Karl Hofer, who

Figure 7.1 A senior staff member of Volkart's Bombay branch with an office clerk, 1941 (VA, Dossier 104: Photos Bombay, Bombay 1941)

had traveled on two trips to India with Georg, Werner and Oskar Reinhart, wrote that one of the attractions of life in India for many Europeans was that "here they could lead the life of a lord surrounded by servants, whereas back home they might merely be lowly laborers."[17]

The company's employee magazine regularly featured ostensibly humorous articles, in which the Indian domestic help was described in an extremely paternalistic tone. For instance, it was reported that an Indian female servant was told by a Volkart employee to remove the belt buckles from his tennis trousers before they were sent to the laundry. But the woman confused buckles with buttons and consequently neatly removed the buttons from all articles of clothing that were sent to be washed. There was also the story of a cook who took a piece of ice that was intended to cool the drinks and wrapped it in a towel before placing it in the sun, and subsequently thought that someone had stolen the ice and simply left behind a soggy piece of cloth. It turned out that he had never seen ice before.[18] Then there was the tale of an Indian office boy named Rama who worked for Volkart and sought help from his superiors because his mother had berated him in the most scurrilous way. The "sahib" followed him to his dwelling where he learned the details of the quarrel from the boy's mother. Rama had taken his sisters' portion of rice with the argument that he needed more food than them because he was the only member of the family with steady employment. When the European Volkart employee heard this, he summoned the lad and ensured that justice was done "like a father, with the palm of one hand, while the other kept the boy tightly over my knee." After this punishment, the boy was determined to quit his job at Volkart, but he was deterred from doing so by his uncle. He then apologized to the European for wrongly attempting to solicit outside help against his mother. "In token of his submission and devotion, he first touched my feet and then his forehead and humbly prayed for my pardon which, of course, could be had for the asking."[19]

Clothing, Clubs and Women

When it came to clothing, Volkart employees also seamlessly fit in with the colonial system. In view of the frequent complaints about the extreme climatic conditions, it is astonishing that Volkart's European employees wore such heavy clothing to work, including full suits with long-sleeve shirts and ties.[20] This was largely motivated by the colonial pretense to stand out from the natives and never renounce the cultural symbolism of European clothing as an icon of civilization, no matter how extreme the conditions.[21] Remarking on the attire of club members in Tuticorin, where he sojourned for an internship in 1902, Georg Reinhart wrote the following:

> As symptomatic of how strictly the English observe social norms, I would like to point out that, even in this remote corner of the world, when attending dinner parties, even small ones, they always wore tailcoats, or at least tuxedos, while the ladies were clad in evening dresses.[22]

Clubs and dinner parties were often the only occasions available to European merchants for amusement and social contacts. Complaints of boredom were commonplace in the letters written by members of the firm stationed in India. Georg Reinhart, for instance, wrote to his parents from Tuticorin:

> My life here is still rather monotonous. . . . Tuticorin is a veritable dump and the few Europeans that one invariably runs into at the club, which is the only attraction in town, fit that mold to a T, otherwise they would not be here.[23]

Even if the entertainment in the clubs was at times somewhat dubious, for most Europeans this was an essential element of their stay in India. In his memoirs, Ammann maintained that "a European who expatriates himself to a country like India . . . *must* have distraction or recreation of some kind, otherwise he is sure to fall into a state of moroseness, if not worse."[24] Membership in the club was also an opportunity to forge contacts with other European businessmen.[25] Accordingly, Volkart instructed its employees that it was essential for them to apply for membership in the club.[26] The firm often even paid their dues and fees.[27]

Since the business world at this time remained a purely male-dominated arena, women were expected to play a key role in the social life of colonial India. Ammann wrote the following:

> In a country like India, and especially in small stations where there are no theatres, no concerts, none of all those many things which in Europe contribute to make life pleasant and interesting, the one thing which helps to make life not only bearable, but agreeable, is sociability and that can only be had where there are ladies, good, gentle and cultured ladies who take an interest in the station's life and their neighbors. I am, of course, speaking of married ladies who know something of life and are ready to take pity on lonely bachelors.[28]

Ammann declined to comment on whether there were affairs between European ladies and unmarried Volkart employees, and there is no information on this in the company archives, nor does the source material reveal any details of love affairs between European employees and Indian women. In Shanghai, though, relationships between European men and local women appeared to be commonplace. The owner of the Swiss trading firm Siber Hegner, which had a branch office in Shanghai, gave the following advice concerning the life of a European employee there:

> As a bachelor you should sleep with the native girls and learn their language through pillow talk. After four years, during your first home leave, find yourself a wife. After all, now you have a slightly better

standing and should be able to reflect this. Then you establish a household in Shanghai.

Likewise, Richard von der Crone, who headed Volkart's Shanghai branch in the late 1930s, recounted that it was possible to hire what he referred to as "Chinese taxigirls"—officially as dance partners, unofficially to go to bed with them. This allowed the young men to gather sexual experiences that they could not have had in Switzerland; after all, in contrast to Zurich, in Shanghai "women were . . . of course not allowed to meddle" in men's affairs.[29]

Up until the turn of the century, very few Volkart employees working in Asia were married. Many of them could not afford a family, not least because the company did not pay for their passage or contribute to the costs of maintaining a household.[30] It was not until living conditions in India became more bearable for Europeans during the twentieth century that more of the employees opted for marriage during their stay in Asia or sent for their families. From the 1950s onwards, the firm also covered the costs of the outward journeys of families and employees and paid child benefits for staff members with children.[31] But the unaccustomed life in the tropics was not easy for many wives. The spouse of a Volkart employee, who moved to India in the 1930s shortly after marrying her husband, was given a stern piece of advice from her father, who admonished her not to drink any whiskey and above all not to start playing bridge, as this led to the "typical tropical stupor." When she arrived in India, she soon made the acquaintance of English wives who spent their entire days playing bridge at the club, since they had homes full of servants and nannies to look after their children, leaving them with nothing else to do. She quickly realized that this was not the life for her and began to play golf. But she soon abandoned this pastime after hitting a ball into the rough, causing a two-meter-long snake to slither toward her out of the undergrowth.[32]

The Indian Employees

Volkart employees came into contact with Indians not only in private but also during daily business activities. Right from the start, the company had collaborated with Indian merchants who worked as brokers or shroffs and were not formally hired by the firm, but instead remained independent middlemen. By contrast, virtually all of the employees during the first decades of the company's history came from Europe. This was also the case with other European trading firms during this era. It was not until the 1870s that Volkart began to engage Indian employees as upcountry purchasing agents. In the 1880s, Volkart also started to hire local personnel to carry out office work. Most of these employees were Hindus or Indians who had converted to Christianity. On Ceylon the company initially hired primarily Burghers: Eurasians whose fathers were from Europe and mothers were from

Ceylon. Later, they were joined by a growing number of Hindus, Buddhists and Christians who had emigrated from India. Many of these employees remained with the firm throughout their entire professional lives and their sons often followed in their footsteps and went to work for Volkart.[33]

Former Volkart employee Heinz Frech recalled that even during the 1950s a strict sense of hierarchy prevailed among the Indian employees (Figure 7.2) that was "somewhat reminiscent of the Hindu caste system," adding that

> every employee, from simple office clerks to high-ranking managers, required at least one assistant. This mania even included the lowest level, the class of clerks known as office peons. No office could function without them, as it was below the dignity of an employee to carry even the most basic document from one desk to the other. The head peon stood at the ready for such tasks. Summoned with one of the handbells that were on every employee's desk, his loud voice immediately rang out to mobilize one of his assistants.[34]

The Indian employees were disadvantaged compared to their European colleagues in many respects. The company hierarchy thus reflected the skewed relationship between Europeans and their Indian subordinates during the colonial era. When taking business trips by train, European employees received first-class tickets from the company, while their Indian coworkers had to travel second class. Likewise, the company provided medical care for

Figure 7.2 The Indian employees of Volkart's Cawnpore agency in 1942 (Fotomuseum Winterthur, Volkart Collection, CD 1, Album Calcutta 1942)

its European employees, but not for the native staff.[35] From the turn of the century onwards, indigenous employees were entitled to a year-end bonus that was the equivalent of half or an entire month's wages, depending on their performance, while European employees had already been enjoying such bonuses since the 1870s. As mentioned earlier, Volkart introduced a retirement fund in 1916 for its European and indigenous employees in India and Ceylon, with equal contributions made by the company and its employees.[36] Prior to that initiative, long-standing employees were rewarded for their loyalty with a special one-off payment.[37]

The company's archives shed little light on how the Indian employees felt about the working conditions at Volkart. The only surviving written record stems from R.S.D. Shenai, who was 24 years old when he was hired by Volkart's Cochin branch in 1914. Sixty years later, he wrote an account of his work for the Swiss trading firm, including a description of a meeting held by the members of the Cochin Chamber of Commerce after the outbreak of World War I. The European merchants gathered there were convinced that the onset of war would have a devastating impact on the trading business, leading them to conclude that it was necessary to dismiss some of the Indian staff and cut the salaries of the remaining natives. The manager of Volkart's Cochin branch, A. Bueler, soundly rejected these proposals. He pointed out that many employees had already been with Volkart for decades and proven that they were reliable and hard-working individuals. Moreover, he said that price increases could be expected, making it more difficult to afford basic necessities like food and clothing. In short, he insisted that he was not going to lay off anyone. Shenai recalled that this statement was greeted with jubilation by the indigenous population of Cochin: "This auspicious news flew around at once like wild fire, and Mr. Bueler was hailed as a 'Dharma Raja' (legitimate Charitable-hearted Ruler)." He went on to say that Volkart enjoyed even greater admiration when the company introduced the Provident Funds in 1916, an initiative that the remaining European companies in Cochin did not emulate until many years later. Shenai thus concluded: "This VENERABLE BROTHERHOOD (V.B.) has become a DHARMA DATA/PITA—(Father of Pious/Providential Charity)! (even though V.B. is not a British Firm)!"[38]

This account is to be treated with caution because it was written upon the request of former Volkart manager Jakob Anderegg, who was working on an internal company history at the time. It thus stands to reason that this narrative may have offered an idealized portrayal of conditions at Volkart. It is also important to note that, although Volkart paid its employees a war compensation that amounted to 10 to 15 percent of their wages as well as generous bonuses during World War I, this hardly made up for the fact that food prices in India had soared by 40–120 percent and rents had risen by 30–40 percent.[39] Nevertheless, the trading firm appears to have provided its Indian employees with comparatively good working conditions. According to the surviving records, serious labor conflicts were a rarity during the colonial era, but one dispute arose in 1920 when the employees of a large number of companies in Bombay demanded higher salaries. The partners at Volkart viewed the demands as legitimate and were prepared to meet them, not least because they recognized that "appropriate payment and good treatment would secure the loyalty of capable workers."[40] But Volkart management in Bombay wanted to conform to the decision of the majority of the companies in the city and not grant the Indian employees any wage increases. Ultimately, it appears that a compromise was reached and Volkart's Bombay branch made a number of adjustments in terms of wages and hiring conditions.[41]

Another example illustrates the company's sensitivity to the mood among its Indian employees. When Georg Reinhart traveled to India and Ceylon on an inspection tour in 1923, the indigenous employees of Volkart's Karachi branch urged the creation of an additional retirement fund because the Provident Funds left some workers, particularly older ones, almost entirely without retirement benefits.[42] Reinhart subsequently wrote to Winterthur to inform the partners that they would have to deal with this problem intensively following his return,

> since there can be no doubt that the Provident Funds fail to meet the demands of humanity and fairness. Moreover, the once so vast differences between native and European staff are increasingly falling by the wayside, and if we have abundantly provided for our Europeans . . . with an extensive and generously endowed retirement fund, it would be unfair for us to intend to do any less for our employees in India—the majority of whom are devoted to our company and to whom we are doubtlessly just as indebted for our success—simply because their skin is dark.[43]

During a visit to the other Volkart branches, Georg Reinhart nevertheless discovered that the majority of the indigenous employees were fully satisfied with the Provident Funds. Although he now refrained from supporting the idea of a new retirement fund, he did feel that it was necessary to introduce a special provision for older and long-standing employees that would provide them with a "small monthly pension . . . until the end of their lives."[44]

Due to a dearth of source material, it is impossible to determine the extent to which Indian employees actually felt that they were full-fledged members of the company. But in their statements to the company management they also used the metaphor of the corporate family, which, as noted in the previous chapter, played an important role in fostering a cultural code for the ties between the firm's owners and their European employees (Figure 7.3). The Indian employees also used this metaphor to remind the owners of their obligations to the workforce. This is reflected in a welcome address delivered by an Indian employee in Tuticorin to Georg Reinhart when he visited the branch in 1927:

Figure 7.3 Georg Reinhart, center, with a garland of flowers, surrounded by the employees of Volkart's Calcutta branch during his trip to India in 1923 (Fotomuseum Winterthur, Volkart Collection, CD 2, Calcutta)

The one reason, among so many, which stands prominently forward to account for the Firm's splendid success in business in all previous years is, we dare say, the mutual trust and confidence between the Firm and its Employees, and the good and honourable treatment meted out to the latter by the former. Honoured Sir, it may not be too much to expect you to regard us, in a metaphorical sense of course, as your dutiful children, fully meriting the confidence which you repose in us, whose one object, as far as our relationship with the Firm is concerned, is the perennial prosperity of the Firm, which, on its part, is the basis of our well-being.[45]

Many years later in the 1980s, a former Indian Volkart employee, speaking on the eve of his retirement, gave the following description of what it felt like to work for the company: "I have thought of the company as my Mother . . . and have given her the devotion one would accord to one's mother. I have also received her love and blessings in full measure."[46] For their part, Volkart managers also saw their relationship with their Indian employees as rooted in the symbolic narrative of the family. The instruction manuals for the branches in India in the early 1920s advised that a "fatherly-friendly tone" toward the Indian employees "would be more effective in achieving the desired result than a harsh manner."[47]

It should be noted, though, that these benevolent words only applied to the Indian office workers, whereas the majority of the more than 5,000 workers in Volkart's employ during the 1920s were Indian day laborers.[48] The scant source material does not allow us to draw any conclusions about their working conditions or the attitudes that the partners and their European and Indian employees had of these workers, but it is safe to assume that their work environment was less favorable in many respects.[49]

Ambivalent Attitudes toward the Colonial Order

Aside from improvements in wages and social benefits, Volkart gradually changed the nature of the tasks that it assigned to Indian employees. For many years, indigenous employees were only assigned routine chores. It was not until the end of World War I that Indian employees were given responsibility for more important tasks, such as translating telegrams, writing letters and compiling order lists. There appears to have been differences of opinion, though, over whether Indians were to be entrusted with independently making purchases and sales, which, even today, remain the core activities of every trading firm. In a letter sent by Volkart's Karachi branch to the headquarters in Winterthur in the late 1920s, managers in India said that "native employees are [suited] for correspondence, statements and other desk work these days," but insisted that they should continue to employ primarily Europeans as buyers and sellers. This was justified with reference to the alleged greater corruptibility of the Indian employees.[50] At Volkart's Bombay office, however, Indian employees were given important tasks at an early stage and were working as upcountry purchasing agents already by the late nineteenth century.[51] Of the 17 buying agencies that were run by Volkart's Bombay branch in 1919 and 1920, only three were headed by Europeans and the remaining 14 were under the aegis of Indian employees.[52]

It is interesting to note that at this time the divide between Europeans and Asians in the Japanese subsidiary Nichizui was far less pronounced than it appears to have been in colonial India. When Georg Reinhart visited Nichizui during his trip to Asia in 1923, he immediately noticed the cooperative atmosphere among Japanese and European employees: "In contrast to the practice in India, where the Europeans assumed prominent positions, there is no noticeable gap here between Europeans and Japanese."[53] The somewhat ambivalent feelings that Volkart's European managers in India had of local staff could be seen as a sign that, due to British colonial rule, they had a far more conflicting relationship with the indigenous population than in Japan. Since there is hardly any surviving source material on working conditions in Volkart's Japanese—and Chinese—subsidiaries, this supposition unfortunately cannot be empirically verified.

The ambivalent attitude toward indigenous staff appears to have been more widespread among European employees in South Asia than among Volkart's partners in Winterthur, who fully recognized their company as a transnational organization with a cosmopolitan approach. In the anniversary publication of 1926, for instance, the firm wrote that it owed its success "primarily . . . to the *esprit de corps* with which we rally around the company flag and that unites us, regardless of our position, nationality or race."[54] And an article in the employee magazine justified the requirement that European employees must learn at least one Asian language by pointing out that this gave them a better insight into "the religious customs, private habits and manifestations of art of the Eastern races, . . . whose culture, although different to ours, is nonetheless in many [ways] of an equal if not higher standard."[55] This appreciation of Asian culture is also reflected by the fact that members of the Indian merchant elite were always portrayed with the greatest of respect in the Volkart archival material. For instance, in a letter to the editor printed in the Swiss weekly magazine *Die Weltwoche* in response to the widespread opinion voiced earlier in this publication that European trading firms in the nineteenth century had only been so successful because they were able to profit from the economic backwardness of Asian countries, Georg Reinhart wrote:

> Not only are India and China ancient cultures whose philosophy, art and science had reached a highly advanced stage at a time when our ancestors still eked out an existence in pile dwellings, but their trade and commerce were already highly developed centuries ago and remain so to this day. When the Volkart Bros. company established its first branch in Bombay in 1851, it was not confronted with backward half savages, but instead encountered a sophisticated trade in cotton, spices, exotic fragrances and other export items.[56]

Particularly in view of the increasingly louder demands for the withdrawal of British colonial troops in the wake of World War I, Volkart officials impressed upon their European employees to treat the indigenous population with respect.[57] In a letter written in 1928, company headquarters urged its European managers in India to act more considerately toward their Indian employees than was the norm on European plantations on the subcontinent at the time: "We demand of our Europeans, specifically those who are in managerial positions, that they distance themselves from the ignorant prejudices concerning the relative value of the two races as commonly exists, for instance, among plantation owners."[58] This was also in the company's business interests. In the 1920s, company owners called on their European employees in India to remain a paragon of virtuous conduct in their dealings with Indian merchants:

> When it comes to doing business with merchants, it goes without saying that their sympathy and devotion to the company can only be won and maintained with polite treatment, while contrary conduct will quickly be the ruin of it. Our most talented buyers and sellers in India owe their success to a great degree to the friendly and respectful treatment that

they have shown their native clients, and particularly to consistently honest and fair trading.[59]

Furthermore, the firm endeavored to integrate both its European and Indian employees into the corporate culture. From the early 1930s onwards, for example, Volkart's Bombay branch held an annual in-company sporting event that was attended by both European and Indian employees and their families (Figure 7.4). They competed in disciplines like the long jump, sack racing, hurdle races, obstacle courses for children and veterans, and an egg-and-spoon race for the ladies.[60]

With the growing criticism of colonial rule, companies doing business in India came under increasing pressure to entrust more indigenous employees with managerial functions.[61] From the mid-1930s onwards, this prompted Volkart to recruit qualified Indians who were trained as district agents in the cotton organization so they could gradually replace their European colleagues. Moreover, many Indian engineers who joined the newly established engineering department in the 1920s rose through the ranks to assume managerial positions.

Other European trading firms in India introduced similar measures during this period. In the 1930s, Volkart's main competitor in the Indian cotton market, Ralli, promoted three indigenous employees—all of whom were the sons of prominent Indians—to the highest managerial level. But within

Figure 7.4 A Swiss company in colonial India: Sporting event involving the Indian and European employees in Bombay to mark the 75th anniversary celebrations of Volkart Bros. on 1 February 1926 (Fotomuseum Winterthur, Volkart Collection, CD 2, Bombay 02)

the company these measures remained controversial, which explains why no more Indians were placed in such managerial positions during the late 1930s.[62] At Volkart the measures to improve the lot of indigenous employees did not meet with unanimous approval either. Company management at the Winterthur head office noted with some annoyance in 1945 that among European managers at the Indian branches "the necessary, radically changed attitude toward the problem of Indianization does not yet exist everywhere." Many branch managers were reluctant to hire Indian employees with top-flight educational backgrounds because they could demand considerably higher salaries than what, until then, had been the norm for Indian personnel. These highly qualified Indians often received wages that were roughly equivalent to the salaries of some European employees. Peter Reinhart said that it was a sign of "a worrisome lack of understanding" when, for instance, the management of Volkart Colombo branch voiced the opinion that "one cannot allow an Indian employee to rise to the same level with regard to salary as is common for a European youngster."[63]

Shortly before India gained its independence, employee organizations emerged in many companies on the subcontinent. On 1 March 1947, the Union of the V.B. Staff was founded. The manager of Volkart's Bombay branch at the time responded very positively to this development, as stated in a booklet that was later published by labor representatives: "[I]n a true democratic manner, [he] welcomed the formation of our Union and congratulated its president for this Staff Organisation." Such a reaction was quite uncommon among companies in India at the time: "We at once became the envy and pride amongst various other brother Unions who were not so fortunate in having their Unions recognised so gracefully." Working conditions were subsequently renegotiated during talks that lasted several days. According to this source, there were two reasons why these negotiations were so quickly crowned with success. First, Volkart employees managed to resist outside influences, specifically attempts by communist and nationalist groups to sway the outcome of the negotiations. Second, it was important that Peter Reinhart, who was on an inspection tour of India at the time, showed a great deal of sympathy for the concerns raised by the employees.[64]

These examples show that the company had a sympathetic ear for the needs of its Indian employees. This was necessary because good business sense precluded Volkart from ignoring the demands of the workforce. Nevertheless, the company's policies in colonial India were characterized by many ambiguities. In the accounts written by Volkart's European employees, the image of India alternated between rapture over the exotic wonderland and a sense of being overwhelmed by the extreme climate and unfamiliar surroundings. Ambivalence also pervaded the contradictory attitudes of the Swiss merchants toward British colonial rule and the differences in opinion between the headquarters in Winterthur and the heads of the Indian branches over whether indigenous employees should be promoted to management positions. In its publications, the firm also tended to reproduce the hierarchy within Indian society. While the members of the Indian merchant elite were treated with utmost respect, company officials had a rather ambivalent attitude toward their Indian office workers. And when it came to their Indian domestic servants, they displayed, at best, an attitude of paternalistic benevolence.

Notes

1 Based on the example of Volkart, it would be extremely tempting to compare the circumstances in India with those in China and Japan during the colonial era, or a non-colonial peripheral area like Latin America. However, since the company archives contain no information on the working conditions in these other non-European countries, such a comparison is not possible.
2 Ammann, *Reminiscences*, 1921, 12–13.
3 Reinhart, *Aus meinem Leben*, 1931, 306–307.
4 Ammann, *Reminiscences*, 1921, 24–27, 31, 43, 55.
5 V.B. News, No. 2, April 1921, 12–13; V.B. News, Nr. 11, June 1924, 12–16. Heinz Frech gave similar descriptions of his hunting trips in the area surrounding Karachi during the 1950s: Frech, *Baumwolle, Stahl und Stolpersteine*, 2001, 55–56.
6 VA, Dossier 12: Tuticorin / Madras, Madras, 8. Miscellaneous information: Madras to Winterthur, 9 December 1938.
7 VA, Dossier 48: Artikel/Abhandlungen/Gedichte/Briefe etc. von ehemaligen Mitarbeitern: W. Haesli, Ballade, 1926.
8 VA, Dossier 48: Artikel/Abhandlungen/Gedichte/Briefe etc. von ehemaligen Mitarbeitern.
9 Anderegg, *Chronicle*, 1976, 130ff., 209–210.
10 VA, Dossier 27: Instruction Manuals: Vorschriften für den Geschäftsbetrieb der indischen Filialen von Volkart Brothers [without date, ca. 1920–1924].
11 VA, Dossier 64: Geschäftsordnung 1915/1921 mit Nachträgen bis 1940 / Upcountry Bookkeeping Instructions 1912–1926 / Upcountry Instructions 1952: General Regulations and Instructions for the Use of Volkart Brothers Up-Country-Agencies. Winterthur 1912, 4.
12 VA Dossier 27: Instruction Manuals: Merkblatt „Tropen-Hygiene" (ca. 1911).
13 Pratt, *Imperial Eyes*, 2008, 8.
14 See Chapter 9 for a more detailed analysis.
15 VA, Dossier 27: Instruction Manuals: Vorschriften für den Geschäftsbetrieb der indischen Filialen von Volkart Brothers [no date, approx. 1920–1924].
16 While no one questioned that Europeans always traveled first class by train, their servants only received third-class tickets: VA, Dossier 64: Geschäftsordnung 1915/1921 mit Nachträgen bis 1940 / Upcountry Bookkeeping Instructions 1912–1926 / Upcountry Instructions 1952: General Regulations and Instructions for the Use of Volkart Brothers Up-Country-Agencies. Winterthur 1912, 3.
17 Hofer, *Erinnerungen eines Malers*, 1953, 150.
18 V.B. News, No. 3, August 1921, 20.
19 V.B. News, No. 7, April 1923, 5–9.
20 Anderegg, *Chronicle*, 1976, 132.
21 Up until the 1830s, Europeans living on the subcontinent often wore Indian clothing and had relationships with Indian women. Afterwards, black tailored suits became the standard attire for the British and other Europeans in India, and even Indian food was increasingly viewed with disdain. More and more Europeans used this as a way of remaining aloof of their Indian surroundings, which they saw as hostile. Collingham, *Imperial Bodies*, 2001.

22 SSW, Nachlass Theodor Reinhart, Ms Sch 84, Briefe von A–G. Reinhart an Theodor Reinhart)/61: Georg Reinhart to Theodor Reinhart, 1902–1903: Tuticorin, 2 April 1902. Not surprisingly, the dress code for dinner parties was not relaxed until after the colonial era. According to Volkart employee Heinz Frech, from the 1950s onwards there was a growing tendency to embrace the American style, which meant that men only wore tuxedos on formal occasions: Frech, *Baumwolle, Stahl und Stolpersteine*, 2001, 50.

23 SSW, Nachlass Theodor Reinhart, Ms Sch 84, Briefe von A–G. Reinhart an Theodor Reinhart)/61: Georg Reinhart to Theodor Reinhart, 1902–1903: Tuticorin, 2 April 1902.

24 Ammann, *Reminiscences*, 1921, 22.

25 Frech, *Baumwolle, Stahl und Stolpersteine*, 2001. 53.

26 VA, Dossier 63: ex GR persönliches Archiv III, Calcutta—Wirtschaftlichkeits Probleme 1928–1931: Werner Reinhart to Winterthur, Bombay, 17 October 1928.

27 VA, Dossier 25: I/P/C Terms of European Staff: Allgemeine Richtlinen Personal, ca. 1966.

28 Ammann, *Reminiscences*, 1921, 22.

29 Zit. nach Steinmann, *Seldwyla im Wunderland*, 1998, 24 and 50.

30 VA, Dossier 1, B) die Teilhaber, 1) Salomon Volkart, 3. Privat-Copierbuch 9.1.1867–1825.8.1870: 29. 12. 1869, Sal. Volkart to Hausheer, Cochin.

31 VA, Dossier 25: I/P/C Terms of European Staff.

32 VA, Dossier 48: Artikel/Abhandlungen/Gedichte/Briefe etc. von ehemaligen Mitarbeitern: Frau Helene Kappeler, Reminiszenzen aus Indien, January 1988.

33 Anderegg, *Chronicle*, 1976, 109, 134–135; VA, Dossier 9: Tellicherry, 2. Table of Events: 1930.

34 Frech, *Baumwolle, Stahl und Stolpersteine* 2001, 25. Based on the source material, it is no longer possible to determine whether the in-company hierarchy actually had something to do with the fact that the Indian employees belonged to different castes.

35 VA, Dossier 64: Geschäftsordnung 1915/1921 mit Nachträgen bis 1940 / Upcountry Bookkeeping Instructions 1912–1926 / Upcountry Instructions 1952: General Regulations and Instructions for the Use of Volkart Brothers Up-Country-Agencies. Winterthur 1912, 4.

36 See Chapter 6.

37 VA, Dossier 24: I/P/C Terms of Local Staff: I. general notes on staff terms.

38 VA, Dossier 24: I/P/C Terms of Local Staff, III. short biogr. notes on some Indian & Pak. Employees: R.S.D. Shenai, born in 1890, Some Memoirs of an Old and Retired employee, joined 1914—retired 1953, written in February 1974.

39 VA, Dossier 24: I/P/C Terms of Local Staff: I. general notes on staff terms.

40 VA, Dossier 24: I/P/C Terms of Local Staff, IV. Branches: General staff terms/ Unions, 1. Bombay: Winterthur an alle Häuser, 11 March 1920.

41 VA, Dossier 24: I/P/C Terms of Local Staff: I. general notes on staff terms.

42 VA, Rapporte von Herrn Georg Reinhart anlässlich seiner Inspektionsreise nach Indien etc. im Jahre 1923: Petition der Angestellten in Karachi an Georg Reinhart, 2 February 1923.

43 VA, Rapporte von Herrn Georg Reinhart anlässlich seiner Inspektionsreise nach Indien etc. im Jahre 1923 (keine Signatur): GR, Karachi to Winterthur, 8 February 1923.

44 VA, Rapporte von Herrn Georg Reinhart anlässlich seiner Inspektionsreise nach Indien etc. im Jahre 1923 (keine Signatur): GR, Colombo, to Winterthur, 6 April 1923.

45 Volkart-Archiv, Dossier 2: Die Teilhaber II, Georg Reinhart: Welcome address of the Indian staff of Volkart Bros. in Tuticorin presented to Georg Reinhart, 19–14–1927.

46 VA, Dossier 24: I/P/C Terms of Local Staff, III. short biogr. notes on some Indian & Pak. Employees: "The End of an Era," article with no source listed [probably from the Voltas employee magazine "We", approx. January 1980].

47 VA, Dossier 27: Instruction Manuals—business guidelines for the Indian branches of Volkart Brothers [no date, ca. 1920–1924].

48 VA, Dossier 64: Geschäftsordnung 1915/1921 mit Nachträgen bis 1940 / Upcountry Bookkeeping Instructions 1912–1926 / Upcountry Instructions 1952: Geschäftsordnung, 15 February 1925.

49 For more on the organization of labor in India under colonial conditions, see Ahuja, *Die Erzeugung kolonialer Staatlichkeit*, 1999.

50 VA, Dossier 8: Karachi, 3. Table of Events: Karachi to Winterthur, without date [ca. spring 1927].

51 See Chapter 2. A similar approach was adopted by Ralli Bros. Although Ralli's upcountry agencies were still run by Greeks, the sub-agencies were headed by Indians: GL, Records of Ralli Bros., Ms. 23836: Historical material on the company, 1902–1952: Leoni M. Calvocoressi, *The House of Ralli Brothers*, 1952.

52 Anderegg, *Chronicle*, 1976, 416.

53 VA, Rapporte von Herrn Georg Reinhart anlässlich seiner Inspektionsreise nach Indien etc. im Jahre 1923: GR, Osaka, to Winterthur, 28 May 1923.

54 Reinhart, *Gedenkschrift*, 1926, 7.

55 V.B. News, No. 2, April 1921, 14.

56 VA, Dossier 19: Winterthur II, 14. write-ups about VB by outsiders and corrections by JA: Leserbrief von Georg Reinhart, abgedruckt in der Weltwoche (ohne Datum).

57 VA, Dossier 27: Instruction Manuals—business guidelines for the Indian branches of Volkart Brothers [no date, ca. 1920–1924].

58 VA, Dossier 26: Finance/Exchange 1887–19773 Inland financing—shroffage agreements, Winterthur an Karachi, 30 August 1928.

59 VA, Dossier 27: Instruction Manuals: Vorschriften für den Geschäftsbetrieb der indischen Filialen von Volkart Brothers [no date, approx. 1920–1924].

60 VA, Dossier 5: Bombay III: India General, 24. Some staff notes/terms, Programme: Volkart Brothers Athletic Sports, Saturday, 24 February 1940, W.I.F.A. Grounds; VA, Dossier 24: I/P/C Terms of Local Staff, I. general notes on staff terms: Bombay to Vevey, 29 February 1940.

61 GL, Records of Ralli Bros., Ms. 23834: Report to the Chairman of Ralli Brothers Limited, April 12th, 1939, 15.

62 VA, Dossier 3: Bombay I, 4. Table of Events 1851–1961/2; Anderegg, *Chronicle*, 1976, 416.

63 VA, Konferenz-Protokolle vom 5. Januar 1945–1927. Juni 1947: Protokoll vom 3. August 1945.

64 VA, Dossier 5: Bombay III: India General, 24. Some staff notes/terms: The Volkart Brothers (Bombay) Staff Union (Estd. 1–3–1947), Registration No. 372, Constitution & Review (For Members Only).

Part III

The De-Europeanization of Global Markets

8 An Era of Crises
Europe After 1918

The reverberating shockwaves of World War I shook the institutional foundations of the global economy. A wide range of structural problems—the debts of the European nations that had fought in the war, the overcapacities in heavy industry and agriculture that had been built up during the war, the protectionist economic policies of many countries and the difficulties of reintroducing the gold standard—plunged the global economy into a crisis that was dramatically exacerbated by the Great Depression.[1] While prior to 1914 the international exchange of products had grown faster than the global production of goods, the reverse was true after the war. Between 1881 and 1913, global trade grew by 40 percent, but slowed to 14 percent between 1913 and 1937.[2]

Nevertheless, the notion that a uniform economic deglobalization took place between 1918 and 1939 must be relativized in two respects.

First, an analysis of the statistical data shows that by the mid-1920s the volume of global trade had returned to a level similar to what had been achieved prior to 1914. It was not until 1929 that the economy suffered a collapse that was, in fact, even more dramatic.[3] Furthermore, not all parts of the world were equally affected by the severe downturn in global trade after 1918. Although the war had a devastating impact on European economies, the US economy emerged from the conflict stronger than ever. In Asia the measures taken during the economic war resulted in a decline in imports from Europe after 1914, which fueled robust economic growth in Japan, China and India.[4] This changed the orientation and structure of the flow of trade. Before the war, Asian imports and exports had predominantly involved Europe, but after 1918 there was an increase in both intra-Asian trade and trade with the US. And while the Europeans had primarily exported textiles and other consumer goods to Asia, after 1918 they increasingly began to ship machinery for the newly established Indian, Chinese and Japanese textile mills.[5]

Second, the deglobalization theory becomes problematic when one looks beyond the global balance of trade and examines the individual players who were responsible for the worldwide exchange of goods. A number of business historians have pointed out that the interwar era was by no means a historic period in which companies restricted their activities to their home markets. In fact, it was during this period that many companies stepped up their investments abroad, in part in reaction to the growing protectionism of the day, and began to do more business on a global scale.[6]

It appears that two opposing trends occurred during the interwar era in Europe.[7] From a quantitative perspective foreign trade declined sharply, as was painfully felt in many European countries, while on a qualitative level this was accompanied by a process of global integration among individual companies. This suggests that the development of the global economy and worldwide economic exchanges should not be viewed as a teleological and homogenous process that can be clearly divided into phases of globalization and deglobalization. Instead, researchers need to be sensitive to the asynchronicities, contradictions and dead ends inherent in such globalization processes, and particularly to the possible disparities between the actions of diverse global players.[8]

"A de-Europeanizing tendency in the global economy"

For the reasons stated above, the interwar era will not be described here as a phase of deglobalization, but rather as an era of de-Europeanization of the global economy.[9] The notion of a uniform deglobalization also needs to be viewed from a more nuanced perspective because not all parts of the world were equally affected by the collapse of foreign trade. Upon closer examination, it becomes clear that this was primarily a European phenomenon. Between 1911–1913 and 1927–1929, Europe's share of global trade declined from more than 62 percent to just under 52 percent.[10] Even though European countries still had a hand in more than half of worldwide imports and exports, this drop in businesses is unmistakable. By contrast, between 1913 and 1924 the US and Canada increased their share of global trade from 14 to 19 percent, while Asian countries saw an increase from 7.5 to 10 percent. The proportion of trade controlled by the remaining world regions remained roughly the same during this period. Between 1913 and 1924, the countries of South America were responsible for only roughly 6 percent of the international exchange of goods, followed by Australia and Polynesia with 3 percent, Central America with between 2 and 3 percent and Africa with slightly more than 2 percent. Of particular note here was the development of the Asian countries, both in the intra-Asian trade and in the trade with the US, Canada and Australia. Whereas in 1913 nearly 16 percent of all imports to the US came from Asia, by 1924 this figure had risen to almost 26 percent. At the same time, the proportion of net US exports that went to Asia rose from 5 to over 11 percent.[11]

In addition to declining exports and imports, Europe also lost importance as an industrial region after World War I. The winners were the US, which had surpassed Europe in 1890, and Japan, which underwent a rapid phase of industrialization during the first decades of the twentieth century.[12] World War I intensified this development. The emergence of an increasingly polycentric structure in the global economy had been observed by several contemporaries. In view of the relative weakness of the European economy, the increasing industrialization in Asia and the growing influence of American capital, German economist Hermann Levy noted back in 1926 that there was "a de-Europeanizing tendency in the global economy in a wide range of economic sectors."[13]

To what extent did this development influence the mindset of individual entrepreneurs during the interwar era? Can the process of de-Europeanization be observed not only on the macro-economic level but also on the micro level? These questions will be tackled in this and the three subsequent chapters, as illustrated by the history of Volkart.

While the structure of the international cotton trade was completely oriented toward Europe during the nineteenth century and controlled by European companies, the dawn of the twentieth century marked a turning point that would lead to a new orientation in the flow of trade from 1918 onwards. Up until the beginning of the twentieth century, imports of American cotton to Europe had been completely dominated by European trading companies, allowing them to rake in the lion's share of the profits from this branch of trade.[14]

Before the outbreak of World War I, only very few American trading companies like McFadden, Weld & Co., Alexander Sprunt and Son and Anderson Clayton & Co. had been able to accumulate sufficient capital to enter into partnerships with European merchant houses or acquire their own warehouses in Europe, which would have helped them to receive loans from European banks. Bolstered by the growing strength of the American economy and the increasing role of the US as a financial center, these trading firms managed to convince American banks to grant them loans to export cotton to Europe, which US lending institutions had viewed as an excessively risky business venture until then. This trend was further intensified by World War I. For instance, Anderson Clayton conducted a large export transaction with Russia in 1914, opened its own branch office in Le Havre in 1916 and established an efficient purchasing organization with its own gins and presses in the American South. After 1918, American cotton traders Anderson Clayton and McFadden increasingly began to run their businesses on a global scale. They opened a number of sales offices in Germany and Britain, followed by branches in China and Japan to meet the ever-growing demand for US cotton among East Asian spinning mills.

For their part, Japanese trading companies pursued a rapid course of expansion during the interwar era and established branch offices in Europe, Africa, North and South America as well as in diverse South Asian and East Asian countries.[15] In addition to controlling most of the cotton imports to Japan and China, by the late 1920s companies like Toyo Menkwa and Nippon Menkwa handled 15 percent of all imports of Indian cotton to Europe. This led British observers in 1930 to issue the following warning in the official bulletin of the Royal Statistical Society: "If Lancashire does not look out she will soon have to buy her Indian cotton from Japanese firms."[16]

New Subsidiaries in Europe

Despite the tumult and uncertainty in the wake of World War I, this was not a period of constant decline and retreat for many internationally active trading companies. Increased foreign investments often came in direct reaction to the economic turmoil after 1918. Since the war had weakened the European economy for years to come, Volkart redoubled its activities in East Asia and made its first attempt to gain a foothold in the US market. It established branch offices and subsidiaries in quick succession in Osaka (1919), Bremen (1920), New York (1920), Shanghai (1921), Calcutta (1922) and Singapore (1924), making Volkart into a truly globally active trading company for the first time.

The establishment of a new subsidiary in Bremen was a direct consequence of the economic problems in Germany. German spinning mills traditionally ranked among Volkart's main buyers of Indian cotton, which made them some of the company's most important customers. But after the war many of these manufacturers suffered from the economic situation in the country. They had particular difficulties receiving bank loans to pay the trading companies for the cotton the moment it arrived in Germany, as had been common before the war.[17] To address this problem, the partners at Volkart decided in 1920 to establish an independent company to import Indian commodities to Germany, working on a commission basis on behalf of the headquarters.[18]

The new subsidiary was primarily established to provide German spinning mills with cotton on credit. This practice had been strictly rejected by Volkart until then, which is why it was outsourced to the new firm. The new subsidiary in Bremen was a success despite the financial difficulties of the German cotton mills. Already during the first season in 1920–1921, Volkart Bremen imported 28 percent of all Indian cotton supplied to Germany. Shortly thereafter, this figure rose to even 32 percent, and after 1932 was still a respectable 22 percent.[19] Another startup did not fare nearly as well. In 1922, Volkart invested in a company in Trieste, Italy called Sicmat—Società Italiana Commercio Materie Tessili—that was to supply raw cotton to Italian and Polish spinning mills, and to textile mills in the former Habsburg monarchy. This minority interest in the firm secured Volkart exclusive rights for sales of Indian raw cotton to Sicmat. In 1928, Sicmat was forced to declare bankruptcy because the company that was contracted to sell the textiles made with Sicmat cotton had lost a fortune speculating on the stock exchange. This bankruptcy resulted in losses of nearly 1.3 million Swiss francs for Volkart and was a huge setback for the firm's sales.[20]

Expanding the Range of Products

Aside from boosting Volkart's business in Germany, the opening of the branch in Bremen had an unanticipated impact on the geographical orientation of the cotton business. Indeed, shortly after the new German company opened its doors it was already endeavoring to enter the American cotton sector.[21] Officials at the headquarters in Winterthur showed little enthusiasm for the plans put forward by the Bremen subsidiary. They cited the fact that the competition in the American cotton sector was fierce and that to compete Volkart would have to establish a purchasing organization similar to the one in India. Such an expansion seemed too risky in the eyes of Volkart executives and they flatly rejected it. But officials in Winterthur were willing to

> enter the sector for exotic varieties such as Peruvian, Brazilian and Argentinean strains, and the markets in Hamburg and Bremen promised to be a bonanza in this respect. This is a field that has not been so thoroughly grazed, because in the details of its operation it more closely resembles Indian than American cotton.[22]

Volkart Bremen subsequently began to import Brazilian, Mexican and Turkish cotton to Germany,[23] thereby benefitting from the fact that these countries had pushed ahead with the cultivation of cotton during the interwar era.[24] To facilitate access to the Brazilian cotton market, in 1924 Volkart opened an agency in São Paulo for the purchase of raw cotton.[25]

Entering the American cotton business remained a hotly debated topic over the years that followed. During the 1920s, the subsidiaries in Osaka and Shanghai joined Volkart Bremen in calling for an expansion into the American market because US cotton was in high demand among East Asian spinning mills. Consequently, the company started to export American cotton in the late 1920s. This was initially a loss-making business, but that changed in 1930 when Volkart became the sole representative of the American Cotton Cooperative Association for sales in India, China, Japan and eventually Central Europe. Virtually overnight the company became one of the largest exporters of American raw cotton.[26] It is worth emphasizing how often the company's subsidiaries had tried to nudge the company in this direction during the interwar era. While the headquarters in Winterthur tended to pursue rather conservative policies with regard to the cotton business and continued to make the trade in Indian cotton the focus of its activities, the subsidiaries made proposals for business innovations that over the long term would permanently alter the trading company's area of activity. As will be shown later in this book, the export of US cotton to East Asia in the early 1930s put the cotton business back in the black after Volkart had suffered bitter losses for a number of years,[27] and the expansion to Brazil allowed Volkart to enter the Brazilian coffee business during the 1940s, making the company into one of the world's leading coffee trading firms after World War II.[28]

The Establishment of a Volkart Bank?

After the commodities trade generated record profits for the trading companies in the sector during the initial postwar years, business suffered a dramatic decline in the mid-1920s. Prices plummeted as a result of the increased cultivation of commodities during the war and in the early 1920s. Worldwide inventories of cotton increased sharply after 1944, while cotton prices dropped by 50 percent between 1924 and 1929.[29] In view of this development, Volkart's profits also declined from 1922 onwards, despite high turnover. Starting in 1926, the company made losses for a number of years.[30] To make matters worse, a number of branches that had been established after 1918 were in the red.[31]

To get the company back on track, the partners at Volkart examined to what extent they should resize the business or perhaps adopt a completely new orientation. In 1928, they received a proposal that called for the foundation of an in-company financial institution. Mr. Rehmer, a member of Volkart's finance department, illustrated in a 16-page exposé how the company could use its extensive network of branches to serve as a commercial bank.[32] If the partners had approved Rehmer's proposal, Volkart would have followed in the footsteps of a number of trading firms since the nineteenth century. Over the years, many financially powerful trading companies had begun to use their business acumen and capital to lend money to other merchants, and had eventually transformed into commercial banks in their own right.[33] Volkart would have fulfilled many of the conditions for such a move. As Rehmer noted, Volkart's finance department regularly shifted considerable sums of money between the individual branches to provide them with the necessary funds for the trading business, and it maintained intensive contacts with commercial banks in various countries. On a smaller scale, Volkart gave advance payments to merchants and plantation owners after 1918 and was prepared to conclude transactions on a credit basis, something that earlier had been categorically rejected for decades.

But there were a number of problems with Rehmer's plan.[34] A member of the executive board warned that such a step would complicate the firm's operations because "we would have to treat the various categories (merchant, banker and manufacturer) from diverse perspectives, which could easily lead to dissatisfaction." To make matters worse, he said that by founding its own bank Volkart would be competing with the banking institutions that the company needed to finance its own commercial transactions: "It is questionable whether we would be able to manage with the funds available to us, particularly in times of crisis."[35] This view was also shared by the partners and the proposal was ultimately rejected.

In the Red during the Crisis of the 1930s

Business went from bad to worse. The stock market crash of 1929 accelerated the collapse of commodities prices. Prices for raw cotton plummeted by another 50 percent between 1929 and 1932, meaning that cotton only cost one-quarter of the price that it commanded in 1924.[36]

Volkart remained in the red and made record losses of 15 million Swiss francs in 1931 (Table 8.1).[37] The company's capital, which had amounted

Table 8.1 Net profits and losses of the Volkart company, 1901–1931 (in millions of pounds sterling). Actual figures expressed in 1913 prices, adjusted for inflation according to the Swiss consumer price index

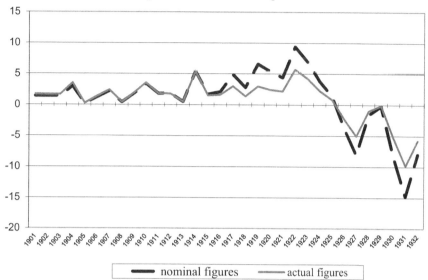

nominal figures   actual figures

(Source: the author's calculations; data from VA, Dossier 61: ex GR persönliches Archiv I, Graphische Tabellen: ratio of share capital to profits and losses)

to 64 million pounds in 1925, had been whittled down by constant losses to roughly half that by the early 1930s. Georg Reinhart felt that the root cause of this development was the massive expansion of business activities after 1918. After all, as he noted, the fields of activity that the company had engaged in before the war—such as importing raw materials to Europe and, to some extent, the import business of European consumer goods to India—continued to be profitable: "One can safely assume," Reinhart said, "that if the company had continued to pursue this 'old' model of business and steered clear of new products and business methods, it would have twice as much capital to its name today."[38]

The large losses of the late 1920s and early 1930s (Table 8.2) eventually threatened the company's creditworthiness. Georg Reinhart noted in 1934 that the banks asked critical questions of the company for the first time ever with regard to "our declining funds, and this calls for extreme caution and prudence."[39] The company reacted by rapidly downsizing its business in the early 1930s. The Singapore branch, which had been opened in 1924 and only made losses ever since, was closed again in 1930 and the other branches underwent intense consolidation.[40] In India, for instance, the company abandoned the seed export business (Table 8.3).[41]

During the Great Depression, Volkart had to rethink its business tactics because the company was increasingly forced to deliver cotton on credit.[42]

Table 8.2 Company assets (share capital + current account) 1920–1932 in pounds sterling

1920	36,328,106
1921	41,837,962
1922	51,721,095
1923	58,947,566
1924	62,609,077
1925	64,270,619
1926	62,017,158
1927	55,599,110
1928	55,763,497
1929	57,086,832
1930	49,808,372
1931	35,329,231
1932	26,653,379

(Source: VA, Dossier 61: ex GR persönliches Archiv I, Allerlei geschäftliche Informationen, Statistiken etc.)

Table 8.3 Turnover of the Indian branches, 1914–1932

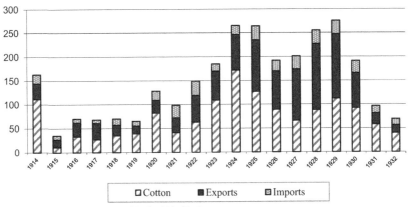

(Source: VA, Dossier 61: Graphische Tabellen)

As late as 1927, Georg Reinhart had reiterated the firm's policy of not granting credit:

> The company has made steady progress according to this principle for 75 years. We have no reason to be less conservative than we were earlier—on the contrary. The large sales that we annually achieve (without granting credit) are fully sufficient to engage our capital reserves and generate an appropriate amount of interest on these funds.[43]

This policy appears to have changed during the 1930s. At any rate, Peter Reinhart noted in a memo in 1959 that prior to World War II it had become "virtually the norm" to accept promissory notes from French spinners. It goes without saying that this entailed a high payment risk. This was a worthwhile approach for Volkart, though, because it allowed it to capture a larger share of the market. Peter Reinhart said that "we owe our position in France to a large extent to our willingness to accept these conditions. It is a key weapon in our battle with the traders in Le Havre."[44]

The political developments in Europe during the 1930s brought additional changes to the business.[45] After the Nazis seized power in 1933, companies were temporarily banned from importing American cotton to Germany. The German regulatory agency for the sector later allocated funds to the spinning mills that they were allowed to use to acquire cotton from import firms based in Germany.[46] Volkart executives felt that these changes would in no way interfere with their business contacts. In fact, since they could benefit from the German price agreements throughout the entire country, they surmised that this might even prove advantageous to the competitiveness of Volkart in the Indian cotton business.[47]

This conclusion is revealing because it shows that Volkart apparently had very few moral qualms about the political turmoil in Europe, which heralded the end of democratic ideals and the demise of the rule of law in many countries and threatened to plunge the continent into a new war. Or, if company officials did have misgivings, there is no evidence of this in the firm's archives. Business transactions with Fascist Italy, Nazi Germany, occupied Czechoslovakia, Austria and Francoist Spain were evidently judged less from an ethical point of view than from the perspective of what impact they might have on the future course of business.[48] Moral considerations also played a secondary role with regard to business transactions in East Asia. In the minutes from a meeting in February 1939, the board of directors went on record as saying that it was "fundamentally opposed" to the proposal put forward by the Japanese subsidiary "to commence business transactions in airplanes, machine guns and finished products that could be used for military purposes of any kind." Nonetheless, it had no objections to supplying "raw materials and semi-finished products that could perhaps also be used to manufacture war material."[49]

The Political Views of the Partners

The company's business attitude toward the rise of fascism and National Socialism and the possible outbreak of a new war was, at best, indifferent. But what about the political views of the partners? Werner Reinhart was very receptive to right-wing ideology. He subscribed to the *Schweizerbanner*, a newspaper published by the *Schweizer Heimatwehr*, and joined this fascist renewal movement in the spring of 1930.[50] In May 1936, Werner Reinhart informed the rector of the German University of Freiburg im Breisgau that he unfortunately could not attend the award ceremony for Nazi poet Emil Strauss, whom he admired greatly, and expressed his regrets that he was "unable to use this celebratory occasion to partake in a neighborly exchange of ideas with our Alemannic brothers on the other side of the border."[51] And in June 1939 he thanked a member of the district leadership of the NSDAP in the southern German town of Donaueschingen for sending him a paper on Germanic culture and, with reference to an earlier meeting at a music festival in southern Germany, made the following comment: "I realized once again how valuable and important it is these days to establish such close contacts across the border. Hopefully this will also be increasingly better understood on our side."[52] Starting in 1933, Werner Reinhart also supported German painter Hermann Burte, who made no secret of his admiration for the Nazis.[53] In a speech given in Freiburg im Breisgau in 1936, Burte spoke of the relationship between Swiss and southern German literature in a manner that the *Neue Zürcher Zeitung* newspaper called "blood mysticism". In Burte's words:

> In Freiburg im Breisgau, in Alemannia, Swiss poets present their works to their [German] neighbors in Baden and bear witness with us to the unity in the spirit of the Alemanni! Over their heads and ours sadly resounds the call of the Alemannic mother of the people: Home, home! Into the night of madness. It will only fall silent when all children of her lineage return home to the green house on the Rhine under the colossal blue stage.[54]

Georg Reinhart was also in contact with Burte and regularly exchanged books with him.[55] While his brother Werner was apparently extremely impressed with Burte's blood-and-soil mysticism, Georg Reinhart flatly rejected it. In reaction to the above speech, he wrote to Burte that, in his opinion, Switzerland had no desire to be annexed by Germany:

> The confederate in Ticino or Sion is closer to my heart than the Alemannian in the Third Reich, despite the kinship of the language. I see the people of the cantons of Ticino, Grisons and Vaud first and foremost as *Swiss* with whom I share the same political ideals, which is certainly not the case these days among the Allemanni in the Third Reich. . . . I believe that every respectable Swiss thinks as I do, and it would thus be wrong to ascribe to us German-speaking Swiss an implausible sense of nostalgia for a land that lies beyond the Rhine.[56]

After Werner Reinhart's death, the fact that he had supported Burte for decades was a source of some embarrassment. Werner Reinhart's heirs decided that Burte would receive no more support after his benefactor's death. Although senior management at Volkart shared Georg Reinhart's aversion to Burte's political views, they decided in 1953 that it would not be in keeping with Werner Reinhart's wishes for Burte to end up empty-handed.

He was granted a monthly stipend of 250 Swiss francs from the firm and a one-time payment of 500 francs from the Volkart Foundation.[57]

World War II

After the outbreak of World War II, Volkart immediately took a range of precautionary measures to forestall as much as possible the negative impacts of the conflict. As with the war of 1914–1918, this new conflagration posed a serious threat to an internationally active trading company. Since the firm anticipated delays in telegraph communications between Switzerland and India caused by the censorship measures of the authorities, it was decided that Volkart's London office would henceforth communicate directly with the Indian branches without previously consulting the headquarters in Winterthur. Furthermore, all outgoing telegrams were subject to an in-company censorship to ensure that no messages were sent that could prove compromising for Volkart.[58] All business contacts with Germany were immediately placed on hold. On September 7, 1939, the company informed its German customers that "following the United Kingdom's entrance in the war, the hitherto cordial business relations between your and our company shall be suspended until further notice." This meant that current orders could no longer be filled. Goods delivered by German companies, but not yet paid for by Volkart, were considered German property and confiscated by the British. Payments due for disbursement to Germany could no longer be transferred and were credited to the corresponding companies by the staff in Winterthur pending a change in the situation.[59] In the fall of 1939, large cotton warehouses belonging to Volkart in Poland were seized. Since the invoicing address was the Volkart branch in London, the Germans came to the conclusion that the cotton belonged to a British company. It was not until Volkart's lawyers managed to convince the Germans that the company's business was conducted out of Winterthur that the confiscated cotton was returned to its owners.[60]

In October 1939, preparations were already underway to move the headquarters in the event of a German attack to allow senior management and part of the workforce to maintain contact with the branches in Asia and the US or flee abroad.[61] In February 1940, it was decided to transfer the company headquarters to the town of Vevey in western Switzerland.[62] This move allowed Volkart to solve a problem that had dogged the company for quite some time. The Swiss corporate code of 1881 stipulated that the name of a general partnership had to reflect a company's actual ownership structure. Since there were no longer any Volkart *Brothers* following the deaths of Salomon and Johann Georg Volkart, the company had to formally move its headquarters to London in 1893 if it intended to retain its name.[63] The revised Swiss corporate code of 1937 tightened this restriction even further by calling for "branch offices of the company whose headquarters were abroad" to declare "the location of the main office." This was an awkward matter for Volkart because it would have had to designate itself as a British company with headquarters in London, and the main office in Winterthur, which was de facto the company's headquarters, would have officially been demoted to a branch office.[64] In the event of a war, Volkart would thus automatically be treated as a hostile company in the regions occupied by the Axis powers. Yet there was a provision in the law that allowed a company to retain its name if the current owners were explicitly named or if a company transferred its headquarters to Switzerland from overseas.[65] The transfer of the headquarters to Vevey offered an elegant solution to this problem by also allowing Volkart to move the nominal headquarters of the firm from London to Switzerland. Indeed, the fact that Volkart "would also achieve its main purpose with this move, namely transferring its headquarters to Switzerland from abroad, would perhaps go unnoticed."[66] In a press release dated late May 1940, the company announced that it would add to the "previously existing company name of 'Volkart Brothers' the addition 'owners Georg Reinhart, Werner Reinhart, Oskar Reinhart and Peter Reinhart'" as a subscript to the company's title. It was only mentioned in passing that this entry would be added to the commercial registry in Vevey, where senior management would have its headquarters until further notice.[67] Thus Volkart formally became a Swiss company again. When the trading company transferred its headquarters back to Winterthur in the summer of 1941, the company was given the above entry in the commercial registry of the canton of Zurich.[68] What's more, the company's letterhead was supplemented with the phrase "Swiss company, founded 1851" to emphasize the Swiss identity of the firm.[69] This addendum had originally been affixed before World War I,[70] but had been left off again from the mid-1930s onwards. It is no longer possible to determine the extent to which British authorities realized that Volkart's headquarters had been transferred from London back to Switzerland. However, the British took very careful note of the fact that the staff of the Winterthur headquarters had been transferred to Vevey out of fear of a German attack. This was interpreted as "evidence of good faith, or at least pro-Ally policy on the part of Messrs Volkart Bros."[71]

It was essential for Volkart not to attract the attention of the British authorities. Already in September 1939, senior management had warned its department heads that any infringement of these regulations, even if it occurred solely as a result of negligence, could lead to "our company being placed on the blacklist, which would be tantamount to the end . . . of our existence as a global trading company."[72] Not surprisingly, all contact was suspended between Volkart GmbH in Bremen and the rest of the company in the fall of 1939. Throughout the entire war, Volkart Bremen remained the exclusive representative for sales of Sandoz paints in Germany, a position that it had held since 1937. This business was highly profitable and largely riskless and covered all of the expenses of the Bremen subsidiary.[73]

Although communications between the headquarters and the branches in London, New York, Shanghai and Osaka—not to mention the offices in India and Ceylon—were not completely suspended throughout the entire war, it often took a number of months for news from Asia to reach Winterthur. Accordingly, the headquarters in Winterthur focused primarily on importing commodities, food and consumer goods to Switzerland.[74] On other continents Volkart also concentrated on niche businesses like trading grain inside India[75] and buying and selling American cotton on the US domestic market. Due to increased demand in the US, Volkart managed to establish an efficient procurement and sales organization that after 1945 was capable of supplying the company's diverse branches with American cotton.[76]

All in all, Volkart was not able to expand during World War II, but instead had to endeavor to maintain its organization "on a reduced scale since the outbreak of the war,"[77] as was noted in the conference minutes from a meeting in 1944. In that sense, the situation was fundamentally different than during World War I, when Volkart was able to achieve record profits thanks to price increases in the commodity sector.[78] The difference arose from the fact that Japan and China, which had been lucrative sales markets for Volkart between 1914 and 1918, had now become theaters of war and, by the same token, the destructive power of military conflicts had increased enormously in the two decades since the end of World War I. In view of the ravages of World War II, Volkart emerged from the war remarkably unscathed. The emotional state of the company owners at the end of the war was portrayed by Peter Reinhart in his 1951 company anniversary speech, in which he emphasized how intergovernmental conflicts led to a remarkable increase in the importance of a company's national affiliation in the global trading business during the initial decades of the twentieth century. Reinhart said that the company had been "incredibly fortunate" during the 1940s for the "simple reason that we, as a Swiss company, with a primarily Swiss workforce, were not directly affected by the war." He went on to say that only very few staff members, all of them employed by foreign subsidiaries, had lost their lives and, in contrast to World War I, not a single employee had been interned.[79]

Notes

1 Osterhammel/Petersson, *Globalization*, 2005, 103–106.
2 Lewis, *Economic Survey*, 1970, 59–72; Jones, *Merchants to Multinationals*, 2000, 84–85.
3 United Nations Statistical Office. *International Trade Statistics*, 1962.
4 Hardach, *Der Erste Weltkrieg*, 1973, 278–280; Kawabe, "Development of Overseas Operations," 1987; Smitka (ed.), *The Interwar Economy of Japan*, 1998; Mutz, "Ein unendlich weites Gebiet," 2006; Parthasarathi, "Global trade and textile workers," 2010, 572–573. See Chapters 9 and 10.
5 Helfferich, *Die Wirtschaft Niederländisch-Indiens*, 1921. See Chapter 11.

6   Jones, *Merchants to Multinationals*, 2000, 86; Jones, "The End of National-ity?", 2006, 164.

7   Fäßler, *Globalisierung*, 2007, 100.

8   Cooper, "What is the Concept of Globalization Good For?", 2001.

9   See for the impact of World War I on global trade in more detail: Dejung/Peters-son (ed.), *Foundations of World-Wide Economic Integration*, 2013.

10 Schlote, "Zur Frage der sogenannten 'Enteuropäisierung' des Welthandels," 1933, 386.

11 Levy, "Die Enteuropäisierung der Welthandelsbilanz", 1926, 331–332.

12 Pollard, *Peaceful Conquest*, 1981, 281.

13 Levy, "Die Enteuropäisierung der Welthandelsbilanz," 329; for a similar line of reasoning, also see Nonn, *Das 19. und 20. Jahrhundert*, 2007, 29.

14 This section of the text is based on the writings of Clayton Garwood, *Will Clay-ton*, 1958, 78–95; Killick, "The Transformation of Cotton Marketing," 1981, 154–168; Killick, "Specialized and General Trading Firms," 1987, 256–263.

15 Ellinger/Ellinger, "Japanese Competition in the Cotton Trade," 1930, 198; Kil-lick, "Specialized and General Trading Firms," 1987, 263; Nakagawa, "Business Management in Japan," 2001, 276.

16 Ellinger/Ellinger, "Japanese Competition in the Cotton Trade," 1930, 201. For the market shares of diverse trading companies in the cotton exports from Bom-bay to Japan, China and Europe during the 1925–1926 season, see Contractor, *A Handbook of Indian Cotton*, 1928, 38–39.

17 VA, Protokolle der Dienstag Konferenzen vom 8. Juni 1920-Okt. 1928: Konfer-enz vom 10. Oktober 1922.

18 VA, Dossier 13: London/Liverpool (VB + Woods&Thorburn) / Bremen, Bremen (incl. Hamburg office): Winterthur to London, Bombay, Karachi, Tuticorin, Tel-licherry, Cochin, Madras, Colombo, 12 February 1920. See also BB, Gebrüder Vol-kart GmbH: Volkart Brothers GmbH, Bremen, to Bremer Baumwollbörse, 1 March 1920 and Bremer Baumwollbörse to Volkart Brothers GmbH, 19 March 1920.

19 VA, Dossier 42: Rechtliches, Cotton Poland 2nd world war: Denkschrift im Auftrag der Firma Gebrüder Volkart in Winterthur (Schweiz) über deren Ansprüche in den besetzten Gebieten des ehem. Polen an die Haupttreuhandstelle—Ost, Ber-lin, 19 June 1940.

20 VA, Dossier 18: Winterthur I, 4 Sicmat: Winterthur an Bombay, 16 July 1929. For more on the Sicmat bankruptcy, also see The Times (London), March 15, 1929, 24 and 26; Dossier 63: ex GR persönliches Archiv III Abbau-Massnahmen Import/Engineering- Div. Bilanzen.

21 VA, Dossier 13: London/Liverpool (VB + Woods&Thorburn) / Bremen, Bremen (incl. Hamburg office), 3. Correspondence: Winterthur to Bremen, 9 June 1922.

22 VA, Dossier 13: London/Liverpool (VB + Woods&Thorburn) / Bremen, Bremen (incl. Hamburg office), 3. Correspondence: Winterthur to Bremen, 9 June 1922.

23 VA, Dossier 13: London/Liverpool (VB + Woods&Thorburn) / Bremen, Bremen (incl. Hamburg office), 4. Note on Volkart G.m.b.H. Bremen 1921–1958 by P.R.: Notiz Volkart G.m.b.H. von Peter Reinhart, 19 May 1958.

24 Kindleberger, *The World in Depression*, 1973, 90.

25 Rambousek et. al., *Volkart*, 1990, 161–162.

26 VA, Dossier 16: USA, Brazil, Mexico, Guatemala/Costa Rica, Turkey, I. USA, 2. Table of Events V.B. Inc.: Notiz von Peter Reinhart vom 20. September 1950: Entwicklung des amerikanischen Baumwollgeschäftes.

27 See Chapter 10.

28 See Chapter 13.

29 League of Nations, *Economic Instability in the Postwar World*, 1945, 85; Kindleberger, *The World in Depression*, 1973, 88; James, *The End of Globaliza-tion*, 2001, 27, 102ff.

30 VA: Dossier 61: ex GR persönliches Archiv I: Graphische Tabellen: Verhältnis von Stammkapital zu Gewinn und Verlust.
31 VA, Dossier 63: ex GR persönliches Archiv III, Mappe: Abbau-Massnahmen Import/Engineering: Div. Bilanzen.
32 VA, Weisse Schachtel: Herr Rehmer. Eine Entwicklungsmöglichkeit. February 1928.
33 Chapman, *Merchant Enterprise in Britain*, 1992, 69–77.
34 VA, Weisse Schachtel: Herr Rehmer. Eine Entwicklungsmöglichkeit. February 1928.
35 VA, Weisse Schachtel: Zum Exposé Herrn Rehmers, ohne Datum.
36 League of Nations, Economic Instability in the Postwar World, 1945, 85; Kindleberger, *The World in Depression*, 1973, 88; James, *The End of Globalization*, 2001, 27, 102ff.
37 VA: Dossier 61: ex GR persönliches Archiv I: Graphische Tabellen: Verhältnis von Stammkapital zu Gewinn und Verlust.
38 VA, Dossier 63: ex GR persönliches Archiv III, Mappe: Abbau-Massnahmen Import/Engineering: Memorandum from GR to WR and E. Neuenhofer, 24 October 1930.
39 VA, Dossier 63: ex GR persönliches Archiv III, Mappe: Abbau-Massnahmen Import/Engineering: Georg Reinhart, Memorandum to Werner Reinhart, 20 September 1934.
40 Rambousek/Vogt/Volkart, *Volkart*, 1990, 141.
41 VA, Dossier 3: Bombay I, 4. Table of Events 1851–1961/2.
42 VA, Dossier 4: Bombay II, 17. General financial correspondence incl. securing exchange 1893, 1927–1928, 1931, 1935: Winterthur to Bombay, Kopie an alle Häuser, 4 September 1931.
43 VA, Dossier 18: 3 Nominal transfer of HO to LONDON from Winterthur: Handwritten note by Georg Reinhart, 1927
44 VA, Konferenz-Protokolle vom 15. Januar 1959–1930. Juni 1965: PR, Office Note, 27. Januar 1959, Eigenakzepte für französische Spinner.
45 In late 1934, the Swiss Association of Transit and Global Trading Companies was established to bolster the domestic political position of Swiss trading firms. For companies involved in the inner European trade, it was above all the clearing transactions with Italy and Germany as well as with Bulgaria and Yugoslavia that posed a problem. Volkart was often represented at the board meetings and, in the fall of 1935, sent a staff member to attend a meeting between the board of directors and the head of the Swiss Federal Department of Economic Affairs. Aside from that, Volkart's involvement in the association was rather limited: WA, Handschriften (HS) 421: Verband schweizerischer Transit- und Welthandelsfirmen, Basel, A 1: Gründungsakte (Copie) und maschinengeschriebene und gedruckte Statuten, 1934; A 2: Protokolle der Vorstandssitzungen 1934–1949.
46 VA, Dossier 18: Winterthur I, 6 Reports PR on his visits to various clients 1938/39, Reise in die Tschechoslowakei vom 5.-11. Nov. 1938, Bericht von Peter Reinhart vom 22.11.38
47 VA, Konferenz-Protokolle Januar 1939–1934. September 1939: Konferenz vom 16. März 1939.
48 This was in stark contrast to the period after World War II in which Volkart, for political reasons, considered halting all business transactions with the East Bloc. For more on this, see Chapter 14.
49 VA, Konferenz-Protokolle Januar 1939–1934. September 1939: Protokoll vom 17. February 1939.
50 SSW, Nachlass Werner Reinhart, Dep MK 391/55: Werner Reinhart, Winterthur, to the Zentralvorstand der Schweizer Heimatwehr, Zürich, 18 February 1930; Werner Reinhart, Winterthur, to Dr. Hs. Bader, Präsident der Schweizer Heimatwehr, Zürich, 3 March 1930.

51 SSW, Nachlass Werner Reinhart, Dep MK 389/32: Werner Reinhart to the Rektor of the Albrecht-Ludwigs-Universität Freiburg i. Br., 5 May 1936.

52 SSW, Nachlass Werner Reinhart, Dep MK 391/134: Werner Reinhart, Winterthur, to the district leadership of the N.S.D.A.P. Donaueschingen, 10 June 1939.

53 VA, Konferenz-Protokolle vom 16. Januar 1953–1956. Januar 1959: BR, Hermann Strübe Burte, 6. Mai 1953

54 Neue Zürcher Zeitung, 3 November 1936.

55 SSW, Nachlass Georg Reinhart, Ms GR 38/88.

56 SSW, Nachlass Georg Reinhart, Ms GR 38/88: Georg Reinhart to Hermann Burte, Winterthur, 6 November 1936.

57 VA, Konferenz-Protokolle vom 16. Januar 1953–1956. Januar 1959: BR, Hermann Strübe Burte, 6. Mai 1953.

58 VA, Konferenz-Protokolle Januar 1939–1934. September 1939: Konferenz vom 4. September 1939

59 VA, Dossier 18: 3 Nominal transfer of HO to LONDON from Winterthur: Rundbrief von Volkart and die deutschen Geschäftsverbindungen, Winterthur, 7 September 1939.

60 VA, Dossier 19: Winterthur II, Korrespondenz Sitzverlegung VB: London/Winterthur/Vevey/Winterthur 1940/1941: Protokoll über die Besprechung mit Herrn Dr. Henggeler 4. März 1940; Dossier 42: Rechtliches, Cotton Poland 2nd world war: Denkschrift im Auftrag der Firma Gebrüder Volkart in Winterthur (Schweiz) über deren Ansprüche in den besetzten Gebieten des ehem. Polen an die Haupttreuhandstelle—Ost, Berlin, 19 June 1940; Anderegg, *Chronicle*, 1976, 453.

61 VA, Dossier 18: Winterthur I, 8 Evacuation of the main part of the Winterthur office to the French part of Switzerland 1940–1941: Bericht über Evakuation des Betriebes, 10.10.39; Winterthur an alle Häuser, 5 December 1939, strictly confidential.

62 VA, Dossier 18: Winterthur I, 8 Evacuation of the main part of the Winterthur office to the French part of Switzerland 1940–1941: Gebrüder Volkart an den Stadtrat von Winterthur, 17. Februar 1940; 1 Table of Events: Winterthur an alle Häuser, 28 February 1940.

63 See Chapter 3.

64 VA, Dossier 18: Winterthur I, 3 Nominal transfer of HO to LONDON from Winterthur.

65 VA, Dossier 18: Winterthur I, 3 Nominal transfer of HO to LONDON from Winterthur; Dossier 19: Winterthur II, Korrespondenz Sitzverlegung VB: London/Winterthur/Vevey/Winterthur 1940/1941: Rechtsanwälte Robert Corti und Rudolf Hofmann, Winterthur to Firma Gebr. Volkart, Winterthur, 8 November 1938; Dossier 19: Winterthur II, Korrespondenz Sitzverlegung VB: London/Winterthur/Vevey/Winterthur 1940/1941: Eidgenössisches Justiz- und Polizeidepartement, Bern, to Herrn Dr. J. Henggeler, Zürich, 16 April 1940.

66 VA, Dossier 19: Winterthur II, Dokumente in Zusammenhang mit Transfer VB Head Office: nach London 1893 / nach Winterthur 1940: Georg Reinhart to Dr. J. Henggeler, Zürich, Vevey, 2 April 1940.

67 VA, Dossier 19: Winterthur II, Korrespondenz Sitzverlegung VB: London/Winterthur/Vevey/Winterthur 1940/1941: Gebr. Volkart, Vevey to Redaktion der Neuen Zürcher Zeitung, Zürich, 29 May 1940 (Pressemitteilung).

68 VA, Dossier 18: Winterthur I, 3 Nominal transfer of HO to LONDON from Winterthur.

69 Konferenz-Protokolle 6. Sept. 1939–1931. Mai 1940: Konferenz vom 19. Dezember 1939.

70 See Chapter 4.

71 NA, TS 13/3826: Naval Prize, Volkart Bros.: Report from Procurator General's Department, May 1940.

72 VA, Dossier 42: Rechtliches, Trading with the Enemy Act, 1939: Zur Zirkulation bei den Abteilungschefs in Vevey und Winterthur, Vevey, 12 September 1939.

73 VA, Dossier 13: London/Liverpool (VB + Woods&Thorburn) / BremenBremen (incl. Hamburg office), 4. Note on Volkart G.m.b.H. Bremen 1921–1958 by P.R.

74 Anderegg, *Chronicle*, 1976, 459; VA, Dossier 18: Winterthur I, 9 War-time activities of Winterthur/Vevey: Bericht über die Tätigkeit der Abteilung 10 von Oktober 1940 bis 31. August 1943, E. Zimmerli, Winterthur, 18. Oktober 1943. Other Swiss trading companies also focused primarily on importing raw materials to Switzerland during the war. For instance, the Winterthur company of Paul Reinhart & Co. managed cotton imports from Syria to Switzerland and helped the Hungarian government to import Turkish cotton in 1941. Private archive of Danièle Burckhardt: Burckhardt-Reinhart, My Fourth Journey to Turkey, 1941. For information on imports of fats and oils for the Swiss soap industry, which were conducted by a syndicate of global trading companies consisting of Volkart, the Union Handelsgesellschaft in Basel and Siber Hegner in Zurich, see Arch Miss 21, Bestand UTC, 4345: Gebr. Volkart, Siber, Hegner & Cie. u.a. 1944, received letters and 4346: Gebr. Volkart, Siber, Hegner & Cie. u.a. 1945, received letters.

75 Anderegg, *Chronicle*, 1976, 477ff.

76 Anderegg, *Chronicle*, 1976, 484–487. See Chapter 14.

77 VA, Konferenz-Protokolle 6. März 1943–1931. Dezember 1944: Konferenz vom 20. Juni 1944.

78 See Chapter 4.

79 Reinhart, "Rede zur Hundertjahrfeier," [1951], 17.

9 Growing Self-Confidence
India After 1918

The interwar era in India differed markedly from the situation prior to 1914. With increasing industrialization, Indian commodities exports steadily declined as more and more raw materials were used within the country. This forced European trading companies to consider whether they should continue to rely on the volatile export business or invest in Indian industrial plants. Meanwhile, political developments on the subcontinent were creating new challenges for European firms. With the Indian independence movement continuing to gain momentum, a non-British company like Volkart found itself particularly under pressure, caught in the middle between the anti-British boycotts of the Indian National Congress and the efforts of the British colonial government to maintain its hold on power.

Changes in the Indian Cotton Industry

The Government of India Act of 1919 gave Indian provincial governments more authority on agricultural policy issues after World War I. The British colonial power felt compelled to take this step as a concession to Indian demands to have a greater say in the running of their country and, from a tactical perspective, to take the wind out of the sails of the mounting independence movement.[1] This resulted in the establishment of diverse new institutions in Bombay designed to monitor the trading sector more effectively and improve the quality of Indian cotton. In 1921, the Indian Central Cotton Committee was founded to oversee the cultivation and trade of cotton. This organization included representatives of both European and Indian companies. Up until then, the trade had been monitored by various business associations that were each able to control only a certain segment of the supply chain. The Bombay Cotton Trade Association, founded back in 1875, enacted regulations for the trade in actual cotton and futures trading and saw to it that there was arbitration between buyers and sellers whenever differences of opinion arose. The fact that only Europeans were allowed into this organization was a source of discontent among Indian entrepreneurs, leading them to establish the Bombay Cotton Exchange as a competing association in 1892. This situation was in turn a source of irritation for the intermediaries, prompting them in 1915 to found the Bombay Cotton Brokers' Association, which primarily focused on regulating commodities futures.[2]

The Indian business community had resisted state control of the trading sector since the early nineteenth century.[3] This changed during the interwar era. Since entrepreneurs—particularly Indian business leaders—could now bring to bear their influence in the Indian Central Cotton Committee, there was relatively little resistance to this new organization, which soon played a very active role in the industry. In 1923, the committee passed the Cotton Transport Act, which authorized the individual Indian states to ban the importing of cotton into their territory if it was merely for the purpose of mixing it with other varieties. In 1925, the Indian government passed the Cotton Ginning and Pressing Factories Act, which called for the marking of every bale of cotton so it could be traced back to the original pressing factory if inspectors determined that the contents had been falsified.[4]

A further measure to improve the quality of Indian cotton was the creation of agricultural cooperatives. These organizations aimed to give cultivators greater control over their cotton and, more importantly, to make them less dependent on loans from moneylenders, whose high interest rates forced many peasants to live in a perpetual state of debt. The Indian government provided the cooperatives with interest-free loans.[5] In addition, the cooperatives organized auctions where cooperatives could sell their cotton. These auctions were for the explicit purpose of circumventing local intermediaries.[6] The cotton brokers tried to subvert this new system by boycotting the merchants who took part in these auctions. But since the auctions were supported by rural communities and village leaders, these attempts to undermine the scheme failed and the new measures proved more successful than originally anticipated by the government.[7] Nevertheless, for quite some time the Indian government failed to develop a state-run or cooperative system to grant agricultural loans. As a result, agricultural loans largely remained in the hands of rural moneylenders who in turn received loans from Indian banks that were established on the subcontinent during the 1920s.[8]

Additional measures to enhance the quality of cotton included the development of irrigation systems in Punjab and Sind and the successful introduction of long-staple American cotton varieties to these regions. All of these steps paved the way for a significant improvement in the quality of Indian cotton from the 1930s onwards. Whereas in 1926 only 6 percent of Indian cotton had a fiber length that was suitable for the manufacture of fine cloth, the proportion of long-staple cotton grown in the country had reached 18 percent by 1932.[9]

Why were these new institutions so successful during the interwar era in making improvements to financing opportunities and cotton quality after the British colonial power had failed with similar projects for decades? One of the main reasons for this was that the British had relied on isolated measures to improve the quality of cotton without carefully considering the social and economic realities in the Indian backcountry. By contrast, the Indian Central Cotton Committee took a more holistic view of the Indian cotton industry. It not only enacted laws to put a stop to fraudulent practices, but also dealt with the commercial aspects of the domestic trade, such as the granting of credit and the setting of prices, which were closely connected with improving the quality of the product.[10] Another key factor was that the Indian Central Cotton Committee was not an institution dominated by the British colonial rulers; Indian entrepreneurs played an important role in the organization. It thus met with far less resistance than an organization like the British agency that was tasked with implementing the Cotton Fraud Act in the late nineteenth century. The initiatives taken by the Indian Central Cotton Committee were also facilitated by the fact that, due to the expansion of the Indian textile industry during World War I and the 1920s, purchasers of Indian cotton were no longer solely located in Europe and East Asia. Indian manufacturers had a great deal of interest in purchasing better quality cotton so they could weave finer and superior quality cloth.[11] In fact, during the interwar era they managed to use long-staple Cambodia cotton grown in India to produce high-quality textiles that could compete with the fine fabrics from Manchester on the Indian market.[12]

The Boom in Indian Industrialization

The boom in the Indian textile industry also changed the structure of the cotton trade. While India had been primarily an exporter of raw cotton until the early twentieth century, now an increasing amount of Indian cotton was spun in local factories. Between the early 1920s and the late 1930s, the use of indigenous cotton in Indian spinning mills steadily increased, rising from 1.8 million bales during the 1923–1924 season to nearly 2.7 million bales by 1935–1936.[13] At the same time, imports of foreign cotton increased because Indian textile mills—like competitors in Japan before them—had begun to blend short-stapled Indian cotton with long-staple cotton from Egypt, East Africa and the US. Whereas prior to 1914 India annually imported an average of 12,000 tons of cotton, during the 1935–1936 season this figure rose to 77,000 and even reached 96,000 in 1938–1939.[14] Although the use of foreign cotton remained relatively marginal in comparison to the quantities of indigenous varieties that were spun in Indian factories, this shows that the boom in industrialization on the subcontinent was accompanied by a reorientation in the flow of trade.

This had an impact on the business of European cotton trading companies, which increasingly sold cotton to Indian spinning mills instead of shipping it to Europe or East Asia. For example, in the 1930s Ralli sold between 40 and 50 percent of its Indian cotton to manufacturers on the subcontinent.[15] On top of this came the import business with foreign cotton. Company officials at the headquarters in Winterthur noted in a letter written in 1931 that Volkart could supply Indian textile mills not only with

Indian cotton "but also with Egyptian and American cotton, for which we have outstanding connections with Reinhart, Alexandria and the ACCA in New Orleans."[16]

Restructuring of Cotton Procurement in the Interior of the Country

The early postwar period was extremely prosperous for many trading companies working in India because war-torn countries generated a huge demand for raw materials. Commodities prices peaked in 1921—and did not begin to decline again until 1935.[17] Sales were also fueled by the growing demand for Indian cotton in India, China and above all in Japan as these countries increasingly industrialized their production.[18] After 1918, this initially generated handsome profits for trading companies like Volkart and its rivals.[19] In 1920, Ralli achieved record sales of 63 million pounds, a result that the company was subsequently unable to repeat.[20] The Japanese trading firm Toyo Menkwa, which had been active in the Indian cotton trading sector since the late 1890s—initially as part of trading giant Mitsui Bussan, after 1920 as an independent company—achieved profits of 308,000 rupees in 1920 and 206,000 rupees in 1922.[21]

The halcyon days did not last long. As a result of the worldwide decline in commodities prices, competition was cutthroat in the Indian cotton trade during the late 1920s. The situation was compounded for exporters in 1927 when the Indian government set the rupee exchange rate at 1 s 6 d after it had been pegged to the British pound since 1893. This placed it 12.5 percent above the 1 s 4 d level prior to 1914. The government wanted to maintain a high rupee exchange rate to avoid a "flight from the rupee" that would have caused India to go bankrupt. But the high rupee exchange rate made Indian exports more expensive, and this not only limited the income of Indian farmers but also had a negative impact on the profit margins of trading firms.[22]

In reaction to the growing pressure on prices, many *jettawala* (Indian cotton traders) in Bombay dispatched their purchasing agents to the interior of the country, where stiff competition pushed up prices as well. Soon prices in the upcountry were higher than those in Bombay.[23] To cover their expenditures, many middlemen saw no option but to increase the weight of the cotton by wetting it down and blending it with extraneous substances.[24] As mentioned earlier, the problem with adulterated and contaminated goods had plagued the Indian cotton trade since the early nineteenth century.[25] Now this practice appeared to be back with a vengeance as desperate cotton traders, under pressure from plummeting prices in the 1920s, tried to enhance their profits by mixing cotton of various qualities and/or wetting down the goods.

Several observers also claimed that not only Indian peasants and petty merchants resorted to such tricks, but also European and Japanese trading companies. "All dealers, whether Europeans, Japanese or Indians, follow this practice," said Arno Pearse, the secretary general of the Manchester-based International Federation of Master Cotton Spinners and Manufacturers' Association, following a trip to India in 1930.[26] The dearth of source material on this subject makes it difficult to judge such a statement or to determine whether Pearse's opinion, i.e., that all cotton trading companies resorted to such fraudulent measures in the late 1920s, also applied to Volkart. At any rate, when the Indian Cotton Committee launched a large-scale investigation into the cultivation and sale of Indian cotton in 1917, a Volkart purchasing agent went on record as saying that his company only used the method of wetting down the cotton to a limited extent to soften the fibers, which reduced the wear and tear on the cotton presses. He also voiced the opinion that the complaints of wetting down Indian cotton were totally exaggerated because the wetted cotton lost most of its moisture by the time it reached Europe, leading him to insist that this practice posed no disadvantage to European spinners.[27] There are no indications in the archives that Volkart resorted to fraudulent methods during the 1920s. However, it cannot be ruled out that the Swiss mercantile house was also trapped in the vicious circle that bedeviled the Indian cotton trade from the late 1920s onwards.

Due to the heavy losses that the company suffered from the mid-1920s onwards, between 1925 and 1927 Volkart slashed the number of buying agencies that it maintained in the backcountry.[28] But this failed to pull the company's cotton business out of the red. In 1932, Volkart's Karachi branch noted in a letter that smaller trading firms like Gill & Co., Patel and Spinner were achieving sales figures that were steadily gaining ground on the two market leaders, Volkart and Ralli. The Karachi staff went on to say that it had proven advantageous for these smaller companies during the crisis that they maintained no expensive buying organizations, in contrast to Ralli and Volkart, but instead made their purchases on the cotton markets of Bombay and Karachi and conducted all of their procurements in the backcountry via Indian intermediaries, known as *artiahs*.[29]

In reaction to these discoveries, Volkart's Karachi branch proposed that the company reduce its purchasing network even further and conduct all future business in the interior of the country via the *artiahs*.[30] Volkart's Bombay branch vehemently opposed this plan, however, and "continued to give priority to the principle of direct purchase." The Bombay staff members also feared even greater problems in collaborating with the *artiahs*:

> Not only does the *artiah* system bear the risk of an uncertain selection, but you also lose opportunities to make profits that come with making your own selection. In our experience, one cannot count on an *artiah* ever delivering something that is above par.[31]

Officials at the headquarters in Winterthur were also skeptical about the proposals from Karachi, which they feared would result in a "tangible deterioration" of the firm's infrastructure.[32] It is no longer clear based on the available source material to what extent Bombay and Karachi actually stopped procuring cotton through their own agencies and instead made purchases from Indian brokers. Nonetheless, the correspondence between Karachi, Bombay and Winterthur is an indication of the widespread opinion among Volkart company officials that the Indian cotton trade was perhaps on the verge of a fundamental realignment.

This point of view largely stemmed from the fact that Volkart's main rivals had to contend with similar difficulties. The Japanese trading companies Toyo Menkwa, Nippon Menkwa and Gosho, which ranked among the top buyers of Indian raw cotton in the 1920s, reduced their activities in the interior of the country during the 1930s and focused on making purchases on the coasts. In 1926, Toyo Menkwa had roughly 156 buying agencies for raw cotton. Like many other trading firms, the company posted record profits in the early 1920s, but it made losses of 287,000 rupees in 1927 and 261,000 rupees in 1928. Even after downsizing its buying agency network, it remained in the red until the early 1930s.[33] And Ralli, which had been one of the leading cotton exporters in India for over half a century, completely withdrew from India in 1931 following huge losses and subsequently handled all of its purchases on the subcontinent via the Greek firm Argenti & Co., which was designated as Ralli's procurement agent.[34]

A Diversification into Indian Industrial Facilities?

In view of the economic developments on the subcontinent, it comes as no surprise that during the 1920s staff members at Volkart repeatedly suggested investing in Indian manufacturing companies. This ultimately could have led to a departure from the import and export business that the firm had pursued until then. Trading in raw cotton remained the most important area of business. This focus on a single product made total sense because company officials knew from years of experience how important it was to have an intimate knowledge of the traded products, as summed up in a letter from the headquarters in Winterthur in 1940:

> People without any special knowledge of the articles that they handle and who have no special connections in the countries with which they work cannot possibly expect to compete against firms who know their business by long experience, which means that they know the tricks of the trade as well as the particularities of their respective districts.[35]

Just how valuable such knowledge was in the volatile overseas trade became clear in 1924 when the newly opened branch in Singapore began to export coconut meat, also known as *coprah*. Although Volkart became the leading exporter of *coprah* in Singapore within a year, the branch lost money due to a lack of experience with this product. The employees of

Volkart's Colombo branch, who were responsible for the calculations, had assumed that the *coprah* lost only 5 percent of its weight due to dehydration during transport. But the actual loss of weight was much higher, resulting in returns that were far lower than what had been calculated.[36] A lack of familiarity with the traded product also led the Colombo branch to make a serious blunder in 1936 when it sold a customer 1,800 tons of Mozambican sugar that was stored in Bombay. Two months before Volkart Colombo had concluded negotiations on the transaction, all sugar exports to Ceylon had been banned by the Indian government. Volkart employees had not realized this, however, and the ordered sugar could not be shipped out of the country. Volkart had to scramble to find another buyer in India and ended up suffering a substantial loss. Senior company officials in Winterthur were extremely annoyed and wrote a letter to the branches involved to remind them of the importance in the trading business of having an intimate knowledge of the product:

> We would most certainly assume that a situation fraught with such difficulties could not arise if this had been a type of transaction that we conclude on a continual basis, and with which we are all familiar in every detail, such as is the case with cotton.[37]

Following the heavy losses incurred by Volkart during the crisis in the commodities trade from the mid-1920s onwards, the managers in the Indian branches repeatedly suggested that the company should become involved in industrial production on the subcontinent. Similar moves had already been made by several trading companies. For instance, Indian merchants had begun to establish their own textile industry after being forced out of the cotton export business by European trading firms in the late 1860s. Indeed, they were the founders of India's industrialization.[38] Starting at the turn of the century, European import-export companies had begun to serve as managing agencies for Indian industrial enterprises.[39] Likewise, in the Atlantic trade it was not uncommon from the mid-nineteenth century onwards for European trading companies to diversify and within a single generation transform into commercial banks, industrial firms or shipping lines after the original trading business had lost its lucrativeness.[40]

In 1927, the head of the Bombay branch suggested that Volkart should also diversify in a similar manner. In view of the severe slump in global trade and mounting competition in the sector, trading companies were forced to engage in increasingly risky operations that led "with startling frequency to crises and collapses for the sectors involved." The Bombay manager recommended a new strategy "that idolizes neither the sales figures nor the percentage of sales that cotton represents for the company." He urged greater involvement in industrial production. But his proposal fell on deaf ears in Winterthur. In a handwritten memo, Georg Reinhart reacted as follows to the letter from Bombay: "As a matter of principle, we (V.B.) intend to remain merchants and not become industrialists."[41] The company management justified this by stating that

> we have no one among our personnel in India who has the requisite experience and expert knowledge to manage such companies, not to mention the necessary sufficiently trained subordinate staff. Additional concerns arise from such an immobilization of capital, which runs counter to our ongoing pursuit of liquidity.[42]

It is entirely conceivable that this attitude was also influenced by the political unrest fomented by the activities of the Indian National Congress and the frequent strikes by textile workers.[43] This would confirm the view offered by Rajnarayan Chandavarkar that the activities of the workers' movement during the first half of the twentieth century had a lasting impact on business decisions in India.[44] Nevertheless, the partners at Volkart showed a willingness to revise their position because, in their view, one could expect

> that the industrialization in India, once calm has returned to the country, will make further progress at the expense of the export trade in raw products. This development could possibly force us to reorient our general business policy, for example, we could compensate for a decline in the export business by seeking out new fields of activity, perhaps with more intensive involvement in the industrial sector.

Accordingly, they asked leading company officials in India "to keep an eye on the course of events and submit to us all possible interesting proposals, even if only of an informative nature for the time being."[45]

Such new opportunities presented themselves again and again during the 1930s. The lack of an efficient banking system often made it very difficult for Indian entrepreneurs to raise the necessary capital to invest in an industrial company.[46] Well-capitalized European companies were able to fill this gap. An example from Ceylon shows just how lucrative it could be to invest in an industrial enterprise. In 1931, the local management of Volkart's Colombo branch decided to purchase a small amount of stock in a local match factory, but without obtaining prior approval from the headquarters in Winterthur.[47] This investment paid off handsomely. After only four years, Volkart had received dividends that were nearly equivalent to the original price of the stock.[48] Despite a wide range of enticing opportunities, the investment in the match factory in Ceylon remained the company's only noteworthy involvement in the industrial sector and, significantly, this deal only came about because local Volkart managers had not waited for a green light from Winterthur. In all other instances, the partners stubbornly adhered to their cautious approach.[49]

The reluctance of Volkart's owners to diversify into the industrial or financial sectors can be interpreted as a sign of the path dependency of the firm's development. Volkart was certainly no exception in this regard. Other lead-ing merchants during the interwar era adopted a similar approach, such as the partners at Ralli, who limited their activities to the trading business for many years.[50] In contrast to Volkart, however, during the late 1920s Ralli abandoned its objections to a diversification strategy and soon acquired industrial enterprises, shipping lines and plantations, and even established its own insurance company.[51] Business historians like Stanley Chapman and Alfred Chandler would view such an across-the-board rejection of diversifi-cation, like the policy pursued by Volkart, as a sign of a backward-looking corporate culture and as one of the negative impacts of owner capitalism.[52] However, the further development of the company casts doubt on the wis-dom of such sweeping statements. After Volkart outmaneuvered the compe-tition and in 1930 was appointed the official representative of the American Cotton Cooperative Association for China, Japan and India, followed later by commissions for diverse other European countries, the company rose overnight to become one of the leading exporters of American raw cotton.[53] This put Volkart back in the black. During the 1937–1938 season, the com-pany achieved record profits of some 1.75 million Swiss francs and the part-ners received large dividends.[54] Company officials interpreted this renewed success in the cotton sector as proof that during a crisis it was particularly wise to focus on one's core business. Peter Reinhart, the son of Georg Rein-hart and a partner in the firm since 1934, sent a letter that same year from Shanghai outlining his observations from his travels through Europe, India, China and Japan:

> The most outstanding impression is that we depend upon the Indian cotton business and everything else is only justified if it either benefits the cotton business or produces direct positive results, or promises to benefit the cotton business in the foreseeable future. . . . It is far easier for us to produce results in all areas of the cotton sector than with cot-ton and every imaginable other item. . . . To sum it up, my idea for the development of the company is as follows: Specialists in trading cotton of all types. . . . Not however: Clumsy amateurs in lace, timepieces and rubber boots.[55]

The Indian Independence Movement and Swiss Loyalty Conflicts

The stock market crash of 1929 initially had relatively few repercussions in Asia. But when a credit crunch hit in 1930 and commodities prices plum-meted, Indian agriculture was plunged into a severe crisis. Fixing the value of the rupee at 1 s 6 d in 1927 had already dealt a severe blow to Indian farmers because it increased their debts with respect to the global market value of the commodities that they produced. When the Great Depression struck, their already meager incomes were cut in half. To make matters worse, banks and wholesalers no longer granted credit to rural moneylenders, who then increased the pressure that they exerted on farmers.[56] Tumbling commodities prices sparked farmers' protests.[57] The Indian National Congress stylized itself as the representative of the victims of the economic crisis and stepped up its boycott of British goods, which had been in place since 1929. Indian activists hoped that this would add weight to their campaign to pressure the government to abolish the salt tax, reduce the land tax, increase tariffs on imports and, ultimately, grant political independence to India.

A staff member of the British intelligence bureau described the objectives of the campaign as follows: "[T]he Congress made it perfectly clear that they were mainly interested in the boycott of British goods only and that they were alive to the efficacy of this boycott programme as a political weapon for the emancipation of India." To illustrate his point, he cited a speech that a leading member of the independence movement had given in August 1930 and in which he urged his audience to boycott British products:

> If you do not get an article made in India and you want it, then please get that article from the bazaar if it is made in any non-British country. And I go further and say that even if you have to pay more for a non-British article please pay and buy it for God's sake. For the country's sake, for the honour of this country, for the freedom of this country, do not buy a single thing made in England.[58]

In addition to British products, British companies were targeted by the boycott campaign, in particular British cotton exporters in Bombay. A flyer by the Congress listed seven leading British export companies, including a company owned by a Muslim merchant, that were ignoring the boycott. All Indian merchants were admonished not to do business with these firms. Frederick Hugh Sykes, who was the governor of Bombay until 1931, wrote in a letter in 1932 "that the cotton market generally is intimidated by the Congress and few dare to deal openly with the boycotted firms."[59] In the opinion of one British observer, this was because most of the indigenous cotton merchants in Bombay were Hindus. Even if they did not agree with the goals of the Congress, they feared the social repercussions that could result from violating the boycott. For instance, a man who became socially ostracized was not even allowed to conduct a proper funeral ceremony following the death of a member of his family: "It is a terrible weapon against a religious and cast-ridden community like the Hindus."[60] For their part, the government exerted pressure on the Indian cotton merchants by making it a punishable offense to refuse to supply British exporters with cotton. Many Indian merchants fled to the interior of the country to escape this dilemma.[61]

In addition to the predicament of Indian merchants, non-British export firms were also under pressure. Sykes accused them in the abovementioned letter of trying to profit from the boycott:

> It is alleged that some of the foreign firms, namely, Swiss and Japanese, are helping the boycotters, and it has been admitted by the Japanese Consul that some Japanese firms have been afraid to do business openly with British firms lest they should find themselves also on the boycott list. In the meanwhile, however, the position is easy for them, since they have not to perform any positive act of boycott in order to obtain from Indian firms the business which would otherwise have gone to their British competitors.[62]

This development was extremely unpleasant for the Volkart company, which Sykes refers to in his letter. For the first time since the end of World War I, the Swiss nationality of the company—which was otherwise of no consequence to its business in India—was once again an issue. This is reflected in a letter sent from Bombay to Volkart headquarters in Winterthur in 1932: "We take the position that, as a foreign company, we must assume a completely neutral attitude in a political sense and under no circumstances shall we stray from this principle in the future." The competition was green with envy that Volkart enjoyed a privileged position as a non-British firm. Ralli allegedly went so far as to lobby the Indian government in a bid to sway opinion against Volkart. The Swiss trading company was convinced that many British companies generally would have been happy to see Volkart added to the boycott list, in part because this would have increased the political weight of the cotton exporters vis-à-vis the government. Moreover, staff members at the Bombay branch said that they were subjected to considerable pressure in an effort to convince Volkart to join forces with the boycotted companies.[63]

The managers at the headquarters in Winterthur welcomed the fact that Volkart's Bombay branch was doing its best to remain as neutral possible during the boycott controversy. This approach was motivated by more than just commercial opportunism. It was both an expression of Volkart's sense of obligation to the British colonial government and its sympathies for the independence efforts of Indian nationalists:

> We owe the British administration our thanks that they have maintained the calm, law and order that has facilitated the economic development of this country and given us the opportunity to pursue our business, safely and unimpeded, for 80 years. On the other hand, one can also feel sufficient sympathy for the justified political aspirations of a great people in order not to follow, through political thick and thin, a government that is nonetheless an imperialist power and, despite all its good deeds, would not, for reasons having to do with its own nature, carry through with the full national development of the country.[64]

If push came to shove, however, Volkart would have to decide in favor of the government because the Congress was not an administrative body.

The company had already found itself on the horns of a similar dilemma in the 1920s when the Indian independence movement under the leadership of Mahatma Gandhi called for civil disobedience. The employees at Volkart's Karachi branch were of the opinion that the political unrest hampered the company's ability to conduct its business: "Transactions with the natives have become far more difficult because a certain category of traders directly seeks to provoke situations that revolve around racial differences when they are bound by contractual obligations that lead to losses."[65] This assessment came in reaction to a letter that the Winterthur headquarters had sent to all branches, calling on the entire workforce to treat the indigenous population with respect:

> It is . . . not a sign of weakness, but rather an imperative of equity and fairness, as well as prudence, when the European becomes aware of this necessity and makes it a guiding principle for his contacts with the natives. For those who have stood for years in the shoes of the feared sahib, who views the natives as inferior human beings to whom he owes little or no measure of consideration, this will be a major adjustment to the new spirit of the times. . . . As a neutral company, we have every interest in respecting this sentiment and adopting an appropriate tact at all times.[66]

A few months later, all signs of such restraint had disappeared. After Gandhi's arrest in 1922, a situation report to the company's customers said that the firm had been "terrorized by Gandhi's supporters" who had pressured Volkart to boycott British textiles. The report also contained the following statement:

> The arrest of this tribune has demolished, at least for the time being, the myth that the government would not dare lay a hand on him, and it must be said that a firmly established government in Oriental countries has it easier than a government that seeks to fully shoulder the weight of its responsibilities and thus reaps the resentment and even the scorn of the Orientals.[67]

Hence, Volkart was interested in maintaining the status quo, which had made it possible to pursue a profitable line of business, while, at the same time, the firm had a certain degree of sympathy for the cause of the independence movement. As a company from a neutral third country, it found itself in a dilemma. In the early 1930s, Volkart was under pressure from both British trading companies and the boycott movement. In March 1932, the president of the boycott committee warned Volkart against continuing to trade in cotton. The company ignored the letter, apparently without suffering any negative consequences.[68] However, out of fear that the firm would be blacklisted, Volkart drew up a contingency plan that would have allowed it to collaborate secretly with Indian cotton brokers to circumvent the boycott.[69]

The boycott was lifted in 1933. The Indian National Congress and the government engaged in protracted negotiations until finally the Government of India Act was enacted in 1935. This legislation consisted of three key elements: it established a federalist structure, gave greater autonomy to the provinces and helped to guarantee the rights of minorities through specific voting laws.[70] The losses that the boycott inflicted upon cotton exporters were relatively minimal, as stated in a government report on the cotton trade in 1932: "The losses of individual European firms are probably not very serious, and the field of loss is limited." The report went on to state that the boycott had not significantly reduced the incomes of farmers.[71] British exporters were able to circumvent the boycott in Bombay by making their cotton purchases in the interior of the country. This apparently went smoothly, despite the boycott.[72]

The political and economic changes on the subcontinent during the interwar era provided the European trading companies with only an inkling of the challenges that awaited them following World War II. After India, Pakistan and Ceylon achieved independence, their newly established governments curtailed commodities exports in an effort to promote their own industries and forced European companies to accept the investment of domestic capital in their companies in South Asia. As a result, the traditional import and export business of European trading companies came to a standstill. In contrast to the anti-British boycotts of the 1930s, however, Swiss companies like Volkart were also affected by this development.[73]

Notes

1 For more on this topic, see Manela, *The Wilsonian Moment*, 2007, 77–97.
2 Dholakia, *Futures Trading and Futures Markets*, 1949, 15–16.
3 See Chapter 2.
4 Contractor, *A Handbook of Indian Cotton*, 1928, 33; Dantwala, *Marketing of Raw Cotton*, 1937, 47–48.
5 NML, Manuscript Section, Purshotamdas Thakurdas Papers, File No. 6: Surat Factory, Kapas, 13 January 1913 to 18 June 1923: Gulabbhai Nagarji Desai, Divisional Superintendent of Agriculture, Northern Division, Surat, to the Deputy Director of Agriculture, Poona, 11 December 1918.
6 NML, Manuscript Section, Purshotamdas Thakurdas Papers, File No. 6: Surat Factory, Kapas, 13 January 1913 to 18 June 1923: R.B. Ewbank, Registrar Cooperative Societies, Bombay Presidency, Poona, to Purshotamdas Thakordas, Bombay, 3 May 1919.
7 NML, Manuscript Section, Purshotamdas Thakurdas Papers, File No. 6: Surat Factory, Kapas, 13 January 1913 to 18 June 1923: Report No. 636 of the Assistant Registrar, 20 April 1919.
8 Gazeteer of Bombay State, Poona District, 1954, 317–323 and 352.
9 Peters, *Modern Bombay and Indian States*, 1942, 50; Ray, *Industrialization in India*, 1979, 61–62.

10 Sethi, "History of Cotton," 1960, 16.
11 NML, Manuscript Section, Purshotamdas Thakurdas Papers, File No. 142: Lancashire Meeting, 2 June 1933 to 20 November 1935: Summarised Report of First Indian Tour by Mr. H.C. Short, Commissioner of the Lancashire Indian Cotton Committee, 30 July 1935; File No. 323: Indian Central Cotton Committee, 28 April 1944 to 12 August 1958: Inaugural speech of Purshotamdas Thakurtas at the Sixth Conference on Cotton Growing Problems in India on 5–2–55.
12 Ray, *Industrialization in India*, 1979, 33.
13 East India Cotton Association. *Bombay Cotton Annual* No. 17, 1935/36, 95.
14 Ray, *Industrialization in India*, 1979, 61.
15 GL, Records of Ralli Bros., Ms. 23834: Report to the Chairman of Ralli Brothers Limited, April 12 1939, 9.
16 VA, Dossier 11: Delhi / Lahore / Calcutta / Chittagong, Calcutta, 4. Correspondence: Winterthur to Calcutta, 16 July 1931.
17 James, *The End of Globalization*, 2001, 104.
18 See Chapter 10.
19 For Volkart's profit figures during this period, see Chapter 8.
20 Ralli Brothers *Limited*, 1951, 12.
21 Naoto, "Up-country Purchase Activities," 2001, 209.
22 Ray, *Industrialization in India*, 1979, 247; Rothermund, "Currencies, Taxes and Credit," 2002, 16–17.
23 Naoto, "Up-country Purchase Activities", 2001, 208.
24 Dantwala. *Marketing of Raw Cotton*, 1937, 44.
25 See Chapter 2.
26 Pearse, *The Cotton Industry of India*, 1930, 30–31.
27 Mr. E. S. Shroff, Agent Messers. Volkart Brothers' Agency, Khamgaon (inquiry from the 18 November 1917), in: Indian Cotton Committee, Minutes of Evidence, Volume IV, 1920, 45.
28 Anderegg, *Chronicle*, 1976, 313–314.
29 VA, Dossier 8: Karachi, 5. Cotton Organisation Inland—general correspondence: Karachi to the Agencys in Ambala, Amritsar, Bhatinda, Lyallpur, Montgomery, Kopie an H.O. und Bombay, 13 December 1932.
30 VA, Dossier 8: Karachi, 5. Cotton Organisation Inland—general correspondence: Karachi to the Agencys in Ambala, Amritsar, Bhatinda, Lyallpur, Montgomery, Kopie an H.O. und Bombay, 13 December 1932.
31 VA, Dossier 8: Karachi, 5. Cotton Organisation Inland—general correspondence: Bombay to Karachi, 5 January 1933.
32 VA, Dossier 8: Karachi, 5. Cotton Organisation Inland—general correspondence: Winterthur to Karachi, copy to Bombay, 7 January 1933.
33 Naoto, "Up-country Purchase Activities," 2001, 209.
34 www.rallis.co.in/aboutus/hist1854.htm (15 May 2009).
35 VA, Dossier 11: Delhi / Lahore / Calcutta / Chittagong: Calcutta, 4. Correspondence: Winterthur to Calcutta, 11 March 1940.
36 VA, Dossier 15, The Far Eastern Organisation, II. Singapore, 2. Table of Events.
37 VA, Dossier 6: Colombo, 7. Import: incl. Swedish Match business, Winterthur to Colombo, London, Bombay, 3 June 1936.
38 Chandavarkar, *Imperial Power and Popular Politics*, 1998, 55–68. See Chapter 2.
39 Ray, *Industrialization in India*, 1979, 262–269.
40 Jones, "Multinational Trading Companies," 1998.
41 VA, Dossier 3: Bombay I, 5. Cotton general correspondence—incl. the boycott of European Firms in 1932: Bombay to Winterthur, 9 November 1927.
42 VA, Dossier 8: Karachi, 18. Miscellaneous correspondence: Winterthur to Karachi, 23 July 1930.

43 VA, Dossier 8: Karachi, 18. Miscellaneous correspondence: Winterthur to Karachi, 23 July 1930.
44 Rajnarayan Chandavarkar theorized that "the pattern of capitalist development in India had been shaped largely by the role of the working classes" (Chandavarkar, *Imperial Power and Popular Politics*, 1998, 3).
45 VA, Dossier 8: Karachi, 18. Miscellaneous correspondence: Winterthur to Karachi, 23 July 1930.
46 Ray, *Industrialization in India*, 1979, 227.
47 VA, Dossier 6: Colombo, 7. Import: incl. Swedish Match business: Colombo to Winterthur, 10 June 1931.
48 VA, Dossier 6: Colombo, 7. Import: incl. Swedish Match business: Colombo to Winterthur, 30 July 1935.
49 VA, Dossier 7: Cochin, 5. Various notes: Winterthur to Cochin, 2 September 1932.
50 Ralli Brothers *Limited*, 1951, 9.
51 Ralli Brothers *Limited*, 1951, 9 and 32–56.
52 Chapman, *Merchant Enterprise in Britain*, 1992, 294; Chandler, *Scale and Scope*, 2004 [1990], 236ff.
53 See Chapter 10.
54 VA, Dossier 59: PR-Privatarchiv: Notizen / Briefe / Personelles etc., Historisches betr. Geschäft: PR and GR und WR, Gewinn & Verlustrechnung 1937–1938, 10 December 38.
55 VA, Dossier 59: PR-Privatarchiv: Notizen / Briefe / Personelles etc., Historisches betr. Geschäft: PR, Shanghai, to Winterthur, 6 June 1934.
56 Ray, *Industrialization in India*, 1979, 247; Rothermund, Currencies, Taxes and Credit, 2002, 16–18.
57 Rothermund, *An Economic History of India*, 1988, 100–101.
58 NAI, Home Department Political Branch, File No. 33/6, 1931: Note prepared by the Director of Intelligence Bureau on 16 February 1931 on the Subject of the Congress Boycott programme.
59 NAI, Home Department Political Branch, File No. 33/6, 1931: F.H. Sykes, Government House, Bombay, to the Earl of Willingdon, 19 March 1932.
60 NAI, Home Department Political Branch, File No. 33/6, 1931: J.R. Abercrombie, European Association (Bombay Branch), Bombay, to H.B. Holme, London, 19 March 1932.
61 NAI, Home Department Political Branch, File No. 33/6, 1931: J.R. Abercrombie, European Association (Bombay Branch), Bombay, to H.B. Holme, London, 19 March 1932.
62 NAI, Home Department Political Branch, File No. 33/6, 1931: F.H. Sykes, Government House, Bombay, to the Earl of Willingdon, 19 March 1932.
63 VA; Dossier 3: Bombay I: 5. Cotton general correspondence—incl. the boycott of European Firms in 1932: Bombay to Winterthur, 4 March 1932.
64 VA, Dossier 3: Bombay I: 5. Cotton general correspondence—incl. the boycott of European Firms in 1932: Winterthur to Bombay, 18 March 1932.
65 VA, Dossier 8: Karachi, 3. Table of Events: Karachi to Winterthur, 24 November 1921.
66 VA, Dossier 7: Cochin, 12. Various generals notes on Cochin as a place: Winterthur an alle Häuser, 6 October 1921.
67 Gebrüder Volkart, *Situationsbericht Nr. 24*, 8 May 1922.
68 VA, Dossier 3: Bombay I, 4. Table of Events 1851–1961–2.
69 VA, Dossier 3: Bombay I, 6. Bombay House brokers: Bombay an Winterthur, 28 June 1932.
70 Rothermund, *An Economic History of India*, 1988, 101–102 and 107.
71 NAI, Home Department Political Branch, File No. 33/6, 1931: Report on Cotton situation, 25 March 32. This had been one of the greatest fears of the British

colonial government: Brit Lib, Mss Eur F 150/4b, Sykes Collection, Correspondence July-October 1932: Letter from India Office, Whitehall, to the Governor of Bombay, 8 July 1932.

72 NAI, Home Department Political Branch, File No. 33/6, 1931: J.R. Abercrombie, European Association (Bombay Branch), Bombay, to H.B. Holme, London, 19 March 1932.

73 See Chapters 12 and 14.

10 Expansion East and West

Extending the Business to China, Japan and the US

The forcible opening of Chinese and Japanese markets by means of imperial gunboat diplomacy allowed Western merchants to expand their activities into East Asia. Already after the Second Opium War (1856–1860), Volkart began to investigate the possibility of selling cotton to China. The Middle Kingdom was traditionally an important market for Indian cotton. In the early 1860s, roughly one-third of all Indian cotton exports went to China.[1] After Volkart signed an agreement in 1869 to be represented in Shanghai by British trading firm Jardine Matheson & Co., the Swiss firm founded its own sales office in the city in 1878. This became an independent branch in 1901, but had to be closed again in 1908 due to unsatisfactory results.[2]

Meanwhile, the rapid industrialization of Japan attracted the attention of European merchants. Between 1887 and 1897, the number of spindles in Japanese spinning mills rose from 76,000 to more than 970,000.[3] This made Japan the leading textile manufacturer in Asia.[4] From 1897 onwards, Japan was the world's main buyer of Indian cotton for half a century, with the exception of the year 1901.[5] It would thus be a vast oversimplification to reduce the history of the Indian cotton trade to the relationship between India and Britain, or between the subcontinent and Europe. Even during colonial times, trade connections with East Asian countries were often just as important, if not more so, as business ties with Europe.[6] During the 1899–1900 season, Volkart exported 10,682 bales of cotton to Japan and 17,077 bales to China.[7] Since Volkart regularly sold over 100,000 bales of cotton to Europe each year during the 1890s, its sales to East Asia were still relatively modest,[8] but the company anticipated that its revenues from the region would someday equal, if not surpass, what it achieved in the European market. In 1899, for instance, the managers of the Bombay branch wrote to the headquarters in Winterthur that, in their opinion, Volkart's future lay to a large degree "in the cotton trade with China and Japan."[9]

The Control of the East Asian Cotton Business by Japanese Trading Companies

Starting with the 1894–1895 season, Volkart had a European employee stationed in Japan as a broker for the sale of Indian cotton.[10] In 1903, the company established its own sales office in Kobe, which, after it moved to Osaka, became an independent Volkart branch in 1917.[11] But exporting cotton to Japan was a difficult undertaking for European trading firms, in large part because the Japanese government temporarily resorted to protectionist measures during the late nineteenth century. One of the restrictions was that Japanese spinners were forced to use Japanese steamships for their cotton imports.[12] These constraints were eased after World War I, but it still remained far from easy for foreign companies to do business in Japan.[13]

Obstacles arose from the fact that Japanese trading companies were able to take considerable business risks and, in some cases, sell their cotton in Osaka for less than what they had paid in India. This was a consequence of the structure of the Japanese cotton industry, which was fundamentally different than the market in Europe and the US. For instance, the cotton trade between the American South and Britain had attracted a wide range of competing firms. Up to 120 trading companies were exporting cotton from the US during the interwar era and roughly two-thirds of these firms focused exclusively on importing to Liverpool. American cotton always passed through several hands before it ultimately arrived at the spinning mills and all of the players involved hedged their operations on the futures market.[14] By contrast, in Japan 80 percent of all cotton imports were handled by three companies: Toyo Menkwa, Nippon Menkwa and Gosho. These three companies were part of large, interconnected financial and business conglomerates known as *zaibatsu*, which owned scores of factories, banks and trading companies. Since trading companies and textile mills often belonged to the same large corporation, they could conclude special agreements that ensured a steady supply and were profitable for both sides. Thanks to their connections to spinning mills, the cotton trading companies achieved such large turnovers that they were able to negotiate price reductions of up to 1 percent on the purchase of large quantities of cotton. Furthermore, they established huge cotton warehouses that allowed them to mitigate the risks of price fluctuations. Accordingly, neither Japanese trading companies nor spinners needed to hedge their transactions on the futures market. And since Japanese trading companies also controlled 80 percent of all textile exports from Japan, it was possible for them to balance out the risks involved in purchasing raw cotton with the yields from sales of textile products.[15]

In addition to the three big leading Japanese cotton trading companies of Toyo Menkwa, Nippon Menkwa and Gosho, there were roughly 50 other companies that imported cotton to Japan during the 1920s. Roughly half of these firms were owned by foreign investors.[16] Although these businesses included renowned American trading companies like Anderson Clayton and McFadden, the foreigners failed to establish direct contact to Japanese cotton mills and for many years remained of only marginal importance in the country.[17]

It was a similar story in China, where for quite some time Europeans had been forced to cede most business transactions to their Japanese rivals, in large part because a considerable share of the textile industry in China

Table 10.1 The eight largest exporters of Indian cotton from Bombay to Japan, China, Europe, November 1925–October 1926

	Japan	China	Europe	Total
Japan Cotton Trad. Co., Ltd.	376,479	72,408	40,165	489,052
Toyo Menkwa Kaisha, Ltd.	344,417	79,566	12,478	436,461
Gosho Kabushiki Kaisha, Ltd.	271,650	61,031	25,031	357,982
Ralli Brothers	21,800	19,075	83,204	124,079
Volkart Brothers	23,900	21,800	86,486	132,186
Sundry Shippers	9,045	1,200	54,587	64,832
Ozu-Burin & Co., Ltd.	55,500	1,300	0	56,800
Forbes, Forbes, Campbell & Co.	0	0	43,759	43,759
Patel Cotton Co.	0	16,970	25,114	42,084

(Source: Contractor, Dorabjee B. A Handbook of Indian Cotton for Merchants, Shippers, Mills, Factory owners and others interested in the Cotton Trade. Bombay 1928, 38–39.)

was in Japanese hands. After its victory in the Sino-Japanese War in 1895, Japan had pushed through agreements allowing it to build its own factories in China. In 1922, 30 percent of all Chinese spindles were in factories that were operated by Japanese firms, followed by 40 percent in 1930 and 44 percent in 1936.[18] This had a direct impact on Japan's share of the cotton trade. For instance, during the 1925–1926 season, the Japan Cotton Trading Co., which belonged to Nippon Menkwa, imported 376,479 bales of Indian cotton from Bombay to Japan and 72,408 bales to China. Toyo Menkwa imported 344,417 bales to Japan and 79,566 bales to China. Gosho imported 271,650 bales to Japan and 61,031 to China. During that same year, Volkart shipped out of Bombay 23,900 bales to Japan and 21,800 bales to China. Ralli exported from Bombay 21,800 bales to Japan and 19,075 bales to China. Although the two large European cotton trading companies lagged far behind their Japanese rivals, exports to China and Japan were extremely important to them because one-third of their cotton sales out of Bombay were to East Asia during the mid-1920s (Table 10.1).

The Establishment of a Subsidiary in Osaka with Japanese Investors

One of the main reasons that the East Asian market became so important during the interwar era was that global trade was still reeling from the aftermath of World War I. The steep decline in European exports after 1914 fueled East Asia's industrialization.[19] Imports of Indian raw cotton to Japan soared during the 1916–1917 fiscal year to 1.6 million bales—more than twice as much as ten years earlier. This trend continued after the war. During the interwar era, 40 to 50 percent of India's cotton exports went to Japan.[20] During the war, Japan edged out Britain as the leading supplier of cotton yarn and textiles for the Chinese market. Whereas 90 percent of all Chinese textile imports came from Britain in 1915, this figure had dropped to just 51 percent by 1920. During the same period, the market share of Japanese textiles imported to China rose from 9 percent to 48 percent.[21]

This development made Volkart even more determined to make inroads into the Chinese and Japanese markets after 1918. While the newly established subsidiaries in Bremen and New York were completely owned by Volkart,[22] indigenous textile manufacturers and merchants had a stake in the company's East Asian ventures after the war. In 1919, the recently opened Osaka branch was transformed into an independent company with Japanese partners, the Nichizui Trading Co., Ltd.[23] The Volkart partners initially only had a 25 percent minority interest in Nichizui, which soon established branches in Tokyo, Nagoya, Kobe and Fukuoka. In addition to cotton, Nichizui imported European machinery, primarily from Swiss companies.[24] Volkart had forged ties with Japanese investors to gain better access to the Japanese market, but the Swiss were also motivated to take this step because Japanese spinning mills generally only paid for their cotton purchases 60 or 90 days after receiving shipments. This ran counter to Volkart's principal of demanding full payment upon delivery of the goods. Nichizui thus became an intermediary that purchased the cotton from Volkart according to the usual terms of payment and sold it to the spinning mills on credit.[25]

The involvement of Japanese businessmen initially helped to open doors for Nichizui in Japan, but it soon became apparent that such a joint venture could also be highly problematic. After Nichizui made outstanding profits during its first year, in 1920 the Japanese economy was plunged into a serious crisis that lasted until the early 1930s.[26] The abrupt end of the economic boom of World War I and the postwar years unnerved the Japanese partners at Nichizui to such an extent that they wanted to liquidate the company again in 1920, despite the fact that Volkart had pledged financial support and amended the contract conditions for the transactions with its Indian branches to allow Nichizui to end the year with positive results. In view of the differences of opinion with its Japanese partners, Volkart considered purchasing a majority interest in the company. But this contravened the basic idea behind establishing Nichizui, namely "to involve as many influential Japanese in the company as possible, and thus boost the business transactions of the kaisha."[27]

Just one year later, Volkart headquarters informed the Bombay branch that it was prepared to purchase shares in Nichizui to acquire a majority stake in the company. The experiences of recent months had shown "that due to the diverse mindsets and points of view, and occasionally diverging interests, it is extremely difficult to achieve a fruitful and harmonious collaboration between Japanese and European directors as well as Japanese and European personnel."[28] During the summer of 1922, the headquarters announced that Volkart had acquired the majority of the shares.

> Only one-third of the shares remain in the hands of the current Japanese shareholders, allowing us to retain the character of a Japanese kaisha,

in accordance with our wishes, while at the same time giving us control of the company as the principal shareholder.[29]

In-company Frictions

Even after becoming the majority shareholder, however, Volkart executives found it far more difficult to oversee Nichizui's transactions than it had been to manage the company's branches in India. Instead of difficulties with intractable shareholders, the Swiss found themselves confronted with the principal-agent problem. When Georg Reinhart visited Nichizui during his trip through Asia in 1923, the company's managing director, Julius Müller, assured him that "the Japanese—now that we have the majority—are now entirely amenable to working according to our intentions." But that was apparently only part of the truth. In his report back to his brothers in Winterthur, Reinhart said that he was extremely concerned that the Japanese members of the board of directors largely maintained a passive demeanor toward Müller. This is problematic "because it would be good if Müller's management of the company were occasionally supervised and perhaps corrected. Mr. Müller wields unlimited power." For instance, the company's balance sheets were approved without debate at the monthly board meetings.

> Given Mr. Müller's personality traits, which you also know only too well, I view this situation as extremely dangerous. In the days when the Japanese still held the majority of the shares, the control and influence of the Japanese co-directors was still sufficiently energetic that Winterthur rarely deemed it necessary to intervene in Nichizui's internal affairs.

He went on to say that now that Volkart had a majority share in Nichizui, it was important to keep closer tabs on Müller and set guidelines concerning the risks that he was allowed to take in the cotton trade. Reinhart was dismayed, for instance, that Müller had repeatedly engaged in speculative transactions with Indian and American cotton, and had even occasionally speculated on the stock exchange. Reinhart immediately put a stop to these practices that contravened the company's articles of association. Likewise, Müller did not apparently realize that, due to its enormous turnover, Nichizui could run into financial difficulties—even if business was flourishing—if it did not have sufficient cash reserves. Reinhart concluded:

> It would be best if we divorced ourselves entirely from the notion that Nichizui is a foreign joint-stock company in which we only have a say . . . through our representatives on the supervisory board. Instead, we must view Nichizui as if no Japanese were involved, in other words, we should treat it just as we do our affiliated companies in Bremen and New York.

He also noted that it would not be a problem if the Japanese partners (Figure 10.1) subsequently decided to withdraw from the firm entirely, "as Nichizui has now been established as a Japanese company and has an excellent Japanese staff to conduct transactions with the Japanese."[30]

It is clear that the partners at Volkart saw themselves confronted with a problem in Japan that they had not encountered in India. They realized time and again that they did not understand the motives of the shareholders and staff of the Japanese subsidiary. For instance, in response to a letter from Osaka written in 1940 outlining the difficulties between the Swiss manager of Nichizui and the employees, a Volkart company official commented that this was yet another indication of "the strange mentality of the Japanese and the strange conditions that we have to deal with."[31] Two years later, Volkart management realized that the Nichizui supervisory board refused to divulge the name of an employee who had misappropriated funds and that they had no intention of taking the man to court. This elicited the following response from the headquarters in Winterthur: "This position apparently conforms with the—incomprehensible to us—mentality of the Japanese that the culprits in cases like this are not held accountable."[32] Such generalized statements, in which business difficulties were explained with a cultural difference, were undoubtedly a reflection of a certain helplessness on the part of the partners.

Figure 10.1 Managers and Japanese partners of Nichizui in 1922, top row from left: Mikuni, Müller, Takashima; bottom row from left: Yamada, Takemura, Yashiro, Yamanaka (VA, Dossier 111: Photos Bremen, London, USA, Mexico, Brazil, Colombia, Singapore/Shanghai/Japan)

At any rate, no such statements were made with regard to the company's Indian branches, where the company owners had much keener insights into the business situation. Furthermore, thanks to their own training in the Indian branch offices, they had an excellent knowledge of the subcontinent. By contrast, in Japan the Volkart partners were completely dependent upon the information that they received from the Swiss manager of Nichizui, who, in the 1920s, was a man that the partners evidently did not trust. During his inspection tour of Japan in 1923, Georg Reinhart came to the conclusion that Müller was hard-working, spoke fluent Japanese, got along extremely well with the Japanese and was intimately familiar with the Japanese character: "He would have been ideally suited as the head of Nichizui if his honesty were above doubt and if his erratic behavior and speculative nature were not cause for grave concern." Indeed, it was only after the fact that Reinhart learned from a European employee that the purchase of the majority interest had been anything but a smooth ride. At the time, the Japanese shareholders had stated during a meeting that they were prepared to sell their shares to Volkart for 50 yen a piece. Then Takashima, who was another Japanese shareholder and had apparently been eavesdropping at the door, walked into the room and talked to the other shareholders in Japanese in an effort to sway their opinion. As a result, they now suddenly demanded 55 yen per share—and ultimately received this amount. Takashima then pocketed half of the difference between this and the formerly agreed price. Müller had neglected to inform the partners at Volkart of this incident.[33]

The bribery payments that remained indispensable for many transactions in Japan at the time were another cause for concern that Reinhart cited:

> According to my inquiries, the process involves Mr. Müller withdrawing the funds in question, which amount to thousands of yen, but he refuses to produce any receipts or vouchers to this effect. These funds—with the exception of a single customer whom Mr. Müller bribes in person—are given by Mr. Müller to our employee Nakagawa, who has the marvelous task of placing these sums of money in the hands of the relevant people to be bribed. According to Mr. Müller's response to my query, he reaffirmed that we can have absolute confidence in Nakagawa, but insisted that we have no possibility of ever receiving a receipt from the bribed individuals.

According to Reinhart, a European employee had noted in one situation that Nakagawa had indeed not kept any of the bribe money for himself. But it remained unclear whether he did so as a rule. And it was just as unclear how honestly Müller dealt with the bribe money that passed through his hands. The fact of the matter was that although Müller bitterly complained about his meager salary and the high cost of living in Japan, he reportedly lived a lavish lifestyle. This prompted Reinhart to write that "one is occasionally inclined to entertain certain doubts about how Müller has amassed such savings." For the time being, however, Volkart could only protect itself from Müller's "shortcomings," as Reinhart referred to them, "by intensifying the monitoring from Winterthur (through queries, statements etc.)."[34]

In 1926, the differences between Volkart and Julius Müller became so untenable that he was forced to leave the company. Müller went to work for Ralli Brothers and, collaborating with this Volkart rival and Japanese partners, established a new import company called Showa Menkwa, which worked in the same sector as Nichizui and was apparently organized in a similar manner. In 1927, he founded his own trading company, Uebersee-Handels AG, with branches in Japan and Switzerland.[35]

Müller's activities not only alienated the partners but also sowed a deep sense of mistrust between the Indian branches and Nichizui. This was a cause for concern among company officials at the Winterthur headquarters. In a letter dated 1929, Volkart tried to mend the fences:

> We admit that during the era of Julius Müller, in which he pursued extremely high-handed business practices with a Japanese shareholder majority, a certain amount of reserve on the part of our Indian branches was understandable, but now that the company owns 80 percent of the Nichizui joint stock the situation is different.[36]

To prevent these persistent in-company tensions from burdening the business, the headquarters had to remind the Indian branches on several occasions that the Japanese subsidiary was an integral component of the Volkart network of branch offices, as reflected in another letter from 1929:

> Since the company owns 80 percent of Nichizui shares, the transactions in the East are of virtually the same degree of interest to us as the ones in India. . . . We therefore ask that all transactions with the East always be viewed from the perspective of the *entire* company.[37]

And in yet another letter company officials wrote that

> the interests of both firms are closely linked, so it makes no sense if an Indian company sought to gain an edge on Nichizui or vice versa. We therefore request that all entities in India come to view Nichizui as if it were a branch of V.B, while, by the same token, Nichizui, and its Japanese shareholders and directors in particular, must realize that their company was primarily established to serve *our* purposes, and that they should thus view themselves as a limb that serves the entire organism of the firm.[38]

The business results of the Indian and East Asian entities were in fact closely connected. The branches in Japan and China often made losses. But since they represented sales channels for cotton imported by Volkart, the transactions could nevertheless be lucrative for the company as a whole.

During the Great Depression, Volkart was heavily burdened by the fixed costs that it was obliged to maintain for its purchasing network in India. The company hoped that it could cover these business expenses by increasing its sales to East Asia. In 1929, the headquarters made the following announcement to its branches: "We need to significantly expand our sales to the East to fully utilize our Indian organization and as a means of counterbalancing temporary fluctuations in sales to Europe."[39] In fact, Volkart's sales figures to East Asia started to rise in 1929–1930, while cotton sales to Europe declined. Nevertheless, during the 1930s Europe remained the company's main sales region for Indian cotton.[40]

Crises and Wars: The Japanese Economy in the 1930s and 1940s

In the early 1930s, the economic crisis spread to East Asia. Japan slid into a recession in 1930, followed by China in late 1932.[41] Due to the economic downturn, Nichizui was unable to pay dividends in 1929–1930. During the 1930–1931 season, the company made losses on its imports of Indian cotton, despite large sales. Nevertheless, the firm was able to make a profit thanks to lucrative transactions with Egyptian and, above all, American cotton.[42] Profits from importing American cotton primarily had to do with the fact that in 1930 Volkart had managed to become the sole representative of the American Cotton Cooperative Association for India and East Asia. In the early 1920s, roughly two-thirds of the raw cotton spun in Japan still came from India. From 1925 onwards, imports of US cotton surpassed the import volume from India.[43] Demand for US cotton continued to rise during the 1930s, soaring from 177,000 bales of raw cotton imported to Japan in 1931 to 250,000 bales in 1936.[44]

Thanks to its role as a representative of the American Cotton Cooperative Association, as well as a collaboration with the Winterthur trading company Paul Reinhart & Co. for deliveries of Egyptian cotton, Volkart was able to use Nichizui to offer cotton in Japan from virtually every major cultivation area in the world. In view of the weakness of the European economy, it was important for a trading company like Volkart to no longer focus exclusively on the import-export trade between India and Europe, but instead handle an increasing number of transactions on a global scale. In Japan the company benefited from the efforts of the local spinning industry during the 1920s to improve the production process. One innovation was to blend inexpensive raw cotton from India and Egypt with high-quality US cotton. This allowed Japanese textile mills to offer a wider range of products and reduce costs at the same time.[45] Furthermore, Volkart benefited from a veritable economic boom in Japan fueled by massive increases in military spending starting in 1931 and the wars in Manchuria and later in China. While the Japanese economy had grown by more than 33 percent during the 1920s, it experienced the phenomenal growth of 72 percent in the 1930s.[46] This also resulted in an increase in cotton imports. In 1936–1937, Japan imported a record 2.4 million bales of Indian cotton.[47] During this fiscal year, Nichizui achieved its largest cotton sales with a total of 533,000 bales that were imported to Japan from India, the US, Egypt, Uganda, Brazil and China.[48]

In the early 1930s, Nichizui also began to export Japanese textiles to Argentina, South Africa and Australia. This is another indication that world trade revolved less and less around Europe.[49] Exports of Japanese consumer goods by Nichizui show that it continued to pursue an independent course during the 1930s, even though Volkart had been the majority shareholder for quite some time. The Japanese subsidiary ventured into the export sector even though the partners at Volkart remained unconvinced of the wisdom of this idea.[50] There were other aspects as well in which Nichizui's insistence on acting as an independent company was a source of concern—and heavy losses—for the parent company. The managers of Nichizui saw it as their main job to generate as much profit as possible. But since their revenues were in yen and the Japanese currency had been heavily devalued in relation to the British pound, which was the currency that Volkart used for its calculations in the rest of the company, this business practice by Nichizui managers caused Volkart to lose 4 million yen in the late 1930s. Because the isolated results achieved by Nichizui were less important to Volkart than the overall results of the company, conflicts of interest arose with the remaining Japanese shareholders who were interested in receiving regular dividends that they hoped would be as high as possible.[51] This led Peter Reinhart to conclude that a business like Volkart's was not suitable for investment from outside capital.[52] This shows that while collaborations with indigenous partners could be extremely effective for launching businesses in foreign markets, they could also lead to considerable amounts of friction in the long run. Consequently, Volkart purchased the last remaining shares from the Japanese partners and became the sole owner of Nichizui in 1939.[53]

An increasing number of Japanese employees left Nichizui from 1939 onwards. They were afraid that the growing trade restrictions of the day would leave them with no future in a foreign trading company. Between 1939 and 1941, Nichizui was only able to conduct a limited number of transactions because imports to Japan were increasingly limited by rigid trade barriers. After Japan declared war on the Allies, all contact was broken off between Nichizui and the various Volkart branch offices. Nichizui was able to conclude only sporadic transactions within the Japanese Empire during the war.[54] The only reason that Nichizui was able to remain active at all during the war was that the majority of its capital had been in Japanese hands when it was founded in 1919. This meant that Nichizui was considered a Japanese company, even though it was well known that all of its shares were owned by Swiss investors from 1939 onwards. In fact, this ownership structure allowed the company to resume business sooner than other foreign trading companies after World War II. In June 1946, Nichizui became one of the first trading companies based in Japan to sign contracts for deliveries of American cotton to Japanese spinning mills.[55] By contrast, imports of machinery, which had been one of Nichizui's main business areas before the war, were not resumed.[56]

The Establishment of a Chinese Subsidiary

After Volkart had closed its Shanghai branch in 1908 due to disappointing results, the company planned a reopening in 1916. But this failed because Volkart could not find suitable personnel.[57] After the end of World War I, the firm made another attempt. The Chinese textile industry had boomed during the war. In 1923, there were 3.6 million spindles in China, or four times as many as prior to 1914.[58] This held out the promise of extremely lucrative transactions for a cotton trading company established on the subcontinent because the majority of the cotton spun in China came from India.[59] Following Volkart's experience in Japan, the company was highly aware of the "disadvantages and difficulties of an entity like Nichizui, with the unavoidable and at times unpleasant objections that could be raised by third parties,"[60] and accordingly opened a branch in Shanghai in 1921 without any investments from local businessmen. At the same time, it realized right from the start that, as confirmed in a letter written by the headquarters in 1923, this new branch, "by virtue of our business principles and payment conditions, had to have its wings clipped, so to speak, and it cannot be said that we are making full use of the business opportunities in China."[61] The main stumbling block was that Chinese spinning mills did not pay for cotton delivers upon delivery, but only following a 15-day delay, which ran counter to Volkart's business principles.[62] The fact of the matter was that these principles made it impossible for the branch in Shanghai to become a major player in the Chinese cotton trade, a realization that led the company to conclude that it had to "revert to the original idea and establish a company, which was theoretically independent of our firm, with the inclusion of indigenous capital," as it had done in Osaka.[63]

In 1924, the Fohka Swiss-Chinese Trading Co. Ltd. was established in Shanghai with a capital of 500,000 taels.[64] The partners at Volkart invested 300,000 taels and Z. K. Woo, the former comprador (i.e., agent) of Volkart Shanghai, invested 110,000 taels. The remaining shares went to the Swiss manager who operated Fohka on behalf of Volkart, along with 12 Chinese businessmen from Shanghai and Nanking.[65] In contrast to Nichizui, which had been founded in Osaka as a Japanese firm, Fohka was established as a company in accordance with Swiss law.[66] This was possible because after the Second Opium War the British and American enclaves were merged to form the Shanghai International Settlement, in which European merchants fell under the jurisdiction of their respective home countries.[67] Fohka was initially founded primarily to handle the cotton trade between China, India, Japan, Europe and the US. However, more areas of business were soon added, such as importing dyes for the Chinese textile sector at the behest of Swiss chemical manufacturer Geigy, importing timepieces and other consumer goods from Europe, importing copper from the US, coffee and sandalwood from India and sugar from Java. Furthermore, Fohka served as an importer of European machinery.[68]

The Compradors as a Link to the Chinese Domestic Market

After the Opium Wars, the Chinese were forced by the European colonial powers to open the country to foreign merchants. Although they had the right to engage in trade throughout the entire country, the Europeans remained primarily in the coastal cities and, up until the 1920s, concluded all transactions with the help of affluent Chinese intermediaries known as compradors.[69] This made the situation in China fundamentally different from the one in India, at least until the early twentieth century. Although up until the 1930s Western merchants in India also relied on the cooperation of indigenous merchants, who served as brokers or shroffs,[70] European traders were able to penetrate the subcontinent with the help of the British colonial government. The Raj ensured a stable single currency, introduced a standardized system of weights and measures and established a court system that Westerners could use with confidence.[71] Moreover, the construction of railroads and telegraph lines allowed European companies to open agencies in the interior of India.

China was a far more formidable challenge for European trading firms. Even in the wake of imperial gunboat diplomacy, which had opened up the country to trade, Westerners found it extremely difficult to do business with Chinese merchants. Obstacles included the language barrier, the complexity of the monetary system, unfamiliar business practices, influential trade guilds and the lack of an extensive railway network like the one in India. Western companies thus had to rely upon the services of compradors, who used their wealth and influence to give Westerners access to areas of business that would have otherwise remained beyond their reach. They received a regular salary for their work and a commission of between 1 and 3 percent of the turnover. The compradors supervised the Chinese employees that they recruited for their Western employers, rented premises and provided information on the Chinese market. They also served as translators and intermediaries for transactions with local businessmen and Chinese bankers. Finally, they were responsible for the procurement of Chinese goods and the sale of imported goods in the interior of the country, as European and American merchants in particular rarely did any business outside treaty ports like Shanghai and Hong Kong up until the 1920s.[72]

The informational asymmetry that arose from the powerful position occupied by the compradors was extremely problematic for Western merchants. The compradors often used their positions to their own advantage, for example, by doing business secretly on the side, which put them in direct competition with their Western employers, or by charging a commission to the Chinese merchants with which Western companies sought to do business, which ultimately made the goods more expensive. Not surprisingly, many Western firms often made heavy losses doing business with China, while the compradors were generally able to make a profit.[73]

Since the late nineteenth century, Western companies had made repeated attempts to circumvent the compradors, but were unable to do so for many years. The first foreigners that managed to dispense with their compradors were the Japanese. The Japanese trading company Mitsui Bussan copied Western firms in 1877 and hired compradors. But in 1891 they began to train Japanese personnel to replace the compradors. Graduates of Japanese institutions of higher education were housed with Chinese families and tasked with learning Chinese. Likewise, they had to wear their hair in Chinese styles and adopt the Chinese mentality to the greatest possible degree. Mitsui was convinced that this was the only way that they could gain the trust of Chinese merchants. Between 1898 and 1901, Mitsui dismissed all of its compradors and replaced them with Japanese employees, causing the company's profits to triple.[74]

For many years, such a strategy was beyond the reach of Western companies due to the greater cultural and geographical distance to China. Like all other Western trading companies, before Volkart established the Fohka Swiss-Chinese Trading Co. Ltd. it was only able to conduct business in China with the help of compradors. When Georg Reinhart visited the Volkart branch in Shanghai (Figure 10.2) in 1923, he wrote the following glowing description in his travel report: "The comprador, Mr. Woo, is a very nice man with a refined sense of Chinese culture. I am sure that we will have no negative experiences with him in terms of the reputability of his character."

Figure 10.2 Office of the Volkart branch in Shanghai in 1922 (VA, Dossier 111: Photos Bremen, London, USA, Mexico, Brazil, Colombia, Singapore/ Shanghai/Japan)

Contacts between European managers and Chinese employees were facilitated in Shanghai from the turn of the century onwards by the advent of a new Chinese middle class,[75] many members of which had a Western education. In his report from Shanghai, Georg Reinhart described a Chinese employee as follows:

> Mister Teng is dwarfishly small and has a horribly pockmarked face, but he is a highly educated man who speaks excellent German without ever having been outside China. He used to be a language teacher and is the man who translates our cotton bulletin into Chinese. He is tasked with correspondence at the office.[76]

Domestic Political Turmoil and Attempts to Expand into the Interior of the Country

With the launch of Fohka, Volkart pursued a strategy similar to that of other Western companies after World War I. After the colonial powers began to lose importance in East Asia during the interwar era and the Chinese economy gained strength, Westerners entered into a growing number of joint ventures with Chinese businessmen.[77] Still, Fohka continued to conduct many of its transactions through its former comprador and current partner, Mr. Woo (Figure 10.3). This proved problematic due to China's

Figure 10.3 The Fohka staff on 1 February 1926 on the occasion of Volkart's celebration of its 75th anniversary at the Great Eastern Hotel, Shanghai. In the front row, eighth from the left, sits the partner and former comprador of Volkart, Z. K. Woo. In the background is the Swiss flag and the flag of the Chinese Republic (VA, Dossier 111: Photos Bremen, London, USA, Mexico, Brazil, Colombia, Singapore/Shanghai/Japan)

precarious domestic political situation. The year 1922 marked the end of the economic boom that the country had enjoyed since the beginning of World War I. The ensuing economic crisis constituted a severe test for the young Chinese Republic and exacerbated the conflicts between provincial rulers and the government, rendering China practically ungovernable. Local warlords controlled large regions of the country. Foreign companies were blackmailed. Gangs of bandits, including discharged soldiers, attacked travelers and massacred entire villages. One night during the spring of 1923, a horde of 1,200 robbers attacked the Blue Express, China's luxury railway line connecting Tianjin and Pukou, and 26 foreign nationals were abducted and forced to march into the mountains. One British man was murdered.[78] Volkart could have easily fallen victim to such a spectacular attack. Indeed, only two days earlier Georg Reinhart had traveled on the same train as part of his journey through China.[79]

In view of the unstable political situation, it soon became clear how problematic it was that Fohka was continuing to conduct business primarily via the former comprador, Mr. Woo. This meant that key connections to the Chinese market were established not by a European employee, but rather by an indigenous businessman with his own personal set of commercial interests. The principal-agent problem intensified to the point that Woo could not be sufficiently controlled by the European managers and partners at Volkart. In 1927, they discovered that Woo had defrauded the company to the tune of 100,000 taels by not paying for a cotton shipment that he had received from Fohka.[80] This swindle was a direct result of the political turmoil. Woo was unable to settle his debts because he was forced to pay protection money to a local warlord. Above and beyond these difficulties, business was not going well for Fohka. Due to careless transactions, the company had suffered losses of 3 million Swiss francs. Consequently, Fohka was liquidated in 1927 and all subsequent transactions in Shanghai were conducted via a branch office that was completely controlled by Volkart.[81]

Despite the political upheaval of the day, the Chinese textile industry made enormous strides during the interwar era. Whereas cotton textiles made up 20–25 percent of all imports in 1920, China was producing all of its cotton goods by 1937, making the country entirely self-sufficient in this respect— although it should be added that more than 40 percent of these textiles were produced by Japanese companies that had launched businesses in China. During the interwar era, the mutual economic dependency of China and Japan grew stronger than at any previous time in history. From the 1920s onwards, Japan was China's most important trading partner. The booming Chinese textile industry meant that an increasing amount of American raw cotton was imported to China. A veritable trade triangle developed between the US, China and Japan. Japanese factories in Shanghai, Tianjin and Qingdao used cheap Chinese labor to produce thread from long-staple American cotton, and this thread was then used to manufacture cloth in Japan.[82]

As in Japan, it was to Volkart's advantage that the company had emerged as a major multinational trading company during the interwar era and, as an agent of the American Cotton Cooperative Association, was able to broker sales of American raw cotton in Asia.[83] In addition to being able to offer Indian and—as a representative of Paul Reinhart & Co.—Egyptian cotton in China, this allowed Volkart to become one of the leading suppliers of US cotton and to compete with the American trading company of Anderson Clayton, which had dominated sales of US cotton in China until then. With American cotton added to its portfolio, Volkart was now able to establish business contacts with Chinese spinning companies that would have been impossible to negotiate if the company was only offering Indian cotton for sale. Between 1930 and 1934, before the shockwaves of the Great Depression had reached China, Volkart was able to secure lucrative business deals and make good on previous losses from Fohka.[84]

In 1927–1928, Volkart opened a second Chinese branch office in Tianjin to sell Chinese raw cotton to Japan, the US, Europe and Australia, and to supply Indian and American cotton to the spinning mills in northern China. Thanks to Volkart's decades of experience in the cotton trade and the company's worldwide corporate structure, it was able to do business in the sector without the aid of a comprador.[85] Volkart was not the only company to conduct business in the interior of the country without the help of a comprador. Other Western trading companies, such as the British mercantile house of Butterfield & Swire, also decided to take this step in the late 1920s, following the lead of Japanese firms that, as mentioned above, had made inroads into China during the late nineteenth century.[86] This backward integration was facilitated by the Chinese government, which was pressing ahead with the construction of infrastructure projects and introducing policies to promote the export sector.[87] Since the early twentieth century, the government had been supporting efforts to expand the cultivation of cotton in northern China, particularly long-staple American varieties. Because production costs in China were significantly lower than in the US, the government hoped that these varieties could replace imports of foreign cotton and that Chinese cotton would sooner or later be able to compete on the world market. After some initial teething problems, production in northern China rapidly increased from the 1920s onwards.[88] Encouraged by this success, in the early 1930s Volkart sent a Swiss employee on an inspection tour in the Xihe district to find out whether it would be possible for the company to establish its own procurement organization in northern China, with cotton gins and presses, based on the approach taken in India during the late nineteenth century. This employee later reported that he was the first Western merchant to inspect the cotton growing regions in the north. He strongly advised against expanding into the interior of the country, however, due to the unstable political situation and rampant corruption. In his opinion, the safest approach for foreign export firms for several years to come was to purchase cotton on the coast in Tianjin.[89] Nevertheless, in 1936 Volkart laid the cornerstone for a procurement organization in the upcountry of northern China to acquire long-staple Chinese cotton for spinning mills in Shanghai. One of the main motivations behind this move was the bunker crop of Chinese cotton during the 1935–1936 season, which made it possible for domestic cotton to compete with imported cotton. As it turns out, Volkart had been considering opening buying agencies for quite some time, as evidenced by a Swiss employee who had received Chinese language lessons for a number of years to gain a level of proficiency that would have allowed him to converse with indigenous merchants and officials without the aid of an interpreter. In other words, the company intended to use backward integration to counter the unstable domestic political situation, but this plan was overtaken by geopolitical events. When the Japanese invaded in 1937, the cotton business in China came to a grinding halt. In October 1938, Japan instituted an export embargo on Chinese cotton. Only exports to Japan were allowed. The buying agencies of Volkart's Shanghai branch were closed after just one season in operation.[90]

The Japanese Occupation and Rise to Power of the Communists

Starting in 1934, the business transactions of Volkart's Shanghai branch suffered from mounting tensions between China and Japan and the severity of the Great Depression. In 1937, for instance, the branch only barely managed to cover its own fixed costs. The attack launched by Japanese troops resulted in the destruction of several of Volkart's cotton warehouses, amounting to losses of 400,000 Swiss francs.[91] Despite the Japanese occupation, Volkart Shanghai achieved record sales in 1939 and 1940. After Japan invaded Indochina in September 1940, spinning mills in China placed large orders for cotton because they feared supply bottlenecks from a possible war in the Pacific. Volkart was able to move large quantities of goods at high prices and, in addition to Indian and American cotton, managed to sell large consignments of Brazilian cotton. Many of the orders were placed by the Japanese-dominated government of northern China in Beijing. A Japanese employee of Nichizui, who had been stationed in China, served as a liaison between Volkart and the Japanese cotton mills. Nichizui had also opened its own buying agencies for cotton in northern China, but the archives contain no further details on its activities.[92]

After the war, business began to pick up again after a more or less continuous lull between 1941 and 1945. Since Chinese spinning mills were strapped for cash, big shippers like Volkart and Anderson Clayton granted generous terms of payment. Volkart's Shanghai branch was able to sell 116,000 bales of cotton during the 1945–1946 season, which amounted to more than 11 percent of all private cotton imports to China. Furthermore, Volkart Shanghai recommended imports of foodstuffs, chemicals and wool, and served as the representative in China for several Swiss mechanical engineering companies, just as it had done before the war.[93] This allowed the branch to achieve the best operating result in its history in 1945–1946.[94] The spirit of optimism for future business opportunities in China—despite the many difficulties—is reflected by a quote from the 1945–1946 annual report of Volkart Shanghai: "China undoubtedly will be one of the biggest markets for the next decade for all sorts of goods and raw materials, but especially for machinery and railway material."[95]

After the communists rose to power, it became increasingly difficult for Western companies to do business in China. Starting in 1949, companies were only allowed to import raw cotton if, in return, thread and textiles were exported from China. The outbreak of the Korean War and the embargo against China put a stop to the cotton trade and ended all imports of machinery from the West. Faced with dismal results, Volkart decided to close its Shanghai branch in 1952. The Chinese government only allowed this move after the company agreed to give its Chinese employees a generous severance package. In addition, the former manager of Volkart Shanghai was not allowed to leave the country before he was prepared to pay a penalty tax of approximately 100,000 Swiss francs for allegedly engaging in illegal currency transactions.[96]

In actual fact, Volkart had conducted a number of illegal currency transactions after the war. For example, the company managed to send half of its record profits from 1945–1946 to Switzerland tax-free. What's more, during the following years the company made profits from currency transactions on the black market and transferred some 120,000 Swiss francs tax-free to Switzerland. For these operations Volkart Shanghai had a separate accounting system in which all documents were promptly destroyed as soon as they were no longer needed.[97]

Expansion to the US

Volkart could not have stepped up its business activities in East Asia after 1918 if it had not expanded to the US at the same time to meet the growing demand in China and Japan for long-staple American cotton. From the late 1880s onwards, Volkart had been represented by John W. Greene & Co. and various other American trading companies in the US. But the partners were not truly satisfied with this solution because Volkart had no branch offices of its own in the US, which was the largest producer of cotton and, starting in the late nineteenth century, the world's leading industrialized nation.[98]

After World War I, the company made another attempt to handle its growing amount of business in the US via a branch of its own, which was established in New York in 1920. This branch office not only brokered purchases of American cotton and served as a source of information on developments in the American cotton industry, but also conducted futures transactions on the New York Cotton Exchange for the branches in Osaka and Shanghai to help minimize the risks of the East Asian cotton trade.[99]

The fact that Volkart's New York office was initially established primarily to conduct futures transactions for the branches in East Asia shows the close connection between the company's decision to open a branch in the US and the expansion of its activities in East Asia. This is an indication of the degree to which Volkart saw its branches spread across three different continents as a single entity in which the individual branches were the organs "that complement each other in their activities and are reliant upon each other," as it was phrased in a letter from the headquarters in 1933.[100]

In 1922, the New York branch was transformed into a new company established in accordance with American law. This new formation was necessary for tax reasons. As their American lawyers explained to the partners, US tax authorities could conclude that Volkart was active in the US as an entire company if the Swiss firm was represented by its own agency there. In this case, in addition to the New York agency having to pay taxes on its income in the US, American authorities could demand that the partners disclose the company's total revenues so the IRS could determine what share of Volkart's income had been earned in the US. In a bid to prevent this, Volkart Brothers Inc. was formally established as an independent company that assumed responsibility for the activities of the New York office. All company shares remained in the hands of the Volkart partners, however.[101]

But this expansion created new problems. There were repeated differences of opinion between the subsidiary in New York and the branches in India concerning the amount to be paid in commissions.[102] Similar problems arose in the transactions between the Indian branches and Nichizui.[103] One of the main reasons for this was that the managers of the individual branches and subsidiaries earned a share of the profits, motivating them to strive for the best possible results for their own operations. By contrast, the partners at Volkart were interested in smooth business operations between the individual branches and optimum results for the entire organization. In a letter written in 1928 to the various branches and subsidiaries, the partners noted that Volkart Brothers Inc. and the rest of the company had a "shared destiny" and that the advantage of having their own subsidiary in New York was that it would "serve as a broker for the American business . . . with greater diligence and interest" than an outside agent would. "This advantage should be worth at least as much as what an outside company would demand for the service," they concluded. Furthermore, they argued that the subsidiary in New York had to receive appropriate compensation for its work as this "bona fide certificate of earnings was required for tax reasons and to prove to the authorities that it has the character of a corporation that is independent of our firm."[104] Hence, a contradiction of sorts existed between the internal organization of the company and the way in which it presented itself to the authorities. In internal communications, the partners insisted upon the unity of the company organization and attempted to minimize as much as possible the different interests of the managers of the individual branches, which could in turn be interpreted as in-company transaction costs. But when it came to the American tax authorities, they had to maintain the appearance that Volkart Brothers Inc. and the rest of the company were two separate organizations.

At the outset, Volkart conducted hardly any export transactions of American cotton via its newly established branch in New York. In response to a suggestion made by the subsidiary in Bremen that Volkart should enter the trade in American cotton, the headquarters in Winterthur responded in 1922 that the company had no interest in pursuing this branch of business: "We know how tough the competition is in America and what tricks large American companies have to use to keep their heads above water." They added that to be successful in the American cotton business required a purchasing organization that was similar to the one in India, after all "if we . . . only purchase from one shipper, we lack any basis whatsoever for establishing a V.B. brand that demands extra high prices from certain customers . . . and we forfeit the so-called shipper's profit by default." In view of the uncertain economic situation, the partners were not prepared to risk taking such a step to expand the business.[105]

Although in 1927 there was talk of sending a buying agent to the Southern states to purchase cotton for the Asian branch offices and Volkart Bremen, company executives clearly stated that they intended to stick with the "repeatedly stressed principle that we as a company have no intention whatsoever of acting as a shipper of American cotton."[106] Contrary to this policy statement, however, the company began to export American cotton to Europe and Asia in the late 1920s. The cotton was purchased from diverse American intermediaries who had to provide assurances regarding the quality of the delivered goods. But the results were miserable. Due to intense competition in the sector, the firm was forced to purchase from smaller suppliers that often could only provide inferior quality merchandise. Volkart frequently had to pay compensation to spinning mills and the company was running the risk of squandering the hard-earned reputation that it had built up over the years as an outstanding supplier of Indian cotton.[107]

Entering the American Cotton Trade

In 1930, Volkart suddenly became one of the largest exporters of American cotton after it managed to become the sole representative in Asia of the recently established American Cotton Cooperative Association (ACCA). Since state-subsidized cotton cooperatives produced roughly 10 percent of the US cotton crop in the 1930s, the ACCA quickly became one of the leading distribution channels for American cotton.[108] Volkart was able to assume this position for the ACCA because the company had an efficient sales organization in India, China and Japan. The firm also benefited from having its own subsidiary in the US. On the day that the ACCA was established, the head of Volkart Brothers Inc. flew from New York to New Orleans, where the headquarters of the ACCA was located, and secured for Volkart the exclusive sales rights for ACCA cotton in China, Japan and India. On the downside, a recently signed agency agreement between Volkart Shanghai and the American cotton trading company McFadden for the sale of American cotton in China had to be terminated before a single transaction had been completed. "It was appealing for the ACCA to work with us," wrote Peter Reinhart in a memo in 1950,

> because we were prepared . . . to pay for the cotton in cash in New York so that they didn't have to deal with the endless problems of the East Asian market. For us, the new agreement meant that we suddenly entered the American cotton trade in a very big way; after all, it was rapidly clear that the ACCA would become a key factor in the American cotton trade right from the start. Its sales were soon comparable with those of Anderson Clayton.[109]

Business flourished because spinning mills in India, Japan and above all China were highly interested in American cotton. After only two and a half years, Volkart had sold 1 million bales of cotton in Asia for the ACCA. On the strength of its imports of American cotton and its ongoing trade in Indian cotton, in the second half of the 1930s Volkart was responsible for one-quarter of all cotton imports to China. Business was also brisk in Japan. In addition to its sales to Japanese spinning mills via Nichizui, Volkart was now also able to supply large Japanese cotton import firms. This allowed for a maximum margin of 5 percent, but it was risk-free because the Japanese trading companies required no deferment of payment and paid for the cotton upon delivery in Japan. Now that Volkart could offer American cotton, the company came into contact with customers that earlier would have been beyond its reach as a supplier of only Indian cotton. The ACCA was so satisfied with Volkart's performance in the Asian trade that in 1933 the company was also able to assume responsibility for sales in Germany, Poland, Czechoslovakia and Switzerland.[110]

Volkart thus successfully entered the American cotton trade not through a backward integration and establishment of its own procurement organization, but rather by tying into an intra-organizational network. However, as with the joint ventures with Japanese and Chinese merchants in establishing subsidiaries in East Asia, the collaboration with the ACCA created a number of new problems. The American cotton from the ACCA was in direct competition with the Indian cotton sold by Volkart. Hence, the Volkart headquarters felt it necessary in 1933 to remind the branch offices in Osaka and Shanghai that they were essentially established as sales channels for the cotton acquired via the company's procurement organization in India. Company officials went on to say that when faced with the choice between purchasing Indian or American cotton, the decision should not be influenced by the anticipated profits on location, but rather by the notion that the greatest benefits to the entire organism must be the criterion for action in every part of the organization. Accordingly, a transaction in Indian cotton, which on paper entails the same degree of risks and opportunities as a given transaction in American cotton, is a better deal for the overall company because it benefits the work of the Indian branch offices.[111]

Increased Importance of Futures Trading

During the 1930s, the branch in New York served primarily as a link between the ACCA and the Volkart sales offices in Asia and Europe. Likewise, Volkart Brothers Inc. began to import Indian and Chinese cotton and, starting in 1933, also Egyptian cotton that was purchased in Alexandria from the branch office there of the Winterthur trading company Paul Reinhart & Co.[112] Finally, Volkart's New York subsidiary also purchased futures on the New York Cotton Exchange to safeguard the company's cotton transactions against fluctuating prices.[113]

In 1931, it was decided that the trading of futures would be handled by a newly established firm, the Volkart Brothers Clearing Co. Since only members were allowed to trade on the exchange,[114] the new company acquired a seat on the New York Cotton Exchange along with seats on various commodity futures exchanges in New York, New Orleans and Chicago. Volkart Brothers Clearing Co. not only conducted its own futures transactions, but also began to perform services for other merchants on US commodity exchanges, such as handling large transactions for cotton and coffee trading companies from Brazil. Countertrades played a large role in these transactions. Volkart indicated that it was prepared to conduct transactions via local merchants at the commodity exchanges in Liverpool and Bombay if the merchants in question were prepared, in return, to conduct exchange operations in the US via the Volkart Brothers Clearing Co.[115] This was profitable because on the diverse exchanges there was always a slight difference between the prices of the futures contracts and the prices of the relevant varieties of cotton. In other words, it could pay off to terminate a futures contract for Indian cotton in Bombay with the intention of concluding one for American cotton in New York if the relative price of American futures in New York was lower than that of Indian futures in Bombay. There was not only an intrinsic connection between the relative prices of individual varieties of cotton, but also between the prices that were paid for futures contracts for these commodities on the individual exchanges.[116] In order to profit from the corresponding differences in prices, in 1938–1939 Volkart opened a dedicated division in Bombay to handle exchange transactions.[117] This shows that futures transactions at the commodity exchanges had become increasingly complex during the interwar era and were progressively becoming a key element of a trading company's operations.

Only a few years earlier, Volkart managers had strictly rejected all exchange transactions that did not serve to safeguard deals with physically existing commodities, but they could not prevent individual branch offices from occasionally engaging in such exchange operations. In 1932, the Volkart branch in Bombay suffered heavy losses from speculative deals on the exchanges. Executives at the headquarters in Winterthur saw this as further proof that "speculative enterprises, as such, have far more negligible prospects of making profits as of making losses" and therefore demanded that "speculative enterprises . . . as such, i.e., disassociated from transactions in actual goods, should be completely eradicated from our code of conduct." Entirely in keeping with traditional commercial practice, they were convinced that there was only "one sure means of increasing sales, and thus also profits, and that is to study the market meticulously on both sides for business opportunities in the purely factual sense of favorable buying and selling."[118] Embarking on large-scale exchange transactions was therefore far more than merely an expansion of the previous area of business. Indeed, by viewing futures trading as a legitimate commercial activity that had earlier been dismissed as pure speculation, Volkart had undergone a fundamental change in attitude on what was widely accepted within the company as the essence of commercial transactions.

Large Government Contracts and Multinational Trading Companies

The global economy of the 1930s was characterized by a primacy of nation-state policies over economic interaction. After the onset of the Great Depression, exchanges of goods and movements of capital were subjected to severe political restrictions. This development was problematic for an internationally active trading company because political interventions by national governments generally impeded cross-border business transactions and, in extreme cases, even rendered them impossible, as Volkart and other companies experienced during World War I.[119]

But the politicization of global trade could also have advantages for a big company like Volkart because it led to major government contracts. Not only did Volkart benefit from the fact that the US government subsidized cotton exports via the ACCA, it also profited in the fall of 1932 when the US government approved 40 million dollars in credit for the export of American cotton to China.[120] The US government, which was under intense domestic political pressure from cotton farmers, hoped that this measure would eliminate America's surplus of cotton and stabilize cotton prices by stimulating demand. The loans had been approved because Rong Zongjing, the head of China's largest cotton mill, Shenxin Textile Mills, had managed to convince the Chinese government that the Japanese invasion would soon result in a shortage of cotton in Manchuria. However, his main motivation was the hope that US cotton loans would lead to declining cotton prices in

China, which would have given his company an advantage over Japanese competitors.

The ACCA was responsible for most of the cotton exports under this agreement and Volkart's Shanghai office was given the job of delivering the cotton in question to the Chinese government.[121] In late September 1933, an initial shipment of approximately 160,000 bales of cotton worth 10 million dollars arrived in Shanghai. But, as it turned out, China had a bumper cotton crop that year and, not surprisingly, virtually none of the Chinese spinning mills purchased the American cotton. By late March 1934, only 90,000 bales of the delivered cotton from the US had been sold. This was a source of aggravation for the US government because the lack of demand dashed all hopes of a price increase on the American market. The cotton credit was subsequently reduced from 40 million to 10 million dollars. For its part, the Chinese government was left with 100,000 bales of unsold cotton, which it then offered to the Japanese spinning mills in Shanghai. However, the government in Tokyo banned the Japanese spinning mills from purchasing the American cotton because they were convinced that the cotton credit had been approved primarily as a means of weakening Japan's influence in China. Faced with this desperate situation, the Chinese government asked Volkart if the company would be willing to repurchase the cotton at a reduced price. Volkart agreed under the condition that the cotton could be reexported, which was not allowed under the Chinese-American agreement. After protracted negotiations with the US government, it was decided that the cotton would be shipped to Germany, where it was ultimately sold at a profit. This transaction was extremely lucrative for Volkart not only because of the large volume involved but also because all of the risk was borne by the governments involved. The Japanese press was outraged at this turn of events and reported that a European company like Volkart had been instrumental in smuggling cotton out of China.

The Establishment of an American Purchasing Organization

As the Great Depression began to subside in 1937, private American cotton trading companies increasingly objected to state subsidies of the ACCA, which was nothing but unwelcome competition for them. This prevented the ACCA from making any more long-term commitments. As a result, Volkart informed the ACCA in the summer of 1938 that it intended to make purchases from other American cotton exporters in the future and the ACCA reluctantly had to consent to this. The collaboration with the ACCA ended in the summer of 1939.[122]

In order to continue to offer American cotton to its customers in various regions of the globe and guarantee the quality of the deliveries, Volkart established Volkart Brothers Inc., New Orleans, in January 1940.[123] This new subsidiary was initially merely intended to ensure the link between American cotton exporters and Volkart's sales organization. But after France was occupied by Germany and Italy, exports to Europe came to a standstill. Instead of supplying European textile mills, Volkart New Orleans changed its plans and decided instead to focus on supplying American textile enterprises with cotton. But in order for this to succeed, Volkart needed buying agencies in the US, which is why Volkart began to establish its own purchasing and sales organization in the US in 1942.[124]

Notes

1 Vicziany, "Bombay merchants and structural changes," 1979, 165–166.
2 VA, Dossier 15: The Far Eastern Organisation, I. Shanghai (incl. Tientsin etc.), 2. Table of Events; Anderegg, *Chronicle*, 1976, 113.
3 Saxonhouse/Kiyokawa, "Supply and Demand for Quality Workers," 1998, 183–184;
4 Fletcher III, "The Japan Spinners' Association," 2001.
5 VA, Dossier 3: Bombay I, 4. Table of Events 1851–1961/2.
6 Beckert, Emancipation and Empire, 2004, 1421; Sugihara (ed.), *Japan, China, and the Growth of the Asian International Economy*, 2005; Akita/White (ed.), *The International Order of Asia*, 2010.
7 Anderegg, *Chronicle*, 1976, 195ff.
8 Anderegg, *Chronicle*, 1976, 756.
9 VA, Dossier 3: Bombay I, 4. Table of Events 1851–1961/2: Bombay to Winterthur, 18 October 1899.
10 Anderegg, *Chronicle*, 1976, 195.
11 VA, Dossier 14: Japan.
12 VA, Dossier 14: Japan, Korrespondenz: Winterthur to Osaka, copies to Bombay, Karachi, Tuticorin, 10 April 1918 (Diktat von E. Müller-Renner).
13 V.B. News, No. 10, March 1924, 8.
14 For more on the importance of futures trading, see Chapter 3.
15 NA, BT 55/5, Board of Trade (Committee Papers), Committee on Civil Research 1928–1929, Sub-Committee on Cotton Industry, Costs of Production in Cotton Industry in Japan: British Consulate, Osaka, to H. Hughes, Director, The Statistical Bureau, Manchester Chamber of Commerce, September 4, 1928, 5; Pearse, *The Cotton Industry of Japan and China*, 1929, 12; Ellinger/Ellinger, "Japanese Competition in the Cotton Trade," 1930, 195–201; Naoto, "Up-country Purchase Activities," 2001, 199–200.; Jeremy, "Organization and Management," 2004, 204–216;.
16 Ellinger/Ellinger, "Japanese Competition in the Cotton Trade," 1930, 198.
17 Killick, "Specialized and General Trading Firms," 1987, 263.
18 Osterhammel, *China und die Weltgesellschaft*, 1989, 264.
19 Dantwala, *A Hundred Years of Indian Cotton*, 1947, 23; Hardach, *Der Erste Weltkrieg*, 1973, 278ff.
20 Bombay Chamber of Commerce, Report of the year 1926.
21 Toshiyuki, "The Changing Pattern of Sino-Japanese Trade," 1998, 145.
22 VA, Dossier 13: London/Liverpool (VB + Woods&Thorburn) / Bremen: Bremen (incl. Hamburg office): Gesellschaftsvertrag vom 31. August 1922 zwischen Gebr. Volkart, Winterthur und Volkart G.m.b.H., Bremen; VA, Dossier 16: USA, Brazil, Mexico, Guatemala/Costa Rica, Turkey, I. USA, 1. VB Inc. New York—1922.
23 The name of the subsidiary is a combination of the Japanese terms "nichi" (Japan) and "sui" or "zui" (an abbreviation of "suisu," meaning Switzerland): V.B. News, No. 10, March 1924, 4.

24 For more on Nichizui's machinery import business, see Chapter 11.
25 V.B. News, No. 10, March 1924, 4ff.
26 Yamamura, "Then Came the Great Depression," 1998.
27 VA, Dossier 14: Japan: Winterthur to Bombay, 2 December 1920.
28 VA, Dossier 14: Japan: Winterthur to Bombay, 2 June 1921.
29 VA, Dossier 14: Japan: Winterthur to Bombay, Kopie an alle Häuser, 17 August 1922.
30 VA, Rapporte von Herrn Georg Reinhart anlässlich seiner Inspektionsreise nach Indien etc. im Jahre 1923: GR, Osaka, to Winterthur, 28 May 1923.
31 VA, Konferenz-Protokolle vom 5. Juni 1940–1931. Juli 1941: Protokoll vom 22. August 1940, Brief vom 17.7.: Takashima/Takemura.
32 VA, Konferenz-Protokolle vom 5. August 1941–1944. März 1943: Konferenz vom 16. Juli 1942.
33 VA, Rapporte von Herrn Georg Reinhart anlässlich seiner Inspektionsreise nach Indien etc. im Jahre 1923: GR, Osaka, to Winterthur, 28 May 1923.
34 VA, Rapporte von Herrn Georg Reinhart anlässlich seiner Inspektionsreise nach Indien etc. im Jahre 1923: GR, Osaka, to Winterthur, 28 May 1923.
35 Anderegg, *Chronicle*, 1976, 358.
36 VA, Dossier 14: Japan: Winterthur an unsere indischen Filialen und an Osaka, Kopie an London, Hamburg, New York, 18 July 1929.
37 VA, Dossier 14: Japan: Winterthur to Bombay, Kopie nach Karachi, Tuticorin, Osaka, Shanghai, 27 June 1929.
38 VA, Dossier 14: Japan: Winterthur an unsere indischen Filialen und an Osaka, Kopie an London, Hamburg, New York, 18 July 1929.
39 VA, Dossier 14: Japan: Winterthur to Bombay, Kopie nach Karachi, Tuticorin, Osaka, Shanghai, 27 June 1929.
40 VA, Dossier 59: PR-Privatarchiv: Notizen / Briefe / Personelles etc., Cotton: EN/K, 4 February 1932.
41 Rothermund, "Chinas verspätete Krise," 1983; Rothermund, "Currencies, Taxes and Credit," 2002, 22; Yamamura, "Then Came the Great Depression," 1998, 279ff.
42 VA, Dossier 14: Japan: Geschäftsbericht der Nichizui Trading Co., Ltd., Osaka, per 31. August 1931, to Bombay, Karachi, Tuticorin, Calcutta; Volkart-Archiv, Dossier 15, The Far Eastern Organisation, I. Shanghai (incl. Tientsin etc.), 5. notes by staff members who were in Shanghai: von der Crone to Anderegg, 3 September 1978.
43 Pearse, *The Cotton Industry of Japan and China*, 1929, 44.
44 Anderegg, *Chronicle*, 1976, 426.
45 Yui, "Development, Organization, and Business Strategy," 2001, 326.
46 Yamamura, "Then Came the Great Depression," 1998, 284–285.
47 Dantwala, *A Hundred Years of Indian Cotton*, 1947, 23–24.
48 Anderegg, *Chronicle*, 1976, 426.
49 Anderegg, *Chronicle*, 1976, 428.
50 VA, Dossier 14: Japan, Korrespondenz: Peter Reinhart, Tatuta Maru, 20 July 1939 to Winterthur.
51 VA, Dossier 14: Japan, Korrespondenz: Peter Reinhart, New York, to Winterthur, 25 June 1938.
52 VA, Dossier 14: Japan, Korrespondenz: Peter Reinhart, Tatuta Maru, 20 July 1939 to Winterthur.
53 VA, Dossier 14: Japan, Short note on the history of Volkart in Japan, 13 March 1986.
54 Anderegg, *Chronicle*, 1976, 428
55 Anderegg, *Chronicle*, 1976, 556–559.

56　For more on imports of machinery to Asia, see Chapter 11.

57　Steinmann, *Seldwyla im Wunderland*, 1998, 147.

58　Osterhammel, *China und die Weltgesellschaft*, 1989, 264.

59　Of the 717,000 bales of raw cotton imported during the 1921–1922 season, 151,000 came from the US and 565,000 came from India: Pearse, *The Cotton Industry of Japan and China*, 1929, 197.

60　VA, Dossier 15, The Far Eastern Organisation, I. Shanghai (incl. Tientsin etc.), 3. Correspondence: Winterthur to Bombay, 30 June 1921.

61　VA, Dossier 15, The Far Eastern Organisation, I. Shanghai (incl. Tientsin etc.), 2. Table of Events: Winterthur to Calcutta, Kopie an alle Häuser, 5 September 1923.

62　VA, Dossier 15, The Far Eastern Organisation, I. Shanghai (incl. Tientsin etc.), 3. Correspondence: Winterthur to Bombay, 30 June 1921.

63　VA, Dossier 15, The Far Eastern Organisation, I. Shanghai (incl. Tientsin etc.), 2. Table of Events: Winterthur to Calcutta, Kopie an alle Häuser, 5 September 1923.

64　The name 'Fohka' was directly inspired by the Chinese pronunciation of Volkart: V.B. News, No. 11, June 1924, 11.

65　BAR, E 2200.290 (Shanghai), Akz. 1, Behältnis 21, V.B.b. ancien 21, Fohka—Swiss-Chinese Trading Co., Ltd. (1924–1935): Minutes of the constituent General Meeting of the Fohka Swiss-Chinese Trading Company Limited, Shanghai, 25 February 1924.

66　Anderegg, *Chronicle*, 1976, 375.

67　Osterhammel, *China und die Weltgesellschaft*, 1989, 149–153; Steinmann, *Seldwyla im Wunderland*, 1998, 12–13.

68　Anderegg, *Chronicle*, 1976, 375–376. For more on imports of machinery to China, see Chapter 11.

69　Osterhammel, *China und die Weltgesellschaft*, 1989, 149 and 181.

70　Also see Chapters 2, 9 and 11.

71　Bayly, *Rulers, Townsmen and Bazaars*, 371; Benton, *Law and Colonial Cultures*, 2002.

72　Hao, "A New Class," 1970; Smith, "Compradores of the Hong Kong Bank," 1983; Osterhammel, *China und die Weltgesellschaft*, 1989, 187; Ray, "Asian Capital," 1995, 485–501.

73　Yang, "The Profitability of Anglo-Chinese Trade," 1993.

74　Cochran, "Three Roads into Shanghai's Market," 1992.

75　Osterhammel, *China und die Weltgesellschaft*, 1989, 245–246.

76　VA, Rapporte von Herrn Georg Reinhart anlässlich seiner Inspektionsreise nach Indien etc. im Jahre 1923: Georg Reinhart, Shanghai, 2 May 1923.

77　Osterhammel, "Imperialism in Transition," 1984.

78　Osterhammel, *China und die Weltgesellschaft*, 1989, 232–233.

79　V.B. News, No. 9 December 1923, 24; Georg Reinhart. *Aus meinem Leben*. Winterthur 1931, 258–259.

80　VA, Dossier 15: The Far Eastern Organisation, I. Shanghai (incl. Tientsin etc.), 5. Notes by Staff Members who were in Shanghai: von der Crone (1938–1954 BM in Shanghai) to Anderegg, 15 August 1978.

81　VA, Dossier 15: The Far Eastern Organisation, I. Shanghai (incl. Tientsin etc.), 2. Table of Events.

82　Osterhammel, *China und die Weltgesellschaft*, 1989, 249; Toshiyuki, "The Changing Pattern of Sino-Japanese Trade," 1998, 152; Yui, "Development, Organization, and Business Strategy," 2001, 332.

83　For a more detailed description, see the last part of this chapter.

84　Anderegg, *Chronicle*, 1976, 430–431; Steinmann, *Seldwyla im Wunderland*, 1998, 146.

85　VA, Dossier 15: The Far Eastern Organisation, I. Shanghai (incl. Tientsin etc.), 5. Notes by Staff members who were in Shanghai: Wolfgang Hegar to Anderegg, 21 December 1975; Anderegg, *Chronicle*, 1976, 433.

86　Sugiyama, "Marketing and Competition in China," 2001, 153–154.

87 Grove, "International Trade," 2001, 101.
88 Pomeranz, *Making of a Hinterland*, 1993, 72–82; Grove, "International Trade," 2001, 101–102.
89 VA, Dossier 15 A: Shanghai Informationen-Buch, 96: Tientsin to Winterthur, 15. October 1933.
90 VA, Dossier 15: The Far Eastern Organisation, I. Shanghai (incl. Tientsin etc.), 5. Notes by Staff Members who were in Shanghai: von der Crone to Anderegg, 3 September 1978; Werner Müller to Anderegg, 10 April 1978.
91 BAR, E 2200.290 (Shanghai), Akz. 1 Behältnis 108, XX.C.13.4. Réparation des dommages de Guerre: Volkart Brothers (1937–1946); Anderegg, *Chronicle*, 1976, 435.
92 VA, Dossier 15: The Far Eastern Organisation, I. Shanghai (incl. Tientsin etc.), 5. Notes by Staff Members who were in Shanghai: von der Crone to Anderegg, 3 September 1978; Anderegg, *Chronicle*, 1976, 491–450.
93 See Chapter 11.
94 VA, Dossier 15, The Far Eastern Organisation, I. Shanghai (incl. Tientsin etc.), 2. Table of Events; Anderegg, *Chronicle*, 1976, 550ff.
95 VA, Dossier 15, The Far Eastern Organisation, I. Shanghai (incl. Tientsin etc.), 3. Correspondence: Balance Sheet Report—Season 1945/1946, Shanghai to Winterthur, 5 October 1946.
96 VA, Dossier 15, The Far Eastern Organisation, I. Shanghai (incl. Tientsin etc.), Mappe: Labour Settlement 1953; Anderegg, *Chronicle*, 1976, 553–554.
97 VA, Dossier 15: The Far Eastern Organisation, I. Shanghai (incl. Tientsin etc.), 5. Notes by Staff Members who were in Shanghai: von der Crone to Anderegg, 3 September 1978.
98 VA, Dossier 16: USA, Brazil, Mexico, Guatemala/Costa Rica, Turkey, I. USA, 2. Table of Events V.B. Inc.
99 V.B. News, No. 1, November 1920, 18; VA, Dossier 16: USA, Brazil, Mexico, Guatemala/Costa Rica, Turkey, I. USA, 2. Table of Events V.B. Inc.
100 VA, Dossier 14: Japan: Winterthur to Osaka und Shanghai, Kopie nach Bombay, Karachi, Tuticorin, New York, 7 November 1933.
101 VA, Dossier 16: USA, Brazil, Mexico, Guatemala/Costa Rica, Turkey, I. USA, 1. VB Inc. New York—1922: Parker, Marshall, Miller & Auchincloss, New York to Messrs. Volkart Bros., New York, 23 January 1922.
102 VA, Dossier 16: USA, Brazil, Mexico, Guatemala/Costa Rica, Turkey, II. New York, 4. Correspondence: Winterthur an alle Häuser, 3 May 1928.
103 VA, Dossier 14: Japan: Winterthur to Bombay, Kopie nach Karachi, Tuticorin, Osaka, Shanghai, 27 June 1929; Winterthur an unsere indischen Filialen und an Osaka, Kopie an London, Hamburg, New York, 18 July 1929.
104 VA, Dossier 16: USA, Brazil, Mexico, Guatemala/Costa Rica, Turkey, II. New York, 4. Correspondence: Winterthur an alle Häuser, 3 May 1928.
105 VA, Dossier 13: London/Liverpool (VB + Woods&Thorburn) / Bremen, Bremen (incl. Hamburg office), 3. Correspondence: Winterthur to Bremen, 9 June 1922.
106 VA, Dossier 13: London/Liverpool (VB + Woods&Thorburn) / Bremen, Bremen (incl. Hamburg office), 3. Correspondence: Winterthur to Bombay, 20 July 1927.
107 VA, Dossier 16: USA, Brazil, Mexico, Guatemala/Costa Rica, Turkey, I. USA: Notiz von Peter Reinhart vom 20. September 1950, "Entwicklung des amerikanischen Baumwollgeschäftes."
108 Garside, *Cotton Goes to Market*, 1935, 289–302.
109 VA, Dossier 16: USA, Brazil, Mexico, Guatemala/Costa Rica, Turkey, I. USA: Notiz von Peter Reinhart vom 20. September 1950, "Entwicklung des amerikanischen Baumwollgeschäftes."
110 VA, Dossier 16: USA, Brazil, Mexico, Guatemala/Costa Rica, Turkey, I. USA: Notiz von Peter Reinhart vom 20. September 1950, "Entwicklung des amerikanischen Baumwollgeschäftes."

111 VA, Dossier 14: Japan: Winterthur to Osaka und Shanghai, Kopie nach Bombay, Karachi, Tuticorin, New York, 7 November 1933.
112 Anderegg, *Chronicle*, 1976, 442.
113 For a more detailed description of the importance of futures transactions in the commodities trade, see Chapter 3.
114 Garside, *Cotton Goes to Market*, 1935, 138–139.
115 VA, Dossier 16: USA, Brazil, Mexico, Guatemala/Costa Rica, Turkey, I. USA, VB Clearing Co., N.Y.—1931; Anderegg, *Chronicle*, 1976, 446–447.
116 Garside, *Cotton Goes to Market*, 1935, 314.
117 Anderegg, *Chronicle*, 1976, 395.
118 VA, Dossier 59: PR-Privatarchiv: Notizen / Briefe / Personelles etc., Cotton: Winterthur to Bombay, 22 March 1932.
119 See Chapter 4.
120 The description of the cotton loans here is based on Osterhammel, *China und die Weltgesellschaft*, 1989, 294; Hosoya, "The United States and East Asia in the mid-1930s," 1990; Cochran, "Businesses, Governments, and War in China," 1990.
121 For more on the role of Volkart and the ACCA in this transaction, see Anderegg, *Chronicle*, 1976, 432; Steinmann, *Seldwyla im Wunderland*, 1998, 148.
122 VA, Dossier 16: USA, Brazil, Mexico, Guatemala/Costa Rica, Turkey, I. USA: Notiz von Peter Reinhart vom 20. September 1950, "Entwicklung des amerikanischen Baumwollgeschäftes,"
123 VA, Dossier 16: USA, Brazil, Mexico, Guatemala/Costa Rica, Turkey, I. USA: Notiz von Peter Reinhart vom 20. September 1950, "Entwicklung des amerikanischen Baumwollgeschäftes."
124 VA, Dossier 16: USA, Brazil, Mexico, Guatemala/Costa Rica, Turkey, II. New York (New Orleans/ Dallas included), 2. Table of Events V.B. Inc.; Anderegg, *Chronicle*, 1976, 443ff.

11 Machinery for Asia

Although it had been one of the primary goals of the British colonizers to transform India into a producer of cash crops like indigo, jute, opium and cotton for world markets, the economy of the subcontinent could not be limited to agricultural production. Starting in the 1860s, India gave rise to an efficient textile industry that was increasingly able to compete with British and continental European textile imports. Indian and, later on, also Chinese and Japanese spinning and weaving mills initially used primarily British machinery, but subsequently also relied on systems from continental Europe and the US. Western manufacturers of machinery often exported their products via trading companies that were established in the relevant countries.[1] Such collaborations were necessary because neither the trading firms nor the manufacturing companies had the requisite knowledge to carry out the exports alone. Trading companies lacked the technical knowledge that was required to install and maintain complex machinery, which meant that manufactures had to send engineers abroad to assist them. For their part, the producers of machinery had no knowledge of the foreign markets and relied on intermediaries who were familiar with local business practices and could provide a sales organization. This shows that the global market for machinery—like the commodities market before it—could only emerge during the late nineteenth century because the players involved were able to establish entrepreneurial networks that spanned several continents.

A Difficult Start

The challenges involved in exporting machinery overseas are reflected in the problems that Volkart faced for quite some time in this business area. Starting in the 1880s, the Volkart engineering department in the Bombay branch endeavored to sell cotton and coconut fiber presses as well as diesel engines, electrical installations and boilers from diverse British manufacturers. But the sales figures were rather disappointing, so Volkart decided to close the engineering department again in 1892.[2]

It was around this time that a number of different Swiss mechanical engineering companies redoubled their efforts to boost exports abroad and, in addition to Latin America and Egypt, shifted their focus to Asian countries like China, Japan and British India.[3] This must have encouraged Volkart to make a renewed attempt in the machinery business. Starting in 1908, the company used its Bombay and Karachi offices to import agricultural implements by John Wallace & Sons in Glasgow and, from 1912, trucks by the Swiss firm Saurer.[4] In 1914, Volkart began to negotiate with Gebrüder Sulzer AG, a highly diversified company that was also based in Winterthur and manufactured a range of products that included diesel engines and refrigeration units.[5] After the matter had been postponed due to the outbreak of the war, the two companies resumed negotiations in the summer of 1922. At issue was whether, and under what conditions, Volkart could assume responsibility for sales of Sulzer machines in India. In accordance with the initial talks, Sulzer was to supply the technical personnel for maintaining the supplied pumps, ice makers and refrigeration units, while Volkart was responsible for marketing the equipment and financing the transactions. Despite the fact that Volkart headquarters in Winterthur was highly interested in such an expansion of its area of activity, the managers of the Bombay branch remained skeptical. Although officials at Volkart Bombay agreed that the machinery import business had a bright future, they were concerned that there were already a large number of well-established companies in India that were working in the sector "exclusively or as their main area of business" and "either had their own large engineering units or more or less well-equipped repair workshops and a technical staff that was familiar with the sector in India." They also pointed out that Swiss machinery was also relatively expensive, which was a particular problem for sales in India where "far less emphasis is placed on quality goods as on relative cheapness." Furthermore, sales of machinery in India were only possible if one was prepared to pay bribes, and the managers of Volkart Bombay reminded the executives in Winterthur that this "path . . . is, to our knowledge, distasteful for both you and us."[6] The Bombay branch was also skeptical of the plans of the headquarters to conduct transactions in the machinery sector on its own account. Volkart Bombay preferred instead to work as an intermediary on a commission basis to avoid having to establish and maintain warehouse inventories of machinery and replacement parts, which could easily be damaged in the tropical climate of India, and to escape having to give guarantees to buyers that deliveries would be on time and machines would function properly.[7] The representation negotiations with Sulzer ultimately failed, partly due to the objections of the Volkart branch in Bombay.

Aside from the inquiry from Volkart, for quite some time the Sulzer company had already been giving some thought to how it could sell its machinery in India. In late 1921, the British firm Bird & Co. in Calcutta was commissioned to import Sulzer machinery.[8] One year later, Heinrich Wolfer, a member of the Sulzer board of directors, traveled to India to sound out the sales opportunities on the subcontinent, which is an indication of how meticulously the manufacturing company planned its exports.[9] Wolfer noted that "the Indian market has to be cultivated directly on location."[10] Up until then, individual company representatives had been convinced that the Indian market could be handled via the Sulzer branch in London because several British companies that were involved in the Indian textile industry had their headquarters in the British capital.[11] But Wolfer insisted that Indian entrepreneurs, especially in Bombay, were the key decision-makers and had to be addressed directly.[12] Moreover, during a trip through the interior of the country, Wolfer gained insights into how the industry worked there and came to the conclusion that the "conditions . . . are generally difficult and unsatisfactory," and went on to say that

> high-quality machines are practically unknown. Maintenance personnel for the machinery are subpar and engineers are usually very poorly educated. . . . There is a deep-seated common practice of always buying the cheapest available product. People have not yet learned how to judge the cost of a machine according to its value for money and maintenance over an extended period of time. It will be extremely challenging for our future Indian personnel to convince customers that a slightly more expensive machine can actually be the cheapest.[13]

He went on to say that this was why it was important for Sulzer to station its own technicians in India. He cited as an example the Schweizerische Lokomotiv- und Maschinenfabrik, which was doing brisk business in India after placing an advertisement that offered customers a "special supervising engineer in attendance."[14] In reaction to Wolfer's report, in November 1923 Sulzer opened its own sales office in Calcutta,[15] which collaborated with Bird & Co. to handle sales throughout the entire subcontinent.[16]

Reestablishment of an Engineering Department

Although Volkart had missed out on its opportunity to represent Sulzer, and its efforts to import technical equipment had failed in the past, in 1923 the company decided to import machinery from British, American and continental European manufacturers to India via the newly opened engineering department in Bombay.[17] Volkart soon had a large number of Indian and European technicians on its payroll for the maintenance and installation of complex equipment (Figure 11.1).[18] This signaled an expansion of the company's entrepreneurial spectrum from the trading business to the area of industrial services. Furthermore, the company rented warehouses and showrooms. Starting in 1927, it opened its own offices and service stations for the machinery business in Madras, Lahore and Calcutta, along with diverse sales agencies in the industrial centers of the subcontinent.[19]

A report by the Swiss consulate general in Bombay from the year 1928 bears witness to how important it was for European manufacturers to be represented in India by a reliable trading company. The report stated that

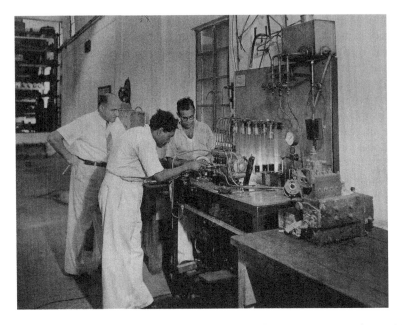

Figure 11.1 Workshops of the Volkart engineering department in Bombay, 1941
(Fotomuseum Winterthur, Volkart Collection, CD 1, Album Bombay 1941)

the consulate was regularly contacted by smaller companies that had "insufficient experience with Indian business life or fall for the empty promises of Indian merchants." These companies regularly asked the consulate for help in collecting outstanding payments. According to the report, the consulate could not be of much assistance because many Indian entrepreneurs were notoriously insolvent and many companies were nothing more than scams. These firms often had their headquarters in remote regions, where the consulate had little influence. The report urged companies to exercise "utmost care" when doing business with India and said that "Swiss manufacturers would be well advised to take their cue from one of the well-known Swiss firms that has been working in India for decades and is intimately familiar with the conditions," adding that if this was not possible they should collaborate with a British firm. But they were advised against working together with an Indian trading company, even if it demanded lower commission fees:

> Even for the well-established foreign, including Swiss, mercantile houses, it is extremely difficult to judge the creditworthiness of the thousands of Indian trading companies, both large and small. It is far more difficult, however, for Swiss manufacturers to form a sound opinion of whether business transactions should be pursued with a certain buyer. . . . The

structure of Indian trading companies can change during the course of a year and partners come and go, without news of these changes being widely known. The wholesale trading companies located here are thus obliged to exercise extreme caution in their selection of customers and must maintain their own information services.

The report went on to say that the business principles "of the Indians" are different than what is commonly found in Switzerland:

The natives often work with slim margins and are generally tempted to extract an extra bit of compensation from European manufacturers merely from the smallest infringement or lapse on the part of the foreigner. There is no other country where the competition is so stiff and where even the smallest merchant, with a minimum amount of capital, speculates to such an extent as in India.[20]

The first Swiss mechanical engineering company that agreed to be represented by Volkart after 1922 was Brown, Boveri & Cie. (BBC) from Baden, Switzerland, which produced electrical engineering systems and had been interested in working together with Volkart for quite some time (Figure 11.2).[21] Over the years that followed, Volkart went on to represent several other Swiss industrial companies on the subcontinent[22] along with diverse manufacturing firms from continental Europe.

Figure 11.2 The construction of a hydroelectric power plant in the Indian town of Pallivasal in 1939 with machines made by Swiss Firms BBC and Escher Wyss, which were represented on the subcontinent by the Volkart engineering department (VA, Dossier 103: Photosammlung Indien Brack und Belmont)

The fact that Volkart primarily represented continental European mechanical engineering companies made the market entry more difficult, however, because British machines were generally used in Indian factories, as reflected by this statement by the top manager of Volkart Bombay in 1925:

> It is, of course, extremely difficult to introduce outside replacement machinery, or to introduce any kind of outside machinery for that matter, in a British system and in a spinning mill or textile mill built by British suppliers, . . . but it should be possible to successfully compete in newly emerging projects, especially since the owners are usually members of the native intelligentsia and have anti-British political leanings.[23]

Volkart imported machinery to some extent on its own account and to some extent on a commission basis, usually for a 5 percent fee.[24] For commission transactions in the overseas trade, it was common for buyers to pay for half of the purchasing price upon ordering and the remaining half upon receipt of the goods.[25] In contrast to other countries, Switzerland granted its manufacturing companies no financial support for their exports overseas, and even Swiss banks appeared to be rather reluctant when it came to financing export orders.[26] It was not until 1934 that Switzerland began to grant state export risk guarantees to promote sales of Swiss industrial products abroad.[27]

The development of the trade in machinery is in many respects characteristic of certain changes that occurred in the importing of Western industrial products during the interwar era. Experience had shown that the free procurement system used until then by the import department was often unsatisfactory. Volkart gradually changed this policy in the 1920s and began to conclude exclusive representation agreements with European and American manufacturing companies.[28] In doing so, it became patently clear that the company needed warehousing facilities because its Indian customers were no longer prepared to accept that their orders only arrived after a lengthy delivery period.[29]

Although importing European textiles was one of the most important areas of business for Volkart in the early years, from the late nineteenth century onwards the company no longer shipped such products to India. Textiles for the Indian market were increasingly manufactured by Indian firms. Volkart supplied these companies not only with raw cotton but also spinning machines and dyes for the textiles, and starting in the 1890s the firm served as an official representative in India for the Berlin-based Actien-Gesellschaft für Anilin-Fabrication (AGFA).[30] Import transactions were not without risk because if prices suddenly declined many Indian merchants were no longer able to pay for their ordered goods.[31] Hence, for its sales of dyes Volkart relied on the services of an Indian guarantee broker who ensured the buyers' willingness to pay. But that was apparently not possible for the trade in machinery.[32] This prompted Volkart to deviate here from its long-standing business principle of "generally delivering no goods to merchants or other import customers without immediate payment." Buyers of machinery were now granted the possibility of a deferment of payment,[33] which shows that during the interwar era Volkart was increasingly prepared in certain sectors to conduct sales transactions on a credit basis. In addition to the machinery sector, this also applied to sales of cotton to French, German, Chinese and Japanese spinning mills.[34]

The Importance of Bribes

Volkart was involved in the business of importing machines not only to India but also to East Asia, a region that in the late nineteenth century had developed to become one of the leading export markets for European machine manufacturers. Starting in the 1890s, large quantities of European machines were exported to Japan, where a rapid industrialization took place during the Meiji period. Although Japan had its own mechanical engineering sector from the turn of the century onwards, up until the 1930s most machinery in Japanese factories was from Europe.[35]

Volkart was represented in Japan by its subsidiary, the Nichizui Trading Co., Ltd., which was founded in 1919. Nichizui focused primarily on importing Indian raw cotton, but was also involved in importing European machinery, the majority of which came from Swiss manufacturing plants (Figure 11.3). Most important of all was the sale of electrical engineering systems made by BBC, which were crucial because during the interwar era Japan was pushing ahead with the construction of hydroelectric power plants

Figure 11.3 Presentation of Swiss industrial products at an industrial trade show in Tokyo, 1922 (VA, Dossier 111: Photos Bremen, London, USA, Mexico, Brazil, Colombia, Singapore/Shanghai/Japan)

to meet the country's growing energy needs.[36] In 1926, Nichizui's engineering department already had 20 European engineers on its payroll who were supported by diverse Japanese sales representatives and technicians.[37]

Sales of machinery in Asia were generally only possible if importers were prepared to pay bribes, even if this was illegal in most countries. Import companies like Volkart had to be extremely careful to ensure that no evidence was left in the form of bookings, receipts or correspondence that could link the company to such practices. For instance, in a letter written by the Volkart branch in Bombay in 1929, it was recommended that payments of large sums of money be made with the help of a commissioning agent or broker, who would openly receive a commission or brokerage fee "without us having to worry about what *they* do with it."[38]

Despite its efficient sales organization for the mechanical engineering sector, Volkart evidently had to continue to rely on local intermediaries who paid kickbacks to help orchestrate business deals. This practice was extremely controversial among the company's executives. Georg Reinhart, for example, was highly critical of it, although he also conceded that "brokerage fees to third parties who help to conclude a business transaction based on Indian norms and views may be considered legitimate as long as they do not exceed a reasonable amount." But he insisted that they definitely had to put an end to "the practice of making payments that cannot be entered into our books" and made special reference here to the trade in machinery.[39] He justified this point of view by saying that doing honest business deals was an "*ethical* matter."[40] At the same time, he pointed out that several employees of Sulzer, as well as the former Swiss manager of Nichizui, had apparently

> amassed large amounts of money through bribes that their employers were forced to pay, but that they pocketed instead of passing on. Such acts of fraud are very easy to commit because, of course, no receipts are kept for illegal commissions.[41]

Despite Georg Reinhart's concerns, Volkart continued to pay bribes to facilitate some of its import transactions during the 1930s.[42] As mentioned earlier, European trading companies had many qualms about paying such inducements. Yet for Western manufacturing companies it was practical because they did not have to deal directly with this unsavory aspect of selling their products in the Asian region and could instead delegate the task to associated trading companies.

The Ordeal of Choosing the Right Representatives

Representatives of European mechanical engineering firms had to contend with highly unfamiliar situations in Asia during the early twentieth century, as revealed by a report submitted by a Swiss representative who had used an office in Kobe to market Sulzer products since 1909. In 1916, he vociferously objected to allegations from the company's headquarters that he had not obtained enough offers in Japan and China. He pointed out that before his arrival in these countries Sulzer had been completely unknown and the company was now annually selling 1 million Swiss francs worth of machinery in East Asia. Furthermore, he insisted that this was only possible because he had undertaken long journeys in which on many occasions he had had no alternative but to travel on native vessels, coal trains and locomotives. He added that he had been forced to

> live for two to three weeks at a time entirely like a native Japanese, sliding around on the floor and using sticks of wood to eat food that most people would find unbearable. To make matters worse, there was the fear for my personal safety in China. All of this to promote the brand and its business.[43]

In view of these difficulties, it seemed advisable for European machinery manufacturers to collaborate with a locally established trading company. After Sulzer opened a sales office in Kobe in December 1925,[44] it decided to work together with Nichizui. But this collaboration was not without its problems. For instance, Nichizui claimed that Sulzer sold its boilers to other import companies in Japan at a lower price[45] and the Sulzer sales office retorted that Nichizui charged commissions that were too high.[46] The upshot of these mutual allegations was that Sulzer continued to rely on Nichizui for some of its imports to Japan, but at the same time began to conduct imports via Japanese trading firms like Suzuki and the Okura Trading Co.[47]

China, like Japan, had been forced by the Western colonial powers to open its ports to foreign merchants and had undergone a similar phase of industrialization in the late nineteenth century. The machinery in Chinese factories was chiefly imported from Europe.[48] Sulzer opened a sales office in Shanghai in 1922.[49] As a rule, Europeans in China could only broker sales with the help of influential indigenous merchants who acted as compradors.[50] During the interwar era, it was extremely difficult for Western industrial companies to forge direct business ties with customers in the interior of the country, as the Sulzer representative in Shanghai noted in a report to the Winterthur company headquarters in 1923. This was in large part because during the 1920s China still had a very limited railway network and most domestic transport was on boats and ships that plied the country's rivers. When Chinese industrialists or civil servants purchased machinery, they sent their trusted representatives to Shanghai to act as buyers. These go-betweens would use the connections of a comprador to contact the import companies, who in turn would contact the machinery manufacturers. All of these intermediaries wanted compensation for their work, usually in the form of commission fees. Furthermore, bribery appeared to be endemic in China, as a Sulzer representative wrote:

> Since people generally don't have a clue when it comes to technical matters, they only take note of the price and the 'squeeze' and, at best,

the name of the company, if they are familiar with it; all other explanations are received with an ironic smile, . . . and this makes the situation especially difficult for us because we are usually more expensive than the others and virtually unknown in China.

Trade in China was also plagued by the unstable political situation and dangerous travel routes: "There is a rather dismal lack of personal safety. The country is crawling with robbers—for the most part discharged or unpaid soldiers—and the seas are full of pirates."[51]

Because it was only possible for machinery manufacturers in China to make their sales with the help of an import company as an intermediary, choosing the right business connections was crucial to success. Instead of working together with European trading companies, though, Swiss machinery manufacturers generally preferred to tailor their approach to conditions in the relevant markets and often opted to collaborate with a Chinese or Japanese import company. This is reflected, for example, in the evaluations that were conducted by BBC in China. In November 1922, BBC Sales Director J. Elink Schuurman visited East Asia. One of the purposes of his trip was to determine whether BBC should be represented by Volkart or by the Chinese firm Sintoon Trading Co. Before his arrival in China, Schuurman indicated that he had trouble taking Sintoon seriously, but these initial reservations were dispelled when he met with company representatives:

> As I saw for myself in Shanghai, Sintoon has outstanding connections throughout China. Volkart, on the other hand, has not yet entered the Chinese machinery market and would have to start from scratch. What speaks in favor of Volkart . . . is that we would be dealing with a Swiss company instead of businessmen who are relatively unknown to us, thus giving us greater financial security.

According to Schuurman, one of the main reasons why BBC ultimately chose Sintoon to represent it was that, unlike other import companies, it "does not require a comprador, an individual who is said to incur not only large costs but also engage in all manner of misconduct."[52] The collaboration with Sintoon was highly successful for BBC, largely because the Chinese trading company carried out the imports on its own account and BBC neither had to rent office space nor work together with a comprador. By contrast, Sulzer began using the services of compradors to conduct business in China in 1922, but despite high turnover only achieved meager results and had to close its sales office in Shanghai in 1937.[53]

In 1928, Winterthur machinery manufacturer Rieter signed a sales representative agreement with Nichizui for Japan.[54] In April 1930, a staff member stationed in Osaka informed Rieter headquarters that Nichizui was also interested in representing Rieter in China. But he pointed out that Nichizui was a company based in Japan that, in view of the anti-Japanese mood in China, could only conduct transactions there via a Chinese firm. He noted that Volkart had a branch office in Shanghai, but said that it mainly worked in the cotton import sector.[55] The headquarters urged that a sales representation solution be found that would make it possible to tackle the markets in China and Japan concurrently. Rieter was in favor of appointing Nichizui as its sales representative in Japan and making it responsible for maintaining contact to the Japanese cotton mills located in China. But when it came to doing business with Chinese cotton mills, Nichizui was not an option because it was a Japanese company. Volkart suggested that its Shanghai branch office could serve as a representative for Rieter with the Chinese cotton mills, but that the transactions would in fact be handled by Nichizui.[56] Rieter had doubts, though, about Nichizui's ability to establish business contacts with Chinese manufacturers and compradors, and instead proposed that Chinese trading company Chien Hsin handle some of its machinery exports. Nichizui, however, opposed the idea of such a dual representation.[57]

In an internal memo, a Rieter staff member subsequently wrote that it was in fact not possible to be represented by two companies in China. He went on to say that if the company chose a Chinese trading company as a representative, Rieter would receive higher prices for its machinery than from Volkart. On the other hand, he felt that working together with a Swiss trading firm represented "a lesser risk." Furthermore, he said that Rieter would have to keep constant tabs on the financial situation of its representative because diverse transactions were to be conducted on a commission basis. He concluded that such information would be "more accessible with Volkart . . . than with Chien Hsin in Shanghai, no matter how financially sound it may be."[58]

A further advantage of being represented by a Swiss import company was that Rieter could receive up-to-date information on the latest economic and political developments in China. For instance, in a letter to Rieter, Volkart included a report from its Shanghai branch office on the current situation in China.[59] Aside from providing more precise market information than Rieter could expect from a Chinese firm, Volkart/Nichizui offered many other advantages. The Swiss company's rather cautious business policies, financial stability and cultural proximity to Rieter all undoubtedly contributed to the manufacturer's decision in December 1931 to appoint Nichizui as its representative in China.[60]

Volkart had also been endeavoring for quite some time to become Rieter's sales representative in India, but the manufacturer instead opted to be represented by another Swiss firm, the import company Sulzer, Bruderer & Co.[61] In early summer 1931, however, the sales department at Rieter was of the opinion that Sulzer, Bruderer & Co. focused too little on selling Rieter machinery and it did not believe in the company's competitiveness. To make matters worse, Sulzer, Bruderer & Co. had negligently allowed documents from Rieter to fall into the hands of Volkart, which at the time served as the representative for German mechanical engineering company Trüt-zschler. According to Rieter officials, Trützschler then copied the machinery made by the Swiss company and successfully marketed it in India. This was extremely aggravating, but it confirmed Rieter's view "that it would be possible to compete with the British in India if we really did the job properly." As a member of the Rieter sales department confirmed to an official at Sulzer, Bruderer & Co., India was a key market for the Swiss manufacturer.[62] He said that due to the crisis in the European textile industry in the early 1930s, there were only three countries in the world where large-scale cotton mills were being established: Russia, China and India. Russia was not a factor for Rieter, as he pointed out, because for political reasons no contracts could be granted to Switzerland. "Business is going well for us in China and more than half of our orders are destined for that country. So you will understand that we cannot simply leave the field to our British rivals in India."[63] Trützschler's success was viewed as proof by Rieter that continental European companies could be successful in India, despite higher prices: "If we can convince the Indians that a new machine—even if it is more expensive—offers advantages, they will purchase it, just as every proper businessman in other countries would." In the fall of 1931, Sulzer, Bruderer & Co. relinquished its role as Rieter's representative in India[64] and, shortly thereafter, Volkart signed on as the Swiss company's representative on the subcontinent and, in exchange, terminated its representation contract with Trützschler.[65]

Losses and Profits

As explained earlier, the engineering department at Volkart succeeded time and again in securing sales representation agreements with leading continental European manufacturers. Nevertheless, this area of business was a loss-making venture for the company over a number of years. For instance, between 1923 and 1933 the machinery import business to India made losses of 4.08 million Swiss francs while losses in Japan were 20,614 francs. Although machinery imports to Japan were at times highly lucrative, profits declined rapidly in the early 1930s.[66] These losses coincided with problems in other sectors. After Volkart made big profits in the early 1920s thanks to its successes in the cotton business, in 1926 it dipped into the red for a number of years.[67] In a bid to turn the situation around, management decided to downsize the company structure and Georg Reinhart urged that they abandon the machinery business, or at least significantly reduce the size of this division, but he ran into resistance from his brother Werner, with whom he co-managed the company.[68]

Apparently Werner Reinhart prevailed on the matter of the machinery import business. At any rate, Volkart strongly expanded its import activities in the area of technical equipment from the late 1920s onwards. In 1928, Volkart established in Bombay the Swiss Engineering Co., which was

100 percent owned by the parent company. The objective of this new subsidiary was to sell and maintain automobiles on the subcontinent.[69] In the mid-1930s, Volkart concluded numerous sales representation agreements with Western companies for imports to India.[70] From 1936 to 1940, the company published the *Volkart Brothers Engineering News*, which, in addition to advertisements for industrial companies represented by Volkart, featured articles on the history of these companies and their products. Since a Western-style consumer society had begun to emerge in India, Volkart imported—aside from large-scale plant installations—an increasing number of air conditioning units, refrigerators and other household appliances (Figure 11.4).[71]

Despite this expansion, the machinery import business to Asia remained fraught with difficulties—and not just for Volkart. Swiss manufacturers also often failed to achieve their anticipated results. Sulzer, for example, planned in the early 1930s to reorganize its import business because the sales results were disappointing due to the relatively high prices of Swiss machinery. The company considered closing its sales office in Calcutta, which it had opened in 1923, and allowing all imports of machinery to be handled by agencies.[72] Aside from Bird & Co., with which Sulzer had collaborated earlier, Volkart was the only other possible sales representative because these were the only two firms that employed technical staff that could supervise the assembly of the machines.[73] In the fall of 1934, a Sulzer representative had a discussion with a Swiss man named Baer who was an employee with Bird & Co. in Calcutta. During their conversation, mention was made of certain advantages to being represented by a British company like Bird, for example, with regard to customs and tariffs.[74] But the Swiss man noted that

Figure 11.4 Showroom for refrigerators in Bombay around 1930 (Fotomuseum Winterthur, Volkart Collection, CD 2, Bombay Gebäude und Büros)

British companies maintained a certain disdain for "continental people," despite all assurances to the contrary:

> The gap between British and continental will always exist, but in such a distant . . . country, where we have to place so much trust in a representative, it is probably better to leave this gap directly between the customer and the representative, and not . . . between the representative and the factory.[75]

The representative was of the opinion that it would be better if Sulzer "gave its representation in India a purely Swiss character" in the future.[76] In other words, he tended to favor granting Volkart the right to represent the company in India. One obstacle to taking on the responsibility of representing Sulzer, though, was that Volkart was already the official sales representative in India for German mechanical engineering company M.A.N., which stood in direct competition with Sulzer. In late September 1939, after Volkart had been forced to renounce its role as the M.A.N. representative due to the outbreak of World War II, negotiations resumed.[77] In March 1940, Volkart became Sulzer's official representative in India. The employees who had worked for Sulzer on the subcontinent henceforth worked in the engineering department of Volkart.[78]

The End of Machinery Imports to Asia

No figures exist on the exports to Asia of the Swiss industrial companies that Volkart represented. It appears that these exports were rather profitable at times. After 1929, for example, Rieter was able to compensate for the drastic decline in business with Germany and Italy in part with major orders from Japan, China and India.[79] BBC's sales to India in the late 1930s also appear to have reaped considerable profits.[80] However, the many changes in representatives and endless litany of complaints about the work of sales agents could be an indication of the difficulties involved in importing goods to Asia. It was doubtlessly not so much the concrete results as the hope that the huge Asian market for machinery imports would someday generate regular profits that motivated import companies like Volkart and the Swiss mechanical engineering companies to persist so stubbornly with their efforts in this sector.[81]

Machinery imports to Asia became increasingly difficult from the late 1930s onwards. Only a limited amount of business was possible in China following the Japanese invasion. During World War II and the civil war that followed, hardly any business transactions could be conducted in this sector. After the communists seized power, Volkart and many other Western companies were forced to close their branches in China.[82] Imports of machinery to Japan also declined as the Japanese mechanical engineering industry grew progressively stronger.[83]

Meanwhile, increased demand in India during World War II had sparked a boom in industrial manufacturing, especially in the production of machinery and chemical products (Figure 11.5).[84] After 1947, the mechanical engineering sector encountered difficulties when the Indian government moved to promote an independent domestic industry. From the 1950s onwards, Volkart transformed all Indian divisions and branches into separate joint-stock companies that gradually merged with Indian firms.[85] In 1954, Volkart's engineering department merged with a subsidiary of Indian industrial giant Tata to form a new company called Voltas, which initially continued to work in the machinery and chemicals import sector. Voltas gradually convinced Western industrial companies like US tractor manufacturer International Harvester and Swiss textile machine manufacturer Rieter, which had earlier imported their products to India via Volkart, to join forces with Indian companies and establish production plants on the subcontinent. During the 1960s, the company also began to manufacture its own refrigeration units.[86]

This shows that entering the machinery import sector eventually led to a corporate diversification toward production, in which the former engineering department evolved to become an industrial manufacturing business. Imports of machinery to Asia thus belong to a highly specific historic phase of the colonial era in which Asia began to develop a consumer culture and in which Western companies, particularly in the textile manufacturing sector, were able to gain a foothold at a time when Asian countries had not yet

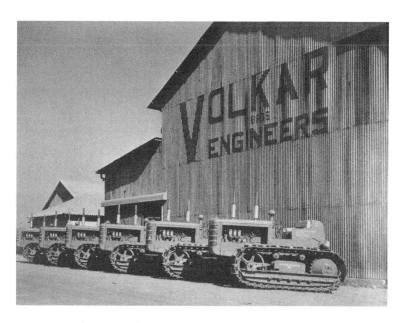

Figure 11.5 Warehouse of the Volkart engineering department in Bombay, 1941 (Fotomuseum Winterthur, Volkart Collection, CD1, Album Bombay 1941)

established their own mechanical engineering industries. This phase came to an end after the colonial era when European and American companies had to produce more and more products in Asian countries if they intended to remain present in that market.

Notes

1 Headrick, *The Tentacles of Progress*, 1988, 361–366; Ray, *Industrialization in India*, 1979, 24ff., 32, 193ff.; Misra, " 'Business Culture' and Entrepreneurship," 2000; Farnie, "The Role of Cotton Textiles," 2004, 410–411.
2 Anderegg, *Chronicle*, 1976, 178f.; Privatarchiv Andreas Zangger: Briefkopierbuch Archibald A. Crawford (1887–1892).
3 Hauser-Dora, *Die wirtschaftlichen und handelspolitischen Beziehungen der Schweiz*, 1986, 246–300; Müller, "Patterns of Technical Innovation," 2001.
4 Anderegg, *Chronicle*, 1976, 237ff.; VA, Dossier 4: Bombay II, 15. Engineering Dept.: Volkart Winterthur to Herren Gebrüder Sulzer A.G. Winterthur, 16 September 1915.
5 VA, Dossier 4: Bombay II, 15. Engineering Dept.: Bombay to Winterthur, 21 July 1914.
6 VA, Dossier 4: Bombay II, 15. Engineering Dept.: Bombay to Winterthur, 25 August 1922.
7 VA, Dossier 4: Bombay II, 15. Engineering Dept.: Bombay to Winterthur, 22 September 1922.
8 Bird was a traditional British managing agency that recruited managers in sectors such as railroad construction, coal mining and jute milling. Ray, *Industrialization in India*, 1979, 267ff.
9 VA, Dossier 4: Bombay II, 15. Engineering Dept.: Winterthur to Bombay, 14 December 1922.
10 KAS, Schachtel 417a: Dr. Hch. Wolfer, Indien-China-Japan 1922–1923: Wolfer, Bombay, to Sulzer, Abt. 1, Winterthur, 22 December 1922.
11 KAS, Schachtel 314: Indien, Indonesien, Pakistan: Indien: Sulzer Bros. London to Dr. Wolfer, Sulzer Bros. Winterthur, 29. October 1921.
12 KAS, Schachtel 417a: Dr. Hch. Wolfer, Indien-China-Japan 1922–1923: Wolfer, Bombay, to Sulzer, Abt. 1, Winterthur, 22 December 1922.
13 KAS, Winterthur, Schachtel 417a: Dr. Hch. Wolfer, Indien-China-Japan 1922–1923: Wolfer, Calcutta, to Sulzer, Winterthur, 18 January 1923.
14 KAS, Schachtel 417a: Dr. Hch. Wolfer, Indien-China-Japan 1922–1923:—Wolfer, Bombay, to Sulzer, Abt. 1, Winterthur, 22 December 1922.
15 KAS, Schachtel 314: Indien, Indonesien, Pakistan, No. 7, Vertreter Ingenieure für Indien & Calcutta: Mitteilung an Herrn Wolfer, Geschäftsverkehr mit S.B. Calcutta, 14 January 1924.
16 KAS, Schachtel 314: Indien, Indonesien, Pakistan, No. 7, Vertreter Ingenieure für Indien & Calcutta: Organisation S.B. Calcutta (zur Besprechung mit Mr. Batho), Winterthur, 18 August 1925.
17 Anderegg, *Chronicle*, 1976, 303–304.
18 "Wir und unser Werk," *Brown Boveri Hauszeitung*, April/Mai 1947, 51; Nr. 4, April 1949, 63; January 1952, 11; Nr. 6, June 1955, 108; October 1960, 300–301.; January 1961, 24; August 1961, 191; March 1962, 81; *Brown Boveri Hauszeitung*, March 1969, 95; January 1970, 27; Juli/August 1971, 286.
19 Anderegg, *Chronicle*, 1976, 304–305.
20 BAR, E 2200.40 (London), Akzession 42, 1928, XX.7, Consulats de Suisse: Consulat général de Bombay: Geschäftsbericht des Schweizerischen Generalkonsulats in Bombay für das Jahr 1927, 6–7 and 37–38.

21 VA, Dossier 4: Bombay II, 15. Engineering Dept.: Winterthur to Bombay, 27 July 1922.

22 In addition to BBC, it represented Rieter, Theodor Bell & Co., Amsler & Co., Schweizerische Werkzeugmaschinen Fabrik Oerlikon, Micafil, Georg Fischer and, from 1940, Sulzer: Rambousek/Vogt/Volkart, Volkart, 1990, 141.

23 VA, Dossier 4: Bombay II, 15. Engineering Dept.: Bericht über die Entwicklung und die Aussichten des Engineering Dept. in Bombay von K. Ringger, 26 November 1925, off Port-Said.

24 Anderegg, *Chronicle*, 1976, 304–305.; Farnie, The Role of Cotton Textiles, 2004, 411.

25 ArABB, B.1.2.3.23.6: J. Elink Schuurman, Kobe, to Brown, Boveri & Cie., Baden, 29 November 1922.

26 V.B. News, No. 10, March 1924, 10.

27 Biotti, *Die Exportrisikogarantie*, 2002.

28 FAN, Bestand Sandoz, M 530.6: Interne Mitteilung. Besprechung mit Herrn Marquart von Gebr. Volkart in Winterthur, am 23. VII. 29, 9 ½ Uhr.

29 VA, Dossier 4: Bombay II, 12. Import Dept.: 30 January 1951—Allgemeiner Rueckblick ueber das Import Geschaeft seit 1926.

30 Anderegg, *Chronicle*, 1976, 199.

31 Anderegg, *Chronicle*, 1976, 236.

32 VA, Dossier 4, Bombay II, 12. Import Dept.: Winterthur an Bombay, 19.11.25.

33 VA, Dossier 64: Geschäftsordnung 1915/1921 mit Nachträgen bis 1940 / Upcountry Bookkeeping Instructions 1912–1926 / Upcountry Instructions 1952: Geschäftsordnung, in Kraft ab 1. Juli 1915, No. 30 (Ergänzung von 1.5.35).

34 See Chapters 8 and 10.

35 Buchheim, *Industrielle Revolutionen*, 1994, 118–128; Flath, *The Japanese Economy*, 2000, 34, 43; Bähr, Lesczenski and Schmidtpott, *Winds of Change*, 2009, 17–135.

36 V.B. News, No. 10, March 1924, 10.

37 VA, Dossier 50: Engineering /Voltas Schriften, Dokumente etc.: Volkart Brothers Winterthur, Switzerland. Exporters of Machinery to India, Japan and China. Technical Advisers, Consulting Engineers. 1926, 6ff.

38 VA, Dossier 61: ex GR persönliches Archiv I, Illegale Kommissionen: Bombay to Georg Reinhart, 25 January 1929.

39 VA, Dossier 61: ex GR persönliches Archiv I, Illegale Kommissionen: Georg Reinhart, Winterthur, to Herr Lieberherr, Bombay, 19 November 1929.

40 VA, Dossier 61: ex GR persönliches Archiv I, Illegale Kommissionen: Georg Reinhart, Memorandum zu Handen der Herren W. Reinhart, E. Neuenhofer, H. Wachter, 10 August 1933.

41 VA, Dossier 61: ex GR persönliches Archiv I, Illegale Kommissionen: Bombay to Winterthur, 4 August 1937.

42 VA, Dossier 61: ex GR persönliches Archiv I, Illegale Kommissionen: Bombay an Winterthur, 4. August 1937.

43 KAS, Schachtel 307: Japan, Korresp. Abt. 1 und 20, No. 6: W. Züblin, Notizen zur Konferenz vom 5. Oktober, Winterthur, 9 October 1916.

44 KAS, Schachtel 307: Japan, Korresp. Abt. 1 und 20, No. 26: Gesellschaftsvertrag vom 1. Dezember 1925.

45 KAS, Schachtel 307: Japan, Korresp. Abt. 1 und 20, No. 9: Bericht von Herrn Egloff, Kobe, Betrifft: K. 46/Nankai Denki Tetsudo K.K., 21 December 1925.

46 KAS, Schachtel 307: Japan, Korresp. Abt. 1 und 20, No. 9: Bericht von Herr Hashizume, Betrifft: Nankai Denki Tetsudo K.K., Kobe, 21 December 1925.

47 KAS, Schachtel 307: Japan, Korresp. Abt. 1 und 20: J. Gastpar to Gebr. Sulzer Winterthur, Kobe, 25 April 1927.

48 Osterhammel, *China und die Weltgesellschaft*, 1989, 273; Osterhammel, *Shanghai*, 1997; Mutz, "Der Sohn, der durch das West-Tor kam," 2005.

49 KAS, Schachtel 299c: China, Nr. 2: Regelung des internen Geschäftsverkehrs zwischen Gebrüder Sulzer AG Winterthur und dem Zweigbureau Shanghai, 25 January 1922.

50 KAS, Schachtel 299c: China: Bericht von E. C. Staudt, Ingenieur für Sulzer in Shanghai an W. Züblin, 10 November 1934.

51 KAS, Schachtel 299c: China, No. 3: Bericht betr. Bureau Shanghai, August 1923.

52 ArABB, B.1.2.3.23.6: J. Elink Schuurman, Kobe, to Brown, Boveri & Cie., Baden, 29 November 1922.

53 Steinmann, *Seldwyla im Wunderland*, 1998, 139–141.

54 HAR, H/i 3556: Vertretungen, 6/30: Vertretungen, Verhandlungen und Verträge: Japan: Agreement of Agency zwischen Rieter und der Nichizui vom 15 November 28.

55 HAR, H/i 3556: Vertretungen, 6/29a: Vertretungen, Verhandlungen und Verträge: China/Nichizui: E. G. Kellner, Osaka, to J.J. Rieter & Cie., Winterthur, Kobe, 12 April 1930.

56 HAR, H/i 3556: Vertretungen, 6/29b: Vertretungen, Verhandlungen & Verträge: Volkart, China: Rieter to Gebr. Volkart, Winterthur, 10 January 1931.

57 HAR, H/i 3556: Vertretungen, 6/29b: Vertretungen, Verhandlungen & Verträge: Volkart, China: Gebr. Volkart, Winterthur, to AG Joh. Jacob Rieter & Cie., Winterthur, 4 November 1931.

58 HAR, H/i 3556: Vertretungen, 6/29b: Vertretungen, Verhandlungen & Verträge: Volkart, China: Notiz zu einem Brief von Gebr. Volkart vom 4. November 1931, no date.

59 HAR, H/i 3556: Vertretungen, 6/29b: Vertretungen, Verhandlungen & Verträge: Volkart, China: Gebr. Volkart, Winterthur, to AG Joh. Jacob Rieter & Cie., Winterthur, 4 November 1931.

60 HAR, H/i 3556: Vertretungen, 6/29b: Vertretungen, Verhandlungen & Verträge: Volkart, China: Rieter to Gebr. Volkart, Winterthur, 17 December 1931.

61 According to Douglas Farnie, Rieter was briefly represented by the Parsi merchant company N. N. Wadia during the 1920s. There is no evidence of this connection in the Rieter company archives, so it is unclear how long it lasted and how successful it was: Farnie, "The Role of Cotton Textiles," 2004, 413.

62 HAR, H/i 3556: Vertretungen, 6/28: Britisch Indien: Verkaufsabteilung Rieter, Winterthur, to Sulzer, Bruderer&Co., Zürich, 29 May 1931.

63 HAR, H/i 3556: Vertretungen, 6/28: Britisch Indien: Verkaufsabteilung Rieter, Winterthur, to Sulzer, Bruderer&Co., Zürich, 29 May 1931.

64 HAR, H/i 3556: Vertretungen, 6/28: Britisch Indien: Rieter to Herren Sulzer, Bruderer & Cie., Zürich, Winterthur, 2 October 1931.

65 HAR, H/i 3556: Vertretungen, 7/26: Konfidentielle Vertreter Korrespondenz: Volkart: Gebr. Volkart, Winterthur, to AG J.J. Rieter&Co., Winterthur, 24 April 1935.

66 VA, Dossier 63: ex GR persönliches Archiv III, Mappe: Abbau-Massnahmen Import/Engineering: Div. Bilanzen.

67 See Chapter 8.

68 VA, Dossier 62: ex GR persönliches Archiv II, Verschiedene Abbauvorschläge im Sinne einer Konsolidierung und Konzentration der Firma 1925–1929: Sparmassnahmen, 9 December 1927; Oberste Geschäftsleitung in Winterthur—Vorbereitung des Rücktritts von G.R. 1930–1945: GR, Richtlinien für die Geschäftspolitik der nächsten Jahre, 13 October 1930; Dossier 63: ex GR persönliches Archiv III, GR, Memorandum I, 23 July 1929; GR, Die Frage des Maschinengeschäftes in Indien und Japan, 5 March 1931.

69 Rambousek/Vogt/Volkart, *Volkart*, 1990, 214.

70 VA, Dossier 4: Bombay II, 12. Import Dept.: 30 January 1951—Allgemeiner Rueckblick ueber das Import Geschaeft seit 1926.

71 VA, Dossier 50: Engineering /Voltas Schriften, Dokumente etc.: *Volkart Brothers Engineering News* (1936–1940).

72 KAS, Schachtel 314: Indien, Indonesien, Pakistan: Indien, No. 7, Vertreter Ingenieure für Indien & Calcutta: Report on Reorganisation of Calcutta Office, Calcutta, 23 October 1930.

73 KAS, Schachtel 314: Indien, Indonesien, Pakistan: Indien, No. 7, Vertreter Ing enieure für Indien & Calcutta: Sulzer Bros. Calcutta, Agents for India & Burma: Gillanders Arbuthnot & Co., to Dr. Wolfer, Calcutta, 30 July 1934.

74 In an effort to protect Indian industry, the Indian government had gradually increased import tariffs during the interwar era: Ray, *Industrialization in India*, 1979, 273.

75 KAS, Schachtel 314: Indien, Indonesien, Pakistan: Indien, No. 8: Volkart Brothers Indien: Besprechung mit Herrn Baer von Bird & Co. Calcutta, vom 10 October 1934, 11 October 1934.

76 KAS, Schachtel 314: Indien, Indonesien, Pakistan: Indien, No. 8: Volkart Brothers Indien: Besprechung mit Herrn Baer von Bird & Co. Calcutta, vom 10 October 1934, 11 October 1934.

77 KAS, Schachtel 314: Indien, Indonesien, Pakistan: Indien, Korrespondenz Abt. 20, Indien: Brown Boveri & Co., Baden, to Gebr. Volkart, Winterthur, 19 October 1939.

78 VA, Dossier 50: Engineering /Voltas Schriften, Dokumente etc.: *Volkart Brothers Engineering News*, Vol. 5, April/May 1940, 14.

79 Müller, "Organizational Change", 2000, Fn. 30.

80 KAS, Schachtel 314: Indien, Indonesien, Pakistan: Indien, Korrespondenz Abt. 20, Indien: Brown Boveri & Co., Baden, to Gebr. Volkart, Winterthur, 19 October 1939.

81 Mutz presents similar arguments for the business activities of Siemens in China: Mutz, "Der Sohn, der durch das West-Tor kam," 2005, 8.

82 KAS, Schachtel 299c: China: Brief der Firmen, die in Shanghai Niederlassungen besitzen an Bundesrat Max Petitpierre, Vorsteher des Eidg. Politischen Departements, Bern, Zürich, 19 June 1950; VA, Dossier 15: The Far Eastern Organisation, I. Shanghai (incl. Tientsin etc.).

83 VA, Dossier 14: Japan, Korrespondenz): Peter Reinhart, Tatuta Maru, 20 July 1939.

84 Ray, *Industrialization in India*, 1979, 250.

85 VA, Dossier 29–34. For more details, see Chapter 12.

86 VA, Dossier 29: Voltas Ltd. (1954): Text von A. H. Tobaccowala, Managing Director von Voltas, anlässlich des 20. Geburtstag von Voltas am 1.9.74; Business India, Dec. 24, 1979—Jan. 6, 1980, Interview with A.H. Tobaccowala, Managing Director of Voltas; TCA, Tata Sons, Rack 3, Box 37, TS-Vol-8, Extracts from the Minutes of Agents' Weekly Meeting: 26 August 1953 and 11 November 1953; TS-Vol-21 und TS-Vol-24. See also www.voltas.com (13 June 2010) and Chapter 12 for more details.

Part IV

State Interventions and Multinational Trading Companies

12 The Consequences of Decolonization

In August 1947, the subcontinent was partitioned into the states of India and Pakistan. Volkart had to launch a number of in-company restructuring initiatives to adapt its business organization to the new political realities. It also had to contend with the aftermath of the pogroms and violent expulsions that accompanied the division of the subcontinent. Virtually the entire Hindu staff of the branch in Lahore disappeared overnight. In the Indian city of Amritsar, directly on the other side of the new border, the employees remained at their posts, but many of the firm's customers fled and only gradually returned after the violence had subsided. Before the partition, nearly all indigenous staff members in Karachi had been Hindus. These employees fled to India in the summer of 1947. Some of them found new jobs in Volkart's Indian branches. Meanwhile, their jobs at the Karachi branch were filled by Muslims who had fled from India to Pakistan.[1] Since key positions in the ports and government agencies of the new Pakistani state were no longer occupied by Hindus, but instead filled by newly arrived Muslims from India, the country's trade infrastructure suffered a temporary total collapse: "Everything was in a mess," complained the Volkart employees from Karachi in their annual report from 1948, adding that "papers and documents got lost, warehouses were overfull, goods stacked outside were buried under a heap and could not be found."[2]

Even more problematic than these temporary disruptions, at least from the perspective of Western companies, was that the partition of the subcontinent resulted in the increasing politicalization of trade issues, a development that occurred in many former colonies after World War II.[3] For instance, the grain imports that Volkart and Ralli had until then handled on behalf of the government were taken over by indigenous trading companies after 1947. According to Volkart's Karachi office, this change occurred because "strong pressure was brought to bear on the food department not to appoint European firms to this job again."[4] The problems faced by foreign companies worsened as time went by. To mark its centennial anniversary in 1951, Volkart ran a series of advertisements that emphasized the firm's many years of activity on the subcontinent. The advertisement in the *Times of India*, for example, was emblazoned with the slogan "Pioneers in the

Past—Planning the Future: Volkart Brothers."[5] To celebrate the company's birthday, the Volkart partners established a foundation with a capital of 3 million Swiss francs to support humanitarian, social and cultural projects on the subcontinent.[6] But the partners were also pursuing business interests. The minutes of a meeting from 1950 reveal that the funds disbursed by the foundation "should have good publicity value" for the company,[7] something that was highly desirable in view of the increasing hostility toward foreign companies.

But it would have taken far more than just a mere publicity campaign to turn the situation around for a firm like Volkart. After achieving independence, the governments of India and Pakistan insisted that foreign companies hire indigenous personnel at every level of the hierarchical ladder. Furthermore, they demanded that such companies take on indigenous entrepreneurs as partners in their Indian and Pakistani subsidiaries. During the summer of 1951, Volkart—in addition to Ralli and Lever Bros.—was singled out as one of those companies in which such an "Indianization" was desirable.[8] Practically at the same time, the Pakistani regulatory agency for imports and exports issued an order requiring all importers to register themselves by filling out and submitting a questionnaire in which, among other things, respondents had to indicate the percentage of Europeans—along with Muslim and non-Muslim Pakistanis—among their staff, how much capital the company owned and what profits had been transferred out of the country since Pakistani independence. It was above all this last demand that outraged the partners at Volkart, who referred to it as "the height of impertinence by the import controller" and, during a board meeting, ventured to ask the agonizing question: "What further insolence can we expect from the emancipation of the Oriental peoples in the coming years?"[9]

In 1952, a European employee was refused entry into India for the first time. Meanwhile, other Europeans working for Volkart on the subcontinent found that they could no longer have their residency permits extended.[10] Volkart company executives had to admit that although the "notion of Indianization" was not new to the company and they had "focused for years" on "supporting young and up-and-coming Indians," they had "proceeded far too cautiously." Now this led to recruitment problems: "First, there is an acute shortage of capable candidates; second, they either have high-ranking positions in Indian companies, where they have better opportunities over the long term, or are working for the government."[11] What's more, in the opinion of one Volkart manager, there still remained

an enormous gap . . . between the European—especially the specifically Swiss democratic—way of thinking and the Indian [way of thinking]. . . . We all agree that in our branch offices the Swiss approach, lightly tinged with British thinking, has prevailed until now. When receiving certain instructions from senior management, an Indian is bound to think first and foremost like an Indian, as his identity as a Volkart employee is of secondary importance. These divergences give rise to the question of whether the team spirit and deep emotional bond with the company shall remain the same.[12]

Despite these concerns, the company intended to sign an agreement with the Indian government, whereby Volkart would commit to increasing its percentage of Indian employees from 40 to 60 percent. The company could nevertheless claim that the percentage of Indian employees at that point in time was already twice as high as what could be boasted by other foreign companies.[13]

The situation was further complicated for Volkart when, shortly after achieving independence, a number of trade unions were formed, both in India and Pakistan. These workers' organizations were able to push through several demands, such as a provision for free medical care, shorter working hours and the creation of employee lounges and libraries for native personnel.[14] The trade unions grew increasingly radical and soon led campaigns with industrial action such as organizing warning strikes, occupying offices and detaining senior management, all of which began to influence the company's policies. For example, in 1956 Volkart stopped its imports of technical equipment to Pakistan, in part due to problems with the workforce.[15] In most cases, however, the company appears to have been able to maintain peaceful industrial relations by appointing a liaison who maintained contact with the trade unions and ensured that management was informed of the concerns of the workforce.[16]

The Establishment of New Subsidiaries with Indian Partners

Aside from intervening in the personnel management of foreign companies, the governments of the new South Asian states attempted to convince Western companies to build new production plants in India and Pakistan. The idea was for them to cooperate with local partners and have their products manufactured under license by indigenous entrepreneurs.[17] Trading companies were also burdened by significant tax increases following the end of the colonial era. As late as the 1920s, only 45 percent of the net profits from business transactions within the British Empire were taxable in India and the tax rate was 6.25 percent. Profits that had been made from transactions outside the Empire were tax-free in India and the extensive cotton exports fell into this category. The company was subject to taxation in Switzerland for these profits, although only one-third of this income was taxable.[18] Even though taxes in India were regularly increased during the interwar era, the company enjoyed extremely favorable taxation conditions during colonial times. But this suddenly changed after decolonization. Now 25 percent of the net profit from the export business and 100 percent of the profit from the import business were subject to taxation on the subcontinent. On top of this, there were taxes that Volkart had to pay in Switzerland and, in some cases, in Britain, which meant that some of the income was subject to multiple taxation.[19]

In view of these difficulties, Volkart executives complained on numerous occasions about this "intolerable . . . convoluted . . . situation."[20] For quite some time, it was unclear how they intended to deal with these problems. The only thing that was certain was that the "extreme consequence" of "liquidating the Indian business" and "removing the invested capital from the country" was out of the question, in large part because they had to face the very real possibility that they might not be able to transfer the proceeds out of the country.[21] Starting in the early 1950s, company officials therefore repeatedly discussed whether it might be appropriate to hive off individual parts of the company in India and transform them into independent entities with Indian equity ownership.[22]

In 1953, Volkart received a request from the Tata company, which was planning on establishing its own company for importing Western machinery and proposed a collaboration with Volkart: "Tatas would be an outstanding match because they would be *equal* partners," said Balthasar Reinhart, one of Georg Reinhart's sons and a partner at Volkart since the mid-1940s, "so no one could be accused of a sell-out or stooge arrangement."[23] Tata was in fact an ideal combination. The company had been founded as a trading firm by Parsi merchant Jamsetji Nusserwanji Tata in 1868. In 1877, the company started working in the area of textile production and became one of the leading Indian industrial conglomerates during the twentieth century. In the early 1950s, the Tata Group was active in the areas of steel manufacturing, electrical power, insurance and mechanical engineering. It was also involved in the production of household goods and the chemical sector, and had its own hotel chain and airline.[24]

During the negotiations between Tata and Volkart, it was agreed that the Swiss would receive a 45 percent minority stake in a newly established firm called Voltas (a portmanteau of the names of the two partners), while the remaining 55 percent would go to Tata. The new company was to pursue as closely as possible a policy of Indianization, which appealed to the Volkart partners because it was "a postulate of the Indian people and would bring significant savings in costs."[25] The new company was managed right from the start by R. H. Schüepp, the former head of Volkart Bombay.[26] Voltas not only absorbed around 2,000 Indian employees, but also the machine shops and warehouses of Volkart's import and engineering departments, and it carried on as the official representative of Western machinery manufacturers.[27]

The new business prospered. Company officials felt that one of the key factors for success was that Voltas systematically marketed machinery and consumer goods in India and, at the same time, could rely on Volkart's established business contacts and sales network.[28] As with Volkart, integrity and reliability served as the cornerstone for Tata's business activities.[29] The newly merged company gathered market information for Western industrial companies, guaranteed deliveries to their destinations and assumed the financing of imports to India. What's more, Voltas had extensive technical knowledge, which was necessary because, in addition to basic products, it installed entire technical units, such as air conditioning systems for buildings.[30]

By the mid-1970s, the workforce at Voltas had tripled to nearly 7,000 employees. The company's capital was increased a number of times during this period and had risen to 62.3 million rupees in 1974 versus 15 million when the company was founded. The share owned by Volkart gradually declined and had dropped to just under 10 percent by the 1960s. The board of directors consisted exclusively of Indians by then.[31] The last Europeans who had been taken on board by Volkart left Voltas in the late 1960s.[32] The range of products also changed. Whereas products manufactured in India only made up 7 percent of Voltas's turnover when the company was established, by 1974 this figure had risen to over 90 percent.[33] This changeover from importing Western products to selling Indian brands was a direct reaction to the nationalization campaigns of the Indian government. Already during the initial rounds of negotiations between Tata and Volkart, it was decided that, when the opportunity arose, the new company would replace imports of certain goods by launching their own production in India.[34] This objective was systematically pursued during the years that followed. In addition to opening its own Voltas factory near Bombay, the Tata Group joined forces with several companies—which had been represented earlier by Volkart and subsequently by Voltas in India—to establish joint production facilities in India. Sales of the products of these new joint ventures were then handled by Voltas.[35]

The launch of Voltas and the collaboration with Indian partners were thus a success right from the start. At the same time, this was cause for some concern among Volkart executives because they realized that the rest of the corporate organization in India could now become more vulnerable to new government regulations, the fear being that the export business would soon also be forced to cooperate with Indian companies.[36] In 1957, in anticipation of a poor harvest, the Indian government temporarily banned the export of cotton and set maximum prices to ensure that Indian spinning mills and textile factories had access to sufficient supplies. Since cotton sales to Indian buyers were far less attractive than exports, largely due to the existing tax laws, in 1960 Volkart considered shutting down its entire cotton purchasing organization in India. Imports of foreign cotton would continue, though. Indeed, although India had been successfully cultivating high-quality cotton since the 1930s, the Indian textile industry still required foreign varieties of cotton for its products.[37]

But before Volkart could implement its plan to close its cotton export division, Peter Reinhart discussed the situation with a manager from Tata who put him in contact with an Indian firm called Patel Cotton Company Private Ltd., which was interested in merging with Volkart's Indian cotton organization.[38] The negotiations between Volkart and Patel were extremely protracted. One problem was that Patel had difficulties raising the necessary capital for a majority holding in the new company. An additional problem was that the Indian staff members at Volkart were better paid and union organized, whereas the employees of Patel had no union representation of their own. Executives at Volkart agreed that one could not treat the personnel as a cost factor, as had apparently been the case in establishing Voltas, but rather that well-trained employees were to be recognized as "a particularly valuable asset, especially in the current situation."[39] The two companies eventually succeeded in sweeping aside these difficulties. Patel acquired Volkart's Indian cotton organization on 1 September 1961. The newly merged entity continued to go by the name of Patel Cotton Company Private Ltd. and Volkart retained a 650,000 rupee stake in Patel, which corresponded to a 20 percent share of the company. In return, Patel received a 40 percent share of the newly established Volkart (Bombay) Private Ltd., which took over Volkart's remaining cotton division and its sales representation for shipping lines.[40]

The plan was for the two firms, Patel and Volkart (Bombay) Private Ltd. to eventually merge, but the move was initially postponed to avoid jeopardizing the cotton export quotas of the two companies. The merger of these "two independent companies with, in some respects, very different approaches" turned out to be more difficult than expected, as company officials were forced to admit in 1962.[41] In 1964, Volkart (Bombay) Private Ltd. changed its name to Volkart (India) Ltd. and ceded the cotton import business to Patel, which changed its name to Patel-Volkart Private Ltd. In 1968, Patel-Volkart finally merged with Volkart (India) Ltd. and the new company went by the name Patel-Volkart Ltd. Since imports of foreign cotton were handled by the Indian government from the early 1970s onwards, and individual Indian states took control of the trade in seeds in the interior of the country and the ginning of seed cotton, it became increasingly difficult for private companies to conduct business in the Indian cotton sector. On the advice of the Tata Group, in 1973 Patel-Volkart Ltd. merged with Gokak Mills Ltd., a spinning company that had close connections to Tata. The new company did a flourishing business because its own spinning mills could purchase cotton under favorable terms and conditions.[42]

After the once-independent branches in Bombay, Madras, Cochin and Tuticorin were incorporated into Volkart (India) Ltd. in 1964, the only remaining independent branch in India was Volkart Tellicherry, which had acquired three coffee plantations in the years 1952 and 1954, despite the fact that during the interwar era the company had rejected the idea of owning its own plantations because they did not appear to be particularly profitable. Thanks to its excellent sales channels in Europe, Volkart rapidly rose to become India's leading coffee exporter, with a volume of 6,000 tons in 1955–1956. During the 1960–1961 fiscal year, the firm even managed to export 11,000 tons, which corresponded to one-sixth of the Indian harvest.

But only three years later, the company's coffee export figures declined once again to just under 4,500 tons. Parallel to this development Volkart expanded the capacity of its coffee processing plants and by the late 1950s was able to process nearly 8,000 tons of coffee per year. The company also purchased coffee from other growers and, in some cases, granted them advances that were paid the moment the harvested beans were delivered to the processing plants. From the mid-1960s onwards, however, Volkart pursued the same divestment strategy as elsewhere in India and endeavored to reduce the company's level of involvement in Tellicherry and transfer ownership of the coffee plantations to an Indian firm. Once again with the aid of the Tata Group, Volkart was able to establish contact with Consolidated Coffee Estates Ltd., which was one of the leading operators of coffee plantations in India and completely managed by Indians. In 1966, the property and personnel of Volkart Tellicherry was transferred to Consolidated Coffee Estates Ltd., for which Volkart received a 20 percent share in the company.[43]

Changes in Pakistan and Ceylon

Independence also had a major influence on Volkart's activities in Pakistan, where, as in India, the company's business was subject to increasingly rigid government regulations. With annual exports of more than 250,000 bales of Pakistani cotton, Volkart was regularly able to achieve positive results up until the early 1970s. But after widespread flooding decimated the cotton harvest in 1973, the government banned all exports and nationalized the cotton export sector with the establishment of a state export organization in October of that year. Henceforth, all cotton that Volkart Pakistan could sell to domestic spinning mills had to be handed over to the state-owned Cotton Export Corporation of Pakistan. The company was subsequently allowed to sell overseas the cotton that was in the ownership of the Cotton Export Corporation at a price that was determined by the government.[44]

The impact of state regulation was also increasingly felt when it came to imports of Western industrial products. In 1963, Volkart responded to the situation by transforming all branches of the company in Pakistan— including the export division and the sales representation for the shipping lines—into a joint-stock company called Volkart (Pakistan) Ltd. This was to make it easier for outside capital to be invested in the company, which was a measure that the government had been urging Volkart to take.[45] In 1977, Volkart sold 70 percent of its shares in the Pakistani subsidiary to the British firm of Peninsular & Oriental Steam Navigation Co. and in return acquired a 30 percent stake in Mackinnon Mackenzie & Co. of Pakistan Ltd., a company that, until then, had been solely owned by Peninsular & Oriental Steam and was in the business of representing shipping lines, airlines and insurance companies in Pakistan.[46] Accordingly, after largely divesting in India, Volkart was only left with minority interests in companies in Pakistan as well.

In Ceylon, which had been a British crown colony until 1948, decolonization also created completely new problems for foreign companies. After the island gained independence, many Indian Tamils who had moved to Ceylon during the colonial era were forced out of their jobs as a result of political pressure from the Sinhalese-dominated government. This was not a minor problem for Volkart because more than half of its office staff and many of the workers in its warehouses had to be replaced by Ceylonese Tamils and Sinhalese.[47] Furthermore, imports by foreign companies were strictly regulated. Starting in 1955, imports from certain countries were reserved for Ceylonese companies, while certain sectors of the trade were taken over by a state import agency. Since business prospects were extremely bleak due to constant price fluctuations, the import division in Colombo was definitively closed in April 1957.[48]

As in India and Pakistan, foreign companies in Ceylon were under intense pressure to employ indigenous workers and bring on board indigenous investors, much to the displeasure of Western firms. "Ceylon is becoming an increasingly hostile environment for investments and foreigners," as it said in the Volkart annual report for the 1961–1962 fiscal year. In order to "pave the way for a perhaps long-overdue Ceylonization," Volkart's branch in Colombo was transformed into a joint-stock company in 1962.[49] This new entity went by the name of Volanka Ltd., a portmanteau of Vo- from Volkart and -lanka from Sri Lanka.[50] Although in 1973 the company was pressured by the government into handing over to a Ceylonese firm the lucrative representation of diverse shipping lines, Volanka prospered—despite endless conflicts with trade unions, tax increases, new government regulations and transport problems. In addition to exporting spices and oils, the export of coconut fiber was extremely profitable. In the 1960s, Volanka acquired several industrial premises and began to produce coconut fiber and matting. In 1975 and 1976, the company's capital was increased twice. It was not until 1983 that the controlling interest was sold to investors from Sri Lanka.[51]

Aside from the concerns of a possible Ceylonization of the company, there was a second reason why in the early 1960s Volkart was eager to have its business in Ceylon handled by a newly established joint-stock company. The fact of the matter was that Volkart Colombo had not been obliged to pay any taxes in Ceylon on the profits gained from its exports to Europe. The company had always successfully argued that Colombo was merely a buying agency and that the profits from exports to Europe were made by the branches in London and Winterthur.[52] This arrangement was extremely advantageous for Volkart because it allowed the company to engage in a bit of tax evasion. During the 1956–1957 fiscal year, the Volkart branch in Colombo recorded on its books net profits of 979,000 rupees, but the company only paid taxes on a profit of 278,000 rupees in Ceylon.[53] In a letter to the Ceylonese government in 1962, Volkart Colombo maintained that the profits that were transferred to Switzerland were by no means lost for Ceylon because the Winterthur headquarters used this money to grant loans that helped to finance the export business from Ceylon. A balance sheet presented to the government was accompanied by the following comment: "You will notice from these figures that during the last 13 years we brought more money into Ceylon than we took out."[54]

But this claim was a bald-faced lie. As noted in an internal memo by the Bombay branch in 1961, Volkart Colombo had been engaging in illegal activity for years.[55] Company officials feared that the Ceylonese government would notice this sooner or later, especially as indigenous employees naturally realized that the prices that the headquarters in Winterthur reported for Volkart Colombo were lower than the actual sales revenues. Moreover, Volkart Colombo was more than just merely a buying agency for the headquarters in Winterthur, as witnessed by the fact that one-third of the branch's turnover came from direct transactions with customers in Japan, Australia and Africa. To make matters worse, the company's profits were not reinvested in Ceylon, but instead siphoned out of the country.[56] The establishment of an independent joint-stock company, which would conduct direct transactions with other Volkart branches, was a maneuver to prevent the government from discovering these practices. This move was also intended to help "place the previous improper extraction of profits out of Ceylon on a legal footing," as it said in the in-company annual report for the 1961–1962 fiscal year.[57]

Multinational Companies and Tax Evasion

Establishing this new entity had the disadvantage that the branch in Colombo would henceforth have to pay taxes on all of its profits in Ceylon—an onerous development that company officials sought to prevent. In 1960, it was noted in an internal memo that for tax reasons Colombo would calculate artificially low prices for its sales to the other Volkart branches, or rather, if necessary, would even enter fictitious sales into the books, whereby the Colombo branch would lose money in sales transactions with the headquarters in Winterthur.[58]

Based on the source material, it is no longer possible to determine whether these proposals were actually implemented. But they do show the options that a multinational company had at its disposal to sidestep the demands of individual governments. The extent to which the company was aware of such dynamics is clearly revealed in an internal memo from 1965, in which the author contended that Volkart had absolutely no interest in accumulating profits in countries like India, Pakistan, Ceylon, Japan and Brazil due to local tax and currency regulations and the market value of the relevant currencies. It was thus argued that every attempt should be made to transfer profits to Switzerland, where they were deposited on special so-called "private accounts." These accounts were then used to pay the salaries and bonuses of the European employees that worked in the corresponding countries. The author of the memo went on to say that this practice was important for employees because they wanted their savings kept at a safe location and in a robust currency. In the US and Europe, where the tax and currency situation was more favorable, such measures were not deemed necessary. The question now was how this proposal could be concretely implemented. The simplest approach was to transfer the money to Switzerland whenever the headquarters in Winterthur was involved in a commercial transaction: "Then the relevant subsidiary can use appropriate pricing to ensure that in Winterthur—in addition to the legitimate earnings that the joint-stock company must receive for its own efforts in organizing the transaction—additional amounts are accrued. In other words, the prices that countries like Pakistan and Ceylon demand for their products are kept artificially low so that at normal sales prices the difference can be deposited in the corresponding private account." One problem remained, however: "It is clear that if these arrangements were to come to the attention of the authorities in the countries concerned they would be viewed as a violation of their tax and currency laws." In this case, the company would take the position that the sales prices of the subsidiaries were normal and the difference between the prices received by the subsidiary in Colombo was the legitimate profit margin of the headquarters in Winterthur. By contrast, in its dealings with the Swiss authorities the company would have to "take the position that these 'outside profits' should under no circumstances be detached from the usual Winterthur profits, but instead be attributed to the overseas profits."[59] The obvious intended goal here was to prevent such revenues from being fully taxed in Switzerland.

These last two examples show that nation-state policies and globally operating companies were increasingly at odds after 1945. Volkart reacted to this situation by launching two initiatives. First, as was noted already in the 1956 annual report, in view of the hostility toward foreign capital in India, Pakistan and Ceylon, Volkart had to rethink the orientation of its business activities:

> In practice this means that we are generally withdrawing from India, Pakistan and Ceylon with the intention of increasingly relying on the Western Hemisphere, and above all that we intend to reduce our import and engineering departments and instead develop the coffee trade.[60]

Second, the company entered into joint ventures with indigenous partners at several locations. By forcing foreign firms to enter into partnerships with domestic companies, the policies of the governments of newfound nations after decolonization fueled Volkart's transformation into a multinational trading company with a distinct holding structure. The company was gradually evolving from "an organization that focused uniquely on the cotton trade and, more recently, the trade in coffee" to an entity consisting of "a number of individual companies that are tailored to the opportunities and needs of the countries concerned," as was stated in the company's 1961 annual report.[61] In that sense, interorganizational networks not only constituted an effective strategy to penetrate new markets, as described in the previous chapters, but also offered an opportunity to withdraw from these markets without suffering major losses.

Notes

1 VA, Konferenz-Protokolle 4. Juli 1947–1928. Juni 1949: Konferenz vom 6. Oktober 1947; Dossier 8: Karachi, 1. Management and 3. Table of Events: VB.
2 VA, Dossier 8: Karachi, 14. Foodgrains business during and for some time after World War II: Karachi Branch Clearing Department Report for 1947–1948, ending 31 August 1948, 18 October 1948.
3 Amsden, *The Rise of "the Rest"*, 2001, 119.
4 VA, Dossier 8: Karachi, 14. Foodgrains business during and for some time after World War II: Karachi Branch Foodgrains Department Report for 1946–1947, ending 31 August 47, 15 September 1947.
5 VA, Dossier 5: Bombay III: India General, 27. Some general events in India between 1851–1976: Times of India, 1 February 1951 und Pakistan Times, 1 February 1951.
6 VA, Partners' Conference (4 June 1946–1931 August 1956): Conference of 7 July 1950. For an overview of the activities of the foundation during the first 10 years of its existence, see Gebrüder Volkart, The Volkart Foundation, [1961].
7 VA, Partners' Conference (4 June 1946–1931 August 1956): Conference of 7 February 1950.
8 VA, Konferenz-Protokolle vom 1. Juli 1949–1919. Dezember 1952: Protokoll vom 2. Juni 1951.
9 VA, Konferenz-Protokolle vom 1. Juli 1949–1919. Dezember 1952: Pakistan Importers' Registration, 25 May 51.
10 VA, Dossier 3: Bombay I, 4. Table of Events 1851–1961/2; Dossier 25: I/P/C Terms of European Staff, Staff Indianisation Corr. 1951–1967/ Pakistanisation -1967: E. Sulger, Die Indianisierung unserer Niederlassungen in Indien/Ceylon/ Pakistan, 21. 2. 1953.
11 VA, Konferenz-Protokolle vom 16. Januar 1953–1956. Januar 1959: Konferenz vom 25. März 1953.
12 VA, Dossier 25: I/P/C Terms of European Staff, Staff Indianisation Corr. 1951– 1967/ Pakistanisation -1967: E. Sulger, Die Indianisierung unserer Niederlassungen in Indien/Ceylon/Pakistan, 21. 2. 1953.
13 VA, Konferenz-Protokolle vom 16. Januar 1953–1956. Januar 1959: Konferenz vom 27. Juli 1953.
14 Anderegg, *Chronicle*, 1976, 520ff.
15 VA, Dossier 8: Karachi, 3. Table of Events: VB.
16 Anderegg, *Chronicle*, 1976, 522.
17 Anderegg, *Chronicle*, 1976, 529.
18 VA, Dossier 28: Notes on Taxation in India, 1. Indian taxation laws—notes thereon; 2. Notes on taxation practices applicable to VB; 9. UK taxation; VA Konferenz-Protokolle vom 16. Januar 1953–1956. Januar 1959: Konferenz vom 23. April 1953.
19 VA, Konferenz-Protokolle vom 16. Januar 1953–1956. Januar 1959: Konferenz vom 23. April 1953.
20 VA, Konferenz-Protokolle vom 16. Januar 1953–1956. Januar 1959: Konferenz vom 25. März 1953.
21 VA, Konferenz-Protokolle vom 16. Januar 1953–1956. Januar 1959: Konferenz vom 25. März 1953.

22 VA, Konferenz-Protokolle vom 1. Juli 1949–1919. Dezember 1952: Protokoll vom 2. Juni 1951.
23 VA, Konferenz-Protokolle vom 16. Januar 1953–1956. Januar 1959: BR, Zu Protokoll, 23. Oktober 1953.
24 Tata Group, Tata, 2009, 6–7.
25 VA, Konferenz-Protokolle vom 16. Januar 1953–1956. Januar 1959: Konferenz vom 17. Dezember 1953 und Konferenz vom 17. März 1954; VA, Bilanzen, 1952/3 und 1953/54, Kurzer Rückblick auf das Jahr 1953/54, 6 October 54.
26 This required the approval of the Indian government: TCA, Rack 3, Box 36 TS-Vol-30.
27 VA, Dossier 29: Voltas Ltd. (1954), 1. Correspondence leading up to formation of Voltas Ltd.: Volkart Brothers, Bombay, to A.D. Shroff, Bombay, 4 May 1954.
28 VA, Dossier 29: Voltas Ltd. (1954), 1. Correspondence leading up to formation of Voltas Ltd.: Interview with A.H. Tobaccowala, Managing Director of Voltas, BusinessIndia, Dec. 24, 1979-Jan. 6, 1980.
29 Tata Monthly Bulletin, 1964, Vol. 9, No. 10, 15; Anderegg, Chronicle, 1976, 596.
30 Tata Review, 1966, Vol. 1, No. 5, 14.
31 VA, Dossier 29: Voltas Ltd. (1954), 4. The formation of Voltas Ltd.
32 Anderegg, Chronicle, 1976, 597.
33 VA, Dossier 29: Voltas Ltd. (1954), 1. Correspondence leading up to formation of Voltas Ltd.: A. H. Tobaccowala, Managing Director von Voltas, 1 September 1974.
34 TCA, Tata Sons, Rack 3, Box 37, TS-Vol-8, Extracts from the Minutes of Agents' Weekly Meeting: 26 August 1953 and 11 November 1953.
35 TCA, Tata Sons, Rack 3, Box 37, TS-Vol-21 und TS-Vol-24; VA, Dossier 29: Voltas Ltd. (1954), 1. Correspondence leading up to formation of Voltas Ltd.: Interview with A.H. Tobaccowala, Managing Director of Voltas, BusinessIndia, Dec. 24, 1979-Jan. 6, 1980; Anderegg, Chronicle, 1976, 598. Western companies that took part in such joint ventures included American firms like International Harvester (tractors) and Carrier (refrigeration systems), and Swiss companies Rieter (spinning mill machinery) and Hoffmann-La Roche (chemical products).
36 VA, Dossier 29: Voltas Ltd. (1954), 1. Correspondence leading up to formation of Voltas Ltd.: Bombay to Winterthur, 15 September 1953.
37 Anderegg, Chronicle, 1976, 603–604.
38 VA, Dossier 30: Patel Cotton Comp., Patel/Volkart Cotton Merger, Volkart Bombay Pvt. Ltd. 1961.
39 VA, Konferenz-Protokolle vom 15. Januar 1959–1930. März 1965: Konferenz vom 18. November 1960.
40 VA, Dossier 30: Patel Cotton Comp., Patel/Volkart Cotton Merger, Volkart Bombay Pvt. Ltd. 1961.
41 VA, Bilanzen, Bilanz 1961–1962.
42 VA, Dossier 30: Patel Cotton Comp., Patel/Volkart Cotton Merger, Volkart Bombay Pvt. Ltd. 1961; Anderegg, Chronicle, 1976, 706–714.
43 Anderegg, Chronicle, 1976, 543–548 and 628–642 VA, Dossier 35: Consolidated Coffee Ltd. (1967), 5. On and after the merger; Rambousek/Vogt/Volkart, Volkart, 1990, 251.
44 Anderegg, Chronicle, 1976, 621 and 688–691.
45 Anderegg, Chronicle, 1976, 624–625.
46 VA, Dossier 34: Volkart Pakistan Ltd. (1963), Reorganisation VPL/MM 1976; Rambousek/Vogt/Volkart, Volkart, 1990, 252.
47 VA, Dossier 6: Colombo, 4. Table of Events.
48 Anderegg, Chronicle, 1976, 602.
49 VA, Bilanzen, Bilanz 1961–1962.

50 VA, Dossier 33: Volanka Ltd. Colombo (1962), Gründung Volanka 1962 + Vorgeschichte: Winterthur an Colombo, 8 October 1959.
51 Anderegg, *Chronicle*, 1976, 684–687; Rambousek/Vogt/Volkart, *Volkart*, 1990, 159.
52 By contrast, exports to Japan, Australia, India, South Africa and the US were taxed in Ceylon, along with the profits from representing shipping lines and insurance companies: VA, Dossier 6: Colombo, 4. Table of Events.
53 VA, Dossier 33: Volanka Ltd. Colombo (1962), Gründung Volanka 1962 + Vorgeschichte: Notiz vom 22.6.1959, Colombo Company.
54 VA, Dossier 6: Colombo, 17. Volanka Ltd.—successor Co. to VB Colombo: VB Colombo to The Controller of Exchange, Central Bank of London, through the Hongkong and Shanghai Banking Corporation, 27 July 1962.
55 VA, Dossier 33: Volanka Ltd. Colombo (1962), Gründung Volanka 1962 + Vorgeschichte: Notiz von VB Bombay, 21.10.61 zur Volanka Ltd.
56 VA, Dossier 33: Volanka Ltd. Colombo (1962), Gründung Volanka 1962 + Vorgeschichte: Notiz von Jakob Anderegg, 16.12.60.
57 VA, Bilanzen, Bilanz 1961–1966.
58 VA, Dossier 33: Volanka Ltd. Colombo (1962), Gründung Volanka 1962 + Vorgeschichte: Notiz von Jakob Anderegg, 16.12.60.
59 VA, Konferenz-Protokolle vom 15. Januar 1959–1930. März 1965: PR, Office note, 22 February 1965.
60 VA, Bilanzen, Bilanz 1955–1956.
61 VA, Bilanzen, Bilanz 1960–1961.

13 Entering the Coffee Trade

The decades following 1945 saw the advent of a new type of enterprise, the multinational corporation, with integrated production systems, branches in several countries and worldwide business activities. One indication of the growing dominance of multinational corporations was that the volume of global direct investments soared from 66 billion to 6,600 billion dollars between 1960 and 2001.[1] A number of different factors contributed to this development: the constant decline in transport costs, the increasing importance of economies of scale and finally, starting in the 1980s, the rise of neoliberal economic policies, in which closed markets were viewed as a negative phenomenon.[2] This development can also be observed in the commodities trade. As shown in the previous chapters, globally active trading companies like Volkart, Anderson Clayton and Cargill had already launched a geographical expansion of their businesses during the 1920s. This trend became more pronounced during the postwar decades. By the 1980s, seven multinational trading companies were responsible for 40 percent of all shipping of non-roasted coffee, and the second-largest company in this business was Volkart, with a global market share of 8 percent.[3]

After 1945, Volkart did an increasing amount of business in South America and rapidly became one of the key players in the coffee trade, and thus in the shipping of the worldwide second-most important commodity after crude oil.[4] This swift transformation offers an ideal opportunity for a more in-depth examination of two aspects of global trade that have already been addressed a number of times in this work. First, an analysis of the structure of the coffee organization reveals how important network-like collaborations with other companies could be for trading companies entering the market. Second, based on the coffee trade, it is possible to describe the relationship between multinational companies and the territorial interests of national governments. Indeed, the coffee trade during the twentieth century was strongly influenced by political interventions and international agreements, so it comes as little surprise that this constantly led to conflicts of interest between political players and international companies. What is surprising perhaps is that the politicization of the coffee trade could actually yield benefits for multinational companies because it allowed them to be awarded large government contracts. This confirms the observation, which has been reiterated in this book, that territorialization and economic globalization are not absolute opposites, but instead should be seen as dialectically interrelated processes.

From Cotton to Coffee

Volkart first began doing business in Latin America during the 1920s when the company opened a procurement agency in São Paulo in response to the high demand for Brazilian cotton in Germany.[5] At the time, the cultivated area for cotton was substantially expanded to address a sharp decline in the price of coffee, the country's leading export commodity, which was suffering from chronic overproduction.[6] As a result, Brazil's annual cotton production rose from around 400,000 bales to more than 2.1 million bales between 1920 and 1940.[7] In addition to its cotton sales to Germany in the 1920s, Volkart began to export Brazilian cotton to Shanghai and Osaka, although these transactions produced rather disappointing results[8] and the partners considered withdrawing from Brazil altogether.[9]

But the company soon found an opportunity to establish a new basis for its business in Brazil. In 1936, a French firm based in Le Havre called the Société d'importation et de commission ancienne maison Louis Reinhart put Volkart in contact with the Brazilian export company Prado Chaves. The Société d'importation ranked among France's leading import companies and had been founded in the mid-nineteenth century by members of Winterthur's Reinhart merchant family, from which Theodor Reinhart also descended.[10] This French firm's activities included importing coffee and cotton to France on behalf of Prado Chaves, which was one of the leading coffee export companies in Brazil. During the 1930s, Prado Chaves had its own plantations with over 4 million coffee trees and, in addition to the coffee trade, was involved in livestock farming and the cultivation of corn, oranges and cotton.[11]

Although Volkart declined to sign a formal representation agreement, it began to work for Prado Chaves by exporting Brazilian cotton to China and Japan. Volkart also made use of the fact that Brazilian cotton had many of the same characteristics as American varieties,[12] but was much cheaper because the agricultural price-support policies of the US government under the New Deal had resulted in a rapid rise in the price of American cotton. Volkart contacted Canadian spinning mills that had been using American cotton and suggested the possibility of replacing it with Brazilian varieties. When the spinning mills reacted positively to this offer, Volkart became the leading exporter of Brazilian cotton to Canada in the late 1930s.[13] After 1939, exports of American cotton came virtually to a standstill because US domestic demand had rapidly increased in reaction to the outbreak of World War II. Cotton mills in Canada, Japan and China subsequently began to purchase enormous quantities of cotton from Brazil, which generated considerable export orders for Volkart. Japan's entry into the war and a lack of cargo space put a halt to this business in 1941.[14]

In the late 1930s and early 1940s, Volkart sent employees to Brazil to sound out further business opportunities there. These representatives advised the company to establish its own branch in Brazil, but the partners rejected the idea out of hand because they were convinced that they already had a top-notch connection in Brazil with Prado Chaves.[15] It gradually became clear, though, that the collaboration with Prado Chaves was problematic because Volkart often had to revise contract conditions at the last minute. As long as such new arrangements could be made within the company, they were manageable for a trading firm like Volkart. However, in a situation like the one with Prado Chaves, where another company was involved, this regularly led to frictions. Another issue that was a much more fundamental problem was that, although Prado Chaves had extensive experience in the coffee business, it was not well versed in the ins and outs of the cotton trade. On a business trip to Brazil after the end of the war, Peter Reinhart remarked that, despite the fact that Prado Chaves was a "perfectly honest and reliable firm," it was "not a *cotton* firm. None of the directors is sure of what he does in the cotton business. They hardly ever go to the classing room and they are inclined to handle cotton exactly like coffee." He went on to say that Prado Chaves had only recently begun to classify the cotton when purchasing it, which explains why the company often did not know exactly what types of cotton it had in stock in its warehouses. Consequently, Volkart had taken in large quantities of cotton from Prado Chaves without being certain whether it actually had the quality that had been agreed upon in the sales contracts with the spinning mills. Furthermore, the Brazilian company had apparently not realized how important it was to offer a wide range of different types of cotton that were tailored to the specific needs of individual textile mills. And finally, according to Reinhart, Prado Chaves had no knowledge of the type of precise calculation that Volkart performed in India, in which the relatively low cost of processing at the company's own gins in the interior of the country was used to offset lower export prices:

> They like to make a small profit on every single item. In particular they are not treating the profits on their inland operations (ginning, crop advances etc.) as part of their total cotton business and never use them to cut prices.[16]

In 1946, when Peter Reinhart took the abovementioned business trip, Volkart had already had its own branch in Brazil for four years. In 1942, after much hesitation, the company established Volkart Irmãos Ltda. in São Paulo. The new subsidiary had been founded in the wake of new bilateral agreements, which stipulated that exports from Brazil could no longer be sent to countries like France, Sweden and Canada if the transactions had been conducted via a company in the US. Since Volkart arranged its exports from Brazil via its subsidiary in New York, this provision would have forced the firm out of the business. The only option at its disposal was to carry out the exports, for appearances' sake, via a Brazilian subsidiary, although in reality there would be no change in the company's usual business practices. Volkart intended to continue to purchase cotton from Prado Chaves and export it abroad. But the launch of the new company was extremely unsettling for Prado Chaves because the Brazilians feared that Volkart would sooner or later establish its own procurement organization in Brazil.[17] These concerns were entirely justified. In fact, senior management officials at Volkart were hardly enthused over "the paradoxical situation" that

> we as a global company in the cotton industry are incapable of acting as shippers in Brazil, and that our goods are perhaps shipped by a smaller company that first has to make a name for itself in the cotton business (with our help!), and that, to make matters worse, we have not even been commissioned as the general representative of Prado Chaves for the European countries.[18]

Despite all the friction, Volkart was still interested in collaborating with Prado Chaves. A solo business venture entailed considerable risks, at least in the opinion of one member of the board of directors who, in 1943, listed an extensive catalogue of obstacles, including "the foreign language, the inadequate auxiliary staff, the sheer difficulties of launching an entirely new organization and, above all, the entirely different business norms in comparison with the superior commercial practices in the East."[19] After the end of World War II, Volkart initially wanted to avoid any move that would spell the end of its collaboration with the Brazilians, not least of all because Prado Chaves had excellent connections to the Brazilian government, and above all to the finance minister:

> These relations and the evident intention of the Brazilian Government to favour the Brazilian firms have on many occasions been most useful. The Brazilian Government is still holding large stocks and by giving advance information about the selling policy or by letting one choose amongst the qualities, it is very easy to facilitate the business of one's friends.[20]

Nevertheless, Prado Chaves remained skeptical of Volkart's intentions and dissolved its connection with the Swiss company in the summer of 1947. Volkart then began to export Brazilian cotton on its own account. Although Brazilian cotton production was declining, the company made outstanding profits. In 1951, Volkart acquired its first cotton gin near São Paulo, followed by the purchase of five additional facilities by 1956.[21] In doing so, Volkart was following in the footsteps of two major American cotton trading companies, McFadden and Anderson Clayton, which had begun to establish their own purchasing organizations in Brazil back in the 1930s to continue to supply their sales branches in Europe and East Asia with raw cotton, despite the decline in cotton exports from the US.[22]

For Volkart the collaboration with Prado Chaves had a positive spin-off effect that would redirect the company along entirely new lines. During the war, Volkart had begun to export Brazilian coffee, which it purchased from Prado Chaves. This business continued after 1945 when Volkart became the sole representative of Prado Chaves in Italy and served as the leading seller in Switzerland.[23] Encouraged by the positive results, Volkart expanded the business in 1950 to Germany, France and the US—and thus entered into direct competition with Prado Chaves, which was already represented by other import firms in these countries. As a result, Prado Chaves rescinded the representation agreement in the spring of 1951, thus bringing to an end the connection between the two companies in the coffee business as well.[24]

Brazil, the Land of Coffee

It was hardly surprising that a trading company established in Brazil would sooner or later begin to export coffee. During the nineteenth century, Brazil had risen to become the world's largest producer of coffee. The country was ideally suited to play such a leading role. Brazil had enormous areas of arable land that could be put to use after clearing the rain forest. The human costs of this development were devastating, however, as indigenous peoples were driven out and had no legally recognized rights to the land. During the first decades of the twentieth century, Brazil produced between 70 and 90 percent of the world's coffee. After Colombia and a number of Central American and African countries began to promote the cultivation of coffee, Brazil's market share dwindled, but even during the 1960s more than 60 percent of the global coffee crop was grown in the South American country.[25]

In view of the country's steadily growing production, the price of Brazilian coffee was in constant decline. The growing affordability of coffee was one of the main reasons why it evolved from a luxury beverage during the nineteenth century to an increasingly common staple of everyday modern life.[26] This in turn sparked government incentives to further increase the amount of cultivated area, which largely explains why the coffee trade was influenced to an ever-growing degree by state interventions.[27] Because Brazilian coffee production had tripled between 1891 and 1902 to 16.3 million bags,[28] global market prices literally collapsed. To prevent growers from going bankrupt, the Brazilian government bought 8 million bags of coffee in 1906. Thanks to the growing demand for commodities during World War I, the government was able to sell its inventory of coffee on the global market, but the problem of overproduction remained. Plantation owners wielded so much influence in political circles that it came to costly state interventions over the following years. In 1917, 1921 and 1925, the government purchased such large shares of the harvest that by the early 1930s it had twice as much as the average annual production stockpiled in state-owned coffee depots. After this coffee spoiled because it had been in storage too long, most of it had to be destroyed. The negative consequence of this government intervention was that, due to prices that were artificially elevated, not only Brazilian growers produced far more than they could sell on the global market, but also other Latin American countries like Colombia began to subsidize the cultivation and export of coffee.

The Great Depression exacerbated the situation even further. Between 1931 and 1937, coffee prices on the global market plummeted from 21.7 cents to 9.8 cents per pound. Scrambling for a solution, the Brazilian government attempted to solve the problem of overproduction with an international agreement. In 1936 and 1937, the leading Latin American coffee producing countries convened and tried to establish binding export quotas, but were unable to broker an accord. From 1938 onwards, Brazil redoubled its exports in a bid to maintain its share of the global market. The outbreak of World War II left Latin America almost completely severed from the European market, causing the depots with unsellable coffee to overflow. Since the military dictatorship that Brazilian President Getúlio Vargas instituted in 1937 began to forge ties with Nazi Germany, the US seized the initiative and in 1940 pushed through the Inter-American Coffee Agreement, which remained in force until 1945. After the end of the war, demand for coffee rapidly recovered. But since production had declined steeply from the levels achieved during the 1930s, prices rapidly rose, prompting growers to increase the amount of cultivation area once again.

Volkart Becomes a Coffee Company

In view of this development, it made perfect sense that a trading company like Volkart, which was well-established in Brazil, sought to gain a foothold in the coffee trade in the early 1950s. After Prado Chaves terminated its collaboration with the Swiss company, it became clear that Volkart would have to become active as an independent shipper in Brazil if it wanted to move beyond a marginal existence in the coffee business.[29] As a first step, the company set up its own coffee divisions in New York and Winterthur by 1953. One year later, Volkart Irmãos in São Paulo opened a coffee procurement office in Santos.[30] In 1958, Volkart began to purchase coffee in the interior of the country and acquired its first plants to process coffee cherries in the cultivation areas.[31] Such backward integration was absolutely essential for a trading company if it intended to expand its operations in the export business—a lesson that Volkart had already learned from its experience in the Indian cotton business. In the 1890s, European and American coffee export companies had begun to dispatch buying agents into the backcountry of Brazil to purchase coffee directly from growers. By establishing their own procurement agencies and processing plants, exporters could achieve a more effective sorting of the beans and develop their own types of coffee. A buying agent for Edward Johnston & Co.—a British firm that ranked among the leading coffee exporters in Brazil at the turn of the century— voiced this opinion in a letter written to the company owners in London in 1900:

> My idea for the future is . . . [t]hat we should make up types . . . of cof-fee well set in color & style & that . . . the types be kept as uniform as possible. A Santos superior should always be the same whether the crop is a good one or a bad one. . . . I think that in this way we should keep up a uniformity in our types (& I trust also in our shipments) which would be to the advantage of our business as a whole.[32]

By developing its own purchasing organization, Volkart was adopting a course in the late 1950s that was very similar to the one pursued by the American trading company Anderson Clayton at roughly the same time. Anderson Clayton had been involved in the Brazilian cotton market since 1932 and diversified into the coffee sector in 1950, making it Brazil's lead-ing exporter of coffee. In the early 1950s, it shipped more than 300,000 bags of coffee out of the country every month.[33] Forging its own buying organization and operating its own processing plants was essential to the company's export business. In a company brochure from the late 1950s, the importance of this approach was described as follows:

> This permits ACCO's [Anderson, Clayton & Co's] interior managers to furnish the company with accurate periodic reports on the progress of the coffee crop, rainfall and other vital weather conditions. This wealth of information enables ACCO to expertly advise and serve the best interests of its customers abroad.

In Santos the coffee purchased in the interior of the country was sorted once again by the firm and blended to create standard company types.[34]

By creating its own purchasing organization, Volkart was also able to increase its turnover in the coffee business within just a few years. The key to this expansion was that, as a multinational trading company, Volkart— like Anderson Clayton before it—managed to achieve economies of scale right from the start and could use its branch in New York to establish links to the most important coffee roasters in the US (Figure 13.1). But it was ultimately the interventionist approach of the Brazilian state that helped the company land its first major contract. In July 1959, Volkart was able to purchase from the state Brazilian coffee agency 250,000 bags of coffee that had been stored as surplus from prior harvests, resulting in a loss of qual-ity during storage. It was possible to sell this surplus at an extraordinarily low price to manufacturers of instant coffee, and Volkart had to agree to export another 250,000 bags of normal quality coffee under the usual terms

Figure 13.1 Volkart promoted the services of its coffee division in this advertisement targeting roasters in the important US market (from: *Tea and Coffee Trade Journal*, no. 10, 1961, 73.

and conditions the following month. Operation 250/250, as it was referred to internally, was a double coup for Volkart that allowed the company to rapidly increase its sales and establish business contacts to a range of major international clients, most notably Nestlé.[35]

During the 1961–1962 season, Volkart's coffee division achieved its first substantial profits.[36] Sales in the US rose from a relatively modest 315,000 bags in the 1955–1956 season to more than 2 million bags in the 1961–1962 season.[37] The annual report on business in the US during the 1961–1962 fiscal year noted that "the outstanding collaboration with General Foods" had been "particularly successful" and allowed Volkart "to dislodge Anderson Clayton from its leading position to a certain degree."[38]

The Competitive Advantages of Multinational Trading Companies

It is remarkable how quickly companies like Volkart and Anderson Clayton were able to establish themselves in the Brazilian coffee sector. There were several reasons for this. Multinational trading companies had considerable financial power and global trade had undergone a general transformation during the second half of the twentieth century. During this period in history, trading firms increasingly began to pay advances to intermediaries and growers. While for many decades Volkart had strictly refused to do business on a credit basis, the company gradually abandoned this principle after 1918. The firm first showed a willingness to accept more sizable credit risks with the cotton sales of its subsidiaries in China and Japan, and continental European spinning mills were granted increasingly favorable terms of payment. This made business transactions more risky for Volkart, yet at the same time the company managed to increase its sales substantially because many competitors were unable, or unprepared, to take similar capital risks.[39] In the mid-1950s, the company granted its first short-term loans to Indian growers after Volkart had made major inroads into the coffee business on the subcontinent.[40] This was the very first time that Volkart granted agricultural loans.

In Latin America it would have been impossible for Volkart to become a major competitor in the global coffee trade so quickly if the company had not had access to considerable financial resources and not enjoyed such a high degree of creditworthiness among American and European banks. Volkart was no exception in this respect. Other multinational trading companies like Ralli, Bunge & Born and Anderson Clayton increasingly served as financiers after 1945 and thus assumed functions that had been largely reserved for commercial banks until well into the interwar era.[41] In the early 1950s, for instance, Volkart financed coffee exports from Brazil by taking out loans from Western banks and passing these on to Brazilian export firms.[42] Likewise, Volkart's attractiveness for Prado Chaves stemmed in large part from the allure of its financial clout. Indeed, the Swiss could take out loans in the US at far more favorable conditions than would have been granted to the Brazilian firm.[43]

Due to their financial strength, trading companies were also valuable partners for the governments of growing countries. For instance, the

Brazilian finance minister asked Volkart for a loan of 10 million dollars in 1960, which, with interest payments, was the equivalent of 45 million Swiss francs. The plan was that Volkart would acquire a fixed-rate loan of 15 million Swiss francs from the three major Swiss banks at an interest rate of 3.75 percent. The remaining 30 million were to be provided directly to Brazil by the banks, but with no right of recourse to Volkart. The Brazilian government offered 340,000 bags of coffee as security. The idea was for the loan to be paid off successively from exports of this coffee to Europe and the US, and the sales on both markets were to be handled by Volkart. The deal eventually fell through when the Brazilian government got cold feet, but this example illustrates the scale of the coffee trade and the key importance of bank loans for conducting transactions.[44]

In addition to their financial strength, trading companies from industrialized countries also enjoyed far better conditions for their futures transactions on the commodity exchanges. In the late 1960s, coffee futures temporarily declined in importance because the International Coffee Agreement, an international commodity accord first signed in 1962, ensured stable global market prices for a number of years. But when the second round of the agreement expired in 1972, the volume of futures transactions increased once again and became enormously important once more in the wake of a severe frost in Brazil that sent world coffee prices soaring in 1975.[45] Peter Reinhart became a member of the New York Coffee Exchange in 1954, which meant that the company henceforth only had to pay half of the usual fees for its futures transactions.[46] As with the cotton trade, the exchange served highly diverse functions in the coffee sector.[47] First, through the establishment of standardized types of coffee, it made it possible to reach agreements on coffee quality. This was especially important following the advent of the telegraph, which allowed coffee to be traded before the actual goods had reached the port of destination—and often before the coffee had even been harvested. Second, operations on the coffee futures market were aimed at safeguarding against the risks of price fluctuations. Since the futures market was primarily based on upcoming developments, such as the size of the anticipated harvest in certain areas of cultivation, it also opened the door to speculative trading, a practice that was long frowned upon among reputable traders. Members of the exchange were thus banned from spreading rumors to influence prices. An American company that did just that was barred from the New York Coffee Exchange in 1888.[48] Third, the grade of the individual coffee shipments was determined by official classifiers who were appointed by the exchange to assign a specific quality to each consignment. Based on this classification, the price difference was determined with respect to the base price, which in most cases was the price of Santos grade no. 4 coffee.

Multinational trading companies like Volkart and Anderson Clayton that were entering the coffee trade were able to continue to benefit from the fact that they could reduce information and transaction costs through the vertical integration of their procurement, production, import and export structures as well as through their worldwide network of branches and their proximity to roasters in the industrialized countries. As late as the 1960s, it still took a number of days, despite the use of the telegraph, before officials in Guatemala discovered—from a message that traveled via Europe—about a frost in Brazil that drove up global coffee prices.[49] Trading companies like Volkart and Anderson Clayton thus paid close attention to the processing of information. In the early 1950s, Anderson Clayton had developed an elaborate system designed to predict future harvests in Brazil. Company representatives regularly visited plantations and inspected the growth of the harvest and made notes on the influence of the weather. These observations were augmented by information that was received directly from the growers. This system allowed for extremely precise forecasts that were immediately incorporated into Anderson Clayton's calculations.[50]

In the coffee trade, as in global trade in a general sense, the reliability of contractual partners was the key to doing business. Assessing the credibility of a partner was facilitated in large part thanks to the relatively manageable number of parties in the coffee sector. Access to the inner circle of coffee traders on the global market was tightly controlled. The New York Coffee Exchange, for example, had a maximum of 312 members. An existing member had to submit the application for an aspiring new member, who then had to be approved by the board of directors.[51] The larger companies always did business with the same partners and could fairly accurately assess both their financial situation and their reputation. Hence, contracts required very few guarantee clauses. When a dispute did arise, the coffee exchange where the contract had been concluded served as an arbitration court. Trading companies endeavored to nip all conflicts in the bud, though, for reasons that William H. Ukers, the longtime editor of the New York *Tea and Coffee Trade Journal*, described as follows in 1935:

> As the quality of most of the coffee sold is a question of good faith on the part of the seller, it is obvious that those shipping inferior grades or qualities, or refusing adjustment in some mutually satisfactory manner, are soon eliminated by discriminating buyers.[52]

As mentioned in earlier chapters, Volkart's ironclad business principle was that agreements would always be respected,[53] and this notion that a trader's word was his bond also applied to the coffee sector. According to Peter Zurschmiede, who headed Volkart's coffee division from 1966 to 1985, the company prided itself on saying that it would even make good on its deliveries if the market collapsed.[54] This self-image is also confirmed by external observers and business partners. Thomas Nottebohm, one of Guatemala's leading coffee traders, said in an interview that it was always very pleasant to do business with the people from Volkart, and often much easier than with representatives from other firms. He always found the Volkart staff to be "Swiss honest" if perhaps a bit "Swiss dry." When he was negotiating with them, he said it was always a matter of "yes or no," the situation was always "quite clear" and agreements were always respected.[55]

Entering the Market in Central America through Collaborations with Local Coffee Companies

Shortly after the company decided to establish its own coffee organization, it began to diversify its operations in a geographical sense. In addition to exporting Brazilian coffee, Volkart soon also began to purchase locally grown coffee from traders in Colombia and shipped the beans to the US.[56] Likewise, Volkart began to purchase coffee in Mexico and, starting in the early 1960s, stationed staff members in African producing countries like Uganda and the Congo who purchased coffee there for Volkart in New York.[57] During the 1960s, Volkart stepped up its business transactions with export companies from Costa Rica and Guatemala. Central American coffee was highly prized, especially in Germany. German emigrants who had launched their own coffee trading businesses in Central America were able to maintain control of coffee exports by paying advances to growers, and they were able to do so because they received loans from import companies in Bremen and Hamburg.[58] As described in more detail later, Volkart managed to enter these new coffee markets by cooperating with Central American coffee companies that were run by German emigrants and by collaborating with a firm that was founded by a Swiss-German merchant. Working together with export companies that were run by German-speaking merchants offered a number of advantages for Volkart. Since the company had not yet acquired Spanish-speaking staff members, it had to rely on partners with whom it could communicate in German or English. Furthermore, Volkart was of the opinion that one could place more trust in European merchants than in their Latin American counterparts.[59] The common language and shared cultural background formed the cornerstone of trust that was so important in international trade. The enormous importance of such confidence in the eyes of the merchants of the day is reflected by a text published in 1950 by the heads of the Association of Coffee Traders in Bremen: "Purchasing products from a specific planting or district is a matter of trust. One should only do business with known, reliable shippers in the country of origin."[60]

One of Volkart's first Central American suppliers was Swiss merchant Hans Waelti's company in Guatemala.[61] In 1962, Volkart stationed two of its own staff members with Waelti to supervise the purchases in Guatemala.[62] Shortly thereafter, Volkart began to work closely in Costa Rica with Café Capris, a company that had been founded in the 1950s under the name of Capris to import European tools and hardware to Costa Rica. In the early 1960s, one of the Capris partners, a German merchant named Karl Schnell, soon found himself in the coffee export business after he sent a number of coffee samples to his business partner's uncle. This uncle was on the board of directors of German food retailer and producer EDEKA, which even today has one of the largest supermarket chains in the country. This is yet another indication of the ongoing importance of social and family ties in the global trade of goods and commodities, even during the second half of the twentieth century. Once it was clear that EDEKA was delighted with the samples, Schnell established Café Capris and began to export coffee to Western Europe and the US.[63] Volkart was one of the companies that marketed Café Capris in Europe. In 1967, Peter Reinhart traveled to Central America to find out whether it would be profitable for the company to operate its own *beneficios* (coffee processing plants) and establish its own purchasing organization. This would have been extremely risky, however, because business transactions in the region very often relied on the granting of loans. To make matters worse, the lack of local knowledge would have made it difficult for a foreign company to enforce contracts. Accordingly, Volkart decided to invest in the export companies with which it had already successfully collaborated. In 1967, Volkart acquired a minority interest of 35.3 percent in Peter Schoenfeld S.A., which had been exporting coffee from Guatemala since the early 1960s and was closely associated with Juan Waelti Sucs. S.A.[64] In 1969, Volkart purchased a 35.2 percent stake in Juan Waelti Sucs. S.A. and purchased 50 percent of the shares in Café Capris.[65]

This collaboration had advantages for both sides because it helped them to reduce information and transaction costs. Such cooperative efforts allowed Central American exporters to gain access to loans that they then used to pay advances to the *beneficios*. It was extremely difficult for export companies in Central America to acquire loans from European and American banks because they lacked large assets that could serve as security and foreign banks were too unfamiliar with local conditions to be able to effectively evaluate the creditworthiness of local exporters.[66] Financially well-connected trading companies like Volkart, on the other hand, could use these investments to more effectively monitor the quality of the coffee exports, which in turn helped them to establish their own types of products with consistent characteristics. Large *beneficios* had already been producing their own product types for decades. But since a multinational trading company like Volkart could establish brands like Pastores, Gloria, Coral, Jade Azul and Miralinda in the global coffee trade during the late 1960s—brands that were based on special blends of coffee from two or three plantations—these types suddenly attracted the attention of roasters in the industrialized countries.[67] By establishing its own blends of coffee, Volkart was able to stand out from other European competitors who at the time merely marketed their coffee according to their suppliers' descriptions of the taste and aroma.[68]

Coffee Quality and Social Inequality

Compared to the large crops that were grown in Brazil, Central America produced a relatively modest amount of coffee. Throughout the entire twentieth century, Costa Rica never managed to capture a market share of more than 1 or 2 percent of global coffee production,[69] despite the fact that the quality of Central American Arabica was extraordinarily high, in large part thanks to the way that the coffee cherries were processed. There are two common ways of handling the coffee cherries after harvest. The dry processing method involves drying the coffee cherries in the sun. Afterwards the fruit that surrounds the beans is removed with a press. The advantages of the dry method are that coffee cherries at different stages of ripeness can be processed—which demands less attention by pickers—and this type of processing only requires minimal investments in equipment. With the wet processing method the pulp hull is softened in fermentation tanks and completely removed during a washing stage. Afterwards, the coffee beans are dried in the sun or machine dried. The wet method allows for the production of much higher quality coffee, but is more capital intensive than the dry processing method. It also requires a greater degree of attention, as the cherries have to be brought to the processing plant one day after the harvest, and the soaking tanks must be meticulously monitored to prevent excessive fermentation, which would alter the taste of the coffee.[70]

The choice of processing method depended to a large extent on the market position and state of the infrastructure in a given country. Dry processing was the preferred method in Brazil because domestic coffee producers were primarily interested in achieving maximum volume while maintaining the lowest possible costs to safeguard the country's share of the global coffee market. In Guatemala most of the coffee was also processed using the dry method, but, in contrast to Brazil, this method was chosen because the transportation network was often inadequate and the coffee had to be carried by mule over long distances to reach the purchasing centers of the exporters. Since the coffee cherries were seven times heavier than the dried beans, it was easier for small farmers in Guatemala to prepare the coffee themselves using the dry processing method before they brought it to market. In Costa Rica, though, where road conditions were better and the coffee could be transported by truck to the processing plants, exporters decided to specialize in the production of high-quality Arabica coffee. This made Costa Rica the first Latin American country to build large plants for the wet processing of coffee.[71]

The processing plants in Costa Rica were either operated by the owners of large plantations or they belonged to companies that focused solely on running their *beneficios* and often collaborated with specific export companies. The fact that high quality was a characteristic of Costa Rican coffee had an impact on the relationship between the processors, who belonged to the national coffee elite, and the small coffee growers. The farmers usually delivered their coffee to the same processors. As competition increased among the *beneficios*, the processors sent their agents to the villages to buy the coffee directly from the small growers. Because the processors received loans from banks or certain exporters, it was possible for them to pay advances to the small growers to secure the delivery of particularly high-quality coffee fruits. The *beneficios* thus effectively became relay stations between foreign capital and local agriculture. The larger *beneficios* processed the coffee from hundreds, if not thousands of small plantations. The ties between farmers and processors were often remarkably stable and also had a noneconomic aspect, as they were referred to as *compadrazgos* (a symbolic kinship of sorts), which reflected both a sense of mutual commitment and the ever-present social hierarchy. Since this arrangement allowed the *beneficadores* to precisely monitor the quality of the incoming raw coffee, it gave them the option of selling their coffee under their own brand name. During the 1950s, there existed over 100 coffee plantation brands in Costa Rica that were recognized as a quality standard in the global coffee trade.[72]

The relationship between agricultural workers and members of the local coffee elite differed widely in the individual producing countries, and this largely had to do with the diverse production methods. In Costa Rica the independent family-owned companies were viewed as the foundation of the coffee economy and the basis for political stability in the country. Indeed, efforts were made to fairly distribute the proceeds from coffee exports among the population. In 1933, the Instituto de Defensa del Café was established (known as the Instituto del Café from 1948 onwards), a semi-public institution that regulated relations between coffee growers, processors and exporters. One of the most important laws introduced by the Instituto concerned the so-called *liquidaciones*, which called for the proceeds from the sale of coffee to be distributed according to an established formula, whereby exporters would receive 2.5 percent, the *beneficador* would get 9 percent and the rest would go to the growers. Because the price that was obtained on the global market was often not established until months after the coffee had been delivered to the processing plant, the money was paid in installments that were spread over a comparatively long period of time. This law was criticized in certain quarters because it gave the *beneficios* few opportunities to make a profit and made it more difficult to invest in new processing plants. To make matters worse, it complicated calculations for exporters, who did not know how much they had to pay for their coffee until the moment it was sold. Nevertheless, this state measure to protect small growers has remained in place until today.[73]

Such social policy measures to balance out inequalities were unique worldwide and largely responsible for the fact that during the second half of the twentieth century Costa Rica remained a stable democracy in comparison to the surrounding countries in the region and was spared the military coups and civil wars that have plagued Latin American politics.[74] In Brazil, for instance, where coffee quality was only of secondary importance, relations between large landowners and farm workers were extremely poor throughout the twentieth century. Tenants were often forced off coffee plantations because they had failed to pay their rent. Workers frequently went on strike to protest unpaid wages and harsh disciplinary measures by landowners. In a number of cases, plantation owners were even murdered by their farmhands. This induced the plantation owners to deploy armed guards to keep the small growers in check or prevent them from fleeing. These constant tensions were one of the main reasons that the vast majority of landowners supported the military coup of 1964. It was entirely in their interest that the military government launched a crackdown on trade unions and left-wing parties, which were calling on agricultural workers to resist their oppressors. Faced with a dearth of effective labor laws to protect workers, day laborers were not highly motivated during the 1970s and production quality suffered as a result.[75]

In Guatemala the military dictatorship introduced a vagrancy law in 1934 that forced poor Indians and Latinos to work in the coffee plantations for a fixed wage. This law was introduced largely at the behest of the Guatemalan coffee elite. After the Guatemalan Revolution in 1944, these forced labor laws were repealed, but relations between landowners and peasants remained poor. While trade unions were allowed in the cities, they were banned in the countryside in a bid to prevent the coffee sector from being adversely affected by labor disputes. After the government of Jacobo Árbenz Guzmán was deposed by a US-backed military coup in 1954, most of the labor laws in the cities were repealed. During the 1960s and 1970s, death squads murdered hundreds of trade unionists and political activists.[76]

There are no indications that Volkart had any connections to any of the military juntas in Latin America. In fact, it appears that the company made every effort to steer clear of domestic political unrest and instead focus on the export business and sales in the industrialized countries. This is not to say that the company did not harbor at least a general sympathy for the anti-communist and decidedly business-friendly military governments of Central and South America, as illustrated by the following statement from the annual report for the 1961–1962 fiscal year: "In South America, in Argentina and even in Peru, there have been unconstitutional but perhaps appropriate interventions by the military following elections with disappointing results."[77]

The production chains in the coffee sectors of Guatemala and Costa Rica had different structures in the mid-twentieth century that were the result of diverse economic policies and differences with regard to political stability, along with various states of development in their transportation networks. Although major coffee growers in both countries had their own processing plants, Costa Rica also had numerous *beneficios* that were operated by independent entrepreneurs, who in turn cooperated with export companies, whereas Guatemala had no independent processors. Instead, Guatemala's processing plants were often owned by export companies—something that did not exist in Costa Rica until the 1980s. This difference was largely because Costa Rica was more politically stable and payment practices were far more reliable than in Guatemala, which made it possible for Costa Rican export companies to conclude contractual agreements with *beneficadores* and pay them advances. In Guatemala such transactions would have been too risky.[78]

Despite these differences, an ever-growing number of links in the commodity chains in Guatemala and Costa Rica fell under the control of multinational companies. This backward integration was closely connected to the intense competition between local export companies and financially powerful foreign companies, which gained importance as exports from Central America continued to rise.[79] During the 1970s, Costa Rican exporters, who were by then often backed by foreign companies, started to invest more and more in *beneficios* with the aim of generating added value and improving the quality of their purchases. In the late 1980s, for instance, Volkart subsidiary Café Capris entered into a cooperation with the Montealegre family, which belonged to the Costa Rican coffee elite and ranked among the country's leading *beneficadores*. The capital requirements of the processors grew during the 1960s because the sorting of the beans was increasingly done by machine, thereby forcing many smaller *beneficios* out of business. When it came to sudden price fluctuations, though, local exporters faced a shortage of liquidity that could only be resolved with an extra injection of capital from foreign partners. Up until the 1980s, this meant that most Central American export companies and processing plants came under the control of multinational coffee trading companies. During this period, Volkart acquired a majority share of Café Capris in Costa Rica along with Juan Waelti S.A. and Peter Schoenfeld S.A. in Guatemala, and, for all intents and purposes, controlled the *beneficios* of the Montealegre family. In the early 1990s, Volcafé—the successor company to the Volkart coffee division that was sold off in 1989—went on to acquire the remaining shares in these companies.[80] As a result of this development, by the late 1990s roughly 65 percent of all exports from Costa Rica were controlled by just four companies, the most important of which was Café Capris, which was responsible for approximately one-quarter of all coffee exports from the country.[81]

The International Coffee Agreement

The global coffee trade after 1945 was influenced not only by the financial power of multinational companies, but also by the political decisions of national governments.[82] Since the early twentieth century, the coffee producing countries in Latin America had repeatedly tried in vain to limit cultivation and introduce export quotas. After the Cuban Revolution in 1959, there was a growing fear in the US that more governments in Latin America would be toppled by communist uprisings. For geostrategic reasons, it suddenly became important to ensure that Latin American coffee growers had a stable income. In 1962, this led to the conclusion of the International Coffee Agreement, which stipulated that growing countries adhere to export quotas that were to be respected by the importing countries and monitored by the International Coffee Organization (ICO) in London. This made the coffee trade one of the few sectors in the international exchange of goods that could be effectively regulated over an extensive period of time based on a political agreement. Within the ICO, the producing countries were allocated a block of 1,000 votes, with an equal number of votes going to the coffee consuming countries, although the US and Brazil, as the largest consuming and producing countries respectively, each had 400 votes. Since all agreements had to be approved with a two-thirds majority, these two countries essentially had a veto right.

The free global coffee market was thus replaced by a cartel agreement that was essentially initiated by the producing countries. An important intermediary role here was played by the national coffee agencies like the Instituto Brasileiro do Café and the Colombian Federación Nacional de Cafeteros. They collected a certain percentage of the sales price of the exports and used this to finance research and technical innovations in the cultivation of coffee. They also granted cheap loans to growers and softened the impact of price fluctuations by increasing payments to growers when global market prices declined.[83] The large coffee companies in the industrialized countries initially stood behind this agreement. Coffee roasters in particular were afraid of price fluctuations and political and economic crises in the producing countries because this generally led to supply difficulties. Since the agreement engendered greater price stability, it became less important to safeguard transactions with futures. As a result, the coffee futures market in New York was temporarily closed in the late 1960s.

The agreement, which was renewed in 1968, 1976 and 1983, had a number of weak points. First, it made no provisions for sanctions to prevent overproduction in individual countries. Consequently, signatory growing countries often produced more coffee than was specified by their export quotas and attempted to exert pressure on the ICO to receive larger quotas. Second, the agreement tacitly accepted that the key players in the chain of the global coffee trade were national governments. It thus gave short shrift to the role of multinational companies, which were often difficult to control through policies and regulations. Third, the agreement did not include all consumer countries. Whereas in 1962 the vast majority (94 percent) of the world's coffee was still consumed in countries that signed the agreement, by the late 1980s this proportion had dropped to 80 percent. For example, many Asian countries—in which the consumption of coffee was steadily increasing—and various East Bloc states were not among the signatory countries. This allowed producing countries to sell part of their harvest to non-member countries, where higher prices were often paid than in countries that had signed the agreement. To make matters worse, multinational companies had the option of bypassing the quotas by importing to Asia or Eastern Europe and subsequently re-exporting the coffee consignments to Western Europe or the US with forged documents as so-called "tourist coffee." Although tourist coffee never amounted to more than 3.5 percent of all coffee shipments, it undermined the agreement—and above all demonstrated the sheer economic power of multinational companies.[84]

Multinational Companies Circumvent Government Controls

Volkart also reacted very positively to the introduction of export quotas in the early 1960s. It was hoped that the agreement would stabilize prices and coffee production could be adjusted to meet global demand.[85] But Volkart soon began to take advantage of the loopholes in the agreement. During the 1965–1966 season, Volkart first started trading so-called "tourist coffee." In an internal company annual report, though, it was explicitly stated that the competition had begun much earlier, and far more blatantly, to conduct transactions in this area.[86] One year later, the successful development of the coffee sector was commented on with the following words:

> Tourist coffee has been crucial to this success, in other words, the discovery and exploitation of loopholes in the system. Nevertheless, it is important not to be too brazen in overstepping the limits of what is legitimate. After some initial misgivings, Dept. 10 has successfully played this game this year.[87]

Such transactions were not entirely without risk. In 1968, a deal was exposed in which Volkart had imported at least 1,600 tons of coffee using forged Swiss import certificates.[88] Based on the available source material, it can no longer be determined whether this led to a change in strategy or whether the company continued to pursue such practices in the 1970s and 1980s.

Such escapades in the export of tourist coffee were not the only example of how Volkart used its global company structure to evade the political control of state governments and international associations. Another means of optimizing profits was to hide revenues from tax authorities. Already back in the days of its collaboration with Prado Chaves, both companies had successfully avoided sales tax by conducting the coffee exports of the Brazilian company on behalf of Volkart.[89] Likewise, during the postwar years profits from countries like India, Pakistan, Ceylon and Brazil were transferred to Switzerland by artificially maintaining low sales prices at the relevant subsidiaries, whereby all profits went to Winterthur. Company officials were completely aware that in doing so they were contravening the tax laws of the respective export countries.[90] Such illegal activities always entailed the risk that, in the event of a conflict, individual employees could denounce the company to the authorities. This happened, for example, in 1965 after Volkart sued the CFO of the Mexican subsidiary Volkart Hermanos for misappropriating funds to the tune of 133,000 dollars. The defendant went into hiding, but not before he fired off a parting salvo by leaking sensitive information to the Mexican tax authorities: "We don't have a completely clear conscience," as was later admitted in a meeting of the board of directors. It was noted, however, that the misdeed concerned here was not tax evasion in the narrower sense of the term, but the in-company accounting system had admittedly "recorded the transactions . . . such that Mexico actually did earn too little" (Mexico refers here to the Mexican subsidiary of Volkart).[91]

The opportunities to engage in tax evasion were enhanced when two multinational companies joined forces. In 1971, Volkart in Brazil made a proposal to Nestlé, whereby Volkart would sell Nestlé 100,000 bags of coffee at slightly overinflated prices. The purchase of the coffee was to be financed through an interest-free loan by Nestlé to Volkart Irmãos. Part of the resulting profit was later to be transferred by Volkart to Nestlé in Switzerland. This deal would have given both companies a profit amounting to several hundred thousand Swiss francs—Volkart because it would have paid no bank interest for the financing of the purchases and would have received a higher price for the sale of the coffee; Nestlé because the transfer of funds to Switzerland would have allowed it to disclose a smaller profit in Brazil and thus pay less tax.[92] The transaction never materialized because Nestlé was afraid that the Brazilian authorities would notice that Volkart's prices were higher than those of the competition. Furthermore, granting an interest-free loan to other companies was in violation of Brazilian financial law.[93] This example illustrates the opportunities that two multinational companies like Volkart and Nestlé—whose collaboration was facilitated by the fact that Peter Reinhart was a member of the supervisory board of Nestlé from 1963 onwards—[94] had at their disposal to circumvent a country's tax authority.

The market power of companies like Nestlé and Volkart also had a tangible influence on the development of an independent coffee industry in the producing countries. In 1967, the head of the coffee division of Volkart New York, Hans Bühler, confidentially informed Nestlé that the Brazilian coffee company Dominium had asked Volkart if it would sell its instant coffee in the US.[95] Nestlé was less than thrilled with the idea that Volkart would help a Brazilian company to compete with its own instant coffee, Nescafé, in the US. Bühler was informed "that we would consider it an unfriendly act were [Volkart] to give the proposal by Dominium serious consideration." After receiving this thinly veiled threat, Volkart turned down the offer to represent Dominium, a decision that was no doubt influenced by Peter Reinhart's involvement with the Nestlé supervisory board and the fact that Nestlé purchased roughly one-third of its coffee from Volkart during the second half of the 1960s.[96]

The roasters in the northern hemisphere put pressure not only on trading companies to stave off competition from Brazil, but also exerted influence on the US government. When the International Coffee Agreement was renegotiated in 1968, the US delegation pushed through its demand that Brazil scrap its government support for domestic producers of instant coffee—regardless of the fact that, at the very same time, the US was subsidizing exports of American commodities like wheat.[97] Although growing countries were able to gain considerable influence over the trade in coffee beans, the global economic balance of power still put them at a clear disadvantage in the area of coffee processing. This observation perfectly supports the tenet of dependency theory that wealthy northern core countries strove to integrate the southern periphery of poor countries into the global capitalist system solely as producers of commodities, and thus forestalled their industrial development.[98]

The End of the Export Quotas and the Return to a Free Market

All of these interventions show that multinational companies like Volkart were able to exert considerable influence on the production chains in the coffee sector during the postwar era. They used this power to their advantage during the 1980s to push for a repeal of the International Coffee Agreement. A number of incidents, most notably the severe frost in Brazil in 1975, made it abundantly clear that the production quotas had fallen short of achieving their main goals, which were to limit cultivation and maintain price stability. Furthermore, the coffee agreement generated a tangle of nerve-racking red tape, as trading companies had to have scores of documents filled out and stamped, and were required to submit export permit applications to often extraordinarily slow-working agencies in the growing countries and send copies of import certificates to London, where they were checked by the ICO.[99] To make matters worse, companies like Volkart, which were relative newcomers to the market, were refused export permits in many producing countries. Paul Moeller, who headed the Volkart coffee division from 1985, served as one of Switzerland's two representatives at the ICO in London—the other being a member of the Swiss embassy staff—and used his influence to combat the coffee agreement. According to Moeller, he would exert pressure both on the government in Bern and on the European continental group of the ICO in London. He thus took a stance that differed markedly from the position adopted by Emil Sulger, who headed the Volkart coffee division in the early 1960s and, as a representative of Swiss coffee traders, had campaigned together with the Swiss government in favor of the coffee agreement.[100] Within the ICO, Volkart enjoyed additional influence by repeatedly sending partners and CEOs of its Central American subsidiaries to London as delegates of their respective countries.[101]

Ultimately, however, it was less the activities of multinational companies than the decisions of national governments that led to the end of the export quotas. During the 1980s, the agreement lost ground because the united front of the producing countries progressively began to crumble. The main problem was that not all signatories benefited equally from the accord. According to a study by the World Bank, the quotas primarily gave an advantage to large coffee-producing countries like Brazil and Colombia, along with diverse African nations. The losers were growers of high-quality Arabica coffee like Mexico, Costa Rica, Guatemala, Honduras, Nicaragua, Ecuador, Peru, India and Papua New Guinea. In the eyes of the World Bank, these countries could have sold larger quantities in a free market. Another important factor was that during the 1980s the US was voicing mounting criticism of the regulation of the global coffee market. As the largest consumer country that was party to the agreement, Washington carried considerable weight, especially now that the Reagan administration was resolutely pursuing a neoliberal course and pushing for a return to a free market. Since the Cold War was drawing to a close, the US no longer saw any geostrategic arguments in favor of sticking with the coffee agreement. The combined opposition of various interest groups eventually brought down the agreement in 1989.

The end of the agreement primarily caused national coffee agencies to lose influence. Many coffee growers initially welcomed this because the coffee agencies were often corrupt and withheld money from the growers that was their rightful share from the coffee exports, or only transferred the funds after lengthy delays. Weakening these state institutions increased the options available to multinational companies in the producing countries. They could now conclude direct business transactions with growers and often drove a hard bargain. Largely as a consequence of this development, the share of the sales price that was meted out to the coffee growers increasingly began to fluctuate—and generally declined. Whereas more than 20 percent of the sales price went to coffee growers during the mid-1980s, this share dropped to 4 percent in the early 1990s, then rose again to nearly 19 percent in 1997–1998, and was somewhat greater than 10 percent at the turn of the millennium.[102]

A Process of Consolidation during the 1970s and 1980s

But it was more than just the end of the quota system that brought about sweeping changes to the global coffee market. Indeed, an increasingly pronounced consolidation process, both among roasters and trading companies, was reshaping the sector.[103] This development began among coffee roasters already in the early twentieth century. The invention of vacuum packaging made it possible for coffee to be stored for a longer period of time without losing flavor. Already by 1935, over 90 percent of the coffee sold in the US was roasted and sold in airtight packaging. Since the industrialization of the roasting process made it possible to achieve economies of scale, this sparked fierce competition that forced many players out of the market. In 1950, the five largest companies in the US roasted more than half of all coffee and had 78 percent of all warehouse inventories. Moreover, the roasters pursued a vertical integration strategy and began to purchase in the producing countries and, in some cases, even started to operate their own coffee plantations.[104]

Competition among the roasters intensified once again during the 1980s, leaving by the end of the decade only four companies—Nestlé, Philip Morris, Sara Lee and Procter & Gamble—that sold over 60 percent of the world's coffee.[105] These companies also changed their purchasing policies during the late 1970s and tended to close their in-house procurement organizations and increasingly outsource their coffee imports to trading companies.[106] They concentrated their production in new roasting plants that were located in the vicinity of large ports of entry and often could process up to 50,000 bags of coffee per month. This change in orientation fueled a rapid increase in the volume of transactions. As late as the 1930s, contracts were regularly concluded for deliveries of as little as 250 bags of coffee. During the 1980s, deliveries of this size were relatively small orders and, with the fundamental breakthrough of containerization,[107] this was often the minimum quantity that large roasting plants would consider ordering. Anything less than that was simply not worth their while. To produce their coffee brands, major roasting plants required coffee shipments of consistent quality. Hence, it was more efficient for them to order large volumes in a standardized quality than it was to process smaller quantities of coffee from diverse suppliers. The roasters thus delegated the responsibility of ensuring the quality of the coffee to the trading companies, which was a task that the roasting plants had previously handled on their own. This transition was only possible because the trading companies, as described earlier, had begun to develop their own standardized types of coffee during the 1960s, and because the establishment of effective procurement organizations could guarantee consistent quality for all shipments. This eventually led to cut-throat competition in the import and export sector. Starting in the 1950s, many long-standing coffee importers in port cities like Hamburg, Bremen, London, Amsterdam, Marseille, Trieste, New York and San Francisco were forced out of business by multinational trading companies.

Volkart was able to establish itself during this period as one of the world's leading coffee trading companies. Between 1965–1966 and 1969–1970, the company boosted its annual sales of coffee from 2.1 million to 4.3 million bags. This meant that the trade in coffee—both in terms of profits and sales volume—had become more important than the trade in cotton, which had constituted the undisputed core business of the company until the 1960s.[108] Volkart had specialized in Brazilian and wet-processed Arabica coffee, which represented 80 percent of the company's coffee transactions. The less coveted, lower quality Robusta coffee, which was primarily consumed in France, only made up 20 percent of the company's sales.[109] During the second half of the 1960s, Brazilian coffee represented half of the company's turnover in coffee. In 1968–1969 and 1969–1970, Volkart annually exported 2 million bags of coffee from Brazil. This export volume declined over the following years to an annual average of just 620,000 bags in 1970–1971 and 1974–1975, with even fewer in 1975–1976 (Table 13.1). Based on the source material, it is no longer possible to determine the reason for this development. As a result of this decline, in 1973 Volkart sold off its coffee processing plants in Brazil, which, in contrast to the facilities in Central America, had never played a key role in the development of the company's coffee business.[110]

Table 13.1 Origin of the coffee traded by Volkart during the 1975–1976 season

Colombia	607,000 bags
Brazil	432,000 bags
other South American countries (Peru, Ecuador, Venezuela)	96,000 bags
Central America (Guatemala, El Salvador Costa Rica, Nicaragua, Honduras)	790,000 bags
Angola	311,000 bags
other African countries (including Kenya, East Africa, the Congo, Cameroon, Ivory Coast, Togo)	536,000 bags
India	68,000 bags
Indonesia	136,000 bags
Papua New Guinea	10,000 bags
diverse other countries	90,000 bags
	3,471,000 bags

(Source: Anderegg, Chronicle, 1976, 660)

During the late 1970s and early 1980s, Volkart invested in coffee export companies in Papua New Guinea, Kenya and Honduras, and in 1983 was able to enter into a joint venture with a local partner to establish Carcafé S.A. in Cartago, Colombia, the world's second-most important producing country after Brazil.[111] In 1975, Volkart also entered the cocoa trade, which was a relatively easy transition because it had a great deal in common with the coffee trade.[112] Up until the mid-1980s, Volkart achieved a global market share of 8 percent in the sector.[113] Nevertheless, the cocoa business was never lucrative for the company because Volkart was unable to establish its own procurement organizations with their own processing plants in the producing countries. Consequently, after only ten years in the business, Volkart left the cocoa trade in 1985.[114]

By the mid-1980s, the global coffee trade was dominated by just seven companies that conducted roughly 40 percent of all sales to the world's roasters. Volkart was the second-most important company in this sector and achieved sales of 5.5 million bags in 1986–1987, which corresponded to a market share of 8 percent. The market leader was Hamburg-based company Rothfos with sales of 7 million bags. Third to fifth places were held by US company Cargill with sales of 4.5 million bags and British firms Rayner and ED&F Man, which each sold 3.5 million bags.[115] One year later, in 1988, Volkart sold 6.5 million bags of coffee worth 1.7 billion Swiss francs.[116] This reflected the massive expansion course that Volkart embarked upon, most notably after Andreas Reinhart took the helm of the company in 1985. After the price of coffee had doubled between November 1985 and January 1986 due to a drought in Brazil, Volkart suffered heavy losses, just like the other trading companies in the business.[117] Since a bitter rivalry raged between the diverse trading companies, to maintain their market share and ease the pressure on prices they generally attempted to squeeze coffee growers and processors. For instance, in the late 1980s Volkart was accused of hiring female employees for only 59 days. The aim here was ostensibly to prevent these women, who sorted coffee beans in the company's Colombian processing plants, from acquiring the status of full-time employees, which would have given them certain rights. It was only after a minimum of 60 days that workers were considered full-time salaried employees under Colombian law.[118]

The market remained highly volatile, making it extremely difficult for companies to stay in the black. A sharp decline in prices in 1986–1987 and the stock market crash of 1987 further exacerbated the situation for intermediaries. In 1988, the German company Rothfos—the world's largest coffee importer—had to withdraw from the market and sold the business to the German Neumann Group.[119] Shortly thereafter, Volkart also pulled out of the coffee business. In the spring of 1989, the company sold its coffee division to the Erb Group, an investment firm based in Winterthur.[120] The former Volkart coffee division further expanded under the name Volcafé and bought up all of the minority stakes in the diverse subsidiaries that still had outside partners. After the Erb Group went bankrupt,[121] Volcafé was sold to British trading company ED&F Man in 2004. The company continued to develop very positively and was the sales leader in the global coffee trade at the beginning of the twenty-first century.[122]

Notes

1 Berghoff, *Moderne Unternehmensgeschichte*, 2004, 140.
2 Roach, "A Primer on Multinational Corporations", 2005, 28–30; Jones, "Multinationals from the 1930s to the 1980s," 2005, 96–99.
3 Gerencia Comercial, La Industria Cafetera Internacional, 1988, 25; Revista de Comércio de Café, Año 66, Julio 1987, 26–27.
4 Topik/Clarence-Smith, "Introduction," 2003, 3.
5 Rambousek/Vogt/Volkart, "Volkart", 1990, 161.
6 Kindleberger, *The World in Depression*, 1973, 90; Stolcke, *Coffee Planters, Workers and Wives*, 1988, 54–59.
7 VA, Dossier 16: USA, Brazil, Mexico, Guatemala/Costa Rica, Turkey, III. Brazil: Volkart Irmãos Ltda., São Paolo & Santos, 1. P.R. Note of 28 September 1950.
8 Rambousek/Vogt/Volkart, *Volkart*, 1990, S. 161.
9 VA, Dossier 16: USA, Brazil, Mexico, Guatemala/Costa Rica, Turkey, III. Brazil: Volkart Irmãos Ltda., São Paolo & Santos, 1. P.R. Note of 28 September 1950.
10 Hauser/Fehr, *Die Familie Reinhart*, 1922, 189ff.
11 Ukers, *A Trip to Brazil*, 1935, 34; Greenhill, *E. Johnston*, 1992, 184; www.pradochaves.com.br/v2/ingles/marca.htm (2 November 2009).
12 Wright/Gerdes/Bennett, *The Packaging of American Cotton*, 1945, 14.
13 VA, Dossier 16: USA, Brazil, Mexico, Guatemala/Costa Rica, Turkey, III. Brazil: Volkart Irmãos Ltda., São Paolo & Santos, 1. P.R. Note of 28.9.1950; Anderegg, *Chronicle*, 1976, 485.
14 Anderegg, *Chronicle*, 1976, 568; Rambousek/Vogt/Volkart, *Volkart*, 1990, 162.
15 Anderegg, *Chronicle*, 1976, 485–486.
16 VA, Konferenz-Protokolle vom 5. Januar 1945–1927. Juni 1947: PR, Trip to Brazil 13 September to 5 October 1946, 27 November 1946.
17 VA, Dossier 16: USA, Brazil, Mexico, Guatemala/Costa Rica, Turkey, III. Brazil: Volkart Irmãos Ltda., São Paolo & Santos, 1. P.R. Note of 28 September 1950.

18 VA, Konferenz-Protokolle 6. März 1943–1931. Dezember 1944: Konferenz vom 22. April 1944.

19 VA, Konferenz-Protokolle vom 5. August 1941–1944. März 1943: Wachter, Exposée für die Konferenz, 3 February 1943.

20 VA, Konferenz-Protokolle vom 5. Januar 1945–1927. Juni 1947: PR, Trip to Brazil 13 September to 5 October 1946, 27 November 1946.

21 VA, Dossier 16: USA, Brazil, Mexico, Guatemala/Costa Rica, Turkey, III. Brazil: Volkart Irmãos Ltda., Sao Paolo & Santos, 1. P.R. Note of 28 September 1950; Anderegg, *Chronicle*, 1976, 571–572.

22 Killick, "Specialized and General Trading Firms," 1987, 259–260.

23 VA, Konferenz-Protokolle vom 5. Januar 1945–1927. Juni 1947, PR, Trip to Brazil 13 September to 5 October 1946, 27 November 1946.

24 VA, Konferenz-Protokolle vom 1. Juli 1949–1919. Dezember 1952: Konferenz vom 3. März 1951; Dossier 16: USA, Brazil, Mexico, Guatemala/Costa Rica, Turkey, III. Brazil: Volkart Irmãos Ltda., São Paulo & Santos, 2. Addl. Information; Anderegg, *Chronicle*, 1976, 573.

25 Ukers, *All About Coffee*, 1935, 153ff. and 323–327; Greenhill, *British Export Houses*, [approx. 1972], 1–18; Nienstedt, *Kaffee-Erzeugung und—Handel*, 1950, 16–17; Ziegler Witschi, *Schweizer statt Sklaven*, 1985; Greenhill, "E. Johnston," 1992, 133, 179–184 and 201; Bates, *Open-Economy Politics*, 1997, 27; Topik, "The Integration of the World Coffee Market," 2003, 32–33; Pereira de Melo, "Coffee and Development," 2003, 366–373; Topik/Samper, "The Latin America Coffee Commodity Chain," 2006, 122–129.

26 Rossfeld (ed.), *Genuss und Nüchternheit*, 2002; Clarence-Smith, "The Global Consumption of Hot Beverages," 2008.

27 Burns, *A History of Brazil*, 1980, 300–311, 352, 401; Lucier, *The International Political Economy of Coffee*, 1988, 118; Talbot, *Grounds for Agreement*, 2004, 47–55.

28 These bags had a standard weight of 60 kilos.

29 VA, Konferenz-Protokolle vom 1. Juli 1949–1919. Dezember 1952: Konferenz vom 3. März 1951; Dossier 16: USA, Brazil, Mexico, Guatemala/Costa Rica, Turkey, III. Brazil: Volkart Irmãos Ltda., São Paulo & Santos, 2. Addl. Information; Anderegg, *Chronicle*, 1976, 573.

30 VA, Konferenz-Protokolle vom 16. Januar 1953–1956. Januar 1959: Konferenzen vom 13. Januar 1954 und vom 7. September 1954; Anderegg, *Chronicle*, 1976, 589.

31 VA, Bilanzen, Bilanz 1957/58; Konferenz-Protokolle vom 16. Januar 1953–1956. Januar 1959: Konferenz vom 7. Januar 1958 und vom 9. April 1958; Konferenz-Protokolle vom 15. Januar 1959–1930. März 1965: JH, Zu Protokoll, 29 June 1960.

32 UCL, Edward Johnston and Co. archives, GB 0103 Johnston, Letter Book: Edward Greene, Santos, to Reginald E. Johnston, London, 15 October 1900.

33 Greenhill. "E. Johnston", 1992, 244.

34 Anderson, Clayton, *Brazilian Coffee*, [1957], 17–18.

35 VA, Bilanzen, Bilanz 1959–1960.

36 VA, Bilanzen, Bilanz 1961/62; Konferenz-Protokolle vom 15. Januar 1959–1930. März 1965: Konferenz vom 27. Juni 1961.

37 VA, Bilanzen, Bilanz 1959–1960 und 1960–1961.

38 VA, Bilanzen, Bilanz 1961–1962.

39 See Chapters 8, 10 and 14.

40 See Chapter 12.

41 Ralli Brothers Limited, 1951, S. 13; VA, Konferenz-Protokolle vom 5. Januar 1945–1927. Juni 1947: PR, Trip to Brazil 13 September to 5 October 1946, 27 November 1946.

42 VA, Konferenz-Protokolle vom 16. Januar 1953–1956. Januar 1959: Konferenz vom 8. November 1954.

43 VA, Konferenz-Protokolle vom 5. Januar 1945–1927. Juni 1947: PR, Trip to Brazil 13 September to 5 October 1946, 27 November 1946.
44 VA, Konferenz-Protokolle vom 15. Januar 1959–1930. März 1965: Konferenz vom 18. November 1960.
45 Marshall, *The World Coffee Trade*, 1983, 143; Talbot, *Grounds for Agreement*, 2004, 65 and 110.
46 VA, Konferenz-Protokolle vom 16. Januar 1953–1956. Januar 1959: Konferenz vom 8. November 1954.
47 The following explanation of operations on the coffee exchange is based on: Ukers, All About Coffee, 1935, 357–364 and 448–450; Marshall, *The World Coffee Trade*, 1983, 144ff.; Topik, "The Integration of the World Coffee Market," 2003, 40–41.
48 Greenhill, *British Export Houses*, [approx. 1972], 27.
49 Interview with Thomas Nottebohm, 2008.
50 *Revista do Comércio de Café*, Vol. 59, No. 645, Março 1979, 20–21.
51 Ukers, *All About Coffee*, 364.
52 Ukers, *All About Coffee*, 1935, 362.
53 See Chapters 3 and 5.
54 Interview with Peter Zurschmiede, 2008. Zurschmiede made similar comments at an international coffee symposium in Santos in 1977: ICO, SG.12: Peter Zurschmiede. World Coffee Situation Now—and an Outlook for the Next Three Years. Lecture given at the Santos Coffee Seminar on 1 June 1977 in Guarujà; see also ICO, RG.12: Peter Zurschmiede. The world coffee situation as seen by an international trader. Presentation given at the International Coffee Symposium at Monte Carlo, October 1979.
55 Interview with Thomas Nottebohm, 2008.
56 For many years, foreign trading companies could not legally invest in coffee farms in Colombia, the worldwide second-largest coffee producer after Brazil; it was not until the 1980s that Volkart was able to buy a stake in a Colombian export company (interview with Peter Zurschmiede, 2008).
57 VA, Konferenz-Protokolle vom 15. Januar 1959–1930. März 1965: Zu Protokoll, 10. Januar 1962; Konferenz-Protokolle vom 15. Januar 1959–1930. März 1965: Zu Protokoll, 10 January 1962.
58 Wünderich, "Die Kolonialware Kaffee," 1994; Wagner, *The History of Coffee in Guatemala*, 2001; Fleer, "La oligarquía cafetalera," 2001, 122–123; Topik, "The Integration of the World Coffee Market," 2003, 43; Rischbieter, "Globalisierungsprozesse vor Ort," 2007.
59 Interview with Paul Moeller, 2007.
60 Verein der am Kaffeehandel beteiligten Firmen, Kaffee. Handel—Pflanzung—Wirtschaftspolitische Bedeutung—Geschichte, 1950, 25.
61 Interview with Paul Moeller, 2007.
62 VA, Bilanzen, Bilanz 1962/63; Konferenz-Protokolle vom 15. Januar 1959–1930. März 1965: Konferenz vom 21. Februar 1964.
63 ANCR: Fondo Northern Railway Co., 001000 (1952); Interview with Jörg von Saalfeld, 2008.
64 Kaffee-Büro, *Fincas Productoras y Exportadores*, 1962.
65 Interviews with Paul Brose, Jürgen Plate, Jörg von Saalfeld and Peter Schoenfeld, June 2008; Anderegg, *Chronicle*, 1976, 719ff.
66 Interview with Paul Moeller, 2007.
67 Peters Solórzano, Formación y Desarollo del Grupo Cafetalera, 1984, 167; Interviews with William Hempstead, Ronald Peters, Thomas Nottebohm and Jörg von Saalfeld, 2008.
68 Interview with Paul Moeller, 2007.
69 Topik/Samper, "The Latin America Coffee Commodity Chain," 2006, 122.
70 Ukers, *All About Coffee*, 1935, 141–147.

71 Ukers, *All About Coffee*, 1935, 143, 173 and 202; Sanders, *A Report on a Visit*, [1954], 1.
72 *Tea and Coffee Trade Journal*, 1957, Vol. 57, Nr. 8, 16 and 54; Herrero Serrano, *Algunas Factores de la Industria Cafetalera*, 1960; Peters Solórzano, *Empresias e Historia del Café*, 1989; Esquivel Prestinary/Van der Laat, *El Papel del Estado*, 1994; Paige, *Coffee and Power*, 1997, 237–238; Topik/Samper, "The Latin America Coffee Commodity Chain," 2006, 130–131.
73 *Tea and Coffee Trade Journal*, 1957, Vol. 57, Nr. 8, 16, 54–57; Paige, *Coffee and Power*, 1997, 65, 77, 223, 234ff.; interviews with Otto Kloeti and Ronald Peters, 2008.
74 Williams, *States and Social Evolution*, 1994; Grandin, *The Last Colonial Massacre*, 2004.
75 Stolcke, *Coffee Planters, Workers and Wives*, 1988.
76 Roseberry, "Introduction," 1995, 19; McCreery, "Coffee and Indigenous Labor in Guatemala," 2003.
77 VA, Bilanzen, Bilanz 1961–1962.
78 Sanders, A Report on a Visit, [1954], 6 and 15; Roseberry, Introduction, 1995, 22; interviews with Jürgen Plate and Jörg von Saalfeld, 2008.
79 Krug/De Poerck, *World Coffee Survey*, 1968, 226; ANACAFE, Exportación Realizada del Café, 1960–1990.
80 Paige, *Coffee and Power*, 1997, 114 and 265ff.; interview with Paul Moeller, 2007; interview with Jörg von Saalfeld, 2008.
81 ICAFE, Exportaciones por Cosecha y Exportador, 1997/98; Chaves Murillo, *Competitividad Internacional*, 2001, 64–65. In 2000–2001, Café Capris even achieved a share of more than 41 percent of all coffee exports from Costa Rica: Campos López/Jiménez Jiménez/Sancho Quesada/Velásquez Quesada, *Propuesta para el Manejo Electrónico*, 2001, 43.
82 Unless noted otherwise, the following descriptions of the coffee agreement are based on Marshall, *The World Coffee Trade*, 1983, 106–121 and 170–171; Bates, *Open-Economy Politics*, 1997; Talbot, *Grounds for Agreement*, 2004, 55–63 and 108.
83 Topik/Samper, "The Latin America Coffee Commodity Chain," 2006, 120.
84 Marshall, *The World Coffee Trade*, 1983, 122–133; Talbot, *Grounds for Agreement*, 2004, 65–80.
85 VA, Bilanzen, Bilanz 1959–1960.
86 VA, Bilanzen, Bilanz 1965–1966.
87 VA, Bilanzen, Bilanz 1966–1967.
88 BAR, E 7110, Akz. 1979/14, Behältnis 35, Lu 730: Telefonnotiz, Bern, 2. Dezember 1968.
89 VA, Konferenz-Protokolle vom 5. Januar 1945–1927. Juni 1947: PR, Trip to Brazil 13 September to 5 October 1946, 27 November 1946.
90 VA, Konferenz-Protokolle vom 15. Januar 1959–1930. März 1965: PR, Office note vom 22. Februar 1965.
91 VA, Bilanzen, Bilanz 1965–1966.
92 HAN, 400–486: Brésil—Matières premières (1970–1979): A. Fürer to O. Ballarin, Cia. Industrial e Comercial Brasileira de Produtos Alimentares, São Paulo, 11 January 1971; Proposal for discussion with Nestlé, Winterthur, 27 January 1971.
93 HAN, 400–486: Brésil—Matières premières (1970–1979): Confidential Note, Mr. A. Fürer, Financial and Accounting Control, 3 February 71; Arthur Fürer, Generaldirektor Nestlé Alimenta AG, Vevey to Peter Reinhart, Gebr. Volkart AG, Winterthur, 25 February 1971.
94 HAN, 10002: Nomination de Mr. Peter Reinhart (Volkart) au Conseil d'Administration de Nestal: Peter Reinhart, Winterthur, to Max Petitpierre, Président du Conseil d'Administration, Nestlé Alimenta S.A., 26 March 1963; Peter Reinhart, Winterthur, to J. C. Corthésy, Nestlé alimenta, Vevey, 8 July 1964.

95 HAN, 1100–1176: J. J. Scheu, Nestlé (no place), to Afico SA, Purchasing Department, Lausanne, 18 January 1967.

96 HAN, 1100–1176: The Nestlé Company, Inc., White Plains, NY, to J. C. Corthésy, Nestlé Alimenta S.A., Vevey, 20 January 1967.

97 Talbot, *Grounds for Agreement*, 2004, 62.

98 For more on dependency theory, see Frank, *Kapitalismus und Unterentwicklung*, 1975; Cardoso/Faletto, *Abhängigkeit und Entwicklung*, 1984; Bernecker/Fischer, "Entwicklung und Scheitern," 1995.

99 Marshall, *The World Coffee Trade*, 1983, 170.

100 Künzi, ". . . womit die Schweiz," 1993, 310; interview with Paul Moeller, 2007.

101 La Nacion (San José), 25 de julio 1972.

102 Paige, *Coffee and Power*, 1997, 259ff.; Talbot, *Grounds for Agreement*, 2004, 80–97, 108–109 and 166ff.

103 Roseberry, "Introduction," 1995, 10.

104 Topik, "The Integration of the World Coffee Market," 2003, 42–46.

105 Talbot, *Grounds for Agreement*, 2004, 103–104.

106 Unless noted otherwise, the following remarks are based on Marshall, *The World Coffee Trade*, 1983, 20–22; Talbot, *Grounds for Agreement*, 2004, 105; Interview with Ernst H. Schaefer, 2008.

107 *Kaffee- und Tee-Markt*, Vol. 34, 1984, Nr. 2, 17–19.

108 Anderegg, *Chronicle*, 1976, 659.

109 Rambousek/Vogt/Volkart, *Volkart*, 1990, 166; interview with Peter Zurschmiede, 2008.

110 Anderegg, *Chronicle*, 1976, 679–680.

111 VA, Dossier 45: Betriebsmitteilungen 1965–1986, Volkart Brothers Ltd. Betriebsmitteilungen 1978–1986: Betriebsmitteilung, 6. April 1983; Betriebsmitteilung, 6. Mai 1985; Rambousek/Vogt/Volkart, *Volkart*, 1990, 249.

112 Anderegg, *Chronicle*, 1976, 663; Rambousek/Vogt/Volkart, *Volkart*, 1990, 166.

113 *Schweizerische Handelszeitung*, 10 April 1986.

114 Rambousek/Vogt/Volkart, *Volkart*, 1990, 166.

115 Gerencia Comercial, La Industria Cafetera Internacional, 1988, 25; *Revista de Comércio de Café*, Año 66, Julio 1987, 26–27.

116 *Tages-Anzeiger*, 9 May 1989.

117 *Schweizerische Handelszeitung*, 10 April 1986.

118 *Weltwoche*, 29 April 1989.

119 Talbot, *Grounds for Agreement*, 2004, 105–106.

120 Neue Zürcher Zeitung, 15. März 1989; Weltwoche, 29 April 1989; Tages-Anzeiger, 9 May 1989; Coffee & Cocoa International, Vol. 16, Number 4, 1989, 4.

121 La Nación (San José, Costa Rica), 13ᵉ de diciembre 2003; *Basler Zeitung*; 14. May 2004.

122 In 2005, Volcafé had a market share of 14 percent of the global trade in raw coffee and thus led Neumann with a share of 12.5 percent, Esteve with 9 percent and Dreyfus with a 7 percent share of the world market: Volcafé, Your partner, 2005, 9. Also see: www.volcafe.com/history/index.html (1 December 2009).

14 The Cotton Trade After World War II

Like the coffee trade, the global cotton trade was increasingly dominated by multinational trading companies after 1945. During the nineteenth century, the leading trading firms primarily specialized in exporting from certain producing countries. Volkart and Ralli focused on cotton exports from India, Reinhart & Co. shipped out of Egypt, while Anderson Clayton and McFadden sold cotton from the US. After the turn of the century, and particularly after World War I, many of these companies gradually began to expand their spheres of operations.[1] This trend accelerated after the end of World War II. Companies like Volkart, Ralli Brothers and Anderson Clayton progressively became multinational trading companies that had branches in every major growing area and sold cotton in every major consumer country. The accompanying consolidation process was largely fueled by the policies of national governments that intervened more and more often in the trading business from the 1930s onwards and started to sell the cotton harvest via state-subsidized cooperatives and national sales organizations.[2] This paved the way for multinational companies to move large volumes of cotton without having to establish their own sales organizations in the areas of cultivation. At the same time, it forced them to achieve economies of scale. Likewise, they increasingly had to handle the financing themselves, relying either on their own capital or bank loans.[3]

Only sketchy figures are available on the volumes that individual trading companies moved, but this information reflects a constant rise in sales. For example, after 1949 Volkart regularly achieved sales of over 1 million bales from a wide range of areas of cultivation. By comparison, in the late nineteenth century the company shipped nearly 100,000 bales and in the early 1920s annually sold between 200,000 and 350,000 bales of Indian cotton.[4] Other companies achieved a similar increase in sales during this period.[5] Steadily rising sales were not limited to companies in the cotton sector, but rather appear to have been a general development in the global trading business. A 1954 survey conducted by the Swiss Association of Transit and Global Trading Companies, for instance, showed that their members' sales had more than doubled since 1929.[6]

Purchasing Cotton in the US

During the 1930s, Volkart rapidly developed to become a globally active cotton trading company. A decisive turning point here was when the company managed to gain a foothold in the American cotton trade. During the summer of 1939, the collaboration with the American Cotton Cooperative Association came to an end and Volkart established a new branch in New Orleans to serve as a relay station between American cotton exporters and the company's sales agents in Asia and Europe. After exports to Europe (1940) and the Far East (1941) came to a grinding halt in the run-up to World War II, Volkart New Orleans began to supply American spinning mills with cotton and establish its own sales organization in the US.[7]

When it entered the US cotton trade, Volkart benefited from a booming market. As the war effort caused demand to skyrocket, American cotton mills doubled their annual consumption from 6 million to 12 million bales. Volkart soon achieved sales of 200,000 bales of American cotton per year.[8] After the end of the war, it became clear that the business with American cotton would soon become a new area of activity for Volkart. The company established a new subsidiary in 1945, the Magnolia Compress & Warehouse Co. Inc., and acquired new warehouses with cotton presses in New Orleans (1945) and Galveston (1949) (Figure 14.1).[9]

Figure 14.1 Volkart's warehouse in Galveston, Texas, 1949 (VA, Dossier 111: Photos Bremen, London, USA, Mexico, Brazil, Colombia, Singapore/Shanghai/ Japan)

After cotton exports to China and Europe surged in the late 1940s, the volume that Volkart was able to purchase via New Orleans was soon out-paced by the growing demand. This prompted Volkart to open new branches in Dallas and Memphis and an extra subsidiary in Pasadena. The American cotton trade was gaining importance for Volkart chiefly because cotton exports from India had virtually come to a standstill after the end of British colonial rule. For instance, the Bombay branch had sold nearly 100,000 bales of Indian cotton in 1949–1950, primarily to Indian spinning mills, while at the same time it had been able to import an impressive 40,000 bales of American cotton to India.[10]

In the early twentieth century, subtle changes began to emerge in the structure of cotton cultivation in the US. After the end of the American Civil War, most US cotton growers were sharecroppers, in other words, poor farming families who were allowed to use plots of land in return for a share of the crops that they produced. Hence, many farms appeared to be independent production units, when in fact they belonged to a single large landowner. Starting in 1910, the old sharecropping system slowly gave way to mechanized plantations where cotton cultivation was organized according to Tayloristic principles.[11]

A consolidation also took place in the area of bank lending during the first decades of the twentieth century. Instead of receiving loans from local intermediaries, as was common in the late nineteenth century, growers increasingly turned to local and regional banks during the twentieth century. Starting in the 1920s, the US government began to pay advances to growers, a practice that became even more common with the New Deal.[12] Since more and more cotton was produced on mechanized large planta-tions and the cultivation was financed by banks and the US government, multinational companies could achieve high sales without establishing an elaborate procurement organization. A backward integration, like the one Volkart had undertaken during the nineteenth century in India, was thus no longer necessary in the US—and, starting in the 1930s, no longer possible after the government decided that cotton could only be ginned by growers themselves. Accordingly, export companies were no longer allowed to oper-ate their own gins.[13] Trading companies could only achieve a strong position in the export business if they had a highly effective sales organization and an excellent line of credit. During the 1946–1947 season, Volkart required bank loans amounting to 25 million dollars to finance its exports from the US and its futures transactions on the American cotton exchanges.[14]

Different Ways of Doing Business

Despite such successes, Volkart encountered certain obstacles as it entered the American cotton business, most notably because many Americans had ways of doing business that ran counter to the approaches that were traditionally taken by the Swiss company. American merchant Harold Saer, who headed the export division of the American Cotton Cooperative Association before he went to work for the Volkart branch in New Orleans in 1940, tended to adopt a specific operative position at the outset of the cotton season— either a *long* position, whereby he purchased cotton for which he did not yet have a buyer, or a *short* position, whereby he used futures contracts to sell cotton that was not yet in the possession of the company. He then eased away from these positions as soon as prices evolved in a direction that would result in the highest possible profit for the company. Who he ultimately sold to, and whether or not this practice might exasperate longtime customers, was of only secondary importance to him. Volkart, like every other trading company, also regularly went short or long. The company, however, took into account not only the evolution of the markets, but also the wishes of its customers. In an in-company set of guidelines published in 1970, Peter Reinhart noted that Saer essentially saw suppliers and customers as a necessary evil and, in contrast to Volkart, did not value them as key elements of the business.[15]

Even though Reinhart was now pointing out three decades later that Saer's approach was no longer viewed as completely wrong, it appears that showing respect and consideration for the needs of customers still remained a vital component of Volkart's corporate culture in the early 1970s.[16] This is reflected in another contemporary internal memo in which the Volkart executive noted that maintaining "friendly relations" to customers, suppliers and agents had a positive impact on the company over the long term, adding that "it is therefore not a question of a conflict between profit and turnover or profit and friendly relations with clients etc., but rather a choice between immediate short-term profits and the long-term interests of the firm." In Reinhart's opinion, there was no doubt that the long-term interests of maintaining customer loyalty were of greater importance than achieving a short-term profit: "Generally speaking, we are inclined to continue our traditional policy of trying to satisfy the buyers, rather than 'hoarding' the goods for profit."[17]

During the mid-1940s, the not particularly customer-oriented business practices of Volkart New Orleans did not sit well with the partners. "[W]e still feel that V.B. New Orleans is not yet sufficiently closely interwoven with the rest of the firm," as they wrote in a letter at the time[18] in which they admitted that Saer was an outstanding merchant, but one

> who . . . thinks and talks differently from what we are used to and who, therefore, built up a rather self-contained organization which, before gaining its maximum value for us, has to be properly incorporated into the wider V.B. organization.

The partners therefore decided to send J.L. Hurscheler—who had until then served as the head of Volkart Bombay—to New Orleans.[19] These efforts appear to have been only partially successful. Ten years later, the partners again received complaints from customers that cotton deliveries from New Orleans regularly contained a number of bales with inferior quality merchandise. The top employees at Volkart New Orleans, including the ever-present Harold Saer, blamed the dockworkers for these problems. The partners, however, came to the conclusion that the branch in New Orleans was using this practice as a means of getting rid of lower quality cotton as inconspicuously as possible. As a result, they decided to focus more attentively on the quality control in New Orleans.[20]

Mixed Results from the US Policy on Subsidies

In the late 1950s, US cotton exports fell into a severe crisis because there was a glut of cotton on the world market. This was partly the result of massive US government subsidies for cotton farmers and exporters since the 1920s.[21] Since these interventions raised global market prices, other countries were encouraged to take their own measures to significantly boost cotton production during the postwar era,[22] including major producers like China and the Soviet Union, but also India, Pakistan, Brazil, Egypt, Turkey, Mexico and diverse sub-Saharan African countries. Global production of cotton more than doubled between 1945 and 1985, from roughly 6 million to more than 15 million tons per year. This increase was also driven by the introduction of new insecticides like DDT, which considerably reduced the chances of a crop failure due to pest infestation.[23] Meanwhile, cotton production in the US was steadily declining. During the 1920s, American growers were still cultivating 44 million acres of cotton, but in the 1950s they only planted 25 million and by the 1960s only 10 million acres. US cotton's share of global exports had dropped to 24 percent by 1965. This was a dramatic decline from the late nineteenth century, when two-thirds of the cotton cultivated in the world came from the US.[24]

Volkart also bore the brunt of this development. The company was able to acquire large quantities of surplus cotton at auctions organized by the US Department of Agriculture. At one such auction in 1956 it was able to purchase nearly 100,000 bales of surplus cotton, and even 130,000 bales at another auction in 1957. These were the largest individual purchases that the company had ever made.[25] Although Volkart was able to achieve impressive sales figures, the results of the US cotton business were disappointingly modest due to the high level of prices and the company's limited scope of action. In 1959, this led company executives to launch an extensive restructuring plan. The branch in New Orleans was closed after a steep decline in the city's importance as a cotton trading center. At the same time, a new branch was opened in Dallas.[26]

These restructuring measures initially bore fruit.[27] But in the mid-1960s, the business options enjoyed by private export companies were again curtailed by a range of government export subsidy programs and the activities of government-supported cooperatives. Volkart's Pasadena branch was its only profitable venture in the US cotton export business. Following a number of good years, Volkart Dallas had swiftly built up such a large organization that it needed an annual turnover of 300,000 to 400,000 bales to make a profit. Such volumes were no longer possible, however, and Volkart's Dallas branch had to be closed in 1966. The company shifted its focus elsewhere and became the representative for Europe, Africa and the Middle East on behalf of one of the leading US cotton cooperatives, the Plains Cotton Cooperative Association of Lubbock, Texas. A similar agency agreement was signed with Memphis-based US cotton merchant W. B. Dunavant & Co., which until then had been primarily active in the domestic market. The Pasadena subsidiary was the only branch of the company that was still active on the US market.[28] Volkart was not the only export firm that was increasingly withdrawing from the American cotton export business. Leading US trading companies like Alexander Sprunt and Son, McFadden and Anderson Clayton abandoned the US cotton sector between the mid-1950s and the mid-1970s.[29]

Interventions by the American government forced private exporters out of the business, but these measures helped to ensure that cotton prices remained relatively stable between 1945 and 1973.[30] This stability made futures transactions on the cotton exchanges obsolete. A similar development occurred during the 1960s in the coffee trade when the International Coffee Agreement stabilized prices and put a halt to transactions on the futures market. As a result, in 1967 the company liquidated Volkart Brothers, Inc. in New York, which had been in charge of the firm's hedging on the commodity exchanges in New York.[31]

Cotton from around the World

Until the late 1940s, Volkart's trade in cotton focused primarily on exports from India. After India and Pakistan gained independence, cotton exports declined as a result of the economic policies of both countries. In 1948–1949, Volkart exported 90,000 bales from the subcontinent, which was just a fraction of the record 650,000 bales that the company had shipped in 1936–1937. That notwithstanding, Volkart was the largest cotton exporter on the subcontinent in 1948–1949. While its export activities declined, the company increasingly supplied cotton to Indian and Pakistani spinning mills. This cotton originated directly from the subcontinent as well as increasingly from Egypt, East Africa and the US.[32]

Since its export activities from South Asia were encumbered by wave after wave of new regulations as the governments of India and Pakistan pushed for foreign companies to collaborate with local enterprises, in 1961 Volkart merged its cotton organization in India with Patel Cotton Co.[33] and sold a majority share of the Pakistani subsidiary to the British company Peninsular & Oriental Steam Navigation Co.[34]

Despite dwindling exports from the subcontinent, during the 1940s Volkart was able to expand its transactions in US, Latin American and African cotton to such a degree that during the 1949–1950 season it achieved a record volume of over 1 million bales. At the ceremony to mark the company's 100th anniversary in 1951, Peter Reinhart was able to proudly proclaim that the Volkart trading company "is now as powerful and productive as ever."[35] Volkart entered into collaborations with established export companies in many countries, for example, in Egypt with the Swiss firms of Paul Reinhart & Co. and H. Kupper & Co.[36] In 1963, Volkart acquired from H. Kupper the export firm White Nile Cotton Trading Co. in Sudan in a bid to increase its sales of Sudanese cotton. In 1970, White Nile was nationalized; thereafter Volkart purchased its Sudanese cotton from a state-run export company. In addition to occasional exports from Burma and Iran, Volkart increasingly focused on exporting from South and Central American countries like Peru, Guatemala, El Salvador, Nicaragua, Colombia and intermittently also from Argentina and Paraguay (Figure 14.2).[37]

During the 1950s, Volkart also gained a foothold in Mexico.[38] Cotton exports from Mexico were initially carried out by the Volkart branches in New Orleans and Pasadena. In 1951, Volkart executives came to the conclusion that it was high time that they established a subsidiary in Mexico because the Mexican government made the issuing of export licenses dependent upon whether the company concerned could prove that it also made sales to the Mexican cotton industry. This made it necessary to establish a branch in Mexico.[39] In 1953, the company opened a new office in the center of Mexico City,[40] followed in 1954 by an agency in Obregon on the west coast of Mexico. After the company acquired its own cotton gins and warehouses there,[41] it managed to "[win over] a number of relatively reliable cotton growers," as was noted in the minutes of a meeting of the board of directors.[42] The investments soon paid off. During the 1955–1956 season, the Mexican subsidiary achieved net profits of 1.5 million dollars.[43]

But not all such expansion initiatives were crowned with success. In 1951, the company decided to establish a cotton ginning and pressing facility in Turkey together with merchant Arthur Lafont, who had been supplying Volkart with Turkish cotton since the late 1940s. Furthermore, Volkart established a Turkish subsidiary, Volkart Brothers (Türkiye) Ltd., with the aim of buying more cotton from Turkish suppliers.[44] The business was much less profitable than anticipated, though, because the cultivation of cotton did not increase to the extent that the Turkish government had proclaimed it would. Likewise, since the Turkish textile industry was booming in the early 1950s, a considerable share of the domestic cotton crop was used by the Turks themselves. Finally, Volkart had not realized that Turkish shipping companies based their freight rates on volume, not weight, as was common in other countries. This meant that the greater material density that Volkart and Lafont could achieve with their presses did not give them a cost advantage over the partially pressed bales that were otherwise the norm in Turkey. In 1958, Volkart thus decided to sell its share of the presses to Lafont and liquidated its Turkish subsidiary in 1959.[45]

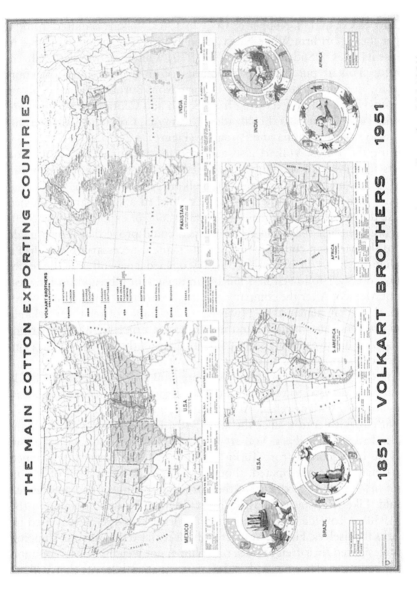

Figure 14.2 Map of the leading cotton growing areas in the world (Swiss National Library, call number 3 M 1951)

Changes in the Sales Organization

Before 1945, no one could have predicted that Volkart would be able to continue so seamlessly with its string of successes from the interwar era. In December 1942, Georg Reinhart told his fellow partners that it was necessary to give careful consideration to how Volkart intended to resume its business transactions after the end of the war. Reinhart evidently had a fairly good notion of the enormous difficulties involved, as witnessed by the following points that he insisted needed to be clarified: "a) which of our former agents in the European countries still exist and which (due to racial persecution or other reasons) have ceased to exist; b) what has become of our customers."[46] Despite the fears of company officials, Volkart was relatively quickly able to rekindle its business contacts after the end of the war. In 1946, Volkart Bremen—along with many other trading companies— imported large quantities of American cotton to Germany on behalf of the United Nations Relief and Rehabilitation Administration. Cotton imports to Germany were controlled by the occupying powers until the early 1950s, when they were again placed in the hands of private companies. After the war, cotton imports were also controlled by the governments of several other European countries. For example, in Britain the state import organization, the Raw Cotton Commission, was not disbanded until 1954.[47]

After 1945, it became common practice for Volkart to accept deferred payments for cotton deliveries to spinning mills in East Asia and Europe. In 1947, for instance, company executives granted French cotton mills a three-month grace period for the purchase of large quantities of Brazilian cotton.[48] And in 1949 Volkart approved deliveries to German textile mills in exchange for promissory notes because this had become an accepted procedure among other importers at the time.[49] Similar payment deferrals had been granted for cotton sales in Yugoslavia and Spain in the late 1940s—although it should be noted that these credits were backed by payment guarantees from local banks—[50] and for sales to Swiss customers starting in the mid-1950s.[51]

Although up until the end of World War II Volkart had only had two branches in Europe—one in Bremen and one in London—in the 1950s the company began to acquire the majority of established import trading companies in various Western European countries. In 1954, for example, it gained a controlling interest in the Liverpool company of Woods & Thorburn and in 1961 the trading house of Sofic in Le Havre. In 1958, Volkart joined forces with its longtime agent in Milan, Italy to establish the Alcott cotton import company. The Liverpool company was closed in 1972 because the textile industry in Lancashire was in decline.[52] By contrast, the subsidiaries in France and Italy were sold to the respective managements in the early 1970s and these companies subsequently served as independent sales agents for Volkart.[53]

From the 1940s onwards, Volkart sold cotton in the Pacific region to spinning mills in Australia, Hong Kong, Taiwan, South Korea, South Vietnam, Thailand, Indonesia, Singapore and the Philippines. In Africa the company had customers in Morocco, Ethiopia and South Africa, and in the Middle East it sold its products to firms in Israel and Lebanon. All sales were brokered by independent trading companies that served as agents for Volkart in the respective countries.[54] The only non-European country after 1945 in which Volkart had a branch that only handled sales of commodities was Japan, where Volkart was able to build upon its subsidiary Nichizui. In 1970, Nichizui was renamed Volkart Japan Ltd.[55] With the help of these diverse subsidiaries and representatives, Volkart moved 1.032 million bales of cotton during the 1960–1961 season, which was a record result for the company at the time. Of this amount, 330,000 bales were shipped to Europe, 170,000 bales went to Japan and 120,000 bales were sold in the Pacific region. A total of 330,000 bales were not exported, but instead sold to domestic spinning mills within the growing countries. Aside from India and Pakistan, this was primarily the case in the US and, to some extent, also in Brazil.[56]

Up until the early 1970s, Volkart hardly did any business with communist countries. As early as 1950, Volkart company officials had assumed the position that "it is not up to us to boycott business transactions [with the countries of the communist bloc] out of a sense of political conviction." Nevertheless, with the exception of Poland and Yugoslavia, the company hardly did any business with East Bloc countries. Any possible concerns that such shipments would support the communist regimes were generally dispelled with the argument that importing commodities not only benefited the buyer but also the seller, which meant that one could not "speak of a unilateral support of this bloc."[57] In 1956, no doubt in reaction to the bloody crackdown on the Hungarian Uprising, instructions were given that, "for ethical reasons, no transactions are to be conducted with the satellite states of Moscow for the time being." One year later, Volkart managers changed their minds once again and said that such a categorical approach could not be maintained. It was decided, however, only in exceptional cases to do business with East Bloc countries and China.[58]

Starting in early 1960s, cotton consumption increased in the Far East. Between 1966–1967 and 1975–1976, Volkart annually imported via Nichizui an average of 238,000 bales of cotton to Japan. During the 1972–1973 season alone, the company imported 667,500 bales to Japan. In 1970, China reopened its doors to Western imports and Volkart resumed importing cotton to China, as it had before 1954.[59] In contrast to Ralli Bros. & Coney, which in 1972 landed a spectacular deal that allowed it to import to China 500,000 bales of American cotton worth more than 150 million dollars, Volkart's business transactions in China were on a rather modest scale.[60]

A Crisis-stricken Period that Began during the 1970s

In the early 1960s, Volkart decided to diversify: "Since our financial resources often exceed what is required for our traditional commercial transactions, and it often does not make sense to use them instead of normal bank loans, we have looked around for other opportunities," as the company wrote concerning its annual results for the 1961–1962 fiscal year. Since Peter Reinhart was a member of the supervisory board of the Union Bank of Switzerland, the company invested 5 million Swiss francs in a capital increase for the bank. Furthermore, a loan was granted to a German department store and a private bank, and an investment was made in the Vulcan Shipping and Development Co., which then acquired a number of oil and liquid gas tankers. Finally, Volkart purchased several real estate holdings in Winterthur and invested in industrial companies in India during the 1970s. Already since the early 1950s, the company had had shares in German publisher Suhrkamp Verlag AG, and during the 1960s it acquired a stake in another German publisher, the Insel Verlag.[61] The partial transferring of the firm's capital to the investment sector appears to have taken place in a rather haphazard manner. It was not until the mid-1980s, after Andreas Reinhart took the helm of the company, that Volkart systematically invested in financial transactions.

Cotton prices remained relatively stable during the 1950s and 1960s. With the onset of the global economic crisis in 1973, prices doubled virtually overnight and remained extremely volatile.[62] By 1988, prices had declined again by 50 percent, and thus essentially returned to the level of the early 1970s.[63] These developments made it increasingly difficult to do business in the trading sector. After the Arab oil-producing countries decided to throttle production in 1973, the following comment appeared in an internal memo at Volkart: "Even to the biggest optimist it must by now be abundantly clear that . . . the days in which 'growth' was the most desirable aim are over. We shall at best enter a period of consolidation, more likely one of recession"[64] During the following two years, the company's cotton division still managed to make a profit—primarily thanks to the new craze in jeans fashions, which fueled a rise in the demand for cotton—but, all in all, things were not looking good for the cotton trade.[65] Cotton production was rising, but demand from the textile industry was declining, leading to falling prices and a growing risk of payment defaults. To make matters worse, as a Swiss company Volkart was hard hit by the decision in 1973 to abandon the fixed-exchange-rate system in favor of a floating-rate system in which the value of a currency is determined by supply and demand. The dollar fell against other currencies, rendering the Swiss franc more expensive. This was highly troublesome for Volkart because the global commodities trade was generally conducted in dollars, while the company's expenditures were largely in Swiss francs. This sent their overhead through the roof.[66]

In the late 1970s, Volkart ranked among the six leading cotton trading companies in the world with an estimated global market share of 10 percent.[67] The end of the fixed-exchange-rate system sparked growing volatility on the commodities markets. This was compounded by additional improvements in communications technologies that allowed market players to keep abreast of the latest changes in supply and demand, which further reduced profit margins and intensified the already stiff competition in the global commodities trade.[68] It goes without saying that Volkart was hard hit by these developments. Although the company achieved a 17 percent year-on-year increase in cotton sales during the 1978–1979 season, the results were bitterly disappointing.[69] In 1979, Volkart was forced to close its cotton department in São Paulo.[70] During the same year, the company also placed limits on its transactions in cotton from Egypt, Peru and Sudan after exports from these countries had become increasingly problematic due to state export monopolies.[71] Already by the mid-1970s, the collaborations in the US with the Plains Cotton Cooperative Association and the W.B. Dunavant trading company had come to an end, temporary reducing Volkart's US cotton exports to a trickle.[72] In 1980, a merger took place between the US subsidiary Volkart Brothers Inc. and the American cotton trading firm of Starke Taylor & Son. Volkart retained an 80 percent majority share in the new company, Volkart Taylor Cooper Inc., which was based in Dallas.[73] All of these steps were part of an initiative to transfer the company's cotton trading operations to the US and the Far East. Meanwhile, the cotton division in Winterthur, which had been the backbone of the company since the 1860s, was severely scaled back.[74]

In 1988, the board of directors decided to divide the company into four independent subsidiaries: Gebrüder Volkart AG as an umbrella organization for the coffee trade, Volcot Holding AG for the cotton trade, Volkart Invest AG for the diverse financial transactions of the company and Volkart International AG for marketing and all commercial transactions outside the commodities trade. The four subsidiaries were united under the umbrella of the Volkart Brothers Holding. The operational center of the cotton trade was transferred entirely to Dallas. In Europe only the subsidiary in Bremen was still active in the cotton trade. According to a company-wide announcement by Andreas Reinhart, who had been the sole owner since 1986, these restructuring measures were in reaction to competitive pressure and the problems created by the weak dollar. "We are convinced that this tightening of the organization will create the necessary simple structures that will allow us to remain successful in the future," he said, adding the following words, which were evidently intended to serve as a rousing pep talk: "We now need your full commitment, the belief in success and, last but not least, a bit of luck. We rely on your complete support in this endeavor."[75]

Volkart Leaves the Trading Business

Subsequent years brought no reprieve for the global cotton trade, which remained fraught with turmoil. It became increasingly difficult to conduct business in the sector due to high oil prices, global overproduction combined with declining world market prices and the global economic crisis in

Japan (from 1991) and other East Asian countries (1997–1998).[76] Volkart stopped trading cocoa in 1985 and coffee in 1989—the coffee trade was thereafter pursued with great success by the independently acting company Volcafé—and instead focused on the cotton trade while, at the same time, it began to diversify into the financial sector.[77] The subsequent years were characterized by a frantic series of restructuring measures as Volkart reshuffled its portfolios. In the late 1980s, the company established a string of new subsidiaries in California, Australia and Hong Kong.[78] In 1990, Volkart acquired Anderson Clayton Co., its long-standing rival and today still one of the leading American cotton trading companies.[79] In 1992, however, Volkart sold its subsidiary in Dallas to the Winterthur cotton trading company Paul Reinhart AG.[80] In 1997, Volkart then sold Anderson Clayton Co. to the Queensland Cotton Holding, the largest cotton processing company in Australia and, at the same time, acquired a majority share in the company.[81]

But even these extensive restructuring efforts failed to produce the desired success. Andreas Reinhart sold the cotton division in the spring of 1999. This was partly taken over by Queensland Cotton and partly further pursued by the previous management, which now operated an independent cotton trading company under the name Volcot.[82] Volkart was henceforth only a holding company. The company managed a number of real estate properties and invested in several ventures, including a company in the US that manufactured cleaning sponges and insulation material made from recycled glass, a resource-efficient tourism project in Portugal, a solar energy company in Switzerland, the cultivation of organically produced cotton in Australia and a company that manufactured organic fungicides in California.[83]

This marked the end of the Volkart trading company's nearly 150 years of corporate history. But the structures that the company had established and the employees who had worked for Volkart left their mark on global trade even after the company withdrew from the active trading business. This shows that the trading sector still played a key role in the global exchange of commodities in the twenty-first century and that corporate structures do not simply disappear, even if a company's capital is transferred into new hands and the business is run under another name.

Notes

1 See Chapters 8 to 10.
2 Bell/Gillham, *The World of Cotton*, 1989, 3–4.
3 Clayton Garwood, *Will Clayton*, 1958, 102; Bowater Organisation, *History and Activities of the Ralli Trading Group*, 1979; Chalmin, *Negociants et chargeurs*, 1985, 5ff.; Killick, "Specialized and General Trading Firms," 1987, 261–262.
4 Reinhart, "Rede zur Hundertjahrfeier," [1951], 16; V.B. News, No. 9, December 1923, 16.
5 Killick, "Response to the Comment," 1987, 271–272.
6 WA, HS 421: Verband schweizerischer Transit- und Welthandelsfirmen, Basel F6: Korrespondenz und zwei Entwürfe, betr. Die Enquête über den Transithandel,

durchgeführt von Prof. Dr. Gsell an der Handelshochschule in St. Gallen, 1953–1958: Der schweizerische Transithandel. Ergebnisse der Enquête 1954, June 1955, 19–20.

7 VA, Dossier 16: USA, Brazil, Mexico, Guatemala/Costa Rica, Turkey, II. New York (New Orleans/ Dallas included), 2. Table of Events V.B. Inc., Notiz von Peter Reinhart vom 20. September 1950, „Entwicklung des amerikanischen Baumwollgeschäftes"; Volkart Bros, *Cotton 1939–1945*, 1945; Anderegg, *Chronicle*, 1976, 443ff.

8 Anderegg, *Chronicle*, 1976, 487.

9 VA, Partners' Conference (4. Juni 1946–1931. August 1956): Konferenz vom 29. September 1947; Dossier 16: USA, Brazil, Mexico, Guatemala/Costa Rica, Turkey, I. USA: Notiz von Peter Reinhart vom 20. September 1950, "Entwicklung des amerikanischen Baumwollgeschäftes"; Anderegg, *Chronicle*, 1976, 566.

10 VA, Partners' Conference (4. Juni 1946–1931. August 1956): Konferenz vom 1. Juli 1948; Konferenz-Protokolle 4. Juli 1947–1928. Juni 1949: Konferenz vom 31. August 1948; Dossier 16: USA, Brazil, Mexico, Guatemala/Costa Rica, Turkey, I. USA: Notiz von Peter Reinhart vom 20. September 1950, "Entwicklung des amerikanischen Baumwollgeschäftes".

11 The mechanization of the picking process made rapid strides during the postwar years in the US. In 1965, over 85 percent of US cotton was mechanically harvested, compared to just 23 percent in 1955. In other countries, though, mechanical harvesting was still highly uncommon during this period in history: Sinclair, *The Production, Marketing, and Consumption of Cotton*, 1968, 5 and 20; Foley, *The White Scourge*, 1997, 64ff., 119–135, 163ff.

12 V.B. News, No. 5, July 1922, 1–6; Garside, *Cotton Goes to Market*, 1935, 170–173.

13 Interview with Paul Alfred Reinhart, 2008.

14 VA, Konferenz-Protokolle vom 5. Januar 1945–1927. Juni 1947: Konferenz vom 16. Oktober 1946.

15 VA, Dossier 44, VBH Guidelines 1970–1983 (written by Peter Reinhart): Peter Reinhart, Cotton and other Commodity Operations and Discretions, 21 May 1970.

16 VA, Dossier 44, VBH Guidelines 1970–1983 (written by Peter Reinhart): Peter Reinhart, Cotton and other Commodity Operations and Discretions, 21 May 1970.

17 VA, Dossier 44, VBH Guidelines 1970–1983 (written by Peter Reinhart): VBH Guidelines No. 16, Winterthur, 18 August 1970: answer to note from 21 May 70.

18 VA, Dossier 3: Bombay I, 2. VB Bombay Management: Winterthur to Bombay (no date).

19 VA, Konferenz-Protokolle vom 5. Januar 1945–1927. Juni 1947: PR, Protocol on conversations with Mr. J. Hurscheler, 19 August 1946.

20 VA, Konferenz-Protokolle vom 16. Januar 1953–1956. Januar 1959: Besprechung zwischen P.R. und J.H. am 21. Juni 1957.

21 Clayton Garwood, *Will Clayton*, 1958, 101; Anderson, "Cotton Marketing", 1999, 675; Walsh, *Building the Borderlands*, 2008, 93–96. To read about the issue of how small farmers in Africa are disadvantaged as a result of the huge subsidies granted to US cotton growers, see Mönninghoff, *King Cotton*, 2006, 220–226.

22 Clayton Garwood, *Will Clayton*, 1958, 101–102; VA, Bilanzen, Bilanz 1959–1960.

23 Munro, *Cotton*, 1987, 6–15; Bell/Gillham, *The World of Cotton*, 1989, 3.

24 Wheeler, *International Trade in Cotton*, 1925, 1; Sinclair, *The Production, Marketing, and Consumption of Cotton*, 1968, 16; Munro, *Cotton*, 1987, 8–21;

Bell/Gillham, *The World of Cotton*, 1989, 4 and 342; Farnie, "The Role of Merchants," 2004, 21.

25 VA, Konferenz-Protokolle vom 16. Januar 1953–1956. Januar 1959: Konferenz vom 20. Juni 1956 und Konferenz vom 7. Mai 1957.

26 VA, Bilanzen, Bilanz 1958–1959.

27 VA, Bilanzen, Bilanzen 1958–1959 and 1959–1960.

28 VA, Bilanzen, Bilanz 1964–1965 and 1965–1966; Anderegg, *Chronicle*, 1976, 581ff.

29 Killick, "Specialized and General Trading Firms," 1987, 261.

30 Munro, *Cotton*, 1987, 338–342.

31 VA, Bilanzen, Bilanz 1966–1967; Anderegg, *Chronicle*, 1976, 570–571. See also Chapter 13.

32 Reinhart, "Rede zur Hundertjahrfeier," [1951], 16.

33 VA, Dossier 30: Patel Cotton Comp., Patel/Volkart Cotton Merger, Volkart Bombay Pvt. Ltd. 1961.

34 Anderegg, *Chronicle*, 1976, 688–691; VA, Dossier 34: Volkart Pakistan Ltd. (1963), Reorganisation VPL/MM 1976; Rambousek/Vogt/Volkart, *Volkart*, 1990, 252. For more information, See Chapter 12.

35 Reinhart, "Rede zur Hundertjahrfeier," [1951], 15–16.

36 VA, Partners' Conference (4. Juni 1946–1931. August 1956): Konferenz vom 15. Februar 1951; Bilanzen, Bilanz 1962–1963. In 1962, the two companies Paul Reinhart & Co. and H. Kupper & Co. had to merge by order of the Egyptian government: VA, Konferenz-Protokolle vom 15. Januar 1959–1930. März 1965: Zu Protokoll, Aegypten, 12.1.1962.

37 Anderegg, *Chronicle*, 1976, 581–583 and 658.

38 For more on the Mexican cotton economy, see Sinclair, *The Production, Marketing, and Consumption of Cotton*, 1968, 20.

39 VA, Partners' Conference (4. Juni 1946–1931. August 1956): Konferenz vom 15. Februar 1951.

40 VA, Konferenz-Protokolle vom 16. Januar 1953–1956. Januar 1959: Protokoll Nr. 1006, Geschäftsleitung, 15. Juli 1953.

41 VA, Konferenz-Protokolle vom 16. Januar 1953–1956. Januar 1959: Konferenzen vom 4. März 1954 und vom 22. Dezember 1955.

42 VA, Konferenz-Protokolle vom 16. Januar 1953–1956. Januar 1959: Konferenz vom 22. Dezember 1955.

43 VA, Konferenz-Protokolle vom 16. Januar 1953–1956. Januar 1959: Konferenzen vom 4. März 1954 und vom 22. Dezember 1955.

44 VA, Partners' Conference (4. Juni 1946–1931. August 1956): Konferenz vom 15. Februar 1951.

45 Anderegg, *Chronicle*, 1976, 574–577.

46 VA, Konferenz-Protokolle vom 5. August 1941–1944. März 1943: Konferenz vom 17. Dezember 1942.

47 Anderegg, *Chronicle*, 1976, 566 and 585.

48 VA. Konferenz-Protokolle vom 5. Januar 1945–1927. Juni 1947, Konferenz vom 6. Juni 1947.

49 VA, Konferenz-Protokolle 4. Juli 1947–1928. Juni 1949: Konferenz vom 24. Mai 1949.

50 VA, Konferenz-Protokolle 4. Juli 1947–1928. Juni 1949: Konferenz vom 15. Juni 1949.

51 VA, Konferenz-Protokolle vom 16. Januar 1953–1956. Januar 1959: Konferenz vom 21. Dezember 1956.

52 VA, Dossier 13: London/Liverpool (VB + Woods&Thorburn) / Bremen: V.B. London; Anderegg, *Chronicle*, 1976, 585–586 and 672–674.

53 VA, Bilanzen, Bilanz 1957/58; VA, Bilanzen, Bilanz 1958–1959; VA, Bilanzen, Bilanz 1960–1961; Anderegg, *Chronicle*, 1976, 586–587.
54 Anderegg, *Chronicle*, 1976, 577–578, 587–588.
55 VA, Bilanzen, Bilanz 1965/66; Anderegg, *Chronicle*, 1976, 559–561 and 681–682.
56 VA, Bilanzen, Bilanz 1960–1961; Dossier 20: VB Organisation 1952–1953: KB, 30 April 1953.
57 VA, Konferenz-Protokolle vom 1. Juli 1949–1919. Dezember 1952.
58 VA, Konferenz-Protokolle vom 16. Januar 1953–1956. Januar 1959: Konferenz vom 21. Februar 1957. Also see: Konferenz-Protokolle vom 15. Januar 1959–1930. März 1965: Zu Protokoll, 15. Dezember 1961; Bilanzen, Bilanz 1961–1962.
59 Anderegg, *Chronicle*, 1976, 656.
60 Bowater Organisation, *History and Activities of the Ralli Trading Group*, 1979, 16.
61 VA, Bilanzen, Bilanz 1961–1962; Anderegg, *Chronicle*, 1976, 645–653.
62 Munro, *Cotton*, 1987, 342.
63 Rambousek/Vogt/Volkart, *Volkart*, 1990, 95.
64 VA, Dossier 44, VBH Guidelines 1970–1983 (written by Peter Reinhart): VBH Guidelines No. 33, Winterthur, 28 December 1973.
65 VA, Dossier 45: Betriebsmitteilungen 1965–1986, Volkart Brothers Ltd. Betriebsmitteilungen 1974–1977: Betriebsmitteilungen of 20 November 1975 and 15 November 1976.
66 VA, Dossier 45: Betriebsmitteilungen 1965–1986, Volkart Brothers Ltd. Betriebsmitteilungen 1978–1986: Betriebsmitteilung of 20 November 1975 and 16 November 1978.
67 The other five cotton trading companies were Ralli Brothers (UK) with a global market share of 10 percent, Mcfadden Valmac (USA) 10 percent, W.B. Dunavant (US) 10 percent, Tokyo Menka Kaisha (Japan) 5 percent and Sumitumo (Japan) 5 percent: Chalmin, "International Trading Companies," 1980, 538.
68 Paul Reinhart, *200 Years Reinhart*, 1988, 5.
69 VA, Dossier 45: Betriebsmitteilungen 1965–1986, Volkart Brothers Ltd. Betriebsmitteilungen 1978–1986: Betriebsmitteilung, 7 November 1979.
70 Rambousek/Vogt/Volkart, *Volkart*, 1990, 164.
71 VA, Dossier 45: Betriebsmitteilungen 1965–1986, Volkart Brothers Ltd. Betriebsmitteilungen 1978–1986: Betriebsmitteilung, 22 February 1979.
72 Rambousek/Vogt/Volkart, *Volkart*, 1990, 162.
73 VA, Dossier 45: Betriebsmitteilungen 1965–1986, Volkart Brothers Ltd. Betriebsmitteilungen 1978–1986: Betriebsmitteilung, 22 May 1980.
74 VA, Dossier 45: Betriebsmitteilungen 1965–1986, Volkart Brothers Ltd. Betriebsmitteilungen 1978–1986: Betriebsmitteilung, 20 June 1980.
75 VA, Dossier 45: Betriebsmitteilungen 1965–1986, Volkart Brothers Ltd. Betriebsmitteilungen 1978–1986: Betriebsmitteilung, 31 May 1988.
76 *Neue Zürcher Zeitung*, 29 December 2000.
77 See Chapters 5 and 13.
78 VA, Bilanzen der Volkart Houchin Inc. 1988–1990; Bilanzen der Volkart (Australia) Pty. Ltd. 1988 and 1989: Annual Report 1988–1989; Bilanzen der Volcot (Hongkong) Ltd.: Annual Report 1988–1989.
79 www.volkart.ch/English/PortraitGeschichteHolding150Jahre.htm; www.emeraldventures.com/team/walterLocher.aspx (19 January 2010)
80 Reinhart AG, "Reinhart", [after 2003]; interview with Paul Alfred Reinhart, 2008; www.thecottonschool.com/PR%20Bio.pdf (19 January 2010).
81 Bilanz, 1. December 1998; www.andersonclayton.com/index.cfm?show=10&mid=7&pid=1; www.alacrastore.com/mergers-acquisitions/Anderson_Clayton_Corp-3163663 (19 January 2010).
82 www.volkart.ch/English/PortraitGeschichteHolding150Jahre.htm; www.volcot.ch (19 January 2010). The Volcot company was liquidated in the summer of 2010.
83 *Tages-Anzeiger*, 1 February 2001.

Conclusion

Based on the history of the Volkart company, the previous chapters of this book have provided an actor-centered overview of global trade from the mid-nineteenth to the late twentieth centuries. This has clearly shown that global markets for products like cotton, coffee and coconut fiber were largely the result of social interactions, often at a very local level. Such an action-theoretical approach serves as a magnifying glass to examine processes that are often overlooked by macro-historical studies. What are the main results?

From a Traditional Merchant House to a Multinational Trading Company

First of all, the Volkart story illustrates why specialized trading companies assumed a key position in the global commodities trade. The firm's specific knowledge was vital to its ability to act as an intermediary between growers and processing plants. It would have taken enormous expense and effort for industrial companies to organize prompt deliveries of commodities like cotton, raw coffee and coconut fiber to guarantee a steady stream of high-quality raw materials for their production plants. The modern commodities trade demands a high degree of business acumen and excellent business ties that are essential to financing transactions, insuring goods and trading on the futures market to safeguard against sudden price fluctuations. And, aside from an intimate familiarity with the products, it took a thorough knowledge of the relevant markets to pave the way for transactions in the producing countries. Trading companies were able to reduce transaction costs by bridging the gaps in information and confidence that are inherent to the overseas trading sector. Furthermore, their ability to achieve economies of scale allowed them to reduce the prices of goods on global markets. By honing these skills and developing these social ties, trading companies laid the cornerstone for an economic structure that was capable of maintaining worldwide trading networks. The emergence of a modern industrial and consumer society would have been virtually unthinkable without such specialized intermediaries.

The history of the Volkart company is a paradigm example of the transition from a mercantile house specialized in a "pre-modern" form of commerce to a multinational company. In the first few years of its existence, Volkart was basically an enlarged family business that focused primarily on a specific, regionally limited area of business, namely the trade between India and Europe. As with many pre-modern trading firms, the company used its business connections, branches and warehouses to sell a wide range of European consumer and industrial goods in the Indian bazaars and ship diverse Indian commodities to Europe. The company had not yet specialized in specific products at this point in time.

The business underwent an extensive reorientation with the advent of telegraph communications, the construction of the Indian railways and the breakthrough of steamship shipping. Since the profit margins in the trade with India were growing narrower, the sector experienced a sweeping consolidation process along with increasing specialization in certain goods. The business of buying and selling on commission disappeared in favor of trading on one's own behalf. Starting in the 1860s, Volkart focused on exporting raw cotton from India. By opening buying agencies and establishing cotton gins and presses in the interior of the country, the company adopted a backward integration model that most notably allowed it to guarantee consistent quality of deliveries and reduce transaction costs by circumventing Indian middlemen. This transition ultimately drove out of business the Indian trading companies that had been responsible for more than half of the cotton exports to Europe until the 1860s.

The second half of the nineteenth century was also marked by a considerable expansion of the business in Europe. The company built an ever-growing network of agencies in key industrial districts. It also maintained outstanding contacts to insurance companies and commercial banks that safeguarded and financed increasingly large shipments. In addition to relying on existing financial institutions, in Europe the company helped to forge the requisite infrastructure for modern global trade by investing in the Bank in Winterthur in 1862 and establishing Swiss Lloyd in 1863. This can be seen as proof of the theory promulgated by many global historians that the capitalist global economy should not be viewed as a process that began in a European core and slowly spread across the entire world, but rather that the emergence of capitalism and the modern world is to be interpreted as the result of global networks.[1]

Another reflection of the transition from a traditional mercantile house to a multinational trading company is that during the late nineteenth century trading companies like Volkart gradually moved away from selling commodities like cotton and coffee with a more or less rough description of the products' features and instead developed their own product types with standardized characteristics that were tailored to the needs of their customers in industrialized countries. By transforming a relatively loosely defined commodity into a proprietary product, they made it easier for manufacturing plants to place orders and could establish their company's product types as unique brands in the global trade of goods and services.

Although the increasing importance of economies of scale in the global trading business led to a similar development among manufacturing companies, there was a clear difference in ownership structures. Since trading companies were less dependent upon long-term investments than industrial manufacturers and merely required short- and long-term loans, most modern trading companies remained in the ownership of families and did not rely on issuing publicly-held shares. Like many manufacturing companies in the late nineteenth century, Volkart had a professional management team that supervised the running of the company's various branches and divisions. But the members of the Volkart and Reinhart families that owned the company remained active at all times in managing the business and always had the last word on important decisions. This had the added advantage that the company's family traditions helped to maintain highly important personal business ties and thus reduced transaction costs.

Trade History as a Relational History of Regions

The Volkart story also offers insights into the importance of diverse regional concepts of global trade.[2] For instance, the company's nationality was rarely an issue. The firm's Swiss origins admittedly played an important role during the two world wars and with regard to the anti-British boycott campaigns of the Indian independence movement in the early 1930s. Especially during the world wars, the subsidiaries of a German or Austrian trading company in the British Empire would have certainly been expropriated, which could have spelled the end of the company concerned. But aside from such exceptional circumstances, a company's national origins were not a decisive criterion, either in the free-trade-loving British Empire or later in the US and Latin America. In the global trading business, a company's success or failure was dictated not so much by its nationality as by its financial strength and access to bank loans, and this was an area where trading firms from industrialized countries enjoyed significantly better opportunities than their rivals in the countries that produced raw materials.

Yet even if the international commodities trade from the late nineteenth century onwards was controlled by a handful of companies from Western Europe, Japan and the US, this does not mean that these enterprises were able to control the entire supply chain from the areas of cultivation to the industrial districts. The enormous distances between growing and industrialized countries were less of a problem here. Already by the late nineteenth century, trading companies were largely able to use insurance policies and futures transactions to minimize liabilities, such as damaged goods or price fluctuations during transport, which had made overseas trade so risky until then. But even on the Indian subcontinent, where the British colonial administration had standardized weights and measures and introduced Western legal norms, it was still impossible for European trading companies to control the first 10 to 20 miles between the inland markets and the farmers' fields because the cultivation of cotton was completely dominated by local moneylenders who handled the selling of the harvest within each district. The enormous influence of Indian moneylenders and intermediaries ultimately defeated the efforts of the colonial administration to convince farmers on the subcontinent to cultivate the long-staple varieties that were so highly prized by the cotton mills in Lancashire.

Hence, despite British colonial rule, India never became the leading cotton supplier of the British textile industry, as British colonial officials had envisioned. Instead, Indian cotton was primarily used in continental Europe during the late nineteenth century, but increasingly sold from the turn of the century onwards in India, Japan and China, where a modern textile industry had emerged. This interplay between local and global developments can be understood as a process of glocalization. The trade flows of Indian cotton show that markets and imperial territories often did not perfectly overlap. Moreover, an increasing amount of American, Egyptian and Brazilian cotton was sold to Asian spinning mills from the 1920s onwards, which proves that industrialization should be seen as a global phenomenon that was perfectly capable of redirecting the flows of global trade.[3] This in turn was an opportunity for multinational trading companies that, thanks to their worldwide network of branches and financial strength, were able to benefit from such shifts in the global economic balance.

Questions of Periodization

An actor-centered approach allows for reflections on the periodization of global trade. The interwar era in particular makes it clear that the history of multinational companies does not necessarily concur with the familiar parameters of political history. Although political events like the two world wars, the establishment of colonial rule and the process of decolonization heavily influenced the activities of trading companies, it could also be said that economic and technical developments—such as the industrialization of Asia and rapid advances in transport and communications from the mid-nineteenth century onwards, and again in the 1970s—had at least just as much influence on the trading business.

Based on the history of Volkart, how is it possible to chronologically structure the development of global trade between the mid-nineteenth century and the end of the twentieth century? It appears advisable here not to select an isolated criterion, but instead to interpret the history of global trade as an overlapping of different time levels.

On the first time level, technical innovations influenced the trading business in waves, such as the rapid advances in railroads, telegraphs and steam shipping in the late nineteenth century and the mounting prevalence of telecommunications, computerization, air traffic and container transport from the late 1970s onwards. In both cases, technical breakthroughs revitalized trade and sparked a large-scale consolidation process. While the first wave of innovations fueled Volkart's meteoric rise as a large company from the 1860s onwards, the technical advances of the late twentieth century exacerbated the volatility of the commodities trade and were a contributing factor to Volkart's decision to withdraw from the trading business.

A second time level reflects the phenomenon of imperialism. The policies of the Western imperial powers opened the Asian markets to Western merchants and had a resounding influence on Asian trade for over a century. Accordingly, the end of the colonial era was for Western trading companies in many ways also synonymous with the relinquishment of their business activities in the Asian region. For instance, Volkart had to withdraw from China after the communists rose to power, and the independence of India, Pakistan and Ceylon made it impossible to continue to pursue the once highly lucrative trading business on the subcontinent.

A third level is engendered by the increasing politicization of global trade. The 1920s marked a key turning point in this regard. Many producing countries increasingly intervened in the export trade to safeguard the incomes of their farmers and landowners in the face of global overproduction and global economic stagnation. After the end of World War II, many former colonies endeavored to reduce their commodities exports in an effort to boost their own industries. At the same time, export quotas were established, such as within the context of the International Coffee Agreement. These state interventions only gradually lost importance toward the end of the twentieth century due to the rise of neoliberal economic policies and the end of the Cold War.[4]

All of these decades—the 1860s, 1920s, 1950s and 1970s/1980s—marked turning points in the history of Volkart. Having said that, however, multinational trading companies were able to react flexibly to such challenges. The end of World War I posed less of a problem for the activities of globally operating trading companies than one might assume based on conventional theories of economic history, which often characterize the interwar era as the age of deglobalization. Trading companies responded to the global economic turmoil of the day by expanding their businesses to new countries and continents. It was certainly no coincidence that Volkart became a genuine global player during the 1920s. On the other hand, political interventions occasionally offered internationally operating companies the possibility of winning large government contracts. Wherever the territorial control of nation-states became too obstructive, companies like Volkart tried to evade their authority. They succeeded in doing so in large part because the geographical horizons of their corporate structure surpassed the sphere of influence of individual governments. Multinational trading companies like Volkart that bought and sold commodities used their extensive reach to shift profits to branches located in areas with low taxation or to circumvent political restrictions like the International Coffee Agreement by dealing in "tourist coffee." This shows once again that national borders and the business areas of multinational companies in the twentieth century were often at cross-purposes, and it indicates that globalization processes were frequently characterized by intense dialectics.

Trade History as Cultural History

The example of Volkart also clearly shows that economic action is always socially embedded and culturally conveyed. The commercial activities of Volkart reflected a cautious approach to business in which speculative endeavors were avoided and every effort was made to respect contractual agreements, regardless of the circumstances. A significant aspect of this approach was that Volkart was a family enterprise, which the business partners viewed as a guarantee for the company's reliability. The firm's corporate culture served as an informal institution that engendered the trust that was necessary to establish and maintain business connections. This culture was eminently important in large part because the global commodities trade was determined by a surprisingly small number of players who often knew each other personally and whose companies and families had maintained business ties for generations. Within such a social context, trading companies could not afford to engage in opportunistic behavior. This also made it worthwhile to maintain long-term business contacts. It is interesting to note that such decisions were hardly made on the strength of price-related considerations, but were instead justified based on the company's traditions. This can be viewed as an indication of the historical path dependency of corporate decisions, and it shows that economic and noneconomic motives cannot be clearly separated from the thoughts and actions of economic players.

The company was far more than an organization that translated nonspecific market signals into the creation of a specific corporate culture and the rendering of specific services. The inner workings of the company can also be interpreted as a culturally influenced interplay of social relations. In the case of Volkart, the concept of an entrepreneurial family served as an important means of solving the principal-agent problem. Although a sophisticated monitoring system was introduced in the 1870s, due to the enormous distances between the individual branches and the essential activities carried out by individual staff members, mere control measures were not enough to prevent opportunistic behavior. Fostering an in-house sense of community was therefore central to the company's success. But employees could also place demands on the company owners based on the concept of an entrepreneurial family. This shows that this cultural concept was much more than a strategic tool that the principals could use to reduce transaction costs. The entrepreneurial family represents a symbolic category that in a certain sense expressed the essence of the company and that all company employees could use to formulate their interests.

This profound degree of in-house stability and the cultivation of ties to business partners allowed the company to establish and maintain long-term collaborations with other merchants. Volkart managed to enter new markets by first conducting transactions via network-like collaborations with local merchants before the company assumed control of subsidiaries in the respective countries. In doing so, the company embarked on a course that resembled the path described as typical for the internationalization of industrial firms.[5] Furthermore, the company worked hand-in-hand with locally established merchants in various parts of the world who served as agents or, in India, as brokers or shroffs.

The enormous importance that such social networks had for the trading business and their frequently astonishing stability show that the question of a company's sphere of activities is often more difficult to pin down than it appears at first glance. From a functional perspective, it would make perfect sense to view the individual merchants who were generally bound by contract to the company as peripheral elements of the firm. If one views a trading company like Volkart as a subnet of global economic interdependencies, then the relationships to agents, brokers, shroffs and compradors represent the nodes where this net began to fray, or rather it marks the place where the European company was intertwined with elements of the global trading network. This leads to another important finding of this study, namely that—at least with regard to the elite corps of each respective merchant class—no cultural divide between a European and Asian way of doing business could be identified. European trading companies were admittedly confronted in Asia with commercial surroundings and a climate that were foreign to them, but they found business partners among the mercantile elite who adhered to sufficiently similar commercial principles to forge fruitful collaborations.

Nevertheless, the cultural aspects of their business transactions should not obscure the fundamental problem of modern global trade. Although Volkart was a company that consistently upheld honorable mercantile values, like other trading companies dealing in commodities it was able to extract exceedingly large profits from the global trading business. By contrast, the agricultural workers and small farmers around the world who cultivated the commodities that Volkart relied upon to do business could, at best, merely eke out a living. This shows that the distribution of profits in the global trading business depended not so much on the moral integrity of individual players as on the structural diversification between industrial centers and agricultural peripheries that has characterized the capitalist global economy of the last two centuries.

Notes

1 Lüthy, "Die Kolonisation und die Einheit der Geschichte," 1991 [1970], 224–227; Bayly, *The Birth of the Modern World*, 2004; Kocka, *Capitalism*, 2016.
2 A flexible approach to regional definitions within the scope of global historic studies is argued by a number of historians, including Feierman, "Afrika in der Geschichte," 2002, 55.
3 For more on industrialization as a global historic phenomenon, see, for example, Osterhammel, *Die Verwandlung der Welt*, 2009, 111.

4 The ability to identify the 1860s and 1970s as decades in which there were fundamental changes in the activities of multinational trading companies offers interesting parallels to the periodization that US historian Charles Maier proposed with his territoriality concept: Maier, "Consigning the Twentieth Century," 2000.
5 Johanson/Wiedersheim-Paul, "The Internationalization of the Firm," 1975.

Bibliography

Archival Sources

Volkart Brothers company archive, Winterthur (VA)
ABB archive Baden (ArABB)
ArABB B.1.2.3.23.6. [Agencies in Asia]
Archive of the Bremen Cotton Exchange (BB)
Volkart Brothers GmbH
Archive of Mission 21, Basel (Arch Miss 21)
Files UTC, 4345 and 4346
National Archive of Costa Rica, San José (ANCR)
Fondo Northern Railway Co., 001000 (1952)
Asociacion Nacional del Café, Guatemala (ANACAFE)
Exportación Realizada del Café, 1960–1990
Baker Library, Harvard University, Historical Collection (BL)
Mss. 761, Stephen M. Weld and Company Collection (Records, 1883–1931)
RBA.9 N413 Neill Bros. & Co.'s Cotton Circular
British Library, London (Brit Lib)
Asia, Pacific and Africa Collections: India Office Records
Diethelm-Archiv, Zurich (DA)
Ca DI 32: Brief von Johannes Niederer, Batavia, an Salomon Volkart, Winterthur, 20. December 1854
Novartis AG company archive, Basel (FAN)
Bestand Sandoz, M 530.6
Guildhall Library, London (GL)
Records of Ralli Bros.
Records of Wallace Brothers & Co. (Holdings) Ltd.
Historical archive of Maschinenfabrik Rieter AG, Winterthur (HAR)
H/i 3556: Vertretungen:
—6/28: Britisch Indien
—6/29a: Vertretungen, Verhandlungen und Verträge: China/Nichizui
—6/29b: Vertretungen, Verhandlungen & Verträge: Volkart, China
—6/30: Vertretungen, Verhandlungen und Verträge: Japan
—7/26: Konfidentielle Vertreter Korrespondenz
Historical archive of Nestlé, Vevey, (HAN)
400–486: Brésil—Matières premières (1970–1979)
1100–1176
4600–4686: Japon—Matières Premières (Commencé 1959)

10002: Nomination de Mr. Peter Reinhart (Volkart) au Conseil d'Administration de Nestal

Instituto del Café de Costa Rica, San José (ICAFE)
Exportaciones por Cosecha y Exportador, 1997/98
Sulzer company archive, Winterthur (KAS)
299c: China
307: Japan, Korresp. Abt. 1 und 20.
314: Indien, Indonesien, Pakistan.
417a: Dr. Hch. Wolfer, Indien-China-Japan 1922/1923.
Library of the International Coffee Organization, London (ICO)
RG.12: Peter Zurschmiede. The world coffee situation as seen by an international trader (1979)
SG.12: Peter Zurschmiede. World Coffee Situation now (1977)
Maharashtra State Archives, Mumbai (MSA)
Revenue Department
National Archives, London (NA)
Board of Trade
Colonial Office
Foreign Office
Treasury Solicitor
National Archives of India, New Delhi (NAI)
Home Department Political Branch
Nehru Memorial Library, New Delhi (NML)
Manuscript Section: Purshotamdas Thakurdas Papers.
Swiss Federal Archive, Bern (BAR)
E2: Auswärtige Angelegenheiten 1848–1895
E 2200: Auslandvertretungen
E 7110: Eidgenössisches Volkswirtschaftsdepartement
Sondersammlungen der Studienbibliothek Winterthur, Handschriftenabteilung (SSW),
Nachlass Georg Reinhart
Nachlass Theodor Reinhart
Nachlass Werner Reinhart
Tata Central Archives, Pune (TCA)
Tata Sons:
—Rack 3, Box 36
—Rack 3, Box 37
University College, London, Special Collections (UCL)
Edward Johnston and Co. archives (GB 0103 JOHNSTON).
Wirtschaftsarchiv Basel, Handschriften (WA)
HS 421: Verband schweizerischer Transit- und Welthandelsfirmen, Basel

Unpublished Individual Sources

Privatarchiv Danièle Burckhardt
Peter Burckhardt-Reinhart, Meine vierte Reise nach der Türkei, 13. August bis 9. Oktober 1941.
Privatarchiv Andreas Zangger
Briefkopierbuch Archibald A. Crawford (1887–1892)

Printed Sources

Alder, Otto. *Jugenderinnerungen eines St. Gallischen Überseers aus den Jahren 1849–1873. Der Familie und Freunden erzählt* (St. Gallen, 1929).

Ammann, August F. *Reminiscences of an Old V.B. Partner, Special Number of the V.B. News, Published by Volkart Brothers and Devoted to the Interests of Their Employees* (Winterthur, 1921).

Anderegg, Jakob. *Volkart Brothers 1851–1976. A Chronicle* (Winterthur, 1976).

Anderson, Clayton & Cía., Ltda. Brazil. *Brazilian Coffee* (Rio de Janeiro, no year given [1957]).

Arndt, Paul. *Deutschlands Stellung in der Weltwirtschaft* (Leipzig, 1913).

Barre, H., "Zur Technik des Baumwollhandels II—VII", *Zeitschrift für Handelswissenschaft und Handelspraxis* 1 (1909), pp. 28–29; 5 (1909), pp. 172–173; 8 (1909), pp. 293–294; 9 (1909), pp. 326–327; 11 (1909), pp. 398–399; 12 (1909), p. 441.

Biedermann, Heinrich. *Lehrbuch des Überseehandels. Organisation, Betrieb, Buchhaltung und Rechnungswesen des überseeischen Export- und Importgeschäftes* (Groß-Lichterfelde-Ost, no year given).

Bombay Chamber of Commerce. *Reports of the Bombay Chamber of Commerce* (1898–1931).

Bowater Organisation. *History and Activities of the Ralli Trading Group. Commodity Merchants for 160 years* (London, 1979).

Bowring, John, *Report on the Commerce and Manufactures of Switzerland. Presented to both Houses of Parliament by Command of His Majesty* (London, 1836).

Contractor, Dorabjee B. *A Handbook of Indian Cotton for Merchants, Shippers, Mills, Factory-Owners and Others Interested in the Cotton Trade* (Bombay, 1928).

Cox, Alonzo B. *Department Bulletin No. 1444. Cotton Prices and Markets* (Washington, 1926).

Crawford, Arthur Travers. *Reminiscences of an Indian Police Official* (London, 1894).

Dantwala, M. L. *Marketing of Raw Cotton in India* (Calcutta, 1937).

———. *A Hundred Years of Indian Cotton* (Bombay, 1947).

Dholakia, H. L. *Futures Trading and Futures Markets in Cotton with Special Reference to India* (Bombay, 1949).

East India Cotton Association. *Bombay Cotton Annual, No. 6* (Bombay, 1924/25).

———. *Bombay Cotton Annual No. 17* (Bombay, 1935/36).

Economic Associates, New York. *World Cotton Position Chart. Disclosing the Dominant Factors for 40 Years of Production—Carryover, Consumption and Developments, Affecting Prizes, 1893–1934* (New York, 1934).

Ellinger, Barnard and Hugh Ellinger. "Japanese Competition in the Cotton Trade" *Journal of the Royal Statistical Society* 18 (1930), pp. 185–201.

Ellison, Thomas. *A Hand-Book of the Cotton Trade: or a Glance at the Past History, Present Condition, and Future Prospects of the Cotton Commerce of the World* (Liverpool, 1858).

Frech, Heinz W. *Baumwolle, Stahl und Stolpersteine. 40 Jahre mit Volkart, Alusuisse und Von Roll* (Frauenfeld, 2001).

Gazeteer of Bombay State (Revised Edition). District Series Volume XX: Poona District (Bombay, 1954).

Gebrüder Volkart. *Calculationstabellen Gebrüder Volkart Winterthur* (Winterthur, 1873).

———. *Situationsberichte der Firma Gebrüder Volkart* (Winterthur, 1921–1925).

————. *Zur Erinnerung an die Hundertjahrfeier der Firma Gebrüder Volkart Winterthur, 1. Februar 1951* [Winterthur, 1951].

————. *The Volkart Foundation 1951–1961* [Winterthur, 1961].

Heine, C. *Die Baumwolle. Ihre Kultur, Ernte, Verarbeitung und der internationale Baumwollhandel* (Leipzig, 1908).

Hesse, Hermann. "Der schwarze König. Ein Gedenkblatt für Georg Reinhart", *Georg Reinhart zum Gedächtnis*, (Verona, 1956), pp. 29–37.

Hofer, Karl. *Erinnerungen eines Malers* (Berlin-Grunewald, 1953).

Indian Central Cotton Committee. *General Report on Eight Investigations into the Finance and Marketing of Cultivators' Cotton* (Bombay, 1929).

————. *Report on an Investigation into the Finance and Marketing of Cultivators' Cotton in Madras (Northerns and Westerns Tract.) 1927–1928* (Bombay, 1929).

————. *Report on an Investigation into the Finance and Marketing of Cultivators' Cotton in Sind* (Bombay, 1929).

————. *Minutes of Evidence Taken Before the Indian Cotton Committee. Volume IV: Commercial. Part I: Minutes of Evidence from United Provinces, Central Provinces, Burma, Sind and Bombay* (Calcutta, 1920).

————. *Minutes of Evidence Taken Before the Indian Cotton Committee. Volume V: Commercial. Part II: Minutes of Evidence from Madras, Bengal, Imperial Officers, Central India, Baroda and Hyderabad* (Calcutta, 1920).

Kindt, Jules. "Notes sur l'industrie et le commerce de la Suisse", in: Ministère de l'Agriculture et du Commerce, ed., *Annales du commerce extérieur, Suisse. Faites commerciaux*, 2 (Paris, 1847), pp. 14–26.

Koenig, Paul. *Der Baumwollweltmarkt in seiner Entwicklung während des Krieges bis zum Friedensschluss* (Berlin, 1919).

League of Nations, *Economic Instability in the Postwar World* (Geneva, 1945).

Levy, Hermann. "Die Enteuropäisierung der Welthandelsbilanz", *Weltwirtschaftliches Archiv* 23 (1926), pp. 329–341.

MacAra, Charles W. *Trade Stability and How to Obtain It* (Manchester, 1925).

Maier-Rothschild, Louis. *Handbuch der gesamten Handelswissenschaften für jüngere und ältere Kaufleute sowie für Industrielle, Gewerbetreibende, Anwälte und Richter. Band II: Buchhaltung und Kontorpraxis* (Berlin, 1914).

Mann, James A. *The Cotton Trade of India. A Paper before the Royal Asiatic Society* (London, 1860).

Müller-Renner, Ernst. "Nachruf im Namen des Personals der Firma Gebrüder Volkart", in: *Zur Erinnerung an Theodor Reinhart, 1848–1919* [Winterthur, 1919], pp. 16–18.

Nicklisch, H. "Zur Technik des Baumwollhandels I", *Zeitschrift für Handelswissenschaft und Handelspraxis*, 10 (1909), pp. 373–377.

Oppel, "Der Handel mit Rohbaumwolle, besonders in Bremen I—II", *Zeitschrift für Handelswissenschaft und Handelspraxis* 5 (1908), pp. 157–162; 6 (1908), pp. 204–211.

Paul Reinhart AG. *200 Years Reinhart* (Winterthur, 1988).

Reinhart AG. *Reinhart. Committed to Cotton Since 1788* (Winterthur, o. J. [after 2003]).

Pearse, Arno S. *The Cotton Industry of Japan and China. Being the Report of the Journey to Japan and China* (Manchester, 1929).

Pearse, Arno S. *The Cotton Industry of India Being the Report of the Journey to India* (Manchester, 1930).

Peters, Thos. *Modern Bombay and Indian States* (Bombay, 1942).

Ralli Brothers' Calcutta Handbook. Volume II. Articles (Calcutta, 1888).

Ralli Brothers Limited (London, 1951).

Ratzka-Ernst, Clara. *Welthandelsartikel und ihre Preise. Eine Studie zur Preisbewegung und Preisbildung.* o.O. [ca. 1910].

Reinhart, Andreas. "Nachwort: die Vision 2000", in Walter H. Rambousek, Armin Vogt and Hans R. Volkart. *Volkart. Die Geschichte einer Welthandelsfirma* (Frankfurt a. M., 1990), pp. 199–200.

Reinhart, Georg. *Gedenkschrift zum fünfundsiebzigjährigen Bestehen der Firma Gebr. Volkart* (Winterthur. 1926).

———. *Aus meinem Leben* (Winterthur, 1931).

Reinhart, Peter. "Rede zur Hundertjahrfeier", in *Zur Erinnerung an die Hundertjahrfeier der Firma Gebrüder Volkart Winterthur, 1. Februar 1951* [Winterthur, 1951], pp. 9–20.

Reinhart, Theodor. *Ausgewählte Schriften aus seinem Nachlass* (Winterthur, 1920).

Remfry, C. O. *Commercial Law in British India* (Calcutta, 1912).

Rivett-Carnac, Harry. *Report of the Cotton Department for the Year 1867–1868* (Bombay, 1869).

Royle, John Forbes. *Culture and Commerce of Cotton in India and Elsewhere* (London, 1851).

Sanders, F. R. A *Report on a Visit to the Coffee Producing Countries of Central and South America, November 1953—February 1954.* Without place or year [1954].

Schlote, Werner. "Zur Frage der sogenannten „Enteuropäisierung" des Welthandels", *Weltwirtschaftliches Archiv* 37 (1933), pp. 381–411.

Schmidt, Fritz. "Die Geschäfte in Baumwolle zu Le Havre I—VIII", *Zeitschrift für Handelswissenschaft und Handelspraxis* 4 (1910), pp. 128–130; 7 (1910), pp. 251–255; 8 (1910), pp. 290–291; 9 (1910), pp. 329f.; 2 (1911), pp. 49–51; 11 (1912), pp. 363–365; 12 (1912), pp. 395–396.

Schmidt, Peter Heinrich. *Der Wirtschaftskrieg und die Neutralen* (Zurich, 1918).

Smith, Samuel. *The Cotton Trade of India. Being a Series of Letters Written from Bombay in the Spring of 1863* (Liverpool, 1863).

Tata Group. *Tata* (Mumbai, 2009).

"Trading with the enemy (Extension of Powers) 5 & 6, cited from 'The British Black List' ", *Harvard Law Review* 30 (1917), pp. 279.

United Nations Statistical Office. *International Trade Statistics 1900–1960* (New York, 1962).

V.B. News. Published by Volkart Brothers, Winterthur, and Devoted to the Interests of Their Employees (1920–1927).

Verein der am Kaffeehandel beteiligten Firmen in Bremen e. V. Kaffee. *Handel—Pflanzung—Wirtschaftspolitische Bedeutung—Geschichte* (Bremen, Bielefeld and Frankfurt a. M., 1950).

Volcafe—ED&F Coffee Division. *Your Partner from Tree to Roasting Plant* (Winterthur, 2005).

Volkart Bros. *Cotton 1939–1945* (New York, 1945).

Wachter, H. "Nachruf im Namen der Arbeitsgemeinschaft der Firma Gebrüder Volkart in Winterthur, gehalten in der Stadtkirche Winterthur am 1. September 1951", in *Zur Erinnerung an Werner Reinhart, 1884–1951*, [Winterthur, 1951], pp. 13–15.

Watson, John Forbes. *Report on Cotton Gins and on the Cleaning and Quality of Indian Cotton. Part I: Summary and Conclusion* (London, 1879).

Weber, Max. "Rede", in: *Zur Erinnerung an die Hundertjahrfeier der Firma Gebrüder Volkart Winterthur, 1. Februar 1951*, [Winterthur, 1951], pp. 25–27.

———. "Rede gehalten am 16. September 1955 anlässlich der Erinnerungsfeier für Herrn Georg Reinhart", in *Georg Reinhart zum Gedächtnis* (Verona, 1956), pp. 9–13.

Wheeler, Leslie A. *International Trade in Cotton* (= United States Department of Commerce, Trade Promotion Series, No. 13) (Washington, 1925).

Wright, John W., Francis L. Gerdes und Charles A. Bennett. *The Packaging of American Cotton and Methods for Improvement* (= United States Department of Agriculture, Circular No. 736) (Washington, 1945).

Zur Erinnerung an Theodor Reinhart, 1848–1919 [Winterthur, 1919].

Periodicals

Bilanz
Basler Zeitung
Brown Boveri Hauszeitung
Cash
Coffee & Cocoa International
Der Landbote (Winterthur)
Kaffee- und Tee-Markt
La Nacion (San José)
Neue Zürcher Zeitung
NZZ am Sonntag
Revista do Comércio de Café
Schweizerische Handelszeitung
Schweizerisches Handelsamtsblatt
Tages-Anzeiger (Zurich)
Tata Monthly Bulletin
Tata Review
Tea and Coffee Trade Journal
The Times (London)
Weltwoche (Zurich)
Wir und unser Werk, Brown Boveri Hauszeitung

Interviews

Interview with Paul Brose, Ciudad de Guatemala, 19 March 2008.
Interview with William Hempstead, Ciudad de Guatemala, 17 March 2008.
Interview with Otto Kloeti, Alajuela (Costa Rica), 28 March 2008.
Interview with Paul Moeller, Winterthur, 26 November 2007.
Interview with Thomas Nottebohm, Ciudad de Guatemala, 18 March 2008.
Interview with Ronald Peters, San José (Costa Rica), 1 April 2008.
Interview with Jürgen Plate, Heredia (Costa Rica), 27 March 2008.
Interview with Paul Alfred Reinhart, Winterthur, 8 July 2008.
Interview with Peter Schoenfeld jun., Tres Rios (Costa Rica), 31 March 2008.
Interview with Jörg von Saalfeld, Heredia (Costa Rica), 27 March 2008.
Interview with Ernst H. Schaefer (telephone), 26 August 2008.
Interview with Peter Zurschmiede, Zurich, 8 February 2008.

Internet Sources

www.alacrastore.com/mergers-acquisitions/Anderson_Clayton_Corp-3163663 (19 January 2010).
www.andersonclayton.com/index.cfm?show=10&mid=7&pid=1 (19 January 2010).
www.emerald-ventures.com/team/walterLocher.aspx (19 January 2010).
www.pradochaves.com.br/v2/ingles/marca.htm (2 November 2009).
www.rallis.co.in/aboutus/hist1854.htm (15 May 2009).
www.thecottonschool.com/PR%20Bio.pdf (19 January 2010).
www.volcafe.com/history/index.html (1 December 2009).
www.volcot.ch (20 January 2010).
www.volkart.ch/English/PortraitGeschichteHolding150Jahre.htm (19 January 2010).
www.voltas.com (13 June 2010).
www.winterthur-glossar.ch/upload/documents/2011/02/19/531.pdf (5 June 2012).

Literature

Ahuja, Ravi. *Die Erzeugung kolonialer Staatlichkeit und das Problem der Arbeit. Eine Studie zur Sozialgeschichte der Stadt Madras und ihres Hinterlandes zwischen 1750 und 1800* (Stuttgart 1999).

Akita, Shigeru and Nicholas J. White, eds., *The International Order of Asia in the 1930s and 1950s* (Farnham and Burlington, 2010).

Allen, John. *Lost Geographies of Power* (Malden MA, 2003)

Altermatt, Claude. *Zwei Jahrhunderte Schweizer Auslandvertretungen.* (Bern, 1990).

Amatori, Franco and Geoffrey Jones, eds., *Business History Around the World* (Cambridge, 2003).

Amsden, Alice H., *The Rise of "the Rest". Challenges to the West from Late-Industrializing Economies* (New York, 2001).

Anderson, Carl G. "Cotton Marketing", in C. W. Smith and J. T. Cothren, eds., *Cotton. Origin, History, Technology, and Production* (New York, 1999), pp. 659–679.

Appadurai, Arjun. "Introduction: Commodities and the Politics of Value" in Arjun Appadurai, ed., *The Social Life of Things. Commodities in Cultural Perspective* (Cambridge, 1986), pp. 3–63.

———. *Modernity at Large. Cultural Dimensions of Globalization* (Minneapolis, 2000).

Arrighi, Giovanni. *The Long Twentieth Century. Money, Power, and the Origins of our Times* (London and New York, 1994).

Austin, Gareth and Kaoru Sugihara. "Local Suppliers of Credit in the Third World, 1750–1960: Introduction", in Gareth Austin and Kaoru Sugihara, eds., *Local Suppliers of Credit in the Third World, 1750–1960* (New York, 1993) pp. 1–25.

Bähr, Johannes, Jörg Lesczenski and Katja Schmidtpott. *Winds of Change. On the 150th Anniversary of C. Illies & Co.* (Munich, 2009).

Bammatter, Emil M. *Der schweizerische Transithandel. Eine Darstellung seiner Struktur und ein Überblick seiner Entwicklung in den Jahren 1934–1954* (Lörrach, 1958).

Bartu Friedemann. *The Fan Tree Company. Three Swiss Merchants in Asia* (Zurich, 2005).

Bates, Robert H. *Open-Economy Politics. The Political Economy of the World Coffee Trade* (Princeton, 1997).

Bayly, Christopher Alan. *Rulers, Townsmen and Bazaars. North Indian Society in the Age of British Expansion, 1770–1870* (Cambridge, 1983).
———. *The Birth of the Modern World, 1780–1914. Global Connections and Comparisons* (Malden, Oxford and Carlton, 2004).

Beckert, Jens, Rainer Diaz-Bone and Heiner Ganßmann, eds., *Märkte als soziale Strukturen* (Frankfurt a. M. and New York, 2007).

Beckert, Sven. "Emancipation and Empire. Reconstructing the Worldwide Web of Cotton Production in the Age of the American Civil War", *American Historical Review*, 109 (2004), pp. 1405–1438.
———. "From Tuskegee to Togo. The Problem of Freedom in the Empire of Cotton", *Journal of American History* 92 (2005), pp. 498–526.
———. *Empire of Cotton. A Global History* (New York, 2014).

Bell, Thomas M. and Fred E.M. Gillham. *The World of Cotton*, (Washington D.C., 1989).

Benton, Lauren. *Law and Colonial Cultures. Legal Regimes in World History, 1400–1900*, (Cambridge MA, 2002).

Berghoff, Hartmut. "Vermögenseliten in Deutschland und England vor 1914. Überlegungen zu einer vergleichenden Sozialgeschichte des Reichtums, in: Hartmut Berghoff and Dieter Ziegler, eds., *Pionier und Nachzügler? Komparative Studien zur Geschichte Großbritanniens und Deutschlands im Zeitalter der Industrialisierung. Festschrift für Sidney Pollard zum 70. Geburtstag* (Bochum, 1995), pp. 281–308.
———. *Zwischen Kleinstadt und Weltmarkt. Hohner und die Harmonika. Unternehmensgeschichte als Gesellschaftsgeschichte* (Paderborn, 1997).
———. "Unternehmenskultur und Herrschaftstechnik. Industrieller Paternalismus: Hohner 1857 bis 1918", *Geschichte und Gesellschaft* 23 (1997), pp. 167–204.
———. *Moderne Unternehmensgeschichte* (Paderborn, Munich, Vienna and Zurich, 2004).
———. "Die Zähmung des entfesselten Prometheus? Die Generierung von Vertrauenskapital und die Konstruktion des Marktes im Industrialisierungs- und Globalisierungsprozess", in: Hartmut Berghoff and Jakob Vogel, eds., *Wirtschaftsgeschichte als Kulturgeschichte. Dimensionen eines Perspektivenwechsels* (Frankfurt a. M. and New York, 2004), pp. 143–168.
——— and Jakob Vogel, eds., *Wirtschaftsgeschichte als Kulturgeschichte. Dimensionen eines Perspektivenwechsels* (Frankfurt a. M. and New York, 2004).

Bernecker, Walther L. and Thomas Fischer. "Entwicklung und Scheitern der Dependenztheorien in Lateinamerika", *Periplus* 5 (1995), pp. 98–118.

Bhattacharya. Bhaswati, Gita Dharampal-Frick and Jos Gommans. "Spatial and Temporal Continuities of Merchant Networks in South Asia and the Indian Ocean (1500–2000)", *Journal of the Economic and Social History of the Orient* 50 (2007), pp. 91–105.

Biotti, Claudia. *Die Exportrisikogarantie als Instrument der Exportförderung. Die Haltung des Schweizerischen Handels- und Industrievereins in der Zwischenkriegszeit und den frühen Nachkriegsjahren. Seminararbeit am Institut für Empirische Wirtschaftsforschung* (Zurich, 2002).

Bonin, Hubert. Christophe Bouneau, Ludovic Cailluet, Alexandre Fernandez and Silvia Marzagalli, eds., *Transnational Companies (19th—20th Centuries)* (Paris, 2002).

Bonus, Holger. "Unternehmen in institutionenökonomischer Sicht", in Clemens Wischermann, Peter Borscheid and Karl-Peter Ellerbrock, eds., *Unternehmenskommunikation im 19. und 20. Jahrhundert* (Dortmund, 2000), pp. 17–29.

Borchardt, Knut. "Globalisierung in historischer Perspektive", in Jürgen Oster-hammel, ed., *Weltgeschichte. Basistexte* (Stuttgart, 2008), pp. 217–238.

Bourdieu, Pierre. *Outline of a Theory of Practice* (Cambridge, 1977).

Braudel, Fernand. *The Wheels of Commerce. Volume II of Civilization and Capitalism, 15th–18th Century* (New York, 1982).

———. *La dynamique du capitalisme* (Paris, 1985).

Broadberry Stephan and Mark Harrison, eds., *The Economics of World War I*, (Cambridge, 2005).

Buchheim, Christoph. *Industrielle Revolutionen. Langfristige Wirtschaftsentwicklungen in Großbritannien, Europa und Übersee* (Munich, 1994).

Burns, E. Bradford. *A History of Brazil* (New York, 1980).

Cameron, Rondo. *A Concise Economic History of the World. From Paleolithic Times to the Present* (New York and Oxford, 1989).

Campos López, Triny, Elizabeth Jiménez Jiménez, Adriana Sancho Quesada and Hans Velásquez Quesada. *Propuesta para el Manejo Electrónico de la Información en el Departamento de Servicios Financieros de Beneficios Volcafe de Costa Rica S.A. Memoria de Seminario, Facultad de Ciencias Económica*s (San José, 2001).

Cardoso, Fernando Henrique and Enzo Faletto. *Abhängigkeit und Entwicklung in Lateinamerika* (Frankfurt a. M., 1984).

Carlos, Ann M. and Stephen J. Nicholas. "Giants of an Earlier Capitalism. Chartered Trading Companies as Modern Multinationals" *Business History Review* 62 (1988), pp. 399–419.

Carrier, James G. eds., *Meanings of the Market. The Free Market in Western Culture* (Oxford and New York, 1997).

———. "Introduction", in: James G. Carrier, ed., *Meanings of the Market. The Free Market in Western Culture* (Oxford and New York, 1997), pp. 1–67.

Cassis, Youssef. *Les Capitales du Capital* (Genève, 2005).

Casson, Mark. "Institutional Economics and Business History. A Way Forward", in Mark Casson and Mary B. Rose, eds., *Institutions and the Evolution of Modern Business* (London and Portland OR, 1998), pp. 151–171.

———. "The Economic Analysis of Multinational Trading Companies", in Geoffrey Jones, eds., *The Multinational Traders* (London and New York, 1998), pp. 22–47.

———."The Family Firm. An Analyses of the Dynastic Motive", in Mark Casson, ed., *Enterprise and Leadership. Studies on Firms, Markets and Networks* (Cheltenham and Northampton, 2000), pp. 197–235.

———. "An Economic Approach to Regional Business Networks", in John F. Wilson and Andrew Popp, eds., *Industrial Clusters and Regional Business Networks in England, 1750–1970* (Aldershot, 2003), pp. 19–43.

Castells, Manuel. "Materials of an Exploratory Theory of the Network Society", *British Journal of Sociology* 51 (2000), pp. 5–24.

Chalmin, Philippe. "International Trading Companies", *Journal of World Trade Law* 14 (1980), pp. 535–541.

———. "Problématique d'un controle des activités des sociétés de négoce international de matières premières", in Claude Mouton and Philippe Chalmin, eds., *Commerce international et matières premières* (Paris, 1981), pp. 25–42.

———. *Négociants et chargeurs. La saga du négoce international des matières premières* (Paris, 1985).

———. "The Rise of International Commodity Trading Companies in Europe in the Nineteenth Century", in Shin'ichi Yonekawa and Hideki Yoshihara, eds., *Business History of General Trading Companies* (Tokyo 1987), pp. 273–291.

Chandavarkar, Rajnarayan. *The Origins of Industrial Capitalism in India. Business Strategies and the Working Classes in Bombay, 1900–1940* (Cambridge, 1994).

——. *Imperial Power and Popular Politics. Class, Resistance and the State in India, c. 1850–1950* (Cambridge, 1998).

Chandler, Alfred D. *The Visible Hand. The Managerial Revolution in American Business* (Cambridge MA and London, 1977).

——. *Scale and Scope. The Dynamics of Industrial Capitalism* (Cambridge MA and London, 2004 [1990]).

—— and Bruce Mazlish, eds., *Leviathans. Multinational Corporations and the New Global History* (Cambridge MA, 2005).

Chapman, Malcolm and Peter J. Buckley. "Markets, Transaction Costs, Economists and Social Anthropologists", in James G. Carrier, ed., *Meanings of the Market. The Free Market in Western Culture* (Oxford and New York, 1997), pp. 225–250.

Chapman, Stanley. *Merchant Enterprise in Britain. From the Industrial Revolution to World War I* (Cambridge, 1992).

——. *The Rise of Merchant Banking* (London, Boston and Sydney, 1984).

Charlesworth, Neil. *Peasants and Imperial Rule. Agriculture and Agrarian Society in the Bombay Presidency, 1850–1935* (Cambridge, 1985).

Chaudhuri, Kirti N. *The Trading World of Asia and the English East India Company, 1660–1760* (Cambridge and New York, 1978).

Chaves Murillo, Johanna. *Competitividad Internacional de la Industria Cafetalera Costarricense. Tesis de la Universidad Nacional, Heredia* (Heredia, 2001).

Clarence-Smith, William Gervase. "The Global Consumption of Hot Beverages, c. 1500 to c. 1900", in Alexander Nützenadel and Frank Trentmann, eds., *Food and Globalization. Consumption, Markets and Politics in the Modern World* (New York, 2008), pp. 37–55.

Clark, Gregory. *A Farewell to Alms. A Brief Economic History of the World* (Princeton and Oxford, 2007).

Clark, Ian. *Globalization and Fragmentation. International Relations in the Twentieth Century* (Oxford, 1997).

Clayton Garwood. Ellen, *Will Clayton. A Short Biography* (Austin, 1958).

Coase, Ronald H. "The Nature of the Firm", *Economica, New Series* 4 (1937), pp. 386–405.

Cochran, Sherman. "Businesses, Governments, and War in China, 1931–1949", in Akira Iriye and Warren Cohen, eds., *American, Chinese, and Japanese Perspectives on Wartime Asia, 1931–1949* (Wilmington, 1990), pp. 117–145.

——. "Three Roads into Shanghai's Market. Japanese, Western, and Chinese Companies in the Match Trade, 1895–1937", in Frederic Wakeman and Wen-hsin Yeh, eds., *Shanghai Sojourners* (Berkeley, 1992), pp. 35–75.

Colli, Andrea. *The History of Family Business, 1850–2000* (Cambridge, 2003).

—— and Mary B. Rose, "Family Firms in Comparative Perspective", in Franco Amatori and Geoffrey Jones, eds., *Business History around the World* (Cambridge, 2003), pp. 339–352.

Collingham, Elizabeth M. *Imperial Bodies. The Physical Experience of the Raj, c.1800–1947* (Cambridge, 2001).

Conrad, Sebastian, *Globalisation and the Nation in Imperial Germany* (Cambridge, 2010).

——. and Andreas Eckert, "Globalgeschichte, Globalisierung, multiple Modernen: Zur Geschichtsschreibung der modernen Welt", in: Sebastian Conrad,

Andreas Eckert and Ulrike Freitag, eds., *Globalgeschichte. Theorien, Ansätze, Themen* (Frankfurt a. M. and New York, 2007), pp. 7–49.

Cooper, Frederick. "What is the Concept of Globalization Good For? An African Historian's Perspective", *African Affairs* 100 (2001), pp. 189–213.

Darwin, John. *After Tamerlane. The Global History of Empire since 1405* (London, 2007).

Das Gupta, Ashin. *Indian Merchants and the Decline of Surat, c. 1700–1775* (Wiesbaden, 1979).

———. *The World of the Indian Ocean Merchant 1500–1800* (Oxford, 2001).

David, Thomas and Bouda Etemad. "Gibt es einen schweizerischen Imperialismus? Zur Einführung", *traverse. Zeitschrift für Geschichte* 5 (1998), pp. 17–27.

Dehne, Philip. "From 'Business as Usual' to a More Global War: The British Decision to Attack Germans in South America during the First World War", *Journal of British Studies* 44 (2005), pp. 516–535.

Dejung, Christof. "Einbettung", in: Christof Dejung, Monika Dommann and Daniel Speich Chassé, eds., *Auf der Suche nach der Ökonomie. Historische Annäherungen* (Tübingen, 2014), pp. 47–71.

———. "Unbekannte Intermediäre. Schweizerische Handelsfirmen im 19. und 20. Jahrhundert", *traverse. Zeitschrift für Geschichte* 1 (2010), Sonderheft „Wirtschaftsgeschichte", pp. 139–155.

——— and Andreas Zangger. "British Wartime Protectionism and Swiss Trading Firms in Asia during the First World War", *Past and Present* 207 (2010), pp. 181–213.

——— and Niels P. Petersson, eds., *Foundations of World-Wide Economic Integration. Power, Institutions and Global Markets, 1850–1930* (Cambridge and New York, 2013).

Dobbin, Christine. *Asian Entrepreneurial Minorities. Conjoint Communities in the Making of the World-Economy* (London and New York, 1996).

Dunning. John H, *Multinational Enterprises and the Global Economy* (Wokingham, 1993).

Dutta, Sudipt. *Family Business in India* (New Delhi, Thousand Oaks and London, 1998).

Engdahl, Tobjörn. *The Exchange of Cotton. Uganda Peasants, Colonial Market Regulations and the Organisation of the International Cotton Trade, 1904–1918* (Uppsala, 1999).

Engel, Alexander. *Farben der Globalisierung. Die Entstehung moderner Märkte für Farbstoffe 1500–1900* (Frankfurt a. M. and New York, 2009).

Epple, Angelika. "Gebr. Stollwercks Aufstieg zum Multinational. Kontrolle und 'Controlling' in Köln, London, Wien und Poszony", in Christian Hillen, ed., *"Mit Gott". Zum Verhältnis von Vertrauen und Wirtschaftsgeschichte* (Köln, 2007), pp. 26–43.

Esquivel Prestinary, Adriana and Paula Lizano Van der Laat. *El Papel del Estado, la Libertad de Comercio y su Tutela Constitucional en la Actividad Económica Cafetalera Costaricense: Hacia una Nueva Ruta. Tesis de la Universidad de Costa Rica* (San José, 1994).

Fäßler, Peter E. *Globalisierung* (Köln, 2007)

Farnie, Douglas A. "The Role of Merchants as Prime Movers in the Expansion of the Cotton Industry", in Douglas A. Farnie and David J. Jeremy, eds., *The Fibre that Changed the World. The Cotton Industry in International Perspective, 1600–1990s* (Oxford and New York, 2004), pp. 15–55.

352 Bibliography

———. "The Role of Cotton Textiles in the Economic Development of India, 1600.1990", in Douglas A. Farnie and David J. Jeremy, eds., *The Fibre that Changed the World. The Cotton Industry in International Perspective, 1600–1990s* (Oxford and New York, 2004), pp. 395–430.

Feinstein, Charles H. Peter Temin and Gianni Toniolo, *The World Economy Between the World Wars* (New York, 2008).

Feierman, Steven. "Afrika in der Geschichte. Das Ende der universalen Erzählungen", in Sebastian Conrad and Shalini Randeria, eds., *Jenseits des Eurozentrismus. Postkoloniale Perspektiven in den Geschichts- und Kulturwissenschaften* (Frankfurt a. M. and New York, 2002), pp. 50–83.

Ferguson, Niall. *The Pity of War. Explaining World War I* (New York, 1999).

———. *The Ascent of Money. A Financial History of the World* (London, 2008).

Fiedler, Martin. "Vertrauen ist gut, Kontrolle ist teuer. Vertrauen als Schlüsselkategorie wirtschaftlichen Handelns", *Geschichte und Gesellschaft* 27 (2001), pp. 576–592.

Fieldhouse, David K. "'A New Imperial System'? The Role of the Multinational Corporations Reconsidered", in Wolfgang J. Mommsen and Jürgen Osterhammel, eds., *Imperialism and After. Continuities and Discontinuities* (London, Boston and Sydney, 1986), pp. 225–240.

Findlay, Ronald and Kevin H. O'Rourke. *Power and Plenty. Trade, War, and the World Economy in the Second Millenium* (Princeton and Oxford, 2007).

Fischer, Thomas. "Toggenburger Buntweberei auf dem Weltmarkt. Ein Beispiel schweizerischer Unternehmerstrategien im 19. Jahrhundert", in Paul Bairoch and Martin Körner, eds., *Die Schweiz in der Weltwirtschaft (15.—20. Jh.)* (Zurich, 1990), pp. 183–205.

Fischer, Wolfram. "Bergbau, Industrie und Handwerk 1850–1914", in Wolfgang Zorn, ed., *Handbuch der deutschen Wirtschafts- und Sozialgeschichte, Band 2: Das 19. und 20. Jahrhundert* (Stuttgart, 1976), pp. 527–562.

———. *Expansion—Integration—Globalisierung. Studien zur Geschichte der Weltwirtschaft* (Göttingen, 1998).

Flath, David. *The Japanese Economy* (Oxford, 2000).

Fleer, Peter. "La Oligarquía Cafetalera y las Elitas Políticas en Guatemala de 1920 a 1944", in Thomas Fischer, ed., *Ausländische Unternehmen und einheimische Eliten in Lateinamerika. Historische Erfahrungen und aktuelle Tendenzen* (Frankfurt a. M., 2001), pp. 119–128.

Fletcher III, W. Miles. "The Japan Spinners Association. Creating Industrial Policy in Meiji Japan", in Steven Tolliday, ed., *The Economic Development of Modern Japan, 1868–1945. From the Meiji Restoration to the Second World War, Volume I* (Cheltenham and Northampton, 2001), pp. 543–569.

Foley, Neil. *The White Scourge. Mexican, Blacks, and Poor Whites in Texas Cotton Culture* (Berkeley, Los Angeles and London, 1997).

Foreman-Peck, James. *A History of the World Economy. International Economic Relations Since 1850* (New York, 1995).

Forster, Simone. *Die Baumwolle. Eine Geschichte ohne Ende.* (Bern [ca. 1985]).

Frank, André Gunder. *Kapitalismus und Unterentwicklung in Lateinamerika* (Frankfurt a. M., 1975).

Frey, Bruno S. *Not Just for the Money. An Economic Theory of Personal Motivation* (Cheltenham, 1997).

Frey, Marc. "Trade, Ships, and the Neutrality of the Netherlands in the First World War", *The International History Review* 19 (1997), pp. 541–562.

Gallagher, John and Ronald Robinson. "The Imperialism of Free Trade", *Economic History Review, New Series* 6 (1953), pp. 1–15.

Ganz, Werner. *Winterthur. Einführung in seine Geschichte von den Anfängen bis 1798* (Winterthur, 1960).

Garside, Alston Hill. *Cotton Goes to Market. A Graphic Description of a Great Industry* (New York, 1935).

Geertz, Clifford. *The Interpretation of Cultures. Selected Essays* (New York, 1973).

Gereffi, Gary and Miguel Korzeniewicz, eds., *Commodity Chains and Global Capitalism* (Westport, Conn. and London, 1994).

Gerencia Comercial—Unidad de Información Comercial. "La Industria Cafetera Internaciónal y su Grado de Concentración", in *Ensayos sobre Economia Cafetera* (ed. Federación Nacional de Cafeteros de Colombia), Año 1, No. (1988), pp. 12–26.

Giddens, Anthony. *The Constitution of Society. Outline of the Theory of Structuration* (Cambridge, 1984).

Goody, Jack. *The East in the West* (Cambridge, 1996).

Gorißen, Stefan. "Der Preis des Vertrauens. Unsicherheit, Institutionen und Rationalität im frühneuzeitlichen Fernhandel", in Ute Frevert, ed., *Vertrauen. Historische Annäherungen* (Göttingen, 2003), pp. 90–118.

Gossler, Claus. *Die Société commerciale de l'Océanie (1876–1914). Aufstieg und Untergang der Hamburger Godeffroys in Ost-Polynesien* (Bremen, 2006).

Grandin, Greg. *The Last Colonial Massacre. Latin America in the Cold War* (Chicago and London, 2004).

Granovetter, Mark. "Economic Action and Social Structure. The Problem of Embeddedness", *The American Journal of Sociology* 91 (1985), pp. 481–510.

Greenhill, Robert. *British Export Houses, the Brazilian Coffee Trade and the Question of Control, 1850–1914. University of Cambridge, Centre of Latin American Studies, Working Papers No. 6.* [ca. 1972].

———. "E. Johnston. "150 Years of Coffee", in Edmar Bacha and Robert Greenhill, eds., *Marcellino Martins & E. Johnston. 150 Years of Coffee.* (no place of publication given, 1992), pp. 131–266.

Greif, Avner. "Institutions and International Trade. Lessons from the Commercial Revolution", *American Economic Review* 82 (1992), pp. 128–133.

Grove, Linda. "International Trade and the Creation of Domestic Marketing Networks in North China, 1860–1930", in Shinya Sugiyama and Linda Grove, eds., *Commercial Networks in Modern Asia* (Richmond, 2001), pp. 96–115.

Guex, Sébastien. "The Development of Swiss Trading Companies in the Twentieth Century", in Geoffrey Jones, ed., *The Multinational Traders* (London and New York, 1998), pp. 150–172.

Guha, Amalendu. *More About Parsi Seths. Their Roots, Entrepreneurship and Comprador Role, 1650–1918. Centre for Studies in Social Science, Calcutta. Occasional Paper No. 50* (Calcutta, 1982).

Guha, Sumit. *The Agrarian Economy of the Bombay Deccan 1818–1941* (Delhi, Bombay, Calcutta and Madras, 1985).

Guinnane. Timothy W, "Trust: A Concept Too Many", *Jahrbuch für Wirtschaftsgeschichte* 46 (2005), pp. 77–92.

354 Bibliography

Hack, Lothar. "Auf der Suche nach der verlorenen Totalität. Von Marx' kapitalistischer Gesellschaftsformation zu Wallersteins Analyse der 'Weltsysteme'?", in Bettina Heintz, Richard Münch and Hartmann Tyrell, eds., *Weltgesellschaft. Theoretische Zugänge und empirische Problemlagen* (Stuttgart, 2005), pp. 120–158.

Häberlein. Mark and Christof Jeggle, eds., *Praktiken des Handels. Geschäfte und soziale Beziehungen europäischer Kaufleute in Mittelalter und früher Neuzeit* (Konstanz, 2010).

Hall, Nigel. "The Liverpool Cotton Market. Britain's First Futures Market", *Transactions of the Historic Society of Lancashire and Cheshire* 149 (1999), pp. 99–117.

Hamid, Abdul. *A Chronicle of British Indian Legal History* (Jaipur, 1991).

Hao, Yen-p'ing. "A "New Class" in China's Treaty Ports. The Rise of the Comprador-Merchants", *Business History Review* 44 (1970), pp. 446–459.

Hardach Gerd. *Der Erste Weltkrieg (= Geschichte der Weltwirtschaft im 20. Jahrhundert, Band 2)* (Munich and Harmondsworth, 1973).

Hardiman, David. "Usury, Dearth and Famine in Western India", *Past and Present* 152 (1996), pp. 113–156.

Harley, Charles K. "The Shift from Sailing Ships to Steamships, 1850–1890. A Study in Technological Change and its Diffusion", in Donald N. McCloskey, ed., *Essays on a Mature Economy. Britain after 1840* (Princeton, 1971), pp. 215–234.

Harnetty, Peter. *Imperialism and Free Trade. Lancashire and India in the Mid-Nineteenth Century* (Manchester, 1972).

Harvey, David. *The New Imperialism* (New York, 2003).

Haskell, Thomas L. and Richard F. Teichgraeber III, eds., *The Culture of the Market. Historical Essays* (Cambridge, 1993).

Hauser, Kaspar and Max Fehr. *Die Familie Reinhart in Winterthur. Geschichtliches und Genealogisches* (Winterthur, 1922).

Hauser-Dora, Angela Maria. *Die wirtschaftlichen und handelspolitischen Beziehungen der Schweiz zu überseeischen Gebieten* (Bern, 1986).

Headrick, Daniel R. *The Tools of Empire. Technology and European Imperialism in the Nineteenth Century* (New York and Oxford, 1981).

———. *The Tentacles of Progress. Technology Transfer in the Age of Imperialism, 1850–1940* (Oxford, 1988).

Helfferich, Emil. *Die Wirtschaft Niederländisch-Indiens im Weltkriege und heute. Vortrag gehalten in der Geographischen Gesellschaft in Hamburg am 7. Oktober 1920* (Hamburg, 1921).

Herrero Serrano, Fernando. *Algunas Factores de la Industria Cafetalera de Costa Rica. Concepción, Actividad, Manejo de Beneficios, Contabilidad. Tesis, Universidad de Costa Rica, Escuela de Ciencias Economicás y Sociales* (San José, 1960).

Herrmann-Pillath, Carsten. *Kritik der reinen Theorie des internationalen Handels. Band 1: Transaktionstheoretische Grundlagen* (Marburg, 2001).

Hettling, Manfred and Stefan-Ludwig Hoffmann. "Der bürgerliche Wertehimmel. Zum Problem individueller Lebensführung im 19. Jahrhundert!", *Geschichte und Gesellschaft* 23 (1997), pp. 333–359.

Hicks, John. *A Theory of Economic History* (New York, 1969).

Hobsbawm, Eric. *The Age of Extremes. The Short Twentieth Century, 1914–1991* (London, 1994).

Holloway, John. "Reform des Staats. Globales Kapital und nationaler Staat", *Prokla. Zeitschrift für kritische Sozialwissenschaft* 90 (1993) Sondernummer "Regionalisierung der Weltgesellschaft", pp. 12–33.

Hosoya, Chihiro. "The United States and East Asia in the mid-1930s. The Cotton and Wheat Loan", in Akira Iriye and Warren Cohen, eds., *American, Chinese, and Japanese Perspectives on Wartime Asia, 1931–1949* (Wilmington, 1990), pp. 73–91.

Howe, Anthony. *Free Trade and Liberal England, 1846–1946* (Oxford, 1997).

Hughes, Alex and Suzanne Reimer, eds., *Geographies of Commodity Chains* (London and New York, 2004).

Hürlimann, Katja. "Eintrag 'Hans Caspar Hirzel' ", *Historisches Lexikon der Schweiz*, www.hls-dhs-dss.ch (14 July 2008).

Isaacman, Allen F. *Cotton Is the Mother of Poverty. Peasants, Work, and Rural Struggle in Colonial Mozambique, 1938–1961* (Portsmouth, 1996).

Isler, Alexander. *Winterthur in Wort und Bild. Eine Festgabe für das eidgenössische Schützenfest vom Jahr 1895 in Winterthur* (Winterthur, 1895).

James, Harold. *The End of Globalization. Lessons from the Great Depression* (Cambridge MA and London, 2001).

———. *Family Capitalism. Wendels, Haniels, Falcks, and the Continental European Model* (Cambridge MA and London, 2006).

Jeremy, David J. "Organization and Management in the Global Cotton Industry, 1800s—1990s", in: Douglas A. Farnie and David J. Jeremy, eds., *The Fibre that Changed the World. The Cotton Industry in International Perspective, 1600–1990s* (Oxford and New York 2004), pp. 191–245.

Johanson, Jan and Finn Wiedersheim-Paul. "The Internationalization of the Firm— Four Swedish Cases", *Journal of Management Studies* 12 (1975), pp. 305–322.

Jones, Charles A. *International Business in the Nineteenth Century. The Rise and Fall of a Cosmopolitan Bourgeoisie* (Brighton, 1987).

Jones, Geoffrey. *British Multinational Banking, 1830–1990* (Oxford 1993).

———, ed., *The Multinational Traders* (London and New York, 1998).

———. "Multinational Trading Companies in History and Theory", in Geoffrey Jones, ed., *The Multinational Traders* (London and New York, 1998), pp. 1–21.

———. *Merchants to Multinationals. British Trading Companies in the Nineteenth and Twentieth Centuries* (Oxford and New York, 2000).

———. *Multinationals and Global Capitalism* (Oxford, 2005).

———. "Multinationals from the 1930s to the 1980s", in Alfred D. Chandler and Bruce Mazlish, eds., *Leviathans. Multinational Corporations and the New Global History* (Cambridge MA, 2005), pp. 81–103.

———. "The End of Nationality? Global Firms and 'Borderless Worlds' ", *Zeitschrift für Unternehmensgeschichte* 51 (2006), pp. 149–165.

——— and Mary B. Rose. "Family Capitalism", *Business History* 35 (1993), pp. 1–16.

Jonker, Joost and Keetie Sluyterman. *At Home on the World Markets. Dutch International Trading Companies from the 16th Century Until the Present* (The Hague, 2000).

Kaffee-Büro, Guatemala. *Fincas Productoras y Exportadores de Café* (Hamburg, 1962).

Kawabe, Nobuo. "Development of Overseas Operations by General Trading Companies, 1868–1945", in Shin'ichi Yonekawa and Hideki Yoshihara, eds., *Business History of General Trading Companies* (Tokyo, 1987), pp. 71–103.

Killick, John R. "The Cotton Operations of Alexander Brown and Sons in the Deep South, 1820–1860", *Journal of Southern History* 43 (1977), pp. 169–194.

———. "The Transformation of Cotton Marketing in the Late Nineteenth Century. Alexander Sprunt and Son of Wilmington, N. C., 1884–1956", *Business History Review* 55 (1981), pp. 143–169.

———. "Specialized and General Trading Firms in the Atlantic Cotton Trade, 1820–1980", in Shin'ichi Yonekawa and Hideki Yoshihara, eds., *Business History of General Trading Companies* (Tokyo, 1987), pp. 239–266.

———. "Response to the Comment of Tetsuya Kuwahara", in Shin'ichi Yonekawa and Hideki Yoshihara, eds., *Business History of General Trading Companies* (Tokyo, 1987), pp. 271–272.

Kindleberger. Charles, *The World in Depression, 1929–1939* (London, 1973).

Kocka, Jürgen. *Unternehmer in der deutschen Industrialisierung* (Göttingen, 1975).

———. "Familie, Unternehmer und Kapitalismus", in Heinz Reif, ed., *Die Familie in der Geschichte* (Göttingen, 1982), pp. 163–186.

———. *Capitalism. A Short History* (Princeton, 2016).

Kracauer, Siegfried. *Geschichte—Vor den letzten Dingen* (Frankfurt a. M., 1973).

Kramper, Peter. "Warum Europa? Konturen einer globalgeschichtlichen Forschungskontroverse", *Neue Politische Literatur* 54 (2009), pp. 9–46.

Krug, C.A. and R.A. De Poerck. *World Coffee Survey* (Rome, 1968).

Künzi, Kilian. "'. . . womit die Schweiz ihrer Politik zugunsten der Entwicklungsländer treu bleiben wird'. Die Schweiz und das Kaffeeabkommen von 1962", *Studien und Quellen. Zeitschrift des Schweizerischen Bundesarchivs, Bern* 19 (1993), pp 305–317.

Landa, Janet Tai. *Trust, Ethnicity, and Identity. Beyond the New Institutional Economics of Ethnic Trading Networks, Contract Law, and Gift-Exchange* (Ann Arbor, 1994).

Landes, David. *The Wealth and Poverty of Nations. Why Some Are So Rich and Some So Poor* (London, 1998).

———. *Die Macht der Familie. Wirtschaftsdynastien in der Weltgeschichte* (Munich, 2006).

Lawson, Philip. *East India Company. A History* (Harlow, 1993).

Lee, Robert, ed., *Commerce and Culture. Nineteenth-Century Business Elites* (Farnham, 2011).

Leimgruber, Matthieu. *Solidarity Without the State? Business and the Shaping of the Swiss Welfare State, 1890–2000* (Cambridge, 2008).

Lendenmann, Fritz. "Die wirtschaftliche Entwicklung im Stadtstaat Zürich", in *Geschichte des Kantons Zürich, Band 2: Frühe Neuzeit—16. bis 18. Jahrhundert* (Zurich, 1996), pp. 126–171.

Lengwiler, Martin. "Das drei-Säulen-Konzept und seine Grenzen. Private und berufliche Vorsorge in der Schweiz im 20. Jahrhundert", *Zeitschrift für Unternehmensgeschichte* 48 (2003), pp. 29–47.

Lesczenski, Jörg. *August Thyssen 1842–1926. Lebenswelt eines Wirtschaftsbürgers* (Essen, 2008).

Lewis, W. Arthur, *Economic Survey 1919 to 1939* (London, 1970).

Lubinski, Christina, *Familienunternehmen in Westdeutschland. Corporate Governance und Gesellschafterkultur seit den 1960er Jahren* (Munich, 2010).

———. "Global Trade and Indian Politics. The German Dye Business in India before 1947". *Business History Review* 89 (2015), pp. 503–530.

Lucier, Richard L. *The International Political Economy of Coffee. From Juan Valdez to Yank's Diner* (New York, 1988).

Lüdtke, Alf. "Gesichter der Belegschaft. Porträts der Arbeit", in: Klaus Tenfelde, ed., *Bilder von Krupp. Fotografie und Geschichte im Industriezeitalter* (Munich, 1994), pp. 67–87.

Lüpold, Martin. "Wirtschaftskrieg, Aktienrecht und Corporate Governance. Der Kampf der Schweizer Wirtschaft gegen die 'wirtschaftliche Überfremdung' im Ersten und Zweiten Weltkrieg", in Valentin Groebner, Sébastien Guex and Jakob Tanner, eds., *Kriegswirtschaft und Wirtschaftskriege* (Zurich, 2008), pp. 99–115.

Lüthy, Herbert. "Die Kolonisation und die Einheit der Geschichte", in Herbert Lüthy, *Wo liegt Europa? Zehn Versuche zu den Umtrieben des Zeitgeists* (Zurich, 1991), pp. 217–236.

Machado, Pedro. *Ocean of Trade. South Asian Merchants, Africa and the Indian Ocean, c.1750–1850* (Cambridge, 2014).

Maier, Charles S., "Consigning the Twentieth Century to History. Alternative Narratives for the Modern Era", *American Historical Review* 105 (2000), pp. 807–831.

Maitte, Corine and Manuela Martini. "Introduction", in: Corine Maitte, Issiaka Mande, Manuela Martini and Didier Terrier, eds., *Entreprises en mouvement. Migrants, pratiques entrepreneuriales et diversités culturelles dans le monde (XVe—XXe siècle)* (Valenciennes, 2009), pp. 9–28.

Manela, Erez, *The Wilsonian Moment. Self-Determination and the International Origins of Anticolonial Nationalism* (New York, 2007).

Mangold, Fritz. *75 Jahre Basler Transport-Versicherungs-Gesellschaft, 1864–1939* (Basel, 1940).

Mann, Michael. "Telekommunikation in Britisch-Indien (ca. 1850–1930). Ein globalgeschichtliches Paradigma", *Comparativ. Zeitschrift für Globalgeschichte und vergleichende Gesellschaftsforschung* 19 (2009), pp. 86–112.

Manning, Patrick. *Navigating World History. Historians Create a Global Past* (New York and Basingstoke, 2003).

Markovits, Claude. "Structure and Agency in the World of Asian Commerce during the Era of European Colonial Domination (c. 1750–1950)", *Journal of the Economic and Social History of the Orient* 50 (2007), pp. 106–123.

———. *The Global World of Indian Merchants, 1750–1947. Traders of Sind from Bukhara to Panama* (Cambridge, 2000).

Marshall, C. F. *The World Coffee Trade. A Guide to the Production, Trading and Consumption of Coffee* (Cambridge, 1983).

McDermott, John. "Trading with the Enemy: British Business and the Law During the First World War", *Canadian Journal of History* 32 (1997), pp. 201–220.

McCreery, David. "Coffee and Indigenous Labor in Guatemala, 1871–1980", in William Gervase Clarence-Smith and Steven Topik, ed., *The Global Coffee Economy in Africa, Asia, and Latin America, 1500–1989* (Cambridge, 2003), pp. 191–208.

McNeill, William H. *The Rise of the West: A History of the Human Community* (Chicago, 1963).

Middell, Matthias. "Der Spatial Turn und das Interesse an der Globalisierung in der Geschichtswissenschaft", in Jörg Döring and Tristan Thielmann, eds., *Spatial Turn. Das Raumparadigma in den Kultur- und Sozialwissenschaften* (Bielefeld, 2008), pp. 103–123.

Misra, A.-M., "'Business Culture' and Entrepreneurship in British India, 1860–1950", *Modern Asian Studies* 34 (2000), pp. 333–348.

Mönninghoff, Wolfgang. *King Cotton. Kulturgeschichte der Baumwolle* (Düsseldorf, 2006).

Mommsen, Wolfgang J. and Jaap A. de Moor, eds., *European Expansion and Law. The Encounter of European and Indigenous Law in 19th- and 20th-Century Africa and Asia* (Oxford and New York, 1992).

Müller, Margrit. "Organizational Change and Decision Making in Business Firms during Periods of Economic Growth and Depression", in Tony Slaven, ed., *Business History, Theory and Practice* (Glasgow, 2000), pp. 209–221.

———. "Patterns of Technical Innovation. Market Relationships, and Institutional Change During the Interwar Period", in Laurent Tissot and Béatrice Veyrassat, eds., *Technological Trajectories, Markets, Institutions: Industrialized Countries, 19th—20th Centuries* (Bern, 2001), pp. 297–329.

———. "Introduction", in Müller, Margrit and Timo Myllyntaus, eds., *Pathbreakers. Small European Countries Responding to Globalisation and Deglobalisation* (Bern, 2008), pp. 11–35.

Munro, John M. *Cotton, 2nd edition* (Burnt Mill and New York, 1987).

Mutz, Mathias. "'Der Sohn, der durch das West-Tor kam'. Siemens und die wirtschaftliche Internationalisierung Chinas, 1904–1949", *Periplus. Jahrbuch für außereuropäische Geschichte* 5 (2005), pp. 4–40.

———. "'Ein unendlich weites Gebiet für die Ausdehnung unseres Geschäfts'. Marketingstrategien des Siemens-Konzerns auf dem chinesischen Markt (1904–1937)", *Zeitschrift für Unternehmensgeschichte* 51 (2006), pp. 93–115.

Nakagawa, Keiichiro. "Business Management in Japan—A Comparative Historical Study", in Steven Tolliday, ed., *The Economic Development of Modern Japan, 1868–1945. From the Meiji Restoration to the Second World War, Volume I* (Cheltenham and Northampton, 2001), pp. 263–282.

Naoto, Kagotani. "Up-country Purchase Activities of Indian Raw Cotton by Toyo Menka's Bombay Branch, 1896–1935", in Shinya Sugiyama and Linda Grove, eds., *Commercial Networks in Modern Asia* (Richmond, 2001), pp. 199–213.

Nelson, Richard R. "Evolutionary Theorising about Economic Change", in Neil J. Smelser and Richard Swedberg, eds., *The Handbook of Economic Sociology* (Princeton, 1994), pp. 108–136.

Nieberding, Anne. "Unternehmerische Sinnkonstruktion", in Karl-Peter Ellerbrock and Clemens Wischermann, eds., *Die Wirtschaftsgeschichte vor der Herausforderung durch die New Institutional Economics* (Dortmund, 2004), pp. 216–225.

Nienstedt, Jost. *Kaffee-Erzeugung und -Handel in São Paulo und Paraná* (Hamburg, 1950).

North, Douglass C. *Institutionen, institutioneller Wandel und Wirtschaftsleistung* (Tübingen, 1992).

Nonn, Christoph. *Das 19. und 20. Jahrhundert* (Paderborn, 2007).

O'Brien, Patrick Karl. "The Great War and the Dislocation of the International Economy 1914–1929", in Wilfried Feldenkirchen, Frauke Schönert-Röhlk and Günther Schulz, eds., *Wirtschaft, Gesellschaft, Unternehmen. Festschrift für Hans Pohl zum 60. Geburtstag* (Stuttgart, 1995), pp. 245–265.

———. "The Deconstruction of Myths and Reconstruction of Metanarratives in Global Histories of Material Progress", in Benedikt Stuchtey and Eckhardt Fuchs, eds., *Writing World History, 1800–2000* (Oxford and New York, 2003), pp. 67–90.

Osterhammel, Jürgen. "Imperialism in Transition. British Business and the Chinese Authorities, 1931–1937", *The China Quarterly*, 98 (1984), pp. 260–286.

———. *China und die Weltgesellschaft. Vom 18. Jahrhundert bis in unsere Zeit* (Munich, 1989).

———. *Shanghai, 30. Mai 1925. Die chinesische Revolution* (Munich, 1997).

———. "Die Wiederkehr des Raumes: Geopolitik, Geohistorie und historische Geographie", *Neue Politische Literatur* 43 (1998), pp. 374–397.

———. "Symbolpolitik und imperiale Integration. Das britische Empire im 19. und 20. Jahrhundert", in Bernhard Giesen, Jürgen Osterhammel and Rudolf Schlögl, eds., *Die Wirklichkeit der Symbole* (Konstanz, 2004), pp. 395–421.

———. *Die Verwandlung der Welt. Eine Geschichte des 19. Jahrhunderts* (Munich, 2009).

——— and Niels P. Petersson. *Globalization. A Short History* (Princeton, 2005).

Offer, Avner. *The First World War. An Agrarian Interpretation* (Oxford, 1989).

Ott, Hugo. "Kriegswirtschaft im 1. Weltkrieg—Ende der Weltwirtschaft?", in Jürgen Schneider et. al., eds., *Wirtschaftskräfte und Wirtschaftswege. Festschrift für Herrmann Kellenbenz* (Bamberg, 1981), pp. 505–524.

Paige, Jeffrey M. *Coffee and Power. Revolution and the Rise of Democracy in Central America* (Cambridge MA and London, 1997).

Parthasarathi, Prasannan. "Global Trade and Textile Workers", in Lex Heerma van Voss, Els Hiemstra-Kuperus and Elise van Nederveen Meerkerk, eds., *The Ashgate Companion to the History of Textile Workers, 1650–2000* (Farnham and Burlington, 2010), pp. 561–576.

——— and Giorgio Riello. "Introduction. Cotton Textiles and Global History", in Prasannan Parthasarathi and Giorgio Riello, eds., *The Spinning World. A Global History of Cotton Textiles, 1200–1850* (Oxford and New York, 2009), pp. 1–13.

Pereira de Melo, Hildete. "Coffee and Development of the Rio de Janeiro Economy, 1888–1920", in William Gervase Clarence-Smith and Steven Topik, eds., *The Global Coffee Economy in Africa, Asia, and Latin America, 1500–1989* (Cambridge, 2003), pp. 360–384.

Perlin, Frank. *The Invisible City. Monetary, Administration and Popular Infrastructure in Asia and Europe, 1500–1900* (Aldershot, 1993).

Peter, Hans. *Salomon Volkart (1816–1893)* (Zurich, 1956).

Peters Solórzano. Gertrud, *Formación y Desarollo del Grupo Cafetalera en la Comunidad Empresarial Costarricense. Trabajo Final de Investigación, Universidad Nacional, Heredia, Costa Rica* (Heredia, 1984).

———. *Empresias e Historia del Café en Costa Rica 1930–1950. Trabajo Final de Investigación, Universidad Nacional, Faculdad de Ciencias Sociales, Escuela de Historia, Heredia* (Heredia, 1989).

Petersson, Niels P. *Anarchie und Weltrecht. Das Deutsche Reich und die Institutionen der Weltwirtschaft 1890–1930* (Göttingen, 2009).

Peyer, Hans Conrad. "Aus den Anfängen des schweizerischen Indienhandels. Briefe Salomon Volkarts an Johann Heinrich Fierz 1844–1845", *Zürcher Taschenbuch auf das Jahr 1961* (Zurich, 1960), pp. 107–119.

———. *Von Handel und Bank im alten Zürich* (Zurich, 1968).

Pfister, Ulrich. "Entstehung des industriellen Unternehmertums in der Schweiz, 18.—19. Jahrhundert", *Zeitschrift für Unternehmensgeschichte* 42 (1997), pp. 14–38.

Pohl, Hans. *Aufbruch der Weltwirtschaft. Geschichte der Weltwirtschaft von der Mitte des 19. Jahrhunderts bis zum Ersten Weltkrieg* (Stuttgart, 1989).

Pointon, Arthur Cecil. *The Bombay Burman Trading Corporation Limited 1863–1963* (London and Southampton, 1964).

———. *The Wallace Bothers* (Oxford, 1974).

Pollard, Sydney. *Peaceful Conquest. The Industrialization of Europe 1760–1970* (Oxford, 1981).

Pomeranz, Kenneth. *The Making of a Hinterland. State, Society, and Economy in Inland North China, 1853–1937* (Berkeley, Los Angeles and Oxford, 1993).

———. *The Great Divergence. Europe, China, and the Making of the Modern World Economy* (Princeton, 2000).

——— and Steven Topik. *The World that Trade Created. Society, Culture and the World Economy 1400—the Present. Second Edition* (New York, 2006).

Pomata, Gianna. "Close-Ups and Long-Shots, Combining Particular and General in Writing the Histories of Women and Men", in Hans Medick and Anne-Charlotte Trepp, eds., *Geschlechtergeschichte und Allgemeine Geschichte, Herausforderungen und Perspektiven* (Göttingen, 1998), pp. 99–124.

Pratt, Mary Louise. *Imperial Eyes. Travel Writing and Transculturation. Second Edition* (London and New York, 2008).

Price, Jacob M. "What Did Merchants Do? Reflections on British Overseas Trade, 1660–1790", *Journal of Economic History* (1989), pp. 267–284.

Purtschert, Patricia and Harald Fischer-Tiné, eds., *Colonial Switzerland. Rethinking Colonialism from the Margins* (Houndmills, 2015).

Rabb, Theodore K. "The Expansion of Europe and the Spirit of Capitalism", *The Historical Journal* 17 (1974), pp. 675–689.

Rambousek, Walter H., Armin Vogt and Hans R. Volkart. *Volkart. Die Geschichte einer Welthandelsfirma* (Frankfurt a. M., 1990).

Randeria, Shalini. "Geteilte Geschichte und verwobene Moderne", in: Jörn Rüsen, Hanna Leitgeb and Norbert Jegelka, eds., *Zukunftsentwürfe. Ideen für eine Kultur der Veränderung* (Frankfurt a. M., 1999), pp. 87–95.

Rankin, George Claus, *Background to Indian Law* (Cambridge, 1946).

Ray, Rajat Kanta. *Industrialization in India. Growth and Conflict in the Private Corporate Sector, 1919–1947* (Delhi, 1979).

———. "The Bazaar. Changing Structural Characteristics of the Indigenous Section of the Indian Economy before and after the Great Depression", *Indian Economic and Social History Review* 25 (1988), pp. 263–318.

———. "Asian Capital in the Age of European Domination. The Rise of the Bazaar, 1800–1914", *Modern Asian Studies* 29 (1995), pp. 449–554.

Reber, Vera Blinn. *British Mercantile Houses in Buenos Aires, 1810–1880* (Cambridge MA and London, 1979).

Reidy, Joseph P. *From Slavery to Agrarian Capitalism in the Cotton Plantation South: Central Georgia, 1800–1880* (Chapel Hill and London 1992).

Reinhart, Carmen M. and Kenneth S. Rogoff. *This Time Is Different. Eight Centuries of Financial Folly* (Princeton, 2009).

Richter, Rudolf and Eirik G. Furubotn. *Neue Institutionenökonomik. Eine Einführung und kritische Würdigung* (Tübingen, 2003).

Riello, Giorgio and Tirthankar Roy, eds., *How India Clothed the World. The World of South Asian Textiles, 1500–1850* (Leiden and Boston, 2009).

Rischbieter, Laura. "Globalisierungsprozesse vor Ort. Die Interdependenz von Produktion, Handel und Konsum am Beispiel 'Kaffee' zur Zeit des Kaiserreichs",

Comparativ. Zeitschrift für Globalgeschichte und vergleichende Gesellschafts-forschung 3 (2007), pp. 28–45.

Roach, Brian. "A Primer on Multinational Corporations", in Alfred D. Chandler and Bruce Mazlish, eds., *Leviathans. Multinational Corporations and the New Global History* (Cambridge MA, 2005), pp. 19–44.

Robertson, Roland. "Glocalization: Time-Space and Homogeneity-Heterogeneity", in Mike Featherstone, Scott Lash and Roland Robertson, eds., *Global Modernities* (London, 1995), pp. 25–44.

Robins, Jonathan. *'The Black Man's Crop': Cotton, Imperialism and Public-Private Development in Britain's African Colonies, 1900–1918, Commodities of Empire Working Paper 11* (2009).

Robinson, William I. *A Theory of Global Capitalism. Production, Class, and State in a Transnational World* (Baltimore and London, 2004).

Rohner, Karl, *Die Schweizer Wirtschaftsvertretungen im Ausland* (Bern, 1944).

Roseberry, William. "Introduction", in William Roseberry, Lowell W. Gudmundson and Mario Samper, eds., *Coffee, Society, and Power in Latin America* (Baltimore, 1995), pp. 1–37.

Rossfeld, Roman, ed., *Genuss und Nüchternheit. Geschichte des Kaffees in der Schweiz vom 18. Jahrhundert bis zur Gegenwart* (Baden, 2002).

Rossfeld, Roman and Tobias Straumann, eds., *Der vergessene Wirtschaftskrieg. Schweizer Unternehmen im Ersten Weltkrieg* (Zurich, 2008).

Rothermund, Dietmar. *Government, Landlord, and Peasant in India. Agrarian Relations under British Rule, 1865–1935* (Wiesbaden, 1978)

———. "Chinas verspätete Krise, 1933–1935", in: Dietmar Rothermund, ed., *Die Peripherie in der Weltwirtschaftskrise. Afrika, Asien und Lateinamerika 1929–1939* (Paderborn, 1983), pp. 225–244.

———. *An Economic History of India. From Pre-Colonial Times to 1986* (London, New York and Sydney, 1988).

———. "Currencies, Taxes and Credit: Asian Peasants in the Great Depression, 1930–1939", in Harold James, ed., *The Interwar Depression in an International Context (Munich, 2002), pp. 15–33.*

———. "Globalgeschichte als Interaktionsgeschichte. Von der Außereuropäischen Geschichte zur Globalgeschichte", in: Birgit Schäbler, ed., *Area Studies und die Welt. Weltregionen und neue Globalgeschichte* (Vienna, 2007), pp. 194–216.

Roy, Tirthankar. *The Economic History of India.* (Oxford, 2011).

Royce, Simon. *The Crimean War and Its Place in European Economic History* (London, 2001).

Satya, Laxman D., *Cotton and Famine in Berar* (New Delhi, 1997).

Saxonhouse, Gary and Yukihiko Kiyokawa. "Supply and Demand for Quality Workers in Cotton Spinning in Japan and India", in Michael Smitka, ed., *The Textile Industry and the Rise of the Japanese Economy* (New York and London, 1998), pp. 183–217.

Schäfer, Michael, *Familienunternehmen und Unternehmerfamilien. Zur Sozial- und Wirtschaftsgeschichte der sächsischen Unternehmer 1850–1940* (Munich, 2007).

Schildknecht, Karl-Heinz. *Bremer Baumwollbörse. Bremen und Baumwolle im Wandel der Zeiten* (Bremen, 1999).

Schlögel, Karl. *Im Raume lesen wir die Zeit. Über Zivilisationsgeschichte und Geopolitik* (Munich, 2003).

Schulte Beerbühl, Margrit and Jörg Vögele, eds., *Spinning the Commercial Web, International Trade, Merchants, and Commercial Cities, c.1640–1939* (Frankfurt a. M., 2004).

Schuyler, Robert Livingston. *The Fall of the Old Colonial System: A Study in British Free Trade, 1770–1870* (New York, 1945).

Scott, James C. *Weapons of the Weak. Everyday Forms of Peasant Resistance* (New Haven, 1985).

Sethi, B.L. "History of Cotton", in Indian Central Cotton Committee, ed., *Cotton in India. A Monograph* (Bombay, 1960), pp. 1–39.

Siddiqi, Asiya. "Some Aspects of Indian Business under the East India Company", in Dwijendra Tripathi, ed., *State and Business in India. A Historical Perspective* (New Delhi, 1987), pp. 78–90.

Siegenthaler, Hansjörg. "Die Bedeutung des Aussenhandels für die Ausbildung einer schweizerischen Wachstumsgesellschaft im 18. und 19. Jahrhundert", in Bernard Nicolai and Reichen Quirinus, eds., *Gesellschaft und Gesellschaften* (Bern, 1982), pp. 325–340.

Siegenthaler, Hansjörg. "Geschichte und Ökonomie nach der kulturalistischen Wende", *Geschichte und Gesellschaft* 25 (1999), pp. 276–301.

Sigerist, Stefan. *Schweizer in Asien. Präsenz der Schweiz bis 1914* (Schaffhausen, 2001).

Simon, Fritz B., Rudolf Wimmer and Thorsten Groth. *Mehr-Generationen-Familienunternehmen. Erfolgsgeheimnisse von Oetker, Merck, Haniel u.a.* (Heidelberg, 2005).

Sinclair, John L. *The Production, Marketing, and Consumption of Cotton* (New York, Washington and London, 1968).

Siney, Marion C. *The Allied Blockade of Germany 1914–1916* (Ann Arbor, 1957).

Sluyterman, Keetie and Hélène J. M. Winkelman. "The Dutch Family Firm confronted with Chandler's Dynamics of Industrial Capitalism, 1890–1940", *Business History* 35 (1993), pp. 152–183.

Smith, Andrew, Kevin D Tennent and Simon Mollan, eds., *The Impact of the First World War on International Business* (New York, 2016).

Smith, Carl T. "Compradores of the Hongkong Bank", in Frank H. H. King, ed., *Eastern Banking. Essays in the History of the Hongkong and Shanghai Banking Corporation* (London, 1983), pp. 93–111.

Smith, Sheila. "Fortune and Failure. The Survival of Family Firms in Eighteenth-Century India", *Business History* 35 (1993), pp. 44–65.

Smitka, Michael, ed., *The Interwar Economy of Japan. Colonialism, Depression, and Recovery, 1910–1940* (New York and London, 1998).

Soutou, Georges-Henri. *L'Or et le Sang. Les Buts de Guerre Economiques de la Première Guerre Mondiale* (Paris, 1985).

Steinmann, Stephan. *Seldwyla im Wunderland. Schweizer im alten Shanghai (1842–1941)* (Zurich, 1998).

Stokes, Eric. *The Peasant and the Raj. Studies in Agrarian Society and Peasant Rebellion in Colonial India* (Cambridge, 1978).

Stolcke, Verena. *Coffee Planters, Workers and Wives. Class Conflict and Gender Relations on São Paulo Plantations, 1850–1980* (New York, 1988).

Subrahmanyam, Sanjay, ed., *Merchant Networks in Early Modern World. An Expanding World: The European Impact on World History, 1450–1800* (Aldershot, 1990).

Subramanian, Lakshmi. "The Castle Revolution of 1759 and the Banias of Surat. Changing British-Indian Relationships in Western India", in Dwijendra Tripathi, ed., *State and Business in India. A Historical Perspective* (New Delhi, 1987), pp. 91–122.

Sugihara, Kaoru, ed., *Japan, China, and the Growth of the Asian International Economy, 1850–1949* (Oxford, 2005).

Sugiyama, Shinya. "Marketing and Competition in China, 1895–1932. The Taikoo Sugar Refinery", in Shinya Sugiyama and Linda Grove, eds., *Commercial Networks in Modern Asia* (Richmond, 2001), pp. 140–159.

—— and Linda Grove, eds., *Commercial Networks in Modern Asia* (Richmond, 2001).

Sulzer, Klaus. "Vom Baumwollzentrum zur Maschinenindustrie. Ein Kapitel Winterthurer Wirtschaftsgeschichte", in *Winterthurer Jahrbuch 1995, 42. Jg.*, (Winterthur, 1995), pp. 9–28.

Tagiuri, Renato and John Davis. "Bivalent Attributes of the Family Firm", *Family Business Review* 9 (1996), pp. 199–208.

Talbot, John M. *Grounds for Agreement. The Political Economy of the Coffee Commodity Chain* (Lanham, 2004).

Teubner, Gunther. "'Global Bukowina'. Legal Pluralism in the World Society", in Gunther Teubner, ed., *Global Law Without a State* (Aldershot, 1997), pp. 3–28.

Thorner, David. *Investment in Empire. British Railway and Steam Shipping Enterprise in India, 1825–1849* (Philadelphia, 1950).

Tilly, Richard. *Globalisierung aus historischer Sicht und das Lernen aus der Geschichte* (Köln, 1999).

Tomlinson, Brian Roger. *The Economy of Modern India, 1860–1970* (Cambridge, 1993).

Topik, Steven. "The Integration of the World Coffee Market", in William Gervase Clarence-Smith and Steven Topik, eds., *The Global Coffee Economy in Africa, Asia, and Latin America, 1500–1989* (Cambridge, 2003), pp. 21–49.

—— and Mario Samper. "The Latin America Coffee Commodity Chain. Brazil and Costa Rica", in Steven Topik, Carlos Marichal and Zephyr Frank, ed., *From Silver to Cocaine. Latin American Commodity Chains and the Building of the World Economy, 1500–2000* (Durham and London, 2006), pp. 118–146.

—— and William Gervase Clarence-Smith. "Introduction. Coffee and Global Development", in William Gervase Clarence-Smith and Steven Topik, eds., *The Global Coffee Economy in Africa, Asia, and Latin America, 1500–1989* (Cambridge, 2003), pp. 1–17.

Torp, Cornelius. "Die Weltsystemtheorie Immanuel Wallersteins. Eine kritische Analyse", *Jahrbuch für Wirtschaftsgeschichte* 1 (1998), pp. 217–241.

——. "Weltwirtschaft vor dem Weltkrieg. Die erste Welle der ökonomischen Globalisierung vor 1914", *Historische Zeitschrift* 279 (2004), pp. 561–609.

Toshiyuki, Mizoguchi. "The Changing Pattern of Sino-Japanese Trade, 1884–1937", in Michael Smitka, ed., *Japan's Economic Ascent. International Trade, Growth, and Postwar Reconstruction* (New York and London, 1998), pp. 132–155.

Trentman, Frank. "National Identity and Consumer Politics", in Patrick O'Brien et al., eds., *The Political Economy of British Historical Experience 1688–1914* (Oxford, 2002), pp. 187–214.

Ukers, William H. *All About Coffee* (New York, 1935).

———. *A Trip to Brazil* (New York, 1935).

Ullmann Hans-Peter. "Kriegswirtschaft", in Gerhard Hirschfeld, Gerd Krumeich and Irina Renz, eds., *Enzyklopädie Erster Weltkrieg* (Paderborn, 2003), pp. 220–232.

Valentinitsch, Helfried. "Ost- und Westindische Kompanien—ein Wettlauf der europäischen Mächte", in Friedrich Edelmayer, Erich Landsteiner and Renate Pieper, eds., *Die Geschichte des europäischen Welthandels und der wirtschaftliche Globalisierungsprozess* (Vienna and Munich, 2001), pp. 54–76.

van Laak, Dirk. *Imperiale Infrastruktur. Deutsche Planungen für eine Erschließung Afrikas 1880 bis 1960* (Paderborn and Zurich, 2004).

Vec, Miloš. *Recht und Normierung in der Industriellen Revolution. Neue Strukturen der Normsetzung in Völkerrecht, staatlicher Gesetzgebung und gesellschaftlicher Selbstnormierung* (Frankfurt a. M., 2006).

Veyrassat, Béatrice. "1945–1990: Bilan des recherches sur l'histoire du négoce international de la Suisse (XVIIIe siècle—Première Guerre mondial)", *Schweizerische Zeitschrift für Geschichte* 41 (1991), pp. 274–286.

———. *Négociants et fabricants dans l'industrie cotonnière Suisse, 1760–1840* (Lausanne, 1982).

———. *Réseaux d'affaires internationaux, émigrations et exportations en Amérique latine au XIXe siècle. Le commerce Suisse aux Amériques* (Genève, 1993).

Vicziany, Marika. "Bombay Merchants and Structural Changes in the Export Community 1850 to 1880", in: Kirti N. Chaudhuri and Clive J. Dewey, eds., *Economy and Society. Essays in Indian Economy and Social History* (Delhi, 1979), pp. 163–196.

von Albertini, Rudolf. *Europäische Kolonialherrschaft 1880–1940* (Zurich, 1976).

Wagner, Regina. *The History of Coffee in Guatemala* (Bogotá, 2001).

Wallerstein, Immanuel. *The Modern World-System, 4 Vols.* (New York, 1974–2011).

———. *Historical Capitalism* (London, 1983).

Walsh, Casey. *Building the Borderlands. A Transnational History of Irrigated Cotton Along the Mexico-Texas Border* (College Station, 2008).

Wanner Adolf. *Die Basler Handelsgesellschaft A.G., 1859–1959* (Basel, 1959).

Washbrook, David A. "Law, State and Society in Colonial India", *Modern Asian Studies* 15 (1981), pp. 649–721.

Weber, Max. *The Protestant Ethic and the Spirit of Capitalism* (New York, 2001 [1930]).

———. *Economy and Society. An Outline of Interpretive Sociology* (Los Angeles, 1978).

Webster, Tony. "An Early Global Business in a Colonial Context. The Strategies, Management, and Failure of John Palmer and Company of Calcutta, 1780–1830", *Enterprise and Society* 6 (2005), pp. 98–133.

Wehler, Hans-Ulrich. *Deutsche Gesellschaftsgeschichte, Dritter Band: Von der 'Deutschen Doppelrevolution' bis zum Beginn des Ersten Weltkrieges, 1849–1914* (Munich, 1995).

Weisz, Leo. *Die Zürcherische Exportindustrie. Ihre Entstehung und Entwicklung* (Zurich, 1936).

———. "Zur Geschichte des europäischen Handels mit Indien. 11teilige Serie", *Neue Zürcher Zeitung*, (20 December 1954–1910 January 1955).

Welskopp, Thomas. "Das institutionalisierte Misstrauen. Produktionsorganisation und Kommunikationsnetze in Eisen- und Stahlunternehmen des Ruhrgebiets während der Zwischenkriegszeit", in Clemens Wischermann, Peter Borscheid and Karl-Peter Ellerbrock, eds., *Unternehmenskommunikation im 19. und 20. Jahrhundert* (Dortmund, 2000), pp. 199–225.

———. "Unternehmensgeschichte im internationalen Vergleich—oder integrale Unternehmensgeschichte in typisierender Absicht", in: Hartmut Berghoff and Jakob Vogel, eds., *Wirtschaftsgeschichte als Kulturgeschichte. Dimensionen eines Perspektivenwechsels* (Frankfurt a. M. and New York, 2004), pp. 265–294.

Welter, Karl. *Die Exportgesellschaften und die assoziative Exportförderung in der Schweiz im 19. Jahrhundert* (Bern, 1915).

Wetter, Ernst. *Die Bank in Winterthur 1862–1912. Inaugural-Dissertation der staatswissenschaftlichen Fakultät der Universität Zürich* (Winterthur, 1914).

Williamson, Oliver E. *The Economic Institutions of Capitalism. Firms, Markets, Relational Contracting* (New York and London, 1985).

Williams, Jeffrey. *The Economic Function of Futures Markets* (Cambridge, 1986).

Williams, Robert G. *States and Social Evolution. Coffee and the Rise of National Governments in Central America* (Chapel Hill and London, 1994).

Wilkins, Mira. *Maturing of Multinational Enterprise. American Business Abroad from 1914 to 1970* (Cambridge MA, 1974).

Wischermann, Clemens. "Unternehmensgeschichte als Geschichte der Unternehmenskommunikation. Von der Koordination zur Kooperation", in Clemens Wischermann, Peter Borscheid and Karl-Peter Ellerbrock, eds., *Unternehmenskommunikation im 19. und 20. Jahrhundert* (Dortmund, 2000), pp. 31–40.

———, Peter Borscheid and Karl-Peter Ellerbrock. "Vorwort", in Clemens Wischermann, Peter Borscheid and Karl-Peter Ellerbrock, eds., *Unternehmenskommunikation im 19. und 20. Jahrhundert*, (Dortmund, 2000), pp. 8–10.

——— and Anne Nieberding. *Die institutionelle Revolution. Eine Einführung in die deutsche Wirtschaftsgeschichte des 19. und frühen 20. Jahrhunderts* (Stuttgart, 2004).

Wong, Roy Bin. "The Search for European Differences and Domination in the Early Modern World. A View from Asia", *American Historical Review* 107 (2002), pp. 447–469.

Wünderich, Volker. "Die Kolonialware Kaffee von der Erzeugung in Guatemala bis zum Verbrauch in Deutschland. Aus der transatlantischen Biographie eines 'produktiven' Genußmittels (1860–1895)", *Jahrbuch für Wirtschaftsgeschichte* 1 (1994), pp. 37–60.

Yamamura, Kozo. "Then Came the Great Depression. Japan's Interwar Years", in: Michael Smitka, ed., *The Interwar Economy of Japan. Colonialism, Depression, and Recovery, 1910–1940* (New York and London, 1998), pp. 264–293.

Yang, Jerry L.S. "The Profitability of Anglo-Chinese Trade, 1861–1913", *Business History* 35 (1993), pp. 39–65.

Yanagisako, Sylvia Junko. *Producing Culture and Capital. Family Firms in Italy* (Princeton and Oxford, 2002).

Yonekawa, Shin'ichi and Hideki Yoshihara, eds., *Business History of General Trading Companies* (Tokyo, 1987).

Yui, Tsunehiko. "Development, Organization, and Business Strategy of Industrial Enterprises in Japan (1915–1935)", in: Steven Tolliday, ed., *The Economic Development of Modern Japan, 1868–1945. From the Meiji Restoration to the Second World War, Volume I* (Cheltenham and Northampton, 2001), pp. 309–340.

Ziegler Witschi, Béatrice. *Schweizer statt Sklaven. Schweizerische Auswanderer in den Kaffee-Plantagen von São Paulo (1852–1866)* (Stuttgart, 1985).

Ziegler, Max. *Der Import ostindischer Baumwolle, insbesondere die Entwicklung der Geschäftsformen (= Mitteilungen aus dem handelswissenschaftlichen Seminar der Universität Zürich. Neue Folge, Heft 45)* (Zurich, 1922).Zimmerman, Andrew. *Alabama in Africa. Booker T.Washington, the German Empire, and the Globalization of the New South* (Princeton, 2010).

Zwierlein, Cornel. *Der gezähmte Prometheus. Feuer und Sicherheit zwischen Früher Neuzeit und Moderne* (Göttingen, 2011).

Name Index

Subject Index

Place Index

For Product Safety Concerns and Information please contact our EU
representative GPSR@taylorandfrancis.com Taylor & Francis Verlag GmbH,
Kaufingerstraße 24, 80331 München, Germany

Printed and bound by CPI Group (UK) Ltd, Croydon, CR0 4YY
01/05/2025
01858416-0002